Feminism and Method

Feminism and Method
Ethnography, Discourse Analysis, and Activist Research

Nancy A. Naples

ROUTLEDGE
NEW YORK AND LONDON

Published in 2003 by
Routledge
29 West 35th Street
New York, NY 10001
www.routledge-ny.com

Published in Great Britain by
Routledge
11 New Fetter Lane
London EC4P 4EE
www.routledge.co.uk

Routledge is an imprint of the Taylor & Francis Group.
Printed in the United States of America on acid-free paper.

10 9 8 7 6 5 4 3 2 1

Library of Congress Cataloging-in-Publication Data

Naples, Nancy A.
   Feminism and method : ethnography, discourse analysis, and activist research / by
   Nancy A. Naples
      p. cm.
   Includes bibliographical references and index.
   ISBN 0-415-94448-1 (alk. paper) — ISBN 0-415-94449-X (pb. : alk. paper)
      1. Feminism—Research. 2. Feminism—Methodology. 3. Women—Research—
Methodology. 4. Action research—Methodology. I. Title.

   HQ1180.N37 2003
   305.42′07′2—dc21

                                                                2003040929

This book is dedicated to
Lionel Cantú
October 7, 1965–May 26, 2002
A generous and insightful soul whose kindness
and lively spirit are sorely missed

Contents

Preface

The work presented in *Feminism and Method: Ethnography, Discourse Analysis, and Activist Research* represents more than twenty years of investigations, self-reflection, and dialogue with other feminist scholars and community activists. As a consequence there are many to thank. First, my special thanks to Emily Clark for her willingness to participate in a dialogue about our work together that is discussed in chapter 10.

For their review of the book manuscript and their inspired suggestions for revision, I thank Leslie Bloom, Sandra Harding, Rosanna Hertz, Dorothy Smith, Gaye Tuchman, and an anonymous reviewer. For their insightful comments on one or more chapters, my thanks to Mary Bernstein, Valerie Jenness, Deborah Fink, Cynthia Truelove, Emily Martin, Judith Howard, Carolyn Allen, Susan Greenhalgh, Carolyn Sachs, Francesca Cancian, Nancy Whittier, Gwendolyn Mink, Wendy Sarvasy, Robyn Wiegman, and numerous anonymous reviewers. Special thanks to Ann Ferguson, Leslie Rabine, John Smith, and James Ferguson for their thought-provoking and challenging suggestions at key points in the development of the analysis presented in chapter 7.

Throughout the book, I include excerpts of my dialogue with many courageous women and other community members in New York, Philadelphia, and Iowa who shared with me their experiences, fears, hopes, and dreams. I am most grateful to them for their willingness to participate in my research with little to gain from it. I also want to acknowledge the many feminist scholars and teachers whose work influenced my development as a feminist researcher, most especially Dorothy Smith, Sandra Harding, Nancy Fraser, Myra Marx Ferree, Marilyn Gittell, Judith Lorber, and Gaye Tuchman.

I have been blessed with the support of good friends and colleagues from whom I have learned a lot of life lessons. They kept me sane during many difficult times—Theresa Montini, Valerie Jenness, Joan Ariel, Francesca Cancian, Belinda Robnett, Sondra Hale, Emily Abel, Karen Brodkin, Kitty Calavita, Nancy Rose, Wendy Sarvasy, Peter Nardi, Deb Fink, Kate Kinney, Dawn Esposito, Susan Stern, and Gilda Zwerman.

Research assistants Gina Battani, Erica Bornstein, Marnie Dobson, Marlene Fisher, Karen Kendrick, Kate Lair, Chrisy Moutsatsus, Jamie Needleman, Morgan Perry, Jennifer Rogers, Kristine Schwebach, Charlene Tung, Clare Weber, and most especially Lionel Cantú (1965–2002) have encouraged me to clarify my approach to feminism and method and have contributed a great deal to my research and praxis. They have also made the journey a lot more interesting and rewarding. I am also grateful to Cynthia Gaunt, Shellin Lubin, Lisa

Mikhail, Brenda Patton, and Chris Schwendiner (1950–1994) for transcribing the research interviews and to Kate Lair for systematizing the references. My sincere gratitude to Arlene Goodwin and Jeanne Monty for their valuable assistance with many details associated with the production of this book. I have also benefited from the expert advice and enthusiastic support I received from Ilene Kalish, my editor at Routledge. I am also grateful to Kim Guinta and Nicole Ellis for their assistance with the book project.

The research reported in this book was funded by a Science and Humanities Research Incentive Grant, Summer Research Awards Program, Undergraduate Research Assistantship Program, and two Faculty University Research Grants from Iowa State University; Cultural Diversity Studies Faculty Research Grant, Labor Studies Grant, and a Faculty Research Grant from the University of California, Irvine; UC MEXUS; Research Fellowship, Center for U.S.–Mexican Studies, University of California, San Diego; Spivack Program on Applied Social Research, Community Action Research Fellowship, American Sociological Association; and the National Institute of Mental Health.

Finally, this book could not have come to fruition without the encouragement and support of my partner, Mary Bernstein, who has been a gentle critic and calming presence.

Acknowledgments

I gratefully acknowledge previous publications for permission to reprint revised versions and excepts from: "A Socialist Feminist Analysis of the Family Support Act of 1988," *AFFILIA: Journal of Women and Social Work* 6(4)(1991): 23–38; "Standpoint Epistemology and the Uses of Self-Reflection in Feminist Ethnography: Lessons for Rural Sociology" by Nancy A. Naples with Carolyn Sachs, *Rural Sociology* 65(2)(2000):194–214; "A Feminist Revisiting of the 'Insider/Outsider' Debate: The 'Outsider Phenomenon' in Rural Iowa," *Qualitative Sociology* 19(1)(1996):83–106; "Towards a Comparative Analysis of Women's Political Praxis: Explicating Multiple Dimensions of Standpoint Epistemology for Feminist Ethnography," *Women & Politics* 20(1)(1999):29–57; "Materialist Feminist Discourse Analysis and Social Movement Research: Mapping the Changing Context for 'Community Control,' " pp. 226–46 in *Social Movements: Identity, Culture, and the State*, eds. Nancy Whittier, David Meyer, and Belinda Robnett, New York, Oxford University Press, 2002; "Bringing Everyday Life to Policy Analysis: The Case of White Rural Women Negotiating College and Welfare," *Journal of Poverty: Innovations on Social, Political & Economic Inequalities* 2(1)(1998):23–53; "The 'New Consensus' on the Gendered Social Contract: The 1987–1988 U.S. Congressional Hearings on Welfare Reform," *Signs: Journal of Women in Culture and Society* 22(4)(1997):907–45; "Deconstructing and Locating 'Survivor Discourse': Dynamics of Narrative, Empowerment and Resistance for Survivors of Childhood Sexual," *Signs: Journal of Women in Culture and Society* (2003); "Feminist Participatory Research and Empowerment: Going Public as Survivors of Childhood Sexual Abuse," by Nancy A. Naples with Emily Clark, pp. 160–183 in *Feminism and Social Change: Bridging Theory and Practice*, ed. Heidi Gottfried, Champaign-Urbana, Illinois University Press, 1996.

PART I

Introduction

CHAPTER 1

Feminism and Method

Throughout my career as a feminist sociologist, I have sought to address the following questions: How does a researcher negotiate the power imbalance between the researcher and researched? What responsibilities do researchers have to those they study? How does participatory research influence analytic choices during a research study? How do strategies of self-reflection alter ethnographic practice? Feminist scholars have consistently raised such questions, suggesting that if researchers fail to explore how their personal, professional, and structural positions frame social scientific investigations, researchers inevitably reproduce dominant gender, race, and class biases.[1] I draw on my empirical work and three different methodological approaches—ethnography, narrative and textual analysis, and activist and participatory research—to demonstrate the *materialist feminist* framework I developed to make visible how power operates during the research process and in the production of narrative accounts.

Over fifteen years ago, feminist philosopher Sandra Harding (1987) asked: "Is There a Distinctive Feminist Method of Inquiry?" In answering the question, she distinguished between epistemology ("a theory of knowledge"), methodology ("a theory and analysis of how research does or should proceed"), and method ("a technique for . . . gathering evidence") (pp. 2–3). She pointed out the "important connections between epistemologies, methodologies, and research methods" (p. 3). Following Harding, I start with the assertion that the specific methods we choose and how we employ those methods are profoundly shaped by our epistemological stance. Our epistemological assumptions also influence how we define our roles as researchers, what we consider ethical research practices, and how we interpret and implement informed consent or ensure the confidentiality of our research subjects. The goal of my approach to teaching research methods in the social sciences and interdisciplinary women's studies is to foreground the epistemological assumptions that guide our choice of different methodologies, how we proceed to implement particular methods, and how we determine what form the written product should take. For example, while researchers who draw on positive or interpretive[2] theoretical traditions might utilize a methodology that generates oral narratives or ethnographic data, what counts as data and how these data are interpreted and reported will vary significantly depending on the specific epistemological stance undergirding the research process. Since there are diverse feminist perspectives, it follows that there are different ways feminist researchers identify, analyze, and report "data."

How one defines the nature of the relationship between researcher and researched also depends on one's epistemological stance. Of course, a researcher does not have complete autonomy in shaping relations with subjects of his or her research. Research subjects have the power to influence the direction of the research, resist researchers' efforts and interpretations, and add their own interpretations and insights. As Leslie Bloom (1998, 35) astutely observes: "The idea that the researcher has 'The Power' over the participant [in a research study] is an authoritative, binary discourse that may function to disguise the ways that 'the flow of power in multiple systems of domination is not always unidirectional' " (Friedman 1995, 18). She concludes with the observation that "power is situated and contextualized within particular intersubjective relationships."[3] As I demonstrate in this book, ethnographers negotiate and renegotiate relationships with the members of the communities they study through particular and ongoing everyday interactions. These interactions are themselves influenced by shifting relationships among community residents. In the chapters to follow, I illustrate my epistemological and empirical solutions to this dilemma and to related problems faced by feminist social scientists.

I share the lessons I have learned through investigations in four areas of my U.S.-based research: first, exploration of women's politicization, community activism, and feminist praxis; second, analyses of the processes of racialization and rural economic development; third, the construction and implementation of U.S. social policy; and finally, analysis of oppositional movements against poverty, racism, sexual abuse, and other inequalities and oppressions. I link important feminist theoretical debates on positionality, interpretive authority, and activist research with case studies to illustrate the strategies I have developed for confronting the particular challenges posed by feminist postmodern, third world, postcolonial, and queer scholars.[4] These challenges include how to explore women's experiences "in similar contexts across the world, in *different* geographical spaces, rather than as *all* women across the world" and how to understand "a set of unequal relationships among and between peoples, rather than a set of traits embodied in all non-U.S. citizens (particularly because U.S. citizenship continues to be premised within a white, Eurocentric, masculinist, heterosexist regime)" (Alexander and Mohanty 1997, xix, emphasis in original).

This book differs from more traditional methods books in the social sciences that detail the techniques of specific methods such as survey research, interview and focus group research, historical research involving archival materials, ethnography, or participant observation.[5] Rarely do such texts make explicit the theoretical assumptions that are implicated in the methods chosen. The argument put forth in most methods books is that the method one chooses should be the most appropriate for specific research questions you wish to answer. While I agree with this sentiment, I also caution that the methods we choose are not free of epistemological assumptions and taken-for-granted understandings of what counts as data, how the researcher should relate to the subjects of research, and what are the appropriate products of a research study. Furthermore, seldom do the authors of traditional methods books acknowledge that the questions researchers ask are inevitably tied to particular epistemological understandings of how knowledge is generated.[6]

This point has been well established in the field of anthropology where over the last 20 years researchers have grappled with the intersection of representation, subjectivity, and power in the practice of ethnography.[7] Third world and postcolonial feminist scholars call on ethnographers to reflect on their research and writing practices in light of political, moral, and ethical questions that arise from the inherent power imbalances between many ethnographers and those they study. Feminist ethnographers have responded to these challenges by examining how certain cultural representations in ethnographic accounts contribute to colonialist practices and further marginalize the lives of third world and other nonwhite peoples, even as they are brought to the center of analysis.[8] Concerns about the dynamics of power inherent in the practice of social research have been raised about methods used in other disciplines as well.

Feminism and Method also differs from feminist texts that critique social scientific research methodologies but fail to offer strategies to negotiate the problems raised. In contrast to these more abstract critiques of social scientific practice, a number of recent publications provide more guidance to feminists in the social sciences interested in finding solutions to the challenging critiques of research practice. These texts also include case examples of empirically based research that highlight feminist research strategies.[9]

A popular book that offers a useful, almost encyclopedic, overview of feminist methods in the social sciences is *Feminist Methods in Social Research* by Shulamit Reinharz (1992). Following a comprehensive review of feminist methods with illustrations from diverse feminist studies, Reinharz identifies ten features that appear consistently in efforts by feminist scholars to distinguish how their research methods differ from traditional approaches. These include the assertion that a feminist approach "aims to create social change," "strives to represent human diversity," and "attempts to develop special relations with the people studied (in interactive research)" (p. 240). However, Reinharz does not attend to the theoretical underpinnings of the research methods she chronicles, nor does she distinguish between the epistemologies that are implicated in the specific methods. What counts as desirable "social change"? How do different feminist theoretical perspectives inform the application of different methods? How do different perspectives influence the strategies considered effective for representing "human diversity"? What types of relationships are possible between a researcher and those she or he studies? In *Feminism and Method*, I attempt to address some of these questions by fore-grounding the theoretical assumptions of different methods I use in my research and presenting some of the empirical solutions I found to the dilemmas posed by contemporary critiques of social research.

Feminism and Method highlights several interrelated feminist epistemologies—namely, standpoint theory, materialist feminism, and "postmodern" theories of discourse and power. A multidimensional *standpoint epistemology* informs how I conduct and interpret ethnographic research. My approach is further enriched by incorporation of insights from racialization theories developed by critical race theorists, most notably Michael Omi and Howard Winant (1986). I also draw on Michel Foucault's theory of discourse for my materialist feminist analysis of oral narratives and texts such as legislative hearings and other policy documents. My efforts to engage in participatory activist research is guided by Dorothy Smith's (1987) standpoint methodology, which she terms *institutional ethnography*, and Nancy Fraser's (1989) analysis of the *politics of need interpretation*. Another theoretical strand that has influenced my methodological practice is *phenomenology*, as articulated in the sociological approaches of *social constructionism* and *symbolic interactionism*.[10] Instead of viewing these theoretical and methodological approaches as distinct and mutually exclusive, I utilize insights from these perspectives to enrich my materialist feminist analytic approach.

Some of the critical historical materialist and feminist theoretical approaches I draw on are defined as "modernist"; others, like Foucauldian discourse analysis, are categorized as "postmodernist." However, I resist the dichotomous distinction between modernist and postmodernist theories that has fueled much recent feminist debate.[11] By defining Foucault's genealogical approach as postmodern and placing it in opposition to Marxism and other frameworks said to be modernist, parties to the debate reduce the complexity of both Foucault's thought and Marxist theories. For example, as political scientist Kathi Weeks (1998) argues, the reduction of Marxism to a limited terrain of "the modern" is accomplished by making "invisible Marxist alternatives to the Enlightenment" (p. 59). By setting up a rigid divide between so-called modernist and postmodernist approaches, this "oppositional logic" succeeds in reducing "modernism to a straw figure, to a homogeneous model of Enlightenment thought" (p. 59). Cultural studies scholar Wendy Hesford (1999) also challenges a divide between modernism and postmodernism that conflates "the deconstruction of the subject with the erasure of human agency" (p. 26). This "modernist-postmodernism paradigm" has been elicited by both adherents and critics of feminist standpoint theories to position standpoint epistemology, since it draws on the Marxist theory, firmly within a modernist paradigm.[12]

Kathy Ferguson (1991) compares and contrasts postmodern genealogical analyses with interpretive standpoint projects like political theorist Nancy Hartsock's as follows: "The interpretivist envisions a more enabling alternative toward which we are invited to struggle, while the genealogist insists that those structures and processes that we take to be thoroughly liberating will also be constraining. The interpretivist holds up for us a powerful vision of how things should be, while the genealogist more cautiously reminds us that things could be other than they are" (p. 333). She concludes that "the advocates of these two projects often speak as if the two were in total opposition to one another. . . . But the two projects connect to one another in important ways" (p. 335).[13] I view my development of a materialist feminist standpoint theory that incorporates important insights of postmodern analyses of power, subjectivity, and language as a powerful framework for exploring the intersection of race, class, gender, sexuality, region, and culture in different geographic and historical contexts.

Organization of the Book

In the next chapter, I discuss the feminist theoretical frameworks that inform my approach to research with particular focus on feminist standpoint epistemologies, postmodern and postcolonial critiques of ethnographic practice, and materialist feminism and discourse analysis. In the next sections, I emphasize three methodological strategies: ethnography, narrative and textual analysis, and activist and participatory research. In part II, I demonstrate the power of materialist feminist standpoint epistemology and reflective practice for feminist ethnography. Part III addresses the usefulness of a feminist materialist discourse analysis for social policy and oral narrative research. Part IV focuses on some of the limits and possibilities for activist and participatory research.

Part II: Standpoint Epistemologies, Reflective Practice, and Feminist Ethnography

Part II outlines how I negotiate the challenges of ethnographic research by drawing on the insights of standpoint epistemology and reflective practice. In chapter 3, I describe how feminist ethnographers center women's standpoint in their fieldwork and highlight knowledge that develops from shifting the ethnographic angle of vision to the everyday lives of women. Women were either viewed primarily in the so-called private sphere of the family or ignored in traditional ethnographic research.[14] Feminist scholars emphasize how women's lives are rendered invisible or marginalized in traditional ethnographies by a presumed separation between public and private spheres.[15] Beginning in the 1970s, researchers informed by a feminist call to describe women's experiences and perspectives in their own words began to make women's lives central in ethnographic and other qualitative accounts.[16] For example, anthropologist Deborah Fink (1986) describes her research on rural women in the Midwestern United States as "feminist in that it is based on the assumption that women have been major participants and have stories to tell that will clarify the events that have shaped rural life and made it distinctive" (p. 7).

Chapter 3 concludes with a discussion of a feminist standpoint perspective on the "insider/outsider" debate (namely, which vantage point is preferable for ethnographic investigation) and calls into question this rigid construction. Rather than viewing ethnographic investigation as unmediated description or interpretation of transparent social reality, my materialist feminist approach seeks to reveal the processes through which both the researcher and those who are the subjects of the research come to select, understand, and interpret the complex social and political processes evident in specific contexts.

In chapter 4, I further develop a feminist standpoint analysis of the "insider/outsider" debate begun in chapter 3. I explore the shifting quality of insider/outsider status in my long-term ethnographic study of economic and social restructuring of two small rural towns in southwest Iowa. The changes in racial and ethnic composition of these historically white European American towns resulted from the expansion of a local food processing plant that contributed to an increase in Mexican and Mexican American residents. The process of racialization documented in the course of the fieldwork demonstrates how insider/outsider positions were ever-shifting and permeable social positions. My conceptualization of what I term the "outsider phenomenon" calls into question the dichotomy between insider and outsider that has been a mainstay of ethnographic analysis. By highlighting the material as well as the discursive processes in and through which "outsiderness" was constructed and reconstituted in rural Iowa, I demonstrate how ethnographers are never fully outside or inside the "community."

In chapter 5, I propose a multidimensional feminist standpoint approach to ethnography that offers a rich resource for comparative analyses of women's political praxis. Patricia Hill Collins, Nancy Hartsock, Donna Haraway, and Dorothy Smith, among others defined as "standpoint theorists," offer somewhat different conceptualizations of what constitute a "standpoint" and how a "standpoint" analysis can contribute to the development of "oppositional consciousness" and feminist praxis.[17] By exploring the different conceptualizations of standpoint and analyzing the implications of each concepualization for ethnographic investigation, I developed a multidimensional standpoint methodology that explores the notion of "standpoint": first, as embodied in experiences of both the researcher and the researched; second, as located and constructed in ongoing relationships in communities; and third, as a methodological strategy, namely, a site through which to begin inquiry (Smith 1987). Through illustrations from my research in both rural and urban settings, I demonstrate that a multidimensional standpoint analysis provides an effective materialist feminist conceptual framework through which to investigate the diversity of women's everyday lives, political analyses, and activism in different locations.

Part III: Feminist Materialism, Discourse Analysis, and Policy Studies

In Part III, I demonstrate the power of a materialist feminist appropriation of Foucauldian discourse analysis for social movement and social policy research. In contrast to the approach I take in Part II where I foreground the epistemological frameworks I use in my ethnographic research to illustrate the power of materialist feminist standpoint theory, Part III emphasizes the empirical findings of my materialist feminist discourse analytic work. Chapter 6 analyzes the changing context for "community control" from the 1960s to the 1990s. I use a materialist feminist discourse analysis to reveal how the shifting patterns of gender, race, class, region, among other social structural forces, shape whose voices are represented and heard within the process of social movement framing of "community control." I also draw on newspaper accounts and archival data, annual reports, and minutes from monthly board meetings, as well as relevant archival data and secondary research for this analysis. The question that motivated this examination was: How do progressive frames achieve wide acceptance and become institutionalized in various social practices but lose the critical feminist or progressive intent?

My materialist feminist use of the term *discourse* contrasts with David Snow and Robert Benford's (1992) conceptualization of the process of "framing" by social movement organizations. First, their definition of "collective action frames" refers to how social movement organizations produce and maintain meaning "for constituents, antagonists, and bystanders or observers" (p. 136). In contrast, my case study of community control explores how "discursive frames" limit what can be discussed or heard in a political context and are not tied necessarily to particular organizations. Second, Snow and Benford view the process of "framing" as "an active, process-derived phenomenon that implies agency and contention at the level of reality construction" (p. 136). In my understanding, the conscious use of certain discursive frames is a process bounded by the discursive field itself. Third, Snow and Benford view "master frames" as successful to the extent they mobilize constituents to engage in collective action.[18] In contrast, I am interested in the extent to which frames chosen by movement actors are open to reformulation and become institutionalized in various social practices but lose the critical feminist or progressive intent.

This discursive analytic approach is also a powerful tool for social policy analysis. Chapter 7 explores the construction of the so-called new consensus between Democrats and Republicans as they began to dismantle the entitlements for women and their families on public assistance in the 1980s. I analyze the broad discursive framing in the congressional hearings that led to the passage of the Family Support Act of 1988, the last legislation that funded the welfare program Aid to Families with Dependent Children. These frames privileged the individualist and coercive behavioral strategies such as workfare and inhibited the incorporation of structural analyses into the construction of welfare reform. Policy analyses typically take one of two forms: (1) institutional studies of the legislative process itself including the influence achieved by varying groups and individuals,[19] and (2) evaluation studies that explore the effectiveness and differential results of policies through an analysis of implementation processes and outcome measures. Each approach offers a window into the complex processes by which state policies are enacted and certain outcomes achieved. However, both approaches render invisible the broader discursive field that shapes what is possible to legislate and to implement. Following my materialist feminist framework, social policies are constituted in discourse and formalized in legislation which, in turn, shape the possibilities for implementation.[20]

Conventional policy analysts typically view their work as an attempt to identify which interests and actors were able to achieve a so-called hegemony within the particular historic moment in which the discussion of welfare reform emerged. In contrast, I employ a Foucauldian definition of discourse (Foucault 1978), which holds that discourse is not the property of individual actors and is itself a "practice" that "is structured and . . . has real effects" (Ferguson 1994, 18).[21]

Part IV: Activism, Narrative, and Empowerment

In Part IV, I address the challenges of activist and participatory research, once again highlighting the value of materialist feminist and reflective practice for feminist praxis. In chapter 8, I examine the experiences of women on public assistance who are completing a four-year college degree using an institutional ethnographic approach to oral narrative analysis. This study was conducted collaboratively with Gina Battani, an undergraduate student at Iowa State University, who was receiving public assistance while completing college. In this chapter, I outline the creative ways the women college students on public assistance manage their child care and educational demands as they face economic and other structural barriers to their success in college.

In chapter 9, I apply a materialist feminist discourse analysis to explore the social and institutional locations from which survivor discourse is generated and how relations of ruling are woven in and through it.[22] I address the construction of the term *survivor*, which is often used to refer those who have experienced some sort of crime or abuse and who have redefined their relationship to the experience from one of "victim."[23] This redefinition can occur as a consequence of personal reformulation, psychotherapy, or in discussions with others who define themselves as survivors. I argue for the importance of locating survivors' discourse in the material sites through which it is produced by survivors of childhood sexual abuse and related traumas. Processes of dialogue and consciousness raising remain central to the establishment of alternatives to the totalizing and depoliticized medical/psychiatric and recovery discourse on treatment of adult survivors. While I acknowledge the limits of rational deliberation for "emancipatory" goals, I argue that engagement with others in struggle can provide a strong basis for understanding the personal, political, and collective possibilities for progressive social action.[24] I believe that the benefits overshadow the risks associated with the use of dialogic and reflective strategies.[25]

In order to produce a materialist feminist analysis of survivor discourse that is grounded in the everyday practices of "knowers" (Smith 1987) who are differentially positioned within "survivor discourse," I draw on Nancy Fraser's approach to "needs talk."[26] In her feminist appropriation of Foucault, Fraser (1989, 157) identifies three forms of "needs talk" used to make claims within the modern welfare state: oppositional, reprivatization, and expert discourses. Fraser argues that these discourses "compete with one another in addressing the fractured social identities of potential adherents" (p. 157). By attending to the relations of ruling embedded in the expert discourse on childhood sexual abuse as well as identifying the processes through which hegemonic assumptions of gender, race, class, and sexuality undergird dominant constructions, I highlight sites of resistance and contradictions posed by oppositional formations. My materialist feminist epistemological approach calls for an intersectional examination of these social locations. I conclude with the hopeful assertion that this approach offers one strategy for foregrounding an oppositional survivors' praxis that can pose a challenge to individualized and depoliticized survivors' discourse. However, strategies that rely exclusively on discursive strategies will remain of limited political power for the development of an oppositional survivor discourse and praxis.

In chapter 10, I illustrate the challenge of conducting feminist participatory research, drawing on a participatory research project I was involved in with another survivor of childhood sexual assault during the early 1990s. Participatory research has been promoted in a variety of arenas by university-based researchers as well as those working in the applied fields of agriculture, education, and economic development. I adopted the approach for work with incest survivors who were involved in an activist research project designed to assess the prevalence of childhood sexual abuse in Iowa and raise the consciousness of social service providers and health professionals about the effects of childhood sexual abuse. My activist research partner and I proposed making the "subjugated knowledges" (Foucault 1972) of survivors salient in discussions of childhood sexual abuse.[27] However, we confronted numerous challenges in our attempts to negotiate the different visions we brought to the activist effort.

Conclusion

Feminist reconceptualizations of knowledge production processes have contributed to a shift in research practices in many disciplines, and require more diverse methodological and self-reflective skills than traditional methodological approaches. Postcolonial, postmodern, and queer theoretical critiques of the practice of social scientific research raise a number of dilemmas that haunt feminist researchers as they attempt to conduct research that makes self-evident the assumptions and politics involved in the process of knowledge production in order to avoid exploitative research practices. Feminist sociologists have responded to the challenges posed by critics of traditional social scientific approaches by developing alternative strategies that remain sensitive to the dynamics of power evident in social research. *Feminism and Method* is my contribution to the ongoing efforts by feminist social researchers interested in producing knowledge for social change and generating research strategies that can help counter inequities in the knowledge production process.

Throughout this book I seek to demonstrate the usefulness of my materialist feminist standpoint epistemology and reflective research strategies for feminist research. The methods I highlight include ethnography, oral narrative and textual analysis, and activist and participatory research. My goal is to move beyond abstract principles and theoretical critique to foreground the feminist epistemologies that undergird different methods and to provide empirical examples that explicate themes central to feminist epistemology of methodologies. The illustrations from my case studies of women's politicization and community activism, racialization and rural economic development, construction and implementation of social policy, and activist research provide a window into some of the many dilemmas I encountered in my journey as a feminist sociologist and the practice-oriented solutions I developed over twenty years of research.[28] In the next chapter, I provide an overview of the feminist epistemologies that inform my work.

CHAPTER **2**

Epistemology,
Feminist Methodology,
and the Politics of Method

Feminist theoretical perspectives were developed in the context of diverse struggles for social justice inside and outside the academy. In their various formulations, feminist theories emphasize the need to challenge sexism, racism, colonialism, class, and other forms of inequalities in the research process.[1] Following the powerful insight of the women's movements of the 1960s that "the personal is political," feminist scholars called for research methods that could challenge "the dualities between 'theory' and 'praxis,' researcher and researched, subject and object" (Richardson 1997, 55).[2] Like many feminist scholars, I address questions in my research that are simultaneously personally, politically, and academically significant. From my earliest memories I have been concerned with understanding and fighting inequality and injustice. Not surprisingly, my academic work focuses on examining the reproduction of, and resistance to, inequalities in different communities, as well as identifying strategies that foster social and economic justice. My growing sensitivity to the formal and informal ways domination is manifest in different research settings helped me negotiate discrimination, sexual abuse, and the relations of ruling that infuse my own life.

In light of my activist goal of challenging inequality in all its complex guises, I was drawn to feminist efforts to conduct research that minimizes exploitation of research subjects.[3] My engagement with different feminist epistemologies led me on a journey from socialist feminism to materialist feminism, and from so-called modernist to postmodernist frameworks. The theoretical frames I have used in the course of diverse investigations over almost twenty years of research are infused with different meanings. What it meant to claim an identity of *socialist feminist* or *materialist feminist* in the early 1980s contrasts significantly with the meanings attached to these theoretical formulations in the first part of the twenty-first century. For example, in reviewing this manuscript, one reviewer commented on my use of the term "socialist feminist" and wrote that "I haven't seen that term used since the early 90's actually." Yet socialist feminist theories were extremely influential for my early engagement with academic feminism. For younger feminist scholars, this framing

13

may not be as salient; however, it remains central to the story I tell of my development as a self-reflective feminist researcher. To deny this category of analysis would be to misrepresent the multiple frames that inform the work I present in *Feminism and Method*.

The categories of feminist theory I draw on to tell my own "origin story" as a feminist scholar overlaps to some extent with the historical shifts in what is said to count as feminist theory. The story I tell in this book illustrates how I engaged with, as well as reformulated, different feminist epistemologies in the context of my own empirical investigations. My story also reflects a process of academic socialization as well as my efforts over time to find the most useful theoretical framework to match what I actually did when I conducted research. In shifting identities from socialist feminist to materialist feminist, I was especially influenced by the work of feminist theorists Patricia Hill Collins, Nancy Fraser, Nancy Hartsock, Sandra Harding, bell hooks, Chandra Mohanty, Chéla Sandoval, and Dorothy Smith. In this chapter, I discuss the epistemologies that inform the empirical investigations to follow and discuss some of the debates that surround their theoretical interpretation, especially in terms of the so-called modernist/postmodernist divide.

In responding to different debates in feminist theory and feminist challenges to social scientific practice, I was pushed to define myself in categories that were seldom of my making. In this regard, I found Dorothy Smith's (1987) origin story of feminist standpoint theory, a powerful illustration of how a "collective story" unfolds:

> Feminist standpoint theory, as a general class of theory in feminism, was brought into being by Sandra Harding (1986), not to create a new theoretical enclave but to analyze the merits and problems of feminist theoretical work that sought a radical break with existing disciplines through locating knowledge or inquiry in women's standpoint or in women's experience. Those she identified had been working independently of one another and have continued to do so. In a sense, Harding created us. (P. 392)

As this quote indicates, the stories we tell about our epistemological journeys are always *interested* stories and form a significant dimension of what I call the "politics of method."[4]

The process of naming my theoretical orientation involved becoming aware of the epistemological assumptions I held about how knowledge is produced and what counts as evidence as I engaged in diverse research projects. I also worked to make self-conscious and articulate the ethical stance I took in the "field." This, in turn, influenced how I conducted and interpreted interview transcripts and other ethnographic resources. These reflective processes also informed the questions that guided my research. My efforts to articulate my epistemological grounding was accomplished in the context of training graduate students to work with me on different research projects and guiding the design and implementation of their own research agendas. In this sense, my movement from identifying as a socialist feminist to a materialist feminist engaged in conversations with postmodern and poststructuralist theories is also a *collective story*. Feminist sociologist Laurel Richardson (1997) defines "a collective story" as one that "tells the experience of a sociologically constructed category of people, in the context of larger sociocultural and historical forces" (p. 14). My students and I are situated in the vibrant and ever-changing field of feminist theory and the development of diverse interdisciplinary formations. It may no longer be necessary to emphasize the plurality of feminist theories and the contestations over the naming, redefinition, and interpretation of each theoretical perspective.[5] However, it is important for my goal in this book to locate myself within certain strands of feminist theorizing in order to explicate my approach to feminism and method. In this introductory chapter, I offer an *interested* overview of the frames that are implicated in the epistemological and methodological stories to follow.

Socialist Feminist Theories of the State

My materialist feminist approach was initially built in dialogue with the work of socialist feminist analysts of the state who drew on Marxist theory to examine how the welfare state helps maintain women's dependence on the family and on low-paid positions inside and outside the home (Pascall 1986). I began graduate training in sociology following a short career as a social worker employed by the YWCA of New York City. I quickly found the arguments posed by socialist feminists of the state useful for understanding some of my experiences as an advocate for pregnant teenagers and adolescent mothers during the 1970s and the shifts in state welfare provision over that decade.[6]

Socialist feminist frameworks focused on the intersection of capitalism and patriarchy in the welfare state.[7] Socialist feminist scholars who examined the gendered implications of the welfare state argued that the state promotes capitalist interests by facilitating women's role as reserve labor and as caretakers to reproduce the labor force.[8] They also explored how the welfare state serves the interest of patriarchy by promoting women's unpaid labor in the home (Miller 1989). However, these are contradictory tendencies.[9] Socialist feminists stressed the contradictions of welfare policy including those emanating from the implicit as well as explicit structuring of gender and racial inequality.[10]

My interest in exploring the contradictory role of the state (broadly defined) in women's lives led me to examine how social policies are constructed and inequalities are contested over time. In 1998, I published *Grassroots Warriors: Activist Mothering, Community Work, and the War on Poverty*, which presents findings from my longitudinal study of women community workers hired in Community Action Programs (CAPs) during the War on Poverty. Through an analysis of the experiences of women community activists from low-income neighborhoods in New York City and Philadelphia, I examined how the state shaped their lives—as workers employed by the state, as unpaid community caregivers who linked others access state resources or gain state protection, and as beneficiaries of state welfare programs. *Grassroots Warriors* illustrates the limits as well as the progressive possibilities of social policy. By emphasizing democratic implementation strategies and grassroots community-based activities, many programs established by the War on Poverty helped expand citizenship for low-income residents in concrete ways that went beyond individual-level practices such as voting or paying taxes.[11] Whether designers of the War on Poverty were conscious or not of the political consequences of community action for low-income communities, the political conflict that followed its implementation led to the termination of support for maximum feasible participation of the poor in community based programs and increased pressure towards professionalization and bureaucratization.

The contradictions of the state identified by socialist feminists include expending resources to counter the consequences of the structural inequities in the economy without challenging these inequalities. The welfare state is constructed as a temporary support for the poor which includes primarily short-term policy solutions that fail to address the underlying problems of poverty. Women reliant on state programs for income assistance, child care, housing, or health care experience the contradictions of the state in every area of their lives.[12] Socialist feminist analysts of the state also note the contradiction between the need to support families where the male breadwinner is absent and the desire to protect "the male breadwinner model" of the family creates an inherent tension in welfare policy from the Progressive Era to the present (Sarvasy 1988, 255).[13] Furthermore, the state's "preference" for the two-parent male and female household, as sociologist Rose Brewer (1988) points out, has historically discriminated against the extended kinship and informal networks established in the Black community.[14]

Underlying the state's reluctance to support "poor adults" is the assertion that the two-parent male and female family and the family wage provide the solution to poverty (Christensen et al. 1988). The emphasis on the two-parent male and female household form in social policy reproduces the gender division of labor inside and outside the home.[15] The family wage kept women's wages low and many families in poverty (Pascall 1986, 26). The structure of social support programs such as social security and child care prevent women from choosing their relationship to paid labor and the family. This contradiction continues in contemporary workfare legislation like the Family Support Act and the Personal Responsibility and Work Reconciliation Act (PRWORA) where women lose welfare benefits if they fail to perform the required work, education or training.[16] In the 2002–03 welfare reform debates surrounding the reauthorization of Temporary Assistance to Needy Families (TANF), the goal of forcing women on public assistance to marry is fostered through financial incentives as well as legislative discourse. In President George W. Bush's plan, states would be required to include marriage promotion strategies in their plans.[17]

In a review of socialist feminist analyses of the welfare state in the early 1990s, I identified additional strategies that were understood to enhance women's oppression and impoverishment: the use of gender and race neutral language to mask the sexist and racist assumptions of social policy; maintaining women in paid and nonpaid care taking roles which are devalued both ideologically and economically; legislating morality; and fragmenting social life in state policy.[18] The "point-of-viewlessness" (MacKinnon 1989, 163) of the state includes the production of supposedly gender- and race-neutral policies and law. For example, the term "unemployment," as Gillian Pascall (1986) notes, "belongs to a male working life rather than a female one" and the gender of the perpretrators of "child sexual abuse" is conveniently hidden (p. 4). Women's differential needs and experiences are masked in discussions of "households" and "families" or the "family wage." Since women are most closely linked to the work associated with households and families, women's labor is hidden within the notion of the family wage.[19] Socialist feminists analyses demonstrate how the state frequently utilizes the ideology of the "deserving" or "truly needy" and "nondeserving" or "abled bodied" poor to justify cutbacks in social welfare.[20]

Feminist scholars of the welfare state also emphasize that racist assumptions are incorporated into the design and implementation of social policy.[21] For example, the Personal Responsibility and Work Opportunity Reconciliation Act, passed in 1996, rendered both legal and illegal immigrants ineligible for Temporary Assistance for Needy Families (TANF), the program that replaced Aid to Families with Dependent Children (AFDC). While the language of welfare policies masked some of the most egregious forms of welfare racism that were apparent in previous versions of the bill and in legislative debate, socialist feminist analysts argued that the concern about the "lazy welfare queen" who reproduces "welfare dependency" in her children was not far beneath the surface.[22]

The use of welfare programs for social control is one of the oldest objectives of social policy.[23] The fear of crime and delinquency has often been used as a justification for intrusive methods of state supervision of the poor.[24] The third contradiction of patriarchal social policy noted by socialist feminists refers to the legislative concerns about the "morality" of the mother versus the economic needs of the child.[25] From the poorhouse to the settlement house, reformers were concerned that the poor adopt "proper" middle-class values, especially as they related to "the work ethic" (Katz 1986). Amendments to the Social Security Act in 1940 incorporated the notion of the "suitable home" to control low-income women's sexual behavior and commitment to work. Public assistance could be withheld if women were not performing in ways acceptable to the local welfare officials.

Socialist feminist analysts drew on historical, comparative, and political economic methods to conduct research on gender and the state. Feminist researchers were especially interested in exploring the design, implementation, and changes in social policy formation.[26] Many feminists examined the themes woven into state policy through historical analyses of texts such as congressional legislation, welfare care records, and law.[27] While socialist feminist analyses revealed how assumptions of gender, race, class, and heteronormativity are inscribed in social policy and how these assumptions contribute to the reproduction of inequalities, they have been somewhat constrained in their analytic power by assuming a somewhat totalized view of patriarchy, capitalism, and racism (see G. Joseph 1981). Consequently, socialist feminist frameworks have been unable to offer an epistemological foundation for exploring "scattered hegemonies" (Grewal and Kaplan 1994) or multiple capitalist, patriarchal, colonialist, and racist formations.[28] Since earlier constructions of feminist analyses of patriarchy and Marxist analyses of class remained central to socialist feminism, it theoretically precluded effective responses to more complex theoretical challenges posed by third world, postmodern, and postcolonial scholars. However, by deepening the analysis of the state to incorporate an intersectional understanding of gendered, racialized, and class-based processes, socialist feminists of the state paved the way for more complex intersectional analyses that also incorporated attention to the heteronormative assumptions of gender and family embedded in social policy.[29]

The conceptualization of a unified state has also been problematic for analysis of different state formations and governing practices as they vary over time, place, and space. The "state" is not a unified phenomenon or institution. Varied manifestations of state formations and practices are observable throughout areas of social life that may or may not have any direct or obvious link to formal state structures. For example, state projects of social control can also be taken up by actors who may not hold formal positions within the state. Critics of socialist feminists constructions of the state as a self-evident and unified formation argue for the necessity of locating and specifying the multiple ways the state appears and shifts over time. They also emphasize the importance of examining the different sites of the state-in-action (for example, in legal practices, tax law, state mental institutions, and corporate welfare).[30] Critics of the unified view of the state also argue that oppressive aspects of the state are often in tension with the progressive possibilities of governing practices. Along with the goal of incorporating a more complex intersectional approach to theorizing and a shift from urban policy research to ethnographic research in the 1990s, I developed a greater appreciation for the insights offered by feminist standpoint epistemology.

Feminist Standpoint Epistemology and Racial Formation Theory

Feminist standpoint theory developed in the context of Black feminist, third world and postcolonial feminist challenges to the so-called dual systems of patriarchy and capitalism approach that was associated with socialist feminist theory. Broadly defined, feminist standpoint epistemology includes Nancy Hartsock's (1983) "feminist historical materialist" perspective, Donna Haraway's (1988) analysis of "situated knowledges," Patricia Hill Collins's (1990) "black feminist thought," Chéla Sandoval's (1991, 2000) explication of third world feminists'[31] "differential oppositional consciousness,"[32] and Dorothy Smith's (1987, 1990a, 1990b) "everyday world" sociology for women.[33] Many theorists whose work has been identified with standpoint epistemologies contest this designation. Dorothy Smith has been particularly vocal about the limits of this classification. She writes: "If I could think of a term other than 'standpoint,' I'd gladly shift, especially now that I've been caged in Harding's (1986) creation of the category of 'standpoint theorists' and subjected to the violence of misinterpretation, replicated many times in journals and reviews, by those who speak of Hartsock and Smith but have read only Harding's version of us (or have read us through her version)" (Smith 1992, 91).

Standpoint epistemology, especially as articulated by Hartsock (1983), draws on Marxist historical materialism for the argument that "epistemology grows in a complex and contradictory way from material life" (p. 117). I find the most useful aspect of standpoint analyses in Hartsock's emphasis on "feminist standpoint" as achieved through a reflective and collective process of struggle and analysis.[34] In her critique of standpoint theory, Katie King (1994) notes the "difficulties with conceptualizing the feminist standpoint as a constructed and mobile position"[35] (p. 71). Other critics of Hartsock's approach point out that she "tends to operate with an overly global conception of women's practice and experience and thus to obscure differences and power inequities among women" (Kruks 2001, 112). Political scientist Sonia Kruks defends the project of standpoint theory against its critics, arguing that: "Because it begins from the social division of labor and from accounts of social reality that emerge from different social practices, there is nothing intrinsic to the theory that would preclude developing an account of a multiplicity of women's standpoints, which would perhaps overlap in some aspects and diverge radically in others" (p. 112–13). Kruks points to Haraway's work on "situated knowledges" to demonstrate the usefulness of "certain postmodern sensibilities" for "acknowledging a multiplicity of different epistemological locations for a nondominative feminism" (p. 113).[36]

By arguing for the development of multiple standpoints that derive from what she terms the "matrix of domination," Collins's (1990) approach to standpoint epistemology evokes Donna Haraway's notion of "situated knowledges." Collins reaffirms her standpoint analysis of Black feminist thought as follows:

> In developing a Black feminist praxis, standpoint theory has provided one important source of analytical guidance and intellectual legitimation for African-American women. Standpoint theory argues that group location in hierarchical power relations produces shared challenges for

individuals in those groups. These common challenges can foster similar angles of vision leading to a group knowledge or standpoint that in turn can influence the group's political action. Stated differently, group standpoints are situated in unjust power relations, reflect those power relations, and help shape them. (P. 201)

She also stresses the importance of *praxis,* the interaction of knowledge and experience, for Black feminist thought. Collins's work, in particular, has influenced Nancy Hartsock to revise her earlier formulation to account for "multiple subjectivities," although critics like Katie King (1994, 87) continue to find that Hartsock's approach lacks an "understanding of the shifting, tactical, and mobile character of subjectivities" found in work by Chéla Sandoval and others influenced by postmodern perspectives (p. 87).[37]

From the perspective of feminist praxis, I found that standpoint epistemology provides a methodological resource for explicating "how subjects are constituted by social systems" as well as "how collective subjects are relatively autonomous from, and capable of acting to subvert, those same systems" (Weeks 1998, 92). However, standpoint theorists utilize different constructions of "standpoint." From my review of the diverse approaches to feminist standpoint epistemology, I identified several major connections among them, as well as some important differences which I detail in chapter 5. One of the most salient themes that link the different perspectives on standpoint is the emphasis on the importance of experience for feminist theorizing and the connection to the women's movement's method of consciousness raising. The second significant theme is the assertion of a link between the development of standpoint theory and feminist political goals. In Harding's (1986) formulation of this connection, "Feminism and the women's movement provide the theory and motivation for inquiry and political struggle that can transform the perspective of women into a 'standpoint'—a morally and scientifically preferable grounding for our interpretations and explanations of nature and social life" (p. 26).

Feminist ethnographers who begin analyses from women's diverse social locations have "contributed significantly to reconceptualization of sociological categories—especially, 'politics,' 'work,' and 'family'—typically used to analyze social life" (Naples 1998a, 3). In my research with urban community workers hired by the War on Poverty, I analyzed the extent to which women's militancy has been masked by the traditional categories used to assess political action.[38] Since much of their efforts occurred outside the formal political establishment, traditional measures of political participation would have underestimated their activism. My analysis of the community workers' oral histories, revealed "a broad-based notion of 'doing politics' that included any struggle to gain control over definitions of self and community, to augment personal and communal empowerment, to create alternative institutions and organizational processes, and to increase the power and resources of the community workers' defined community—although not all of these practices were viewed as 'politics' in the community workers' terminology" (Naples 1998b, 179). I conceptualized their community work as "activist mothering" which I defined as "political activism as a central component of mothering and community caretaking of those who are not part of one's defined household or family" (p. 11). This analysis offered "a new conceptualization of the interacting nature of labor, politics and mothering—three aspects of social life usually analyzed separately—from the point of view of women whose motherwork historically has been ignored or pathologized in sociological analyses" (p. 112–13).[39]

Mareena Wright (1995) also uses standpoint analysis of rural women's everyday experiences to reconceptualize models of work that are limited by the separation of unpaid household labor from paid labor. She develops a "multidimensional continuum model of women's work" (p. 216) that "contradicts old [dual spheres] notions that household work is somehow different or less significant to society than is waged work" (p. 232). By substituting the dual spheres model, Wright's multidimensional continuum model reorients how we understand (p. 232) such as women's labor decision-making processes, women's life course patterns, and our current social policies, especially those regarding the care of children and the elderly.[40] Virginia Seitz (1998) also draws on standpoint theory for her examination of white, working-class Appalachian women's understanding and practice of class struggle. Seitz examines how women from southwestern Virginia successfully "challenged the coal company, the state, and, eventually-working-class men" (p. 213) and contested taken-for-granted constructions of gender and working-class politics. As Seitz emphasizes, however, "sharing the same . . . set of experiences does not necessarily translate into shared political analyses, organizational strategies, and leadership style" (p. 213). In illuminating the "powerful ways in which these women drew upon their gender, class, and racialized ethnicity as 'Appalachians' to help wage a successful strike against the powerful Pittston Coal Company," Seitz illustrates the partiality of standpoints as they intersect in and through different women's political understandings and self-expression (p. 213).

Feminist ethnographers emphasize the significance of locating and analyzing particular standpoints in differing contexts to explicate relations of domination embedded in communities and social institutions.[41] For example, Christina Gringeri (1994), in her examination of rural development from the diverse perspectives of women home-workers and rural development officials in two Midwestern communities, helps explain how rural development strategies are perceived differently by planners and by those who pay the costs of development (also see Naples 1997). Even when they do not directly evoke standpoint epistemology in their work, feminist ethnographers such as Ruth Behar (1993), Sondra Hale (1991), Lila Abu-Lughod (1993), Suad Joseph (1988), Dorrine Kondo (1990), Susan Krieger (1983), and Maria Mies (1982) demonstrate the value of *positionality* for developing strong self-reflective research strategies as well as for ethnographic analysis.

The concept of *positionality* foregrounds how women can strategically "use their positional perspective as a place from where values are interpreted and constructed rather than as a locus of an already determined set of values" (Alcoff 1988, 434). As I argue in Part II of this book, reflective practice informed by standpoint analyses of positionality encourages feminist scholars to examine how gendered and racialized assumptions influence which voices and experiences are privileged in ethnographic encounters.[42] Since the conceptualization of "standpoint" has multiple meanings depending on which approach to standpoint epistemology is referenced, I prefer the term *positionality* when referring to subjectivity and subjective knowledges. The notion of positionality provides a conceptual frame that allows one to "say at one and the same time that gender is not natural, biological, universal, ahistorical, or essential and yet still claim that gender is relevant because we are taking gender as a position from which to act politically" (Alcoff 1988, 433). In my approach, the "position" from which one acts politically is also subject to investigation. I simultaneously take as the starting point, the intersection of gender, race, class, and political context in social actors' political praxis.

Another conceptual resource I draw on for my ethnographic research approach is found in the theory of racial formation developed by sociologists Michael Omi and Howard Winant (1986). Their conceptualization of *racialization* counters certain analyses of standpoint that treat it as fixed in time and space and unproblematically attached to specific and identifiable individuals or groups (Hennessy 1993). According to racial formation theory, race is "a constituent of the individual psyche and of relationships among individuals, . . . an irreducible component of collective identities and social structures" and "contested throughout social life" (p. 23). Winant (1994, 43) defines racialization as "a repertoire of coercive social practices driven by desires and fears, as a framework for class formation, or as an ideology for nation building and territorial expansion, to name but a few" (p. 43). Racialization is also evident in global processes and racial projects that circumscribe "the political terrain upon which racially defined groups could mobilize within civil society, thus constituting these groups as outside civil society" (Winant 1994, 43). In my view, racialization processes are salient in all dimensions of standpoint analysis. Therefore, the concept of racialization is useful for analyzing the shifts in racial-ethnic constructions and interactions over time. Analyses of racialization processes can be extended to incorporate sensitivity to class, sexuality, and gender as well as other dimensions upon which difference is constructed and domination operates.

My development and elaboration of different dimensions of standpoint epistemology revealed a tension between theorists who considered standpoint theory to be firmly grounded in the modernist concerns of feminist political goals and those who viewed standpoint epistemology as anticipating many of the postmodern calls to avoid grand narrative constructions of identity and construct power as multiple and productive. Using a Foucauldian articulation of power, education theorist Jennifer Gore (1992) analyzes power "as exercised, rather than as possessed" (p. 59). This approach, she argues, requires more attention to the microdynamics of the operation of power as it is exercised in particular sites" (p. 59). I view standpoint epistemologies as powerful tools for exploration of the "microdynamics of the operation of power" and find in some strands of standpoint theorizing, sustained attention to the way power infuses investigation and the textual products of such efforts.[43] Therefore, the power of standpoint theorizing can be enhanced by incorporation of insights from postmodern and postcolonial perspectives on power, subjectivity, and language.

Postmodern, Postcolonial, and Third World Feminist Challenges

Postmodern feminist scholars emphasize the ways disciplinary discourses shape how researchers see the worlds they investigate and how "without critique of the metanarratives that theoretically and practically sustain the structures and discourses of" (Luke 1992, 37) academia, research operates to reinsert power relations, rather than challenge them.[44] Many feminist ethnographers have grappled with the challenges posed by postmodern critics and are "divided about the merits and shortcomings of postmodern theorizing" (D. Wolf 1996b, 6). Sociologist Diane Wolf explains that some feminist scholars "have found useful the sensitivity postmodernism demonstrates toward a greater multiplicity of power relations. Postmodernist theorizing has created opportunities for further innovation in research methods and the post-fieldwork process, particularly representation and writing" (p. 6). However, many other feminist scholars "are concerned that the overly textual focus of postmodernism renders the lived realities of women irrelevant" (D. Wolf 1996b, 6). For example, anthropologist Margery Wolf (1996, 215) is concerned that feminist ethnographers "are letting interesting critical positions from outside feminism weaken our confidence in our work; perhaps we are taking too seriously the criticisms of our process by those who have never experienced it" (p. 215).

Rural sociologist Carolyn Sachs (1996) fears that a postmodern emphasis on "fractured identities" and "the multitude of subjectivities" could lead to "total relativism" that precludes political activism (p. 19). Concerns about the depoliticizing consequences of postmodern theories are a consistent thread in feminist debates on the value of postmodernist theories for feminist praxis. Women's Studies scholars Jacqui Alexander and Chandra Mohanty (1997) express concern that

> postmodern theory, in its haste to dissociate itself from all forms of essentialism, has generated a series of epistemological confusions regard-

ing the interconnections between location, identity, and the construction of knowledge. Thus, for instance, localized questions of experience, identity, culture, and history, which enable us to understand specific processes of domination and subordination, are often dismissed by postmodern theories as reiterations of cultural "essence" or unified, stable identity. (P. xvii)

Postmodern analyses of power have destabilized the practice of ethnography (Clifford 1990). If power infects every encounter and if discourse infuses all expressions of personal experience, what can the ethnographer do to counter such powerful forces? This dilemma is at the heart of a radical postmodern challenge to social scientific practice in general. As sociologists Jaber Gubrium and James Holstein (1997) note, "Postmodernist inquiry tends to veer away from how members of society interact to produce their lives and experience, turning more toward the representational practices used by those claiming the authority to offer 'true' representation" (p. 76).[45] Many social scientists committed to empirical investigation worry that postmodern theories of representation undermine their research enterprise, leading not only to neverending self-criticism but also, and more troubling, to "empirical nihilism" (Gubrium and Holstein 1997,109).

In attempting to generate "a new language of qualitative method" for the social sciences, Gubrium and Holstein combine the diverse theoretical traditions of naturalism, ethnomethodology, "emtionalism" (which focuses on "the affective, visceral, and subjective dimensions of experience" and postmodernism (p. 56). They adopt Pauline Rosenau's (1992) articulation of "a more affirmative variant of the idiom" of postmodernism and bracketing it from skeptical postmodernism which, they note "is enamored with a nihilistic vision of a world of ungrounded representation" (Gubrium and Holstein 1997, 79). Yet, even with such "bracketing" strategies, the fundamental premises that undergird divergent perspectives combined under the rubric of one approach to methodology, if brought to the surface, could destabilize the coherence of the internal set of meanings of the resulting epistemological stance.[46]

My strategy for negotiating these challenges has been one of praxis, namely, to generate a materialist feminist theoretical approach informed by postmodern and postcolonial analyses of knowledge, power, and language that speaks to the empirical world in which my research takes place. By foregrounding the everyday world of poor women of different racial and ethnic backgrounds in both the rural and urban United States and by exploring the governing practices that shape their lives I have worked to build a class conscious and antiracist methodological approach (Alexander and Mohanty 1997, xxxiii).[47] While acknowledging the limits of my own angle of vision and reflective practice to disrupt the power imbalances inherent in the research enterprise, my feminist praxis led me beyond the modernist/postmodernist divide to draw on some of the many valuable insights of Marxist, postcolonial, and postmodern perspectives on power and knowledge.

While postcolonial and third world feminist scholars point to the myriad of ways relations of domination infuse ethnography,[48] they also offer some guidance for negotiating power inherent in the practice of fieldwork. Postcolonial feminist scholars charge that the practice of ethnography among marginalized groups is historically tainted by ethnocentric biases in traditional ethnographic practice as well as feminist research.[49] Further, as philosopher Sandra Harding (1998, 12) emphasizes, ethnocentrism is more than a set of "false beliefs and bad attitudes" held by individual scholars; it is structured into the institutional and academic practices so as to produce relationships oppressive to indigenous cultures in the so-called first world as well as third world countries. Harding (1998) asserts:

> What is most startling, and disturbing, from such a perspective of insti-
> tutional, societal, and civilizational eurocentrism is to realize that even
> individuals with the highest moral intentions, and with the most up-to-
> date, state-of-the-art, well-informed, rational standards according to
> the prevailing institutions and their larger cultures, can still be actively
> advancing institutional, societal, and philosophic eurocentrism. (Pp.
> 14–15)

Feminists are not exempt from "assumptions of privilege and ethnocentric universality, on the one hand, and inadequate self-consciousness about the effect of Western scholarship on the 'third world' in the context of a world system dominated by the West, on the other" (Mohanty 1991a, 53). Unfortunately, as Chandra Mohanty emphasizes, these factors "characterize a sizable extent of Western feminist work on women in the third world" (p. 53).

Mohanty calls for "careful, politically focused, local analyses" to counter the trend in feminist scholarship to distance from or misrepresent third world women's concerns.[50] She draws on Maria Mies's (1982) work on lace makers in Narsapur, India, to illustrate this ethnographic approach:

> Mies's analysis shows the effect of a certain historically and culturally
> specific mode of patriarchal organization, an organization constructed
> on the basis of the definition of the lace makers as "non-working house-
> wives" at familial, local, regional, statewide, and international levels. The
> intricacies and the effects of particular power networks not only are em-
> phasized, but they form the basis of Mies's analysis of how this particular
> group of women is situated at the center of a hegemonic, exploitative
> world market. (Mohanty 1991, 65)

Furthermore, Mohanty remarks, "Narsapur women are not mere victims of the production process" (p. 65). Instead, they resist, challenge, and subvert the process at various junctures" (p. 65).[51]

Alexander and Mohanty (1997) recommend "grounding analyses in particular, local feminist praxis" as well as understanding "the local in relation to larger, cross-national processes" (p. xix). The authors contributing to *Women's Activism and Globalization: Linking Local Struggles with Transnational Politics* (Naples and Desai 2002) show the diverse strategies women have developed to "organiz[e] against the gendered, racialized, and regionalized[52] processes of global capital expansion" and militarization and for sustainable agriculture (Naples 2002b, 13). As coeditor Manisha Desai argues:

> Many resistance strategies embody a radical critique not just of global capital but also of preexisting social inequalities based on race, class, gender, sexuality, and nationality among others. Many activist women's efforts focus, to varying degrees and in various ways, on developing concrete economic alternatives based on sustainable development, social equality, and participatory processes though such economic initiatives have not been as successful at the transnational level (Basu 2000). These "counter hegemonies" have succeeded in transforming the daily lives of many women at the local level. This, in my view, is what gives women's agency immense potential. (P. 32)

In assessing the power of transnational feminist networks for struggles against "existing inequalities," Desai points out that these activist associations "are forged not on preconceived identities and experiences but in the context of struggle and as such are more reflexive about these inequalities" (p. 33).

Despite the valuable efforts of feminist ethnographers to produce more balanced accounts of third world women, some postcolonial critics fear that "a 'non-colonialist' (and therefore non contaminated?) space remains a wish-fulfillment within postcolonial knowledge production" (Rajan 1993, 8). In my own ethnographic practice, I have found that materialist feminist theory informed by standpoint epistemology offered methodological strategies that can serve as effective responses to postmodern and postcolonial challenges to ethnographic practice. While I continue to hold deep reservations that any of the major dilemmas inherent in ethnographic practice can be consistently overcome, I remain optimistic that with a commitment to strong reflective strategies, especially ones that include, whenever possible, dialogue and respectful engagement with the subjects of our research, the context and form of the dilemmas can be brought to the surface and become part of the ethnographic story. This contrasts with more traditional ethnographic accounts that deny the power of the ethnographer as well as the subjects of ethnographic encounters and ignore how ruling relations infuse all our research efforts, regardless of method. Taking up the poststructuralist[52] insight of the inherent link between "language, subjectivity, social organization, and power" (Richardson 1997, 88), I turn now to discuss another method for feminist research, discourse analysis, and highlight the power of a materialist feminist appropriation of Foucault for social policy research.

Materialist Feminism and Discourse Analysis

Materialist feminism, in its more recent formulation, engages with historical materialist and postmodern theories of self, agency, and discourse.[53] For example, in their introduction to *Materialist Feminism: A Reader in Class, Difference, and Women's Lives*, Rosemary Hennessy and Chrys Ingraham (1997) describe materialist feminism as "the conjuncture of several discourses—historical materialism, marxist and radical feminism, as well as postmodern and psychoanalytic theories of meaning and subjectivity" (p. 7). Materialist feminists view agency "as complex and often contradictory sites of representation and struggle over power and resources" (Hesford 1999, 74).

Materialist feminism, as I reconstruct its intellectual history, has its roots in socialist feminist theory and has been particularly influenced by the theoretical critiques of African American, Chicana, and third world feminists[54] who, in turn, contributed to the development of diverse feminist standpoint epistemologies as discussed above.[55] I found the work of Gloria Anzaldúa, and Cherríe Moraga especially helpful for broadening the intersectional framework of feminist standpoint epistemology. For example, in the preface to *This Bridge Called My Back*, Moraga passionately ties the political consciousness of women of color to the material experiences of their lives. This "politics of the flesh" (Moraga 1981, xviii) does not privilege one dimension and artificially set it apart from the context in which it is lived, experienced, felt, and resisted. In fact, literary scholar Paula Moya (1997) argues that Moraga's "theory in the flesh" provides a powerful "non-essentialist way to ground . . . identities" for the purposes of resistance to domination (p. 150).[56]

Contemporary formulations of materialist feminism[57] are also informed by Michel Foucault's analysis of discourse. For example, Chéla Sandoval (2000) argues that "the theory and method of oppositional and differential consciousness is aligned with Foucault's concept of power, which emphasizes the figure of the very *possibility* of positioning power itself" (p. 77, emphasis in original).[58] However, Foucault is an unlikely resource for feminist praxis given two features of his work: his neglect of the dynamics of gender in his analysis of power and his displacement of the subject as a central agent for social change.[59] However, as Vikki Bell (1993) argues, "Foucault's politics . . . has its emphasis on local resistance and the questioning of discursive categories that surround us"—two political projects that have much in common with feminist praxis (p. 55).[60] Foucault argues that "power is not overt domination of one group by another, but the acceptance by all that there exists 'an ideal, continuous, smooth text that runs beneath the multiplicity of contradictions, and resolves them in the calm unity of coherent thought'" (Foucault 1972, 155, quoted in Worrall 1990, 8–9). Discourses are defined as "historically variable ways of specifying knowledge and truth—what is possible to speak of at a given moment" (Ramazanoglu 1993, 19). They are not merely "groups of signs (signifying elements referring to contents or representations) but [are] practices that systematically form the objects of which they speak" (Foucault 1972, 49).

Foucault's work is especially relevant for social policy research given his interest in issues of governance and "governmentability" (Foucault 1979). Drawing on Foucault's notion of "governmentality," science studies scholar Nancy Campbell (2000) demonstrates how conventional approaches to "[p]olicy analysis typically misses the cultural assumptions . . . which then exert unacknowledged effects on the policymaking process and policy outcomes."[61] To understand how, what she terms *governing mentalities* affect policymaking and policy implementation, Campbell argues for "a mode of analytic attention that does not divide social structure from discourse, and proceeds with a historical contextualization of our political rationality" (p. 54). In her exploration of the "gender-coded and racially marked" U.S. state policy on illegal drug use, Campbell reveals how "notions of dependency, femininity, and sexual deviance" (p. 36) are mobilized to "target the behaviors of the 'dangerous classes' but excuse those of the dominant" (p. 9). As mentioned in my discussion of socialist feminist theories of the state, women, especially women of color, are particularly disadvantaged by cultural constructions of morality that are formed within a white, middle-class cultural ideal. As Campbell (2000, 7) demonstrates in her analysis of drug policy, "cultural values are installed in public policy in ways that do not always yield policies that are practical, ethical, or just," and, I would add, seldom achieve the goals they are explicitly designed to address. In order to examine how "cultural values" are woven into public policy as well as social movement frames designed to make claims for social justice, I developed a materialist feminist approach to discourse analysis. I illustrate the value of this approach for policy analysis in Part III of *Feminism and Method*.

Discourse analysis of policy explores what can be said and what can be heard within the legislative arena. Legislators and others who participate in the policy formation process must draw on recognizable discursive frames in order to enter discussions about welfare reform or other social policy. Such a process is illustrative of what Foucault describes as discursive strategies. However, as philosopher Gary Gutting (1989) points out, Foucault's "archaeology turns away from the subject and toward the conditions that define the discursive space [or discursive field] in which speaking subjects exist" (p. 244). Feminist critics of Foucault caution that the turn from the subject undermines the political agency of women and others who are interested in contesting the dominant power relations (McNay 1992; Ramazanoglu 1993). Foucault's approach also masks the important feminist insight that social policies target gendered and racialized subjects. By utilizing discourse analysis within a materialist feminist epistemology, I argue that the dynamics of gender, race, and class are brought into the frame more effectively than is possible with a non-feminist Foucauldian approach.

Embedded in both the processes that generate a legislative outcome are the *relations of ruling* that structure the daily lives of those who are the objects of legislative discourse (Smith 1990a, 1990b). In Smith's materialist feminist approach, "the objectified forms, the rational procedures, and the abstracted conceptual organization create an appearance of neutrality and impersonality that conceals class, gender, and racial subtexts" (1990b, 65). Foucauldian discourse analysis offers an explicit methodology to reveal the discursive strategies that reinforce as well as reveal the limits of power. As Michel Foucault (1978) explains: "Discourse transmits and produces power; it reinforces it, but also undermines and exposes it, renders it fragile and makes it possible to thwart it" (p. 101). However, Dorothy Smith differentiates her materialist feminist approach from Foucault's in significant ways. Smith (1987) argues for a feminist sociology that will reveal "the actual practices of actual people" that abstractions both "express and conceal" (p. 213). As she explains: "Those of us who have written what Sandra Harding (1986) has explored as 'standpoint epistemologies' learned that there are indeed matters to be spoken and spoken of that discourse does not yet encompass" (1993, 183–84).

Materialist Feminism, Institutional Ethnography, and Activist Research

In Part IV of *Feminism and Method*, I foreground my efforts to conduct activist and participatory research. In chapter 9, I utilize *institutional ethnography*, Smith's (1987) materialist feminist methodology, to examine how relations of ruling are infused in the everyday life of women college students on public assistance. The practice of institutional ethnography focuses on how women's actual everyday experiences are mediated and defined by text-based sociological and other institutionally related discourses. Those who adopt an institutional ethnographic approach link their work to a variety of traditions including phenomenology and ethnomethodology as well as Marx's historical materialism and poststructuralism.[62] Institutional ethnographers examine how ruling relations are woven into the production of texts used to organize people's activities in various locations such as schools or government agencies or professional offices.[63] A materialist feminist institutional ethnographic investigation makes it possible to disclose to those we work with (for example, in a particular institutional setting like education) how their daily lives are organized by processes of ruling and how these processes can be contested. It is this aspect of Smith's "institutional ethnographic" approach that contributes to its power for feminist activist research. The institutional and political knowledges that feminist researchers uncover through their investigations illustrate the link between institutional ethnography and feminist activism. In the context of activist research, analysts explore the institutional forms and procedures, informal organizational processes, as well as discursive frames used to construct the goals and targets of the work that the institution performs. Smith's approach ensures that a commitment to the political goals of the Women's Movement remains central to feminist research by foregrounding how ruling relations work to organize everyday life.[64] With a "thick" understanding of "how things are put together" it becomes possible to identify effective activist interventions. However, as Devault (1999, 53) explains, "using research results effectively to promote change requires the pragmatic evaluative and strategic skills of activism, honed through more daily participation in front-line work than most researchers can manage . . . These comments point to a final element of institutional ethnographic investigation: to be fully realized, such inquiries should be conducted with an eye to their use by specific groups."

In one of the most poignant examples of the power of institutional ethnography for activist goals, Ellen Pence (1996) created what she termed "the safety and accountability audit" to explore how criminal justice and law enforcement policies and practices can be enhanced to ensure the safety of women who are the victims of domestic violence and to ensure the accountability of the offender. Pence (2002) developed the safety audit to examine the process by which "workers are institutionally organized to do their jobs by the forms, policies, philosophy, practices, and culture of the institution in which they work." Pence's safety audit has been used by police departments, criminal justice and probation departments, and family law clinics in diverse settings across the country. Pence asserts that her approach is not a "performance review of individual employees." Instead, "It examines the institution or system and how it is set up to handle domestic violence cases. Safety and Accountability Audits involve mapping the system, interviewing and observing workers and analyzing paperwork and other text generated through the handling of domestic violence cases."[65]

Institutional ethnographic research is not designed to focus primarily on the content of specific social actors spoken experiences. Dorothy Smith (1999) explains that she resists providing content to the standpoint of social actors because "I want it to function like the arrow you see on maps of malls that tells you 'you are here! The metaphor of a map directs us to a form of knowledge of the social that shows relations between various and differentiated local sites of experiences without subsuming or displacing them" (p. 130). Smith's mapmaking strategy helps an investigator map the activities that coordinate and reproduce oppressive systems and provides a useful tool for activist research. It also helps capture the nuances, contradictions, and less formal processes, institutional processes that intersect in particular social or institutional locations. This knowledge can be used as a resource for social change efforts, providing an assessment of how power operates in local practices of ruling and where activist interventions might be most successful.

The social maps generated from institutional ethnographic investigations are "through and through indexical to the local sites of people's experiences, making visible how we are connected into the extended social ruling relations and the economy." Since the "product could be ordinarily accessible and usable, just as a map is," it offers a guidepost for activist interventions (Smith 1999, 94–95). The goal of activist research is to produce an analysis that retains the integrity of political processes, specific events, diverse actors, and social context while revealing the broader processes at work that may not have been visible to the individual participants or even to the researcher at the time they were engaged in the struggle or when they conducted the research (Naples 1998a).

In an effort to democratize the research process, many feminist researchers argue for adopting participatory strategies that involve community residents or other participants in the design, implementation, and analysis of the research.[66] This analytic process can be further deepened when dialogic reflective strategies are adopted. This form of reflective practice is a collective activity involving ongoing dialogue between and among participants and co-researchers. Sociologist Susan Stern demonstrates in her activist research with parents from the predominantly African American high school her daughter Sarah attended, that conversational strategies can become an integral part of daily life, and politicization, and ethnographic analysis. In small groups or as conversation partners, participants in the conversational research project can assess findings and refocus research questions.[67] Stern (1998) points to the significance of friendship in providing grounds for more egalitarian conversation-based activist research and demonstrates how "[c]onversation-based research builds on ordinary friendship conversations in which exploration of the personal realm grows to include investigation of shared social conditions" (p. 110).[68] Dialogue among participants in an activist project helps in the development of grassroots analyses of personally experienced problems that are inevitably politically constituted.[69]

Analysis of community activism or the process of politicization can be deepened by making one's activist experiences and standpoint visible. Activist researchers have been ambivalent about writing themselves into the narrative record. On the one hand, this strategy can lead to a more honest account of the social movement activities or activist organization in which they participated. Incorporating one's activist experiences and positionality into the analysis can result in a deeper understanding of the political strategies chosen and the process of politicization (Naples 1998a). On the other hand, such a strategy may be viewed as an attempt to create a more "true" or "authentic" depiction of the field encounter, thus once again privileging the researcher's voice over others whose lives were the subject of the inquiry. In addressing this dilemma sociologists Kathy Charmaz and Richard Mitchell (1997) find a middle ground between "deference to subjects' views" and "audible authorship" and stress that they "do not pretend that our stories report autonomous truths, but neither do we share the cynic's nihilism that ethnography is a biased irrelevancy" (p. 194). They offer a strategy for writing an ethnographic account where "the writer remains in the background and becomes embedded in the narrative rather than acting in the scene. The reader hears the writer's words, envisions the scenes, and attends to the story, not the story teller" (p. 214). In chapter 4, I present a similar writing strategy that enriches both the presentation of the ethnographic findings and the reflective analysis.

In addition to the value of reflective practice and dialogic strategies for collective action and activist research, they can also enrich the practice of ethnographic research more broadly. These interrelated processes are especially useful for making conscious what's at stake for us as feminist researchers in the work we do and how our investments inform what we can know about the processes that shape our lives and those of our respondents. In order to render visible what is at stake in the knowledge production process, reflective practices provide valuable tools throughout the research and writing process. The goal of reflective practice is "to avoid creating new orthodoxies that are exclusionary and reifying" (Grewal and Kaplan 1994, 18). The next chapter explores some of the reflective strategies developed by feminist ethnographers who have been influenced by standpoint epistemologies.

Conclusion

In this chapter, I discussed the theoretical strands that have influenced my approach. I described the challenges posed by postmodern and postcolonial scholars and discussed how feminists have participated in these debates and responded with innovative methodological strategies such as reflective techniques, standpoint epistemologies, feminist discourse analysis, and activist and participatory research. My materialist feminist approach to research was developed in dialogue with socialist feminist theories of the state and was subsequently transformed by incorporating the insights of feminist standpoint epistemologies and postmodern and postcolonial feminist perspectives. More specifically, my epistemological stance was enriched by "conversations" and practical application of the work of Dorothy Smith, Sandra Harding, Nancy Hartsock, Nancy Fraser, Patricia Hill Collins, Donna Haraway, Chéla Sandoval, Chandra Mohanty, and Michel Foucault.

Every research study I have conducted or have been fortunate to participate in required both personal and professional resources, and often it was difficult to separate one type of resource from the other. Along with greater understanding of the phenomena I was investigating, I also came away with greater self-awareness that in turn improved my skill as a researcher. Each research project and research site posed new challenges and offered different lessons. In the next three sections of *Feminism and Method*, I present the lessons I learned in three different methodological approaches: ethnography, discourse analysis, and activist and participatory research. The themes I address include how to negotiate the multiplicity of approaches to feminist standpoint epistemology and to assess their relevance for feminist ethnographic practice; how to generate a materialist feminist analysis of discourse; and how to negotiate the tensions between feminist activist goals and research strategies.

PART II

Standpoint Epistemologies, Reflective Practice, and Feminist Ethnography

CHAPTER 3

Standpoint Analysis and Reflective Practice

In my effort to deal with the dilemmas of power in fieldwork, I have developed a strong reflective ethnographic practice that acknowledges how relationships in the field blur what counts as "data," takes into account the contradictions of friendship in fieldwork, and openly confronts ethical dilemmas faced in fieldwork-based friendships to enhance fieldwork agendas. My approach has been influenced by feminist standpoint, postmodern, and postcolonial researchers who have developed innovative methodological strategies designed "to seriously and self-reflexively 'deconstruct' our practices so that we can 'reconstruct' them with fewer negative consequences" (Richardson 1990, 118).[1] Postmodern analysts of ethnographic practice emphasize how relationships between researchers and those whose lives they study are dynamic and ever-changing. Furthermore, from this perspective on power, I argue, members of the groups or communities we research are also active participants in the research process and can play powerful roles in shaping what we come to know about their lives and the communities in which they live and work.

In considering how ethnographers determine how to position themselves in relationship to the individuals they study, Richardson (1990) asks: "How is it possible to situate ourselves as participant observers in the lives of others and not affect them? The social skills that we use to do ethnographies attach us to real human beings. They connect us to people in deeply human ways. And then, we become (solo) authors of 'true' texts, which have unintended, often hurtful, consequences for those who have trusted us" (p. 118). In this chapter, I explore how feminist researchers informed by standpoint theoretical frameworks employ reflective practice to counter the reproduction of inequalities in ethnographic investigation. Although not a complete solution, feminist ethnographers have used reflective strategies effectively to become aware of, and diminish the ways in which, domination and repression are reproduced in the course of research and in the products of their work. Furthermore, I argue, sustained attention to these dynamics can enrich ethnographic account as well as improve ethnographic practice.

By utilizing reflective practice informed by standpoint epistemology, researchers are able to make visible what is privileged as ethnographic data as well as identify "the historical force and potentially creative role of subjectivity" (Weeks 1998, 92)—ours as well as those whose lives we seek to understand. Standpoint epistemologies, especially as articulated by Dorothy Smith, stress that "our social relations—for example, our gender or class relations—are not constructed by outside forces, but rather are constituted in and through our everyday practices" (Weeks 1998, 90–91). This framework offers "a more dialectical conception of the relationship between system and subject, one in which women are not just passive products of social forces but also active participants" (p. 91). The purpose of this chapter is to demonstrate how feminist ethnographers have used standpoint analysis to position themselves within the cultural groups or communities they study and to construct reflective strategies for field research. By adopting reflective strategies, feminist ethnographers work to reveal the inequalities and processes of domination that shape the "field." Reflective practice includes an array of strategies that begin when one first considers ethnographic fieldwork. How one presents the research, who should be the initial contact, what form of dress and address (more or less formal, more or less personal), and where one should live and work while conducting fieldwork are all aspects of reflective practice. These examples refer to a more embodied and somewhat thin view of reflexivity. However, by deepening and extending the process of reflective practice to other dimensions of ethnographic research, ethnographers can generate more complex analyses of the relations of ruling and the development of oppositional consciousness.

Challenges of Ethnographic Practice

Feminists who adopt ethnographic techniques do so at a time when the practice of conventional ethnography is under challenge from a number of directions. Postmodern critics caution that claims to authority in ethnographic accounts belie the looseness of the connection between representational accounts and "an independent social reality" (Hammersley 1992, 2). Furthermore, critical anthropologists argue, "The data which ethnographers use is a product of their participation in the field rather than a mere reflection of the phenomenon studied, and/or is constructed in and through the process and analysis and the writing of ethnographic accounts" (Hammersley 1992, 2). Taking heed of these cautions along with feminist critiques of the objectification of women and others in academic practice and discourse, feminist ethnographers sought to create methodologies and writing strategies designed to challenge the separation between researched and researchers. Diane Wolf (1996b) emphasizes that:

> Power is discernible in three interrelated dimensions: (1) power difference stemming from different positionalities of the researcher and the researched (race, class, nationality, life chances, urban-rural background);

(2) power exerted during the research process, such as defining the research relationship, unequal exchange, and exploitation; and (3) power exerted during the postfieldwork period—writing and representing. (P. 2)

For example, anthropologist Dorinne Kondo (1990) describes how her biography influences her ethnographic account of identity in a Japanese workplace. She explains how "the questions I asked and the responses I received, even the writing of the ethnographic text, occupy a space within a particular history of a specific ethnographer and her informants as we sought to understand each other within shifting fields of power and meaning" (p. 8). As a consequence, Kondo stresses, her textual product is necessarily "partial and located" and "screened through the narrator's eye/I."

Another illustration of this reflective approach can be found in Karen Kendrick's (1998) investigation of battered women's shelters in Orange County, California. Kendrick notes how pressures from governmental officials, funding sources, and professionals in law and social welfare displaced battered women and other community members as central players—a finding consistent with other research in this field. In addition to analysis of organizational history and institutional change, Kendrick describes how her understanding of what it meant to be a feminist, i.e., strong, independent, resistant to patriarchal control, impeded her ability to seek help as a "battered woman." She felt that if she came out as a "battered woman," it would signify that she was a "bad feminist." Further, when Kendrick initiated her research on the politics of battered women's shelters, she expected to find a very vocal radical feminist perspective among the shelter staff, one that contrasted sharply with the perspective of the police and lawyers, for example. With the materialist feminist tool of institutional ethnography, Kendrick's research led her to a much richer analysis of the politics of race, class, sexuality, gender, and institutionalization as they intersected in constructing "battered woman" as the target of shelter work. By drawing on Dorothy Smith's institutional ethnographic approach, Kendrick and other researchers are provided with a feminist epistemological approach that Smith developed directly out of her activist engagement with academic knowledge production.

In response to the explication of how power infuses ethnographic investigation, some feminist ethnographers argue that reflective and dialogic techniques can be employed to reveal how power and difference construct encounters in the field. However, some of the strategies utilized by feminist ethnographers, such as attempting to develop more intimacy and egalitarian relationships between subjects of research and themselves, has led to the recognition of other dilemmas in fieldwork. Tamar El-Or, who is Lecturer of Sociology and Anthropology at the Hebren University in Jerusalem, conducted research among those living in Gur Hassidim, a suburb of Tel Aviv close to her home. She describes how intimacy between researchers and informants can mask the objectification of the researched. El-Or (1997) states:

> Intimacy thus offers a cozy environment for the ethnographic journey, but at the same time an illusive one. The ethnographer wants information, this information happens to be someone else's real life. The informant's willingness to cooperate with the ethnographer might arise from different motivations, but it usually ends when the informant feels that he/she has become an object for someone else's interests. So it seems that intimacy and working relationships (if not under force or fallacy) go in opposite directions. (P. 188)

El-Or concludes her postmodern analysis with the following statement about her post-fieldwork relationship with Hanna, one of her key informants: "We can't be friends because she was my object and we both know it" (p. 188).

In a similar vein, Sociologist Judith Stacey (1991) argues that the appearance of friendship with subjects in ethnographic research could result in greater exploitation than in other approaches: "For no matter how welcome, even enjoyable, the field-worker's presence may appear to 'natives,' fieldwork represents an intrusion and intervention into a system of relationships, a system of relationships that the researcher is far freer than the researched to leave" (p. 113). Stacey suggests that "the postmodern ethnographic solution to the anthropologist's predicament is to acknowledge fully the limitations of ethnographic process and product and to reduce their claims" (p. 115). She draws on James Clifford's analysis to emphasize the limits of ethnographic research: "Ethnographic truths are thus inherently *partial*—committed and incomplete" (Clifford 1986, 7, quoted in Stacey 1991, 116, emphasis is Clifford's). Stacey points out, however, that postmodern strategies cannot counter feminist concerns about the "inherently unequal reciprocity with informants; nor can it resolve the feminist reporting quandaries" (p. 117).

Feminists sociologists interested in developing strategies for reflective practice have turned to social constructionist, symbolic interactionist, and ethnomethodological perspectives of authors such as Harold Garfinkel (1967), Erving Goffman (1976), and Candace West and Don Zimmerman (1987) for methodological guidance. West and Zimmerman, in an influential article, argue that "gender is fundamental, institutionalized, and enduring; yet, because members of social groups must constantly (whether they realize it or not) 'do' gender to maintain their proper status, the seeds of change are ever present" (Lorber 1987, 124). As Barrie Thorne (1995) points out, " 'Doing gender' is a compelling concept because it jolts the assumption of gender as an innate condition and replaces it with a sense of ongoing process and activity" (p. 498). Yet gender is more than a performance: Its structures are not always visible either to the performers or to the ethnographic researchers.[2] Reflective practice can help make visible how daily interactions in the field shape ethnographic interpretation.

Limits and Possibilities of Reflective Practice

Feminist researchers use self-reflection about power as a tool to deepen ethnographic analysis and to highlight the dilemmas of fieldwork.[3] The call for reflective practice has also been informed by the critiques of third world and postcolonial feminist theorists who argue for self-reflexive understanding of the epistemological investments that shape the politics of method and the "intellectual frameworks in politics" (Alexander and Mohanty 1997, xviii).[4] Educational theorist Patti Lather (1992) questions whether praxis can be salvaged through reflective practice "in a post-foundational era" (p. 121). She examines whether it is possible to develop "a reflexivity that attends to the politics of what is and is not done at a practical level in order to learn 'to "read out" the epistemologies in our various practices' " (Hartsock 1987b, 206, quoted in Lather 1992, 121).

Cultural studies scholars have also questioned the call to reflective practice arguing that taken to the extreme, "constant reflexivity" can make "social interaction extremely cumbersome" (Hurtado 1996, 29). In contrast, the call to "accountability" is said to offer a more collective approach than "individual self-assessment of one's perspective" that the term "reflexivity implies" (p. 29). Psychologist Aída Hurtado argues that the process of accountability involves a "political assessment in reference to the group memberships the individual identifies with, to whose members, therefore, she or he has implicitly agreed to listen" (p. 30). However, from the point of view of ethnographic practice, it is seldom clear to whom one should be "accountable" and therefore I prefer the term *reflective practice*. I use the term to indicate both individual self-assessment and collective assessment of research strategies. Hurtado emphasizes that a "reflexive mechanism for understanding how we are all involved in the dirty process of racializing and gendering others, limiting who they are and who they can become" is a necessary strategy to help dismantle domination (p. 124). Such reflective strategies can also help ethnographers bring to the surface "their own privilege and possible bias" as well as "addressing the differences between different constituencies" (p. 160) within the communities they study as well as our their disciplinary communities.

Reflective practices can be employed throughout ethnographic investigation and implemented on different levels, ranging from remaining sensitive to the perspectives of others and how we interact with them to a deeper recognition of the power dynamics that infuse ethnographic encounters.[5] In this regard, Rachel Wasserfall (1997) distinguishes between "weak" and "strong reflexivity." She explains that "the 'weak' reading of reflexivity is a continued self-awareness about the ongoing relationship between a researcher and informants, which is certainly epistemologically useful: the researcher becomes more aware of constructing knowledge and of the influences of her beliefs, backgrounds and feelings in the process of researching" (p. 151). All ethnographers, regardless of theoretical approach, must practice "weak reflexivity." Elijah Anderson (1976), studying the public life of men in a poor black neighborhood on Chicago's South Side, strategically situated himself on the barroom side of Jelly's, a corner bar and liquor store, because the barroom provided a better opening for outsiders than the adjoining liquor store, which was frequented by "regulars." Over time he was able to gain the confidence of a local resident, who then sponsored his incorporation into the group of men who formed the regular clientele. Although Anderson was of the same race as his informants, he felt that his more privileged class background interfered with gaining his informants' trust.

In contrast to "weak reflexivity," the "strong" reflexivity recommended by feminist methodologists challenges "the authority of the author and/or of the power difference in the field" (Wasserfall 1997, 151–52). Wasserfall concludes "that the careful monitoring of one's own subjectivity, which is at the core of any use of the term [*reflexivity*], does not have in all situations a potential to keep distortion away" (p. 152). This dilemma is felt especially in field encounters where the researchers' personal and political beliefs differ radically from those of the persons they study.[6] Wasserfall (1997) remains skeptical about the effectiveness of self-reflective techniques in fieldwork where community residents' worldviews differ from the researcher's. To illustrate her point, she refers to her study that explores how Moroccan Jews living in a cooperative village in Israel formed their ideas about national identities and gender. Although Wasserfall was also an Israeli citizen, she "differed strongly from her informants" on "attitudes toward the Palestinian question, how to achieve peace, and the future of Israeli society" (pp. 154–55). Neither "weak" nor "strong" self-reflective strategies helped Wasserfall negotiate the tension she experienced, although she could understand how such different worldviews were formed. In the end, she worried that her representation of these Moroccan Jews perpetuated certain stereotypes about them "in the Israeli context" (p. 155).

Reflective Practice and the Use of Oral Narratives

Ethnographers frequently draw on biographical narrative or life history approaches to gain further understanding of the historical and cultural experiences that shape personal and interpersonal relationships in diverse communities. I draw on the life history method in much of my scholarship on women's community activism and value this methodology for exploring the development of and shifts in political consciousness and diverse political practices over time without artificially foregrounding any one dimension or influence.[7] I utilized the life histories generated through my research to explore the experiences of those employed by the state-funded antipoverty programs and who remained in related employment in the mid-1980s. Three areas of investigation guided the interviews I conducted: the development of a biography of the activist woman's personal and work history; an exploration of the activist woman's political participation and political analyses; and the community worker's perceptions of community problems, changes over time, and visions of "community." Consequently, the in-depth interview generated a focused life history of key events in each woman's life through a reconstruction of early childhood experiences, community work, political activities, employment histories, family and other significant relationships. This approach offered a "context in which to examine the development of political consciousness" (Mohanty 1991a, 33) as well as an opportunity to explore conflicts and tensions in the community workers' self-definitions.

However, such narratives can not be taken up unproblematically.[8] Oral narratives are "forms of both empowerment and subjection to alternative forms of authority" (Rice 1992, 337). Furthermore, anthropologist Kamala Visweswaran (1994) demonstrates the power of feminist ethnographic narratives that view "identities" as "multiple, contradictory, partial, and strategic" (p. 50). In her view: "The underlying assumption is, of course, that the subject herself represents a constellation of conflicting social, linguistic, and political forces. Individual narratives can be seen as both expressive and ideological in nature. However the category 'experience' is utilized not to pin down the truth of any individual subject, but as a means of reading ideological contradictions" (p. 50). For example, feminist sociologist Susan Chase's (1995) approach to oral narratives includes attention to "*how* women tell their stories" (p. 5). Rather than treat the narratives as "evidence" in an unmediated sense of the term, Chase is interested "in understanding relations among culture, narrative, and experience—in understanding how women make sense of their experiences by narrativing them within a particular cultural context" (p. x). In contrast, Leslie Bloom (1998, 65) adopts a "progressive-regressive method" derived from Sartre's (1963) notion of "spirals" in a life to examine "how the individual surpasses her or his conditioning, thereby manifesting what he calls 'positive praxis.' " She argues that:

> Feminist narratology benefits from the progressive-regressive method because locating points on the spiral makes systematic the difficult task of selecting critical stories from the narratives for interpretation. It also benefits from the progressive-regressive method because it encourages the interpreters or biographers to check, refine, and examine their own interpretations. This is especially helpful for researchers who recognize the instability of their own authority as interpreters. (P. 70)

I see these two approaches to narrative analysis as offering important cautions and reflective strategies for research.[9]

In 2001, I published an introspective ethnography about my father's funeral.[10] The reflective process I employed included feedback from friends, some of whom appear in the story. This reflective and dialogic strategy provided me with an analytic distance from the experiences described. As both interpreter and subject of the interpretation, I found myself in a complicated relationship to the narrative I produced.[12] There are many who critique this form of storytelling, namely, the privileging of one particular account over the multiple stories that could be told about the same phenomenon or set of experiences.[13] Self-disclosure or "going public" (Naples with Clark 1996) with painful life events, emotional difficulties, and personal failures has been criticized within and outside of feminism, within and outside of the academy, and in multiple arenas from the arts to literature to academic research. Anthropologist Ruth Behar (1995) notes that: "No one objects to autobiography, as such, as a genre in its own right. What bothers critics is the insertion of personal stories into what we have been taught to think of as the analysis of impersonal social facts" (pp. 12–13).

Defined by some as "confessional modes of self-representation" (S. Bernstein 1992), using the first-person point-of-view and centering one's own experiences as a basis for knowledge claims—once a privileged strategy for the production of feminist scholarship—is now viewed with suspicion by many.[14] Those theorists critical of this move to discredit experiential theorizing argue that the decentering of women's experiences in feminist scholarship is a consequence of the growing acceptance of certain feminist projects within the academy, thus diminishing the necessity of taking an oppositional stance with regard to knowledge production.[15] In contrast, I believe that the process of critical reflection informed by the theoretical insights of feminist standpoint epistemologies can help uncover the complex dynamics involved in the production of everyday life.[16] Anthropologist Susan Greenhalgh (2001) describes her analysis of her experiences as a patient misdiagnosed with fribromyalgia as an "auto-ethnography." She argues that this approach "is an especially productive vehicle . . . because it allows me to use the patient's own contemporaneously penned words to describe her illness experience [in a way] that remains close to the patient's original experience" (p. 53).

Linked to this debate about the value of going public with painful life experiences is the question that Gloria Watkins poses to herself as bell hooks in a concluding chapter to *Yearning: race, gender, and cultural politics* (hooks 1990b), "Why remember the pain?" (p. 215). The question relates to the "opening remarks" on "disclosure, what it means to reveal personal stuff" in *Talking Back: thinking feminist, thinking black* where hooks (1989) described her uneasiness and reluctance to speak out and reveal her personal feelings and experiences (p. 1). She replies to the question, "why remember the pain?" as follows:

> Because I am sometimes awed, as in finding something terrifying, when I see how many of the people who are writing about domination and oppression are distanced from the pain, the woundedness, the ugliness.

That it's so much of the time just a subject—a "discourse." . . . I say re-member the pain because I believe true resistance begins with people confronting pain, whether it's theirs or somebody else's, and wanting to do something to change it. And it's this pain that so much makes its mark in daily life. Pain as a catalyst for change, for working to change. (P. 215)

Hooks's perspective on going public with one's pain as a "catalyst for change" is found in much of the written work of Black and Chicana feminists.[17] This theme is also evident in discussions by activists in the movement against violence against women and is typically a feature of "Take Back the Night" marches and other public demonstrations.

However, many feminist scholars point to the "difficulty and danger of transforming private pain into public and political acts" (Hesford 1999, 120). In her analysis of the National Clothesline Project begun in 1995 to raise public consciousness about violence against women, Wendy Hesford notes the contradictions of self-disclosure and asks, "Whose experiences remain silent?" (p. 130). However, she also recognizes the value of survivors' public expressions in that "survivors' stories have far too long been coded as culturally unspeakable" (p. 133). Hesford argues for the importance of examining "both the production and the reception of survivor discourse to see how meanings are altered by particular contexts" (p. 134).

Narratives can also be used, as in Dorothy Smith's institutional ethnographic approach, to explore the links between everyday life experiences and broad-based social structural processes (M. Campbell 1998). Marjorie De-Vault and Liza McCoy (2001) explain that "when interviews are used in this approach, they are used not in order to represent subjective states, but to locate and trace the points of connection among individuals working in different parts of institutional complexes of activity" (p. 752). In other words, "interviewing is one tool for investigating a web of social relations" (p. 752). Dorothy Smith (1990a) developed her institutional ethnographic approach as a consequence of her critique of "the practices of thinking and writing . . . that convert what people experience directly in their everyday/everynight world into forms of knowledge in which people as subjects disappear and in which their perspectives on their own experience are transposed and subdued by the magisterial forms of objectifying discourse" (p. 4). Institutional ethnographic analysis provides the methodological framework for my exploration of the material consequences of local discourses and institutional practices for social, cultural, political, and economic processes. I also draw on this approach for exploring how locally constituted material structural conditions contribute to shifts in discursive constructions and social processes. These embedded processes are implicated in the social construction of inequality.

The Shifting Nature of Insider/Outsider Status

One of the most intensely contested debates in the ethnographic literature has been whether an insider's standpoint is more advantageous than an outsider's. Insider research is usually defined as the study of one's own social group or society. Advocates of "insider" research assert that non-natives may be unable to gain the deeper understandings of cultural practices and beliefs that are available to insiders. Insiders have greater linguistic competence than outsiders, can blend in more easily, and are less likely to affect social settings. Advocates of "outsider" research, on the other hand, insist that non-natives can be more objective in observing and analyzing social contexts and cultural beliefs.[18]

A feminist standpoint perspective on the insider/outsider dichotomy contests this rigid construction. Wasserfall's study illustrates the challenges in negotiating between insider and outsider identities in fieldwork settings. Such fluidity of fieldwork identities calls into question taken-for-granted constructions of ethnographers as either "insiders" or "outsiders" to the communities they study (El-Or 1997). Sharon Bays (1998) demonstrates how her insider/outsider identity was renegotiated throughout her fieldwork with Hmong women in the central California town of Visalia. Bays, who was born in Visalia, formed relationships with Hmong women while gardening and participating in the county's Forum on Refugee Affairs. As she began her study, she pondered: "Why would Hmong women want to talk with me? Why would they trust me with the intimate stories of their lives?" (P. 305). She found her answer by exploring the "politics of positionality" (Scott and Shah 1993) in her relationships with the community. Bays (1998) reports:

> Although I no longer live permanently in Visalia, I am an insider in the broader community, tied by family, friends, and work to local issues and events. On the one hand, I conducted research on very familiar turf. This facilitated my entrance to areas of my research that, for instance, examined government programs affecting refugee families. On the other hand, my Visalia insider's position did not necessarily allow easy access to Hmong families. (P. 305)

In other words, her insider's identity was circumscribed by her racial-ethnic and class positions. Her active participation in the community's social life repositioned her with the Hmong women as someone interested in community affairs and willing to struggle alongside them. By working directly with older Hmong women in the garden, for example, Bays was drawn into debates on water use among other important topics. Because she participated directly in their activities, she "was no longer limited to the fringes of Hmong communal debates" (p. 305).

Brackette Williams (1996) also illuminates the blurring of outsider and insider in her ethnographic study of elderly African Americans in rural Alabama.

She powerfully demonstrates how her racial identity as an African American woman was perceived in different ways depending on her changing relationship to others in the community she studied. Her research was designed to explore how "kin-based urban and rural networks formed and operated in relation to the services provided by formal, extra-home agencies" (p. 80). Williams describes how she was perceived as "kinfolk" or "skinfolk" by community members, and how these varying perceptions shaped the data she generated in the field. Although she was of the same racial-ethnic background as her informants, she was an outsider to the community. At the outset of her fieldwork Williams (1996) asked herself the following questions:

> Yet other than being symbols of my racially defined historical and cultural past, alive and well and living in an Alabamian present, who were these particular people to me and who was I to them? How might our joint and separate efforts to answer this question influence the project in which I was involved? How might it be influenced by the place from which I came—Baltimore, by way of Arizona—one place an acceptable "heard from" locale from which Black folks could "legitimately" hail, the other a cultural nether land of the Black world? (P. 80)

Shortly after she began her fieldwork, Williams recognized that questions of kinship as well as racial identification framed how she was perceived by the community residents. She writes: "In the end, it was 'Whose child are you?' and 'Who let you come way off down here all by yourself?' that provided the context within which other aspects of my identity were defined, valued, and sorted out across interactions and the social spaces I encountered" (p. 80). The information she gathered and her analysis of the field experience were shaped by her efforts to negotiate her identity and to justify her work: "Who was I to be doing what I was doing, and why was I doing it to them or other members of their community?" (p. 81).

Information did not flow from community members to Williams as researcher; instead she often found herself used "as a potential source of information and insight into the behavior of" others with whom she was associated who had recently moved to the area and were also defined as "strangers" (p. 81). She concludes, "there was no generic kinship or fully generalizable skinship from which I, or any category of informant, could construct an interracial, cross-class, extra spatial identity for the concept of participant-observation" (pp. 91–92). Williams (1996) calls for fieldworkers to perform ongoing self-reflection or "homework" to "continually try to figure out the power implications of who they are (or, better put, how they are being construed and by whom) in relation to what they are doing, asking, and observing" (p. 73).

Williams reports that, because of her insider status as a member of the same racial-ethnic group she studied, she worked under expectations that others, defined as outsiders, do not experience.[19] In a similar vein, Zavella (1996) referring to Maxine Baca Zinn's (1979) analysis of her research with Mexican Americans, writes that: "insider researchers have the unique constraint of always being accountable to the community being studied" (p. 139). As argued above, however, so-called outsider researchers can be granted conditional insider status based on some fixed features of one's identity, such as gender, race, or cultural background. However, this insider status is always conditional and must be negotiated throughout fieldwork experience. How one recognizes and negotiates these shifting relationships can be greatly enhanced by the application of strong and dialogic reflective strategies employed throughout ethnographic investigation and in the production of ethnographic accounts.

Conclusion

Feminist and other critical theorists alert researchers to the power dynamics of ethnographic investigation and to the different investments often masked in ethnographic research. Dynamics of power influence how problems are defined, which knowers are identified and are given credibility, how interactions are interpreted, and how ethnographic narratives are constructed.[20] This chapter anticipates the development of two arguments found in the subsequent chapters. In chapter 5, I discuss the different approaches to standpoint epistemology that have been influential in feminist ethnographic work. In chapter 4, I further develop my feminist analysis of the insider/outsider debate and demonstrate that such either/or representations are problematic because they are static and overly simplistic. I explore the shifting quality of insider/outsider status in my long-term ethnographic study of two small rural towns in southwest Iowa. As an outsider to these communities, I was taken into confidence by others who themselves felt like outsiders. Because definitions of "insider" were, for the most part, mythical constructions, most residents perceived themselves as "outsiders." The changeable nature of insider/outsider status in these rural towns was highlighted along with changes in the racial-ethnic composition that resulted when a local food-processing plant expanded and Latino workers were recruited. By foregrounding the racialization process, I was able to discover the permeability and shifting nature of insider/outsider positions. How we negotiate the power we wield and the resistance we face in fieldwork depends strongly on the reflective practices we employ. The reflective practices we employ are, in turn, influenced by what we understand as a "standpoint" and how we assess our positionality in the field.

CHAPTER 4

The Insider/Outsider Debate
A Feminist Revisiting

A materialist feminist approach to ethnography offers a critically valuable lens through which to view the "insider" versus "outsider" debate, i.e., whether it is more effective to conduct fieldwork as an insider or an outsider to the communities you study.[1] This epistemiological framework requires that ethnographers reexamine taken-for-granted assumptions about what constitutes "indigenous" knowledge and how researchers draw on their commonalities and differences to heighten sensitivity to others' complex and shifting worldviews. In this feminist revisiting of the insider/outsider debate, I argue that the insider/outsider distinction masks power differentials and experiential differences between the researcher and the researched. The bipolar construction of insider/outsider also sets up a false separation that neglects the interactive processes through which "insiderness" and "outsiderness" are constructed.

Outsiderness and insiderness are not fixed or static positions. Rather, they are ever-shifting and permeable social locations that are differentially experienced and expressed by community members. By recognizing the fluidity of outsiderness/insiderness, we also acknowledge three key methodological points: as ethnographers we are never fully outside or inside the "community"; our relationship to the community is never expressed in general terms but is constantly being negotiated and renegotiated in particular, everyday interactions; and these interactions are themselves enacted in shifting relationships among community residents. These negotiations are manifest in local processes that reposition gender, class, and racial-ethnic relations among other socially constructed distinctions.

In this chapter, I explore the relevance of findings from an ethnographic study of two rural Iowa towns for the insider/outsider debate. The study was designed to examine how economic and social restructuring is reshaping the lives of rural residents in the Midwest (see Appendix B). One theme pervading the data gathered in the field is the extent to which residents with a diversity of social, economic, and demographic characteristics experienced feelings of alienation from the perceived community at large. In fact, most people interviewed in-depth stated that they considered themselves "outsiders" to the community for a variety of reasons. In this feminist revisiting, I highlight the fluidity of outsiderness and insiderness; center attention on power in ethnographic encounters; and challenge reductive and essentialist notions of "standpoint." The concept of "outsider phenomenon" highlights the process through which community members are created as "others"—a process in which all members participate to varying degrees—and by which feelings of "otherness" are incorporated into self-perceptions and social interactions. The identification of the outsider phenomenon is especially noteworthy given the continued salience of *gemeinschaft* in accounts of rural small-town life offered by residents and nonresidents alike (see Naples 1994).

The outsider phenomenon does not describe a specific social identity as in Simmel's construct or set of statuses as in Robert Merton's (1972) formulation[2]; rather it refers to the interaction between shifting power relations in this rural context and the personal and interpersonal negotiations adopted by residents to resist further differentiation from the perceived community. As another "newcomer" to these towns, I am drawn into these processes and inevitably become a party to the renegotiations as I and my research assistants interact with residents over time. A feminist approach to fieldwork includes a sensitivity to issues of power and control in the research process and argues for a self-reflective practice (see Reinharz 1992). Furthermore, the materialist feminist approach utilized in this analysis draws upon "postmodern notions of the subject in conjunction with a theory of the social which is congruent with feminism's political goals" (Hennessy 1993, 3–4). This approach challenges the perspectives derived from attempts to identify outsiders and insiders with reference to ahistorical ascribed or achieved social identities as in Simmel's (1921) conceptualization or to externally identifiable statuses as in Merton's (1972) classic argument.

Revisiting a Chapter in the Sociology of Knowledge

The insider/outsider debate is simultaneously a contestation over divergent epistemological assumptions, methodological strategies and political claims-making. Merton's analysis of this debate appeared in 1972 and addressed issues raised by Black scholars who were challenging the dominance of white intellectuals in academic institutions and disciplinary knowledge production by claiming epistemic privilege for Black intellectuals.[3] Merton believed that when Black scholars posited such epistemic privilege, this "Insider doctrine" would lead to a polarization of claims and a more entrenched ethnocentrism in intellectual activity. He also feared that by "affirming the universal saliency of race and by redefining race as an abiding source of pride rather than stigma, the Insider doctrine in effect models itself after the doctrine long maintained by white racists" that judged a person's value on the basis of his or her "racial pedigree" (p. 20).[4] The more effective intellectual position to strive for, he argued, is one that allows for assessment of the "distinctive contributions . . . to social knowledge" offered "in our roles as Insiders or Outsiders" (p. 41).[5]

Merton (1972, 11) characterized the insider/outsider debate as "the problem of patterned differentials among social groups and strata in access to certain types of knowledge." Merton argued that since we each hold multiple statuses, "we are all, of course, both Insiders and Outsiders, members of some groups and, sometimes derivatively, not of others" (p. 22). Merton recognized the multiplicity of statuses upon which people could feel part of one group or another and, when a part of a particular group, further differentiate from one another on the basis of these contrasting status sets. However, he did not provide the framework through which to analyze how different statuses become differently valued, how power differentials influence conflicts among members who share a particular status, and how statuses could be revalued or reassigned. More importantly for the purposes of this analysis, his approach does not offer a methodological strategy through which to explore how these processes are manifest in community contexts and how individual members actively participate in their construction.

Since Merton firmly believed that "criteria of craftsmanship and integrity in science and learning cuts across differences in the social affiliations and loyalties of scientists and scholars" (p. 42), he did not deal with the fundamental challenge brought by Black intellectuals of the early 1970s. Black scholars who argued for the epistemic privileging of Black intellectual perspectives accurately pointed out how white privilege and racist practices infused the academic enterprise. Merton never directly responded to their claim. He did recognize that the structure of racial inequality that segregated whites and Blacks generated more systematic opportunities for Blacks to observe whites while "the highly visible whites characteristically did not want to find out about life in the black community and could not, even in those rare cases where they would" (p. 30). He also agreed with Kenneth Clark's (1965) powerful point that "privileged individuals" will "shield themselves from the inevitable conflict and pain which would result from acceptance of the fact that they are accessories to profound injustice" (quoted in Merton 1972, 39). Despite his recognition that racial inequality placed Blacks and whites in different social locations to generate different knowledges in their everyday lives and that whites may not want to address structures and processes of inequality, Merton failed to apply this analysis to the structure of academic institutions and disciplinary knowledges. He assumed the value neutrality of intellectual activity and believed that "commitment to the intellectual values dampens group-induced pressures to advance the interests of groups at the expense of these values and of the intellectual product" (p. 42).

In contrast, feminist scholarship has been particularly effective in identifying the processes by which power and relations of ruling are inherent in disciplinary practices. Following Dorothy Smith, I view power as woven in and through the institutions that contour women's daily activities as well as in the academic disciplines that shape official knowledge about them. Women and others who are not typically found in positions of power within educational institutions are objectified in academic practices and constructed in ways that distort or render invisible their experiences and their everyday activities.[6]

Feminist analysts further contest the firm belief expressed by Merton (1972) that adherence to "intellectual values" inevitably lead to a more objective, value-neutral "intellectual product" (p. 42).[7] Of course, this issue is not a uniquely feminist one. For example, Gary Fine (1993) writes: "Objectivity is an illusion—an illusion snuggled in the comforting blanket of positivism—that the world is ultimately knowable and secure" (p. 286). Feminists take this critique of objectivity further when they argue that a belief in the value neutrality of social scientific and other intellectual practices, in fact, serves to mask the relations of ruling embedded in the production of knowledge in the academy.

Situating Knowledges and Modes of Inquiry

The feminist theoretical commitment to explicate the intersections of gender, race-ethnicity, class, and other social structural aspects of social life without privileging one dimension or adopting an additive formulation[8] has influenced the development of diverse feminist standpoint theories exemplified by the different approaches of Patricia Hill Collins (1990, 1991) and Dorothy Smith (1987, 1990a, 1990b). Collins (1991) offers a contemporary analysis of the value of "insider within" theorizing that mirrors the claims of Black scholars contested by Merton. Drawing upon Simmel's assertion that strangers "see patterns that may be more difficult for those immersed in the situation to see" (Collins 1991, 36), Collins argues that "personal and cultural biographies [are] significant sources of knowledge" for "outsiders within" the academy (p. 53). She explains that since working-class Black women are "much more inclined to be struck by the mismatch of [their] own experiences and the paradigms of sociology itself" (p. 50), they are more likely to identify "anomalies" between their experiences and those represented by normalized yet distorted sociological accounts (p. 51).[9] Collins's argument parallels, to a certain extent, Smith's (1987) analysis of women's "bifurcated consciousness."[10] Yet there are significant differences between Collins's and Smith's standpoint theoretical perspectives.

Smith, who differentiates her theoretical framework from Collins's, argues that her approach "does not privilege a knower" (or subject of research) whose expressions are disconnected from her social location and daily activities (D. Smith 1992, 91). Rather, Smith starts inquiry "with the knower who is actually located: she is active; she is at work; she is connected with particular other people in various ways. . . . Activities, feelings, experiences, hook her into extended social relations linking her activities to those of other people and in ways beyond her knowing" (p. 91). This mode of inquiry calls for explicit attention to the social relations manifest in women's everyday activities as well as the deeply felt expressions of outsiderness. However, it does not end

at the level of individual women as "knowers" but is "directed towards exploring and explicating what [they do] not know—the social relations and organization pervading [their] world but invisible in it" (p. 91). Yet such an inquiry
also involves the researcher's engagement with individual knowers who are
shaping and reshaping the researcher's own understanding. As Smith (1992)
asserts: "The project of inquiry from the standpoint of women is always reflective. Also, it is always about ourselves as inquirers—not just our personal
selves, but our selves as participants" (p. 94).

Neither Smith nor Collins offers strategies for how a researcher interested
in exploring women's differing standpoints should navigate relationships with
the different individuals she encounters. Each theorist does highlight the significance of dialogue for the development of knowledges that more accurately
capture the "nature of the matrix of domination" (Collins 1990, 236) or "relations of ruling" (Smith 1987). Not surprisingly, their approaches to the nature
of this dialogue differ. Collins (1990) emphasizes the "partial, situated knowledge" of groups like African American women, Latina lesbians, Puerto Rican
men, and "other groups with distinctive standpoints" who together can contribute to a broadened understanding of "the nature of the matrix of domination" through dialogue across their different standpoints (p. 236). In contrast,
Smith stresses ongoing dialogue between the inquirer and the subjects and objects of inquiry where "the inquirer is always exposed to the discipline of the
other—sometimes the others' direct response, but more often how people's
activities are actually coordinated." Both Collins and Smith agree that the goal
of such dialogue is to decenter dominant discourse, and to continually dis-
place and rework it to determine how power organizes social life and what
forms of resistance are generated from social locations outside the matrix of
domination or relations of ruling. The dialogic strategy that formed a central
component of the method I employed to gather and assess information in my
fieldwork is closer to Smith's representation. On a few occasions, I participated
in group discussions that brought together people from diverse social locations within the two towns. This strategy is similar to the dialogic strategy
Collins recommends.

Yet two questions remained when I considered how to proceed in my research with rural residents in Iowa. First, whose perspectives should be privileged in a dialogic process when I encounter the competing, and sometimes
overlapping, viewpoints of groups represented within the towns—single mothers
working in the factories, single mothers on public assistance (two of many
overlapping categories), newly arrived Mexican factory workers, longer term
Mexican American residents, low-income white European American women
married to Mexican men, full-time homemakers, full-time family farmers,
low-income elderly residents, and so on. The second and somewhat more
challenging question relates to how to locate myself in relationship to different
residents.

A key aspect of Collins's (1990) analysis of Black feminist thought that does offer a partial methodological strategy is found in her discussion of the "ethic of caring" (pp. 215–16). She describes the "ethic of caring" with reference to three interrelated dimensions: an emphasis on "individual uniqueness," "the appropriateness of emotions in dialogues," and "the capacity for empathy." These dimensions of the ethic of caring spoke directly to my own partial solutions to the questions raised above. Yet, as the following analysis will illustrate, emphasizing the uniqueness of individuals within a particular context, valuing emotions in dialogues designed to uncover how ruling relations are experienced and resisted in everyday life, and using empathy with different residents as methodological strategies further demonstrate the challenge faced when applying the insights of feminist standpoint theories in the course of an ethnographic study. In fact, here we face the tension between a conceptualization of standpoint as embodied in particular knowers and one that defines standpoint as constructed in community (see chapter 5). For, as Donna Haraway (1988) argues: "Situated knowledges are about communities, not about isolated individuals. The only way to find a larger vision is to be somewhere in particular" (p. 590).

I will illustrate the outsider phenomenon through excerpts from the narratives of a small but diverse subset of women interviewed in order to problematize the notion of "women's standpoints."[11] Standpoints within the outsider phenomenon are rooted in material conditions structured by class divisions, gender and racial inequality, among other dimensions of inequality. By shifting the standpoint to those who are marginal to the mythic community insider, certain less visible features of daily life are brought into view.[12] Furthermore, from a materialist feminist perspective, standpoints are simultaneously constructed in discourse that, in turn, generates a more fluid conceptualization of standpoint than offered in many critiques of standpoint epistemology. In my analysis of the outsider phenomenon, I explore the material processes through which outsiderness is constructed as well as the material effects this discursive construction has on the residents in these two rural towns.

For clarity of presentation and space considerations, I am forced to present the analysis of the outsider phenomenon and its implication for ethnographic fieldwork in this rural setting in separate sections. Although separating the description of the outsider phenomenon from methodological considerations does not do justice to the process by which I identified and subsequently analyzed this construct (and was personally implicated in its construction), I must now utilize just such a false division in the following presentation.

"Newcomers" and "Outsiders": The Dynamics of Gender and Class

Contrary to popular belief, residents of rural communities frequently experience the sense of alienation and fragmentation often attributed to urban life. The growth in industrial capitalism revealed a variety of political perspectives, social statuses, and perceived outsiderness within the supposedly egalitarian rural communities. Adams (1992, 372) found in her historical study of agrarian activism in Southern Illinois that "although this society is frequently character-ized as egalitarian, differentials in wealth, status, and political power existed" (p. 372).[13] The diversity of political perspectives and economic circumstances among rural residents is documented in historical studies and continues to typify rural communities in contemporary America. Changes in the rural economy enhance the variety of perspectives and experiences among residents. Three significant shifts are evident: first, the change in women's work from on-farm to factory and from part-time nonfarm to full-time nonfarm labor, which, in turn, contributed to and accompanied a restructuring of gender roles and household composition; second, a growing disparity between the few wealthy farmers and business owners and those living on the economic margin of the rural economy; and third, increased racial-ethnic diversity in small rural communities in certain areas in the Midwest.[14] The two towns, Southtown and Midtown (pseudonyms), chosen for this study illustrate these three patterns.

Southtown and Midtown are located 20 miles apart in one of the most rural counties in Iowa. Each town has a population of fewer than 1,500 residents. Racial-ethnic diversity varies between the two towns. Southtown's population is made up almost entirely of white European Americans. Beginning in the early 1990s, Midtown experienced an increase in the number of Mexican and Mexican American residents who moved to the area for employment in a lo-cally owned and recently expanded food-processing plant. The social, demo-graphic, and economic changes reshaping the experiences of residents in these two towns contribute to the salience of the "newcomer" status in their spoken accounts.[15] The category of "newcomer" was used by residents to refer to a wide array of individuals and groups including those who had resided in these com-munities for a decade or more. Recipients of Aid to Families with Dependent Children (welfare assistance that preceded Temporary Assistance to Needy Families) and food stamps in both towns, many of whom have lived in these communities for extended periods of time, were frequently defined as "new-comers" as were racial-ethnic minorities regardless of their length of residency.

Perceived newcomer status is only one aspect of outsiderness. Martha Brand moved to Southtown over a decade ago and continued to feel like an outsider. Residents who were born in the area and left only later to return as adults to raise their children in these towns also described themselves as out-siders. Barbara Drake was born in Southtown, married someone from another area in Iowa, and returned to Southtown after her children were born. Barbara explained that "when you're an outsider, which is what we basically are, mov-ing into a different community . . . you have no name there, even . . . though the kids' grandparents live here, their last name isn't the same." While Martha moved to Southtown as an adult and Barbara left for a number of years, Amy Grove lived in Southtown her entire life. But Amy also expressed that she "always had the feeling of being the outsider, of being inferior" because, she explained:

> We just grew up on a farm and we didn't have much. . . . And then when I got out of eighth grade, out of country school and went to high school, well, I was a country bumpkin, and it was . . . very difficult because here were all these kids that knew one another, and here you were coming in from a country school. And you knew your one classmate. So I would have to say it was really difficult!

Women in both towns, regardless of newcomer designation, who did not adhere to traditional gender roles reported feelings of outsiderness. They sensed disapproval from neighbors and other community members that increased their sense of rejection and isolation. Women whose marital status changed from married to single frequently described themselves as outsiders. As Jenny Sands, who divorced after ten years of married life in the community explained: "It's not a place for a single parent really, . . . 'cause it's very couple- or family-oriented." Jenny's feelings of isolation mirrored those expressed by many women, married and single, on public assistance.

Residents who worked at the local factories reported feeling marginal to the more economically secure town residents they defined as insiders. However, economic security formed but one dimension of a broader, more fluid category of "prestige," which, in turn, formed another dimension by which some community members were defined by others as insiders. Not all those perceived to have secure and middle-class incomes were viewed as having prestige. Barbara Drake who works in a Southtown sewing factory explained that in Southtown those with prestige could "get by with a lot of things where others don't." Barbara thinks that prestige carries "privileges" such that certain families are protected from exposure in the local media if they are involved in any transgressions. According to Barbara, those with prestige are those who have lived in the area "forever," whose "folks were raised around here" along with their grandparents, "and on down the line." These community members could "do no wrong," Barbara said. Drawing from her own standpoint analysis, she believed that she is more aware of the power differences within the community because she is a relative newcomer. She said that as an outsider "when you sit back and kind of look, you can see probably things that the people that lived here for a long time don't see."

Overall, a majority of the community residents, especially women, interviewed reported feelings of alienation from the wider community. Women were particularly affected by the discursive construction of outsiderness. Men were rarely found in the role of single parent or expected to secure household provisions by using food stamps or going to the food pantry. Even when a man stepped outside the traditional family form and divorced or lived openly with a woman who was not his wife, he did not describe the same sanctions reported by the women who had similar marital or household arrangements. Women working at the local factories, growing up in poverty, receiving public assistance, moving to these communities as adults, leaving and returning as adults after marriage to a local farmer, living as a single mother, or otherwise living in a nontraditional family form all expressed feelings of isolation and outsiderness. Ironically, those who were defined by others as insiders, also said they felt like outsiders who would never be accepted. I often left Midtown and Southtown after a field trip asking: "Who are the insiders here?" I have yet to meet a community resident who feels completely like the mythical community insider, although several people presented themselves as more "legitimate" members of the community than others. Those named as insiders, such as the owners of the food-processing plant and the local bankers, also felt like outsiders as they perceived other community residents' resentment of their economic success and political clout. Erin Landers, one of the plant owners and a longtime resident of Midtown, reported that she felt a number of community members, particularly older residents who knew her and her husband as children, resented their financial success. She also experienced hostility from community members who were displeased with the number of Mexican and Mexican Americans who had moved to Midtown for employment in the plant.

Yet embedded in the outsider phenomenon were the patterns of inequality that shaped social life in these two rural towns. While those with more political and economic resources also felt outside for reasons often associated with their power and wealth, those with fewer resources were more disadvantaged by the social control processes associated with the outsider phenomenon. The mythic construction of a *gemeinschaft*-like "community" fed into the outsider phenomenon. The idealized construction of what it meant to be a part of the "community" and of who were "legitimate" community members served as both an internalized and externalized means of social control. When someone spoke up to challenge the construction, they were formally silenced or ostracized. Others silenced themselves for fear that they would disrupt the fragile sense of community. Consequently, many members felt alienated from the mythic community yet were careful not to share their feelings with others who they perceived as more connected to the community. As long as those on the margins felt silenced by the outsider phenomenon they would not challenge the power base and definition of the situation that privileged a small elite who controlled town politics and economic development. The Mexican and Mexican American residents offer further insight into the dynamics of social control evident in the outsider phenomenon. The racialization process led to a number of events and discursive shifts highlighted the fluidity of the outsider phenomenon.

Racialization Processes in Midtown

Mexicans and Mexican Americans were most likely to fit the tacit definition of newcomer as they were among the most recent arrivals in Midtown. However, the term *newcomer* was also used to differentiate between "Americans" and others viewed as temporary and, oftentimes, "illegitimate" residents. Under this formulation, Mexican Americans were frequently categorized along with undocumented Mexican workers as illegal and posing numerous problems for the so-called legitimate members of the community. However, the racialization process in Midtown demonstrates that such a totalizing conceptualization of the Mexican and Mexican American residents was unstable and, consequently, quickly fell apart in the face of interactions with different agents of the state—a process I will illustrate below. Viewing these residents as one undifferentiated group was further compromised as young Mexicans and Mexican Americans entered the school system, were adopted by local families, dated white European American teenagers, or married local white residents.

Whiteness formed an unspoken, but powerful backdrop to the construction of community in both towns. As the number of Mexicans and Mexican Americans increased in Midtown (the percentage grew from less than 1 percent in 1991 to almost 10 percent in 1995), residents became increasingly vocal about the threat the increased racial-ethnic diversity posed to their quality of life. Racial formation theory helps capture "the processes by which racial meanings are attributed, and racial identities assigned" and infused in material practices and institutional arrangements in a particular society.[16] Racialization, the process by which racial formation develops, is fluid and multifaced and provides an analytic tool that allows us to map the changing and contested negotiation of different racial-ethnic groups and subgroups as they insert themselves and are inserted into new social, political, and economic environments. In this case study, race-ethnicity served as a powerful marker through which outsiderness is further constructed and experienced.

Workers of color, especially Mexican and Mexican American workers, have always been overrepresented among the migrant agricultural workers in the Midwest, yet, for the most part, they have not remained as permanent residents in the rural communities. The shacks and trailers of the migrant labor camps huddled at the edges of rural communities remain a symbol of the migrant laborer's marginal, nonresident status in the communities that employs him or her. As permanent residents, Mexicans and Mexican Americans continue to face discrimination and harassment from neighbors, business owners, and health care providers as they attempt to make a home in the small towns. Newly devised housing segregation strategies in Midtown placed Mexican and Mexican American residents in the trailer park at the edge of town or in the least desirable rental properties and further highlighted their marginal and presumed temporary status.

The Mexican and Mexican Americans moved to Midtown from three different areas: some had moved directly from Mexico City, others had come from rural Mexican towns with previous stops in other rural parts of the United States, and some had moved from Los Angeles or other urban areas within the

United States. The fragmentation within the Mexican and Mexican American community enhanced the feelings of alienation expressed by the different residents. On the other hand, the Mexicans and Mexican Americans were treated as one separate and homogenous community within Midtown despite differences in immigration status, citizenship, and region of birth. As Anna Ortega, a U.S. citizen in her 30s who moved from Laredo to Midtown with her family, explained: "But a lot of the Americans think that because we're brown everybody comes from Mexico, and it's not like that, you know. Because you can be Mexican, Hispanic, and you can come from Texas; you can come from Chicago. . . . You can be born and raised in California. . . . [They think]: 'They're from Mexico. They're all illegals.'" Ortega distinguished herself from the white European American residents who she defined as Americans. The process of racialization creates a boundary between "real Americans" (read: white European Americans) and other Americans. These boundaries are maintained by ideological constructions as well as material practices and institutional arrangements (see Naples 1994). Those citizens who do not fit the narrow definition of American feel themselves outside the category despite their legal status.

Racialization is an ongoing process through which patterns of inequality are reshaped and resisted. The dynamic racialization process shaped our relationships with community members as our ethnographic identities were repositioned by shifts in constructions of "community" that accompanied ongoing social, demographic, and political changes. The ongoing community efforts to incorporate or resist incorporating the Mexican and Mexican American residents was further revealed when I hired Lionel Cantú, a bilingual Chicano graduate student, to assist me in Midtown.

Mr. Cantu's first field trip followed on the heels of a raid by agents from the Immigration and Naturalization Service (INS) in 1992. This event helped reorganize racial formation in Midtown. The INS had been contacted about the possibility that illegal workers were employed in the food-processing plant. Competing stories blame, respectively, an older white resident, the police, "outside" complaints, and a disgruntled worker. Informants report that as many as 100 Mexicans were arrested and a large percentage were discovered to be undocumented and subsequently deported. The INS raid contributed to a reshaping of outsiderness as expressed by many residents interviewed after the raid. Many Mexican and Mexican American as well as white European American residents witnessed the deportation of coworkers and neighbors. The tension created by this and other raids in Midtown generated anxiety among many, including those with U.S. citizenship and legal working papers. Since legal residents had also been picked up in the raids and driven to Omaha before they were released without transportation home, their fears were well founded.

The consequences of this anxiety was experienced by Mr. Cantú, who arrived on his first trip to Midtown in a four-door sedan with Omaha plates. Initially he could not find many Mexicans and Mexican Americans willing to talk with him until word-of-mouth confirmed that he was not an INS agent.

INS intervention made visible the contradictions in the construction of the outsider in Midtown. While INS activities served to confirm white European American residents' fears that there were, at least initially, many undocumented Mexican workers in the plant, it also highlighted the fact that many other workers were legal, even "legitimate" members of the community. In addition to the reported growing acceptance of the Mexicans and Mexican Americans on the part of some white European American residents, several white residents also reported an increased awareness of the oppressive features of INS interventions.

A similar, and in many ways, more interesting shift in perception occurred in response to perceived unfair treatment of the Mexican and Mexican American residents by the local police. The local police, all of whom are residents of the town, were constructed as separate from the community in much the same way as the INS agents. The fear of deportation and harassment by INS officials was reinforced by ongoing harassment by local police. Many white European American residents reported that the police targeted Mexicans and Mexican Americans to a greater extent than the white youth who were often the cause of certain problems. Some reported that the Mexicans and Mexican Americans were arrested for drinking when drunk white residents would be escorted home or ignored. As the contact between the white European Americans and Mexicans and Mexican Americans increased, the awareness of police harassment grew. Sympathetic white residents have complained about the unfair treatment and established alliances with some of the Mexican and Mexican American residents. Such an informal coalition may have contributed to the police chief's resignation a year after the INS raid.

The documented shift in discursive construction of outsiderness with regard to the Mexican and Mexican American residents as well as the illustrative material changes highlight the fluidity of standpoints when viewed over time. Yet the tensions between white European American and Mexican and Mexican American residents remain. As my field investigations focused increasingly on the experiences of the Mexican and Mexican American residents and the process of racialization in Midtown, I was also repositioned by formerly receptive informants, especially those who held positions of power in the town. This repositioning was furthered when Mr. Cantú joined the project. Where I found no difficulty moving freely about the town, Mr. Cantú reported being followed by the police, having his mail tampered with, and fearing for his safety. Mr. Cantú's hire coincided with my move from Iowa State University to the University of California. With this move, I lost one key component of my insider designation which, in turn, further revealed the fluidity of this status. Since both factors occurred simultaneously, it is difficult to identify which one contributed more to a new mistrust expressed by previously receptive informants.

Mr. Cantú quickly won the trust of many Mexican and Mexican American residents, a trust that would have been difficult for me to gain as an Anglo, non-Spanish-speaking researcher.[17] In fact, when Anna Ortega was concerned with increasing police harassment in the town, she phoned Mr. Cantú in California for assistance. After some deliberation, we decided to mobilize my network of contacts in Iowa who were working as advocates for Latino residents in other parts of the state. My hesitation in connecting her with these advocates related to fear of exposing her position as an informal recruiter of numerous Mexican and Mexican American workers and their families. When Mr. Cantú returned her call and asked if we could give her name to several people whom we thought might be able to assist her in dealing with the town officials, she agreed. As a recruiter and as a Latina, she felt more responsible for the well-being of those she brought to Midtown than was evidenced by the plant owners who, we suspect, initially sponsored her activities.

The Personal Politics of Fieldwork

Incorporation into the racialization process in Midtown and my dilemma over how to negotiate a more activist involvement in the town formed but two key tensions I confronted. The racialization process was illustrative of the ways in which the ethnographic field shifted over time and limited my ability to take one unchanging position on any methodological dilemma. Returning to the strategies adopted in response to these dilemmas, I will highlight how the "ethic of caring" (an emphasis on "individual uniqueness," "the appropriateness of emotions in dialogues," and "the capacity for empathy" [Collins 1990, 215–16]) in ethnographic encounters helped deepen my understanding of outsiderness even as it raised further dilemmas.

The more I elaborated the diverse experiences of outsiderness, the more I recognized the futility of privileging any particular perspective. Yet each strategy I adopted to counter a reductionist standpoint analysis revealed the limits of such efforts. For example, one strategy I used to gain a broader understanding of the social construction of community included gathering in-depth information from diverse perspectives—a commonplace fieldwork method. With the help of my research assistants, I gained access to a diversity of residents, many of whom we interviewed in-depth. I also utilized group discussions with selected community members where they helped set the agenda, to a certain extent, and maintained watch over the research process. This technique is recommended by many researchers who are engaged in collaborative or activist research projects.[18] In these small group discussions, I posed specific questions about the two towns that were generated from my interviews and other data gathering efforts. Responses from the group helped clarify my findings (or hunches) and, in some instances, redirected my investigations. These discussions often occurred in the course of other activities and sometimes included residents of nearby communities as well as Midtown and Southtown.

These often impromptu dialogues were enriched by the presence of nonresidents as they further highlighted the differences between nonindigenous but contiguous perspectives and indigenous constructions. However, never did one group include a variety of perspectives from within the two towns. Mexicans and Mexican Americans seldom met informally with non-Spanish-speaking white residents. Low-income residents rarely spoke openly about their perceptions and experiences in a group discussion with those they perceived as more economically secure for fear of disapproval by other community members.

Such dialogic strategies with particular knowers within the communities also overlapped with a second, more traditional ethnographic strategy—residing with local families during field trips. Entry into the field and, more particularly, the choices I made regarding where each member of the research team should reside inevitably placed each of us in dialogue with certain members of each town more than with others. I stayed with a local social service worker and her family on their family farm in Southtown. One research assistant, Ms. Perry, stayed in Southtown with a local minister and her family. Another team member, Ms. Schwebach, stayed with a young single woman on a small acreage she rented just outside of Southtown. Mr. Cantú and a fourth researcher, Ms. Bornstein, resided with a couple who ran a bed and breakfast on their large farm at the edge of Midtown. All four households provided safe and rich places in which to discuss some aspects of the research and to further explore indigenous views on the economic and social changes reshaping their communities. Not surprisingly, these four families did not present a full range of perspectives on social life in these two towns despite their differences in political, economic, and social locations. I sought reflections on life in rural Iowa from those with whom we stayed, yet I also viewed the more extended dialogues with them as further data—not as more accurate representations. Since each member of the research team had differing angles of vision through which to observe and interact with certain residents, each of us inevitably formed somewhat contrasting views of social life in these towns. During the so-called debriefing sessions I held with members of the research team after each field trip, I often was amazed by the conflicting perceptions. These sessions also highlighted for me that the growing familiarity and empathy with different residents did shape what each research team member identified as the most significant questions to pursue.

This strategy of "passionate detachment" (Haraway 1988, 585)—defined in this study as developing close relationships with residents and reflecting upon these relationships after each field trip—was somewhat successful. However, I found this strategy challenging to sustain as fieldwork roles and relationships shifted over time. Two of us developed friendships with women in whose houses we stayed and with several other community members.[19] In addition, a number of the Mexicans and Mexican Americans began to perceive Mr. Cantú's role as the Spanish-speaking member of our research group as advocate more than researcher or friend, given that he initially stayed in the home of one of the Mexican American residents. These shifts in perception and relationship raised additional dilemmas that often led to the necessary privileging of one social identity over the other.[20] Building relationships is, of course, a necessary part of gaining trust and access in ethnographic encounters.[21] Less acknowledged in much of the fieldwork literature are the emotional consequences for the researcher when, over the course of fieldwork, more distanced relationships are transformed into friendships.[22] During debriefing sessions each member of the research team expressed personal concerns for the well-being of different community members and debated how to intervene effectively to assist them in their personal crises or to help in their fight against discriminatory practices. Such growing identification with the personal troubles and political tensions in the two towns developed directly out of the engaged and dialogic feminist methodological strategies I adopted for this study. Yet these strategies do not offer solutions to the dilemmas they foster.

Emotions are always present in personal interactions in ethnographic work.[23] Here the feminist perspective is useful in reminding us that emotions can form an important basis for understanding and analysis.[24] Collins (1990) reports that for Black feminist thought "emotion indicates that the speaker believes in the validity of an argument" (p. 215). To extend her argument to fieldwork strategies, by "developing the capacity for empathy" (p. 216), a feminist researcher broadens the grounds upon which individuals will share deeply felt experiences. Rather than attempt to keep a distanced stance in an effort to achieve more "objective" analyses, feminist researchers acknowledge that power is infused in social relations including in relationships between researchers and "informants." The ethic of caring forms one strategy to break down power differentials and experiential differences between the researcher and the researched. On the other hand, the limits of such an approach must also be acknowledged for, as Sondra Hale (1991) cautions, "in the 'feminist interview,' the closeness and intersubjectivity remain artificial and temporary" (p. 134).[25] Furthermore, in research with subjects whose personal ethics and political positions may differ profoundly from the researcher's, as in the case of ethnographic work and in-depth interviews with white supremacists, relationship-building may pose other challenges. However, working from an ethic of caring may be even more important in these circumstances.[26] For example, Kathleen Blee (2002) was able to achieve rapport with racist women activists in her study of women who participated in organized white supremacist groups in the United States. However, she notes that "the intense and conflicting feelings that male racists hold about women, especially women professionals and women outside the racist movement" would undermine such efforts when the researcher is female (p. 204). Yet, she also points out that "male scholars have had little more success."

As I gathered data in Midtown and Southtown and identified the outsider phenomenon, I further explored the notion of outsiderness to get underneath residents' public presentations of self that typically masked the dynamic processes and experiences of exclusion. I shared my own feelings to a certain extent and explored the similarities and differences between mine and those of the community residents interviewed using the multiple strategies just illustrated.[27] This intersubjective approach coupled with my methodological reflections and personal experience of the outsider phenomenon reinforced my already critical stance toward reductionist analyses of insider and outsider standpoints.

By drawing upon the ethic of caring as a methodological strategy, I further revealed two major limits of the outsider/insider debate: the neglect of the interactive processes through which insiderness and outsiderness are constructed and the illusive search for the most objective position from which to assess truth. Both Collins and Smith argue that certain standpoints provide a more reliable vantage point from which to explore "how things work" (D. Smith 1990, 34) especially with regard to the matrix of domination or relations of ruling. Yet, Collins and Smith offer two contrasting views of standpoints. For Collins, standpoints are analogous to diverse social locations organized by gender, race, and class, among other dimensions. For Smith (1992), "to begin with the categories [such as gender, class, or race] is to begin in discourse" (p. 90). In contrast, Smith's approach is designed to shift the standpoint from "text-mediated discourse or organization" to the "actual site of the body" where a woman as knower is "actually located" in order to discover "the social relations and organization pervading her world but invisible in it" (p. 91).[28] Since a primary goal of feminist research is to uncover how inequality is reproduced and resisted, how we draw on our capacity for empathy and dialogue is directly related to a deep commitment to this political project. Consequently, I took inspiration from both Collins and Smith. The use of dialogue, emotion, and empathy helped clarify the relationship between individual narratives and broader processes like racialization and the outsider phenomenon that are hidden from an individual knower's direct sight.

Conclusion

My materialist feminist analysis challenges the false divide between insider and outsider research and between so-called objective or scientific and indigenous knowledge. Smith's (1992) conceptualization of standpoint as a place to begin to explore how relations of ruling are manifest in everyday life and as "a *method of inquiry*, always ongoing, opening things up, discovering" offered a broad methodological strategy designed to avoid reducing standpoint to the expressions of a particular knower (p. 88, emphasis in original). Collins's analysis of the ethics of caring and the role of dialogue in Black feminist thought reflects the interpersonal methodological strategies I adopted to negotiate my relationship with different "knowers" in the encounters in Midtown and Southtown. I incorporated these methodological strategies into a broader materialist feminist analysis to explore the construction of standpoints in discursive as well as materialist practices. The discursive shifts in the notion of outsiderness were woven in and through material practices and simultaneously had material effects on individual expressions and interpersonal experiences—both of which became empirical resources for my understanding of the outsider phenomenon. The discursive construction of outsiderness served to control who felt entitled to speak out and who could be trusted to hear.

This materialist feminist revisiting of the outsider/insider debate demonstrates the limits of Simmel's, Merton's, and other standpoint analyses that neglect the interaction between shifting power relations in a community context.[29] As "newcomers" to these rural towns, I and my research assistants were implicated in these processes and inevitably became a party to the renegotiations as we interacted with different community members whose "positions" were shifting over time. Identification of the outsider phenomenon and my methodological reflections on the interactions between my own outsider feelings and those of community members highlighted for me how processes of inequality and resistance shaped social life in these small towns.

In particular, the process of racialization in rural Iowa demonstrated how insider/outsider positions were ever-shifting and permeable social locations. Standpoints within the outsider phenomenon are informed by material processes that organize class divisions and gender and racial inequality, among other dimensions. However, individuals as actors and knowers within these small communities do not embody a particular and unchanging standpoint. What we choose to define or locate as standpoints must also be open to interrogation throughout the course of fieldwork. Donna Haraway (1988, 584) argues that " 'subjugated' standpoints are preferred because they seem to promise more adequate, sustained, objective, transforming accounts of the world" but also cautions that: "Subjugation is not grounds for an ontology; it might be a visual clue. Vision requires instruments of vision; an optics is a politics of positioning. Instruments of vision mediate standpoints; there is no immediate vision from the standpoints of the subjugated" (p. 584). By viewing standpoint as a mode of inquiry and utilizing an ethic of caring in ethnographic encounters, I was able to identify and analyze a phenomenon of outsiderness that was hidden from the view of individual knowers within the community. This materialist feminist revisiting of the insider/outsider debate focuses careful attention on the "instruments of vision" we use in ethnographic encounters and acknowledges the powerful role we play in shaping what can be seen.

As my discussion of Collins's and Smith's approaches demonstrates, despite important thematic continuity across the different perspectives on standpoint theorizing, there are a number of critical differences in how different theorists define what constitutes a standpoint and how researchers analyze "experience." I categorize these approaches as follows: standpoint as embodied in social identities, as a communal or relational achievement, and as an axis point of investigation. In the next chapter, I detail these three dimensions and contest a reductive reading of feminist standpoint approaches.

CHAPTER 5

Standpoint Epistemology
Explicating Multiple Dimensions

In this chapter, I outline the multiple dimensions of my methodological approach to materialist feminist standpoint analysis, illustrate its utility for exploring women's political praxis, and highlight the dilemmas of my multidimensional standpoint approach for comparative analysis. While I illustrate each strand of standpoint theorizing with reference to particular authors, some theorists contribute to more than one strand. Furthermore, my presentation should not be viewed as a comprehensive review of standpoint theories more generally. It is designed as an outline of the dimensions of standpoint analysis that I find most useful in constructing a comparative approach to ethnographic research on women's political praxis.

I illustrate the dilemmas I encountered in developing a comparative ethnographic analysis of women's political praxis with my research with community workers from different racial-ethnic backgrounds identified in two very different contexts: (1) in low-income neighborhoods in New York City and Philadelphia interviewed in the mid-1980s and mid-1990s; and (2) in two small towns in rural Iowa interviewed between 1990 and 1996. I discuss this research by exploring community workers' "standpoints" from three points of view: as (1) embodied, (2) constructed in community, and (3) an axis point of investigation. Within each of the three dimensions of standpoint epistemology, ethnographers must explicate how to treat "experience" and negotiate shifting intersections of race, class, and gender as well as account for changes over time in the social, political, and economic context.

In reviewing the literature on the different approaches to standpoint epistemology, I identified a number of powerful connecting links among them. They include the significance of experience for the development of feminist theory and the connection between standpoint theory and the feminist political goals of the women's movement. However, when I explored the implications of different standpoint frameworks for ethnographic research on women's political praxis, I identified crucial differences in the way theorists understand what constitutes a standpoint and how researchers analyze "experience." I categorized these approaches as follows: standpoint as embodied in social identities, as a communal or relational achievement, and as an axis point of investigation.

67

I begin by outlining in greater detail than in the previous chapters some of the key criticisms of standpoint epistemology leveled by postmodern and poststructural critics and highlight two primary limitations of their critique: (1) failure to address the central goal of standpoint epistemology—namely, to develop alternative methodologies that challenge masculinist and white middle-class bias in traditional scientific and social scientific positivist research strategies; and (2) misunderstanding of the multiple dimensions of "standpoint" embedded in standpoint theoretical perspectives. I review some of the main points of connection among these differing standpoint approaches with particular attention to what each approach "counts as experience" (Scott 1992) for, as Scott argues, this "is neither self-evident nor straightforward; it is always contested, always therefore political" (p. 37). The goal of this chapter is to demonstrate the power of materialist standpoint methodology for ethnographic research on women's political praxis by explicating the multiple dimensions of feminist standpoint epistemology.

Standpoint Epistemology and Its Critics

Most theorists associated with feminist standpoint epistemology (for example Patricia Hill Collins, Sandra Harding, Nancy Hartsock, Dorothy Smith) begin their analyses by questioning the "truth claims" of positivist research methods and by offering methodological strategies linked to feminist political praxis. Sandra Harding (1991) seeks to reinvent science from the point of view of feminist and postcolonial theoretical and political concerns.[1] Nancy Hartsock (1987) argues that "an analysis which begins from the sexual division of labor . . . could form the basis for an analysis of the real structures of women's oppression, an analysis which would not require that one sever biology from society, nature from culture, an analysis which would expose the ways women both participate in and oppose their own subordination" (p. 175).

Few of the most vocal postmodern critics of standpoint theory offer methodological alternatives to those posed by standpoint theorists. Those who do offer alternative research strategies often limit their approaches to textual or discursive modes of analysis. For example, following an assessment of the limits and possibilities of feminist standpoint epistemologies for generating a "global social analytic," literary scholar Rosemary Hennessy (1993) posits "critique" as materialist feminist "reading practice" (p. 91).[2] She then argues that "critique understands consciousness as ideologically produced" (p. 92) and therefore effectively resists the charge of essentialism. In revaluing feminist standpoint epistemology for her method, she reconceptualizes "feminist standpoint" as a "critical discursive practice, an act of reading which intervenes in and rearranges the construction of meanings and the social arrangements they support" (p. 91). Such a redefinition of standpoint provides a very limited vantage point for feminist investigations of women's political praxis. Although Hennessy starts her analysis by calling for attention to the material conditions that shape women's social lives, she reduces "feminism as a standpoint" to a discursively produced phenomenon. Hennessy's methodological "innovation" effectively renders other methodological strategies outside the frame of materialist feminist scholarship. Furthermore, Hennessy's strategy fails to provide a methodological solution to the primary goal she specifies, namely, to develop a "way of thinking about the relationship between language and subjectivity that can explain their connection to other aspects of material life" (p. 37). In a recent revisiting of her position "that economic, cultural, and political facets of social life are mutually determining," Hennessy acknowledges a shift in her thinking as she came to recognize that "this retreat from class analysis in the academy in the eighties and nineties began to seem one of neoliberalism's most effective ideological weapons" (2000, 12).

Poststructural critics of feminist standpoint epistemology within the social sciences also conclude their analyses with calls for discursive strategies. For example, after assessing Smith's standpoint epistemology, sociologist Patricia Clough (1993) argues for a "feminist, psychoanalytically oriented semiotic approach" that does not rely on "actual experience" (pp. 178–79). By misreading Smith's notion of "standpoint" as reducing subjectivity "to a determined position within the structure" (p. 179), Clough creates what Smith (1993) refers to as a "StrawSmith" (p. 180). Clough then calls for shifting the starting point of sociological investigation from experience or social activity to a "social criticism of textuality and discursivity, mass media, communication technologies and science itself" (p. 179). In contrast, Smith offers feminist ethnographers a place to begin inquiry that envisions subjects of investigation who can experience aspects of life outside discourse. Smith's methodological goal is "to develop inquiry into the social relations in which that experience is embedded, making visible how it is put together and organized in and by a larger complex of relations (including those of ruling and the economy)" (p. 184).

Ignoring Smith's "everyday world" approach, many critics of feminist standpoint epistemology have centered their criticism on the way certain standpoint theorizing reduces women's "ways of knowing" (Belenky et al. 1986) to essentialized categories associated with women's social identities. However, standpoint theorists do not insist that sustained vision from women's vantage point provides "an accurate depiction of reality" as Hawkesworth (1989) charges. Donna Haraway (1988), for example, argues that: "Feminist objectivity is about limited location and situated knowledge, not about transcendence and splitting of subject and object. It allows us to become answerable for what we learn how to see" (p. 153). In their responses to Susan Hekman's (1997) assessment of feminist standpoint theory that appeared in *Signs*, Nancy Hartsock, Patricia Hill Collins, Sandra Harding, and Dorothy Smith all emphasize that feminist standpoint theorizing is designed to investigate how power works rather than some apolitical or abstract "truth." As Harding (1997) explains, "it seems to me that Hekman distorts the central project of standpoint theorists when she characterizes it as one of figuring out how to justify the truth of feminist claims to more accurate accounts of reality. Rather, it is relations between power and knowledge that concern these thinkers" (p. 382).

The appeal to women's embodied social experience as a privileged site of knowledge about power and domination forms one central thread within standpoint epistemologies. However, as Alison Jaggar (1989) argues, "women's standpoint" should not be equated with women's viewpoint or actual experiences (p. 48). Rather, *standpoint* "refers to a way of conceptualizing reality that reflects women's interests and values and draws on women's own interpretation of their own experience" (Jaggar 1983, 387). Nancy Hartsock (1983) writes that "a standpoint carries the contention that there are some perspectives on society from which, however well intentioned one may be, the real relations of humans with each other and with the natural world are not visible" (p. 117). In reworking Marx's historical materialism from a feminist perspective, Hartsock's stated goal is to explicate "the genderedness of relations of domination." She offers the concept of "a feminist standpoint . . . as a basis for understanding the sexual or erotic form taken by gendered power relations" (p. 151). For Hartsock, "the feminist standpoint" offers a "vision of reality" that is "deeper and more thoroughgoing than that available to the worker" and embodied in Marx's notion of the proletarian standpoint (p. 234). Hartsock (1983) states that her goal in articulating "a feminist standpoint" is a "modest one" and further argues that "women's lives provide a related but more adequate epistemological terrain for understanding power. Women's different understanding of power provides suggestive evidence that women's experience of power relations, and thus their understanding, may be importantly and structurally different from the lives and therefore the theories of men" (p. 151).

Hawkesworth (1990) challenges this historical materialist claim and argues that:

> To claim there is a distinct women's "perspective" that is "privileged" precisely because it possesses heightened insights into the nature of reality, a superior access to truth is to suggest there is some uniform experience common to all women that generates this univocal vision. Yet, if social, cultural, and historical differences are taken seriously, the notion of such a common experience becomes suspect. In the absence of such a homogeneous women's experience, standpoint epistemologies must either develop complicated explanations of why some women see the truth while others do not, a strategy that threatens to undermine the very notion of a "women's standpoint," or collapse into a trivial and potentially contradictory pluralism that conceives of truth as simply the sum of all women's partial and incompatible views. (P. 138)

The dual dilemmas identified by Hawkesworth (creating a hierarchy of standpoints[3] or resorting to "judgmental relativism" [Harding 1991, 139]) are closely linked to analyses that rely exclusively on an embodied construction of standpoint. However, rather than view standpoints as individual possessions of disconnected actors, most standpoint theorists attempt to locate standpoint in specific community contexts with particular attention to the dynamics of race, class, and gender.

African American and Chicana feminists have been especially critical of standpoint theorizing that constructs a totalizing view of women's experiences, taking white Western women's social lives as the framework for analysis.[4] However, they also face challenges associated with embodied standpoint analysis as they attempt to articulate the construction of standpoint from the point of view of women of color. Patricia Hill Collins (1990) addresses the intersection of gender and race in her articulation of Black feminist thought. Remaining sensitive to the critiques of essentialism, Collins (1990) concludes her analysis by emphasizing that "despite African-American women's potential power to reveal new insights about the matrix of domination, Black women's standpoint is only one angle of vision" (p. 234). Yet by constructing even this partial standpoint as an angle of vision achieved by African American women, she also falls into the "trap" of essentializing Black women's experience to a certain extent—namely, by masking dimensions of class and sexuality among other axes of difference that fracture Black women's social location (see White 1990). Patricia Clough (1994) aims her criticism of Collins's approach right to the heart of embodied standpoint analyses when she emphasizes that privileging "experience, especially the experience of oppression" in any form, even with attention to the partiality of that experience is a problematic theoretical move (p. 103).

Diversity and Continuity within Standpoint Epistemology: The Matter of Experience

While constructions of standpoint as embodied in specific women's experiences are most vulnerable to charges of essentialism, standpoint theorists typically resist focusing their analyses on individual women removed from their social context. In fact, Hartsock and Collins both emphasize that "standpoints" are achieved in community, through collective conversations and dialogue among women in marginal social positions. According to Collins (1990), standpoints are achieved by groups who struggle collectively and self-reflectively against "the matrix of domination" that circumscribe their lives (p. 234). Hartsock (1983) also emphasizes that "a 'privileged' standpoint is achieved rather than obvious, a mediated rather than an immediate understanding . . . an achievement both of science (analysis) and of political struggle" (p. 288). In this regard, Chéla Sandoval's analysis of *oppositional consciousness* has much in common with Hartsock's. Although Sandoval locates her analysis in a postmodern frame and Hartsock resists such a move, the legacy of historical materialism links their work within a broadly defined feminist standpoint epistemology. In fact, Hartsock (1996) acknowledges the power of Sandoval's analysis for challenging essentialized views of identity and identity politics. Like Sandoval, Hartsock (1996) believes that "the development of situated knowledges can constitute alternatives: they open possibilities that may or may not be realized. To the extent that these knowledges become self-conscious about their assumptions, they make available new epistemologies and political options" (p. 271).

A number of important analyses of women's political activism bear out these materialist feminist claims.[5] Working-class and third world feminist scholarship are especially clear about the import of marginalized and localized understandings for effective political action. For example, Terry Haywoode (1991) emphasizes that the key to effectiveness of the urban working-class women activists she worked with in the 1970s and 1980s was the way they understood the social organization of community, for "women know a great deal about community life because it is the stuff of their every day experience" (p. 183). This form of "working-class feminism" built upon women's kinship and friendship networks and relied on the often invisible work of "center-women" (Sacks 1988) who facilitated the development and mobilization of these networks. Chandra Talpede Mohanty (1997) describes how daily struggles and resistance to global capitalist ideologies make visible "the common interests of Third-World women workers" that can serve as the basis for organizing across differences and national boundaries. Cherríe Moraga (1981) also argues that the political consciousness of women of color develops from the material reality of their lives.[6]

For Collins (1990), dialogue among "subjugated" groups (defined as "African American women, African American men, Latina lesbians, Asian American women, Puerto Rican men, and others with distinctive standpoints") enhances the development of truth claims that can approach an "objective" understanding of the relations of domination in the following way: "Each group speaks from its own standpoint and shares its own partial, situated knowledge. But because each group perceives its own thought as partial, its knowledge is unfinished. Each group becomes better able to consider other groups' standpoints without relinquishing the uniqueness of its own standpoint or suppressing other groups' partial perspectives" (p. 236).

In considering Collins's claim, Susan Mann and Lori Kelley (1997) caution that consensus-building strategies privilege the majority perspectives and "those with the greatest power and resources have no reason to give up their privilege simply because they understand oppression better" (p. 403). Again we confront the limits of standpoint analysis that is detached from the community context where relations of domination could be brought into the analytic frame. By constructing groups who share similar racial, ethnic, gender, and sexual identities as potentially articulating a similar standpoint, Collins is masking other differences within each defined group. Since Collins's goal is to articulate Black feminist thought, she does not investigate how standpoints are differently achieved within other racial-ethnic groups. However, her approach could be broadened to examine the construction of standpoints in ways that remain sensitive to the differences within and across groups. As Collins (1998) explains:

> Theorizing from outsider-within locations reflects the multiplicity of being on the margins within intersecting systems of race, class, gender, sexual, and national oppression, even as such theory remains grounded in and attentive to real differences in power. This, to me, is what distinguishes oppositional knowledges developed in outsider-within locations *both* from elite knowledges (social theory developed from within centers of power such as Whiteness, maleness, heterosexuality, class privilege, or citizenship) and from knowledges developed in oppositional locations where groups resist only *one* form of oppression (e.g., a patriarchal Black, cultural nationalism, a racist feminism, or a raceless, genderless class analysis). In other words, theorizing from outsider-within locations can produce distinctive oppositional knowledges that embrace multiplicity yet remain cognizant of power. (P. 8, emphasis in original)

How we extrapolate "situated knowledges" (Haraway 1988) from the everyday world for theoretical analytic purposes continues to challenge ethnographers and other feminist researchers of women's political praxis.[7] As Chandra Mohanty (1995) argues, "we cannot avoid the challenge of *theorizing* experience. For most of us would not want to ignore the range and scope of the feminist political arena" (p. 71, emphasis in original). This is especially unavoidable if the focus of one's research is the dynamics of women's political praxis. Joan Scott's (1992, 25) critique of how historians use "experience" as "uncontestable evidence and as an originary point of explanation" directly challenges early feminist attempts to rewrite women's history and to document women's subjectivity and agency. Her challenge has been taken to heart by many researchers operating inside and outside feminist frameworks. Her call is not to discard experience in historical research but to contextualize and historicize its usage. Yet, as Kathleen Canning (1994) points out, "Scott's arguments foregrounds the discursive in the construction of women's work while leaving obscure its relationship to the social context in which it emerged" (p. 379). Like Canning, I am also interested in exploring the complex interplay of the material or nondiscursive practices and the discursive patterns and disruptions that contour women's life and, more particularly, influence their political praxis. In this regard, Canning (1994) and I join Dorothy Smith in the goal of keeping "both subjects and the objects of the discourses" in the methodological frame (p. 383).

Yet, at another level, Scott and Smith are engaged in similar projects; namely, to challenge the taken-for-granted practices of their respective disciplines that render invisible or domesticate women's work as well as their everyday lives. Scott (1992) summons historians to view experience as "not the origin of our explanation, not the authoritative (because seen or felt) evidence that grounds what is known, but rather that which we seek to explain, that about which knowledge is produced" (p. 26). In this regard, we might identify a parallel here with Smith's (1996) "everyday world" perspective in which she defines experience as "always social and always bear[ing] its social organization" (p. 1). For Smith, "a sociology for people proposes to explore from experience but beyond it, beginning in the living as people can speak of it rather than in the pregivens of theoretically-designed discourse" (p. 1). Smith's (1992) mode of inquiry calls for explicit attention to the social relations embedded in women's everyday activities. However, it does not end at the level of the individual women as "knower" but is "directed towards exploring and explicating what she does not know—the social relations and organization pervading her world but invisible in it" (p. 91).

Commenting on Susan Hekman's (1997) "revisiting" of feminist standpoint theory, Dorothy Smith (1997) argues that "experience is a method of speaking that is not preappropriated by the discourses of the relations of ruling" (p. 394). Here Smith's construction of experience should be differentiated from Scott's historical reference and related to their different disciplinary foci (although, of course, this should not be read as reifying the methods employed by researchers within each discipline since sociologists also employ historical methods and historians also gather data from living "informants"). Smith ties her understanding of experience to the collective conversations of the women's movement that gave rise to understandings about women's lives which had no prior discursive existence. She explains: "When we assembled *as* 'women' and spoke together *as* 'women,' constituting 'women' as a category of political mobilization, we discovered dimensions of 'our' experience that had no prior discursive definition" (p. 394, emphasis in original). Smith makes a crucial distinction between the political import of experience and the epistemological claim to the truth of what is spoken (a key aspect of Hekman's critique of standpoint theorizing) when she writes: "The authority of experience is foundational to the women's movement (which is not to say that experience is foundational to knowledge) and has been and is at once explosive and fruitful" (p. 394). For Scott, experience is embodied in particular textual products that are, by extension, the result of patterns of exclusion, interpretation, and power. In this regard, ethnographers also confront the thorny dilemmas of inclusion, interpretive authority, and power as we grapple with the construction of individual narratives from interviews and other field-based research methods.

Since many postmodern and poststructural critics of standpoint epistemology present a narrow interpretation of what constitutes a standpoint, they often equate it with some notion of unmediated experience. However, a careful review of standpoint theoretical perspectives reveal multiple approaches to the construction of standpoint: as embodied in women's social location and social experience, as constructed in community, and as a site through which to begin inquiry. With a multidimensional standpoint framework, I have been able to explore the specificity of women's experiences in different social locations as well as to compare across different times and places. The goal of my multidimensional approach to standpoint analysis is to move beyond a fractured account of differences to a broader understanding of how relations of ruling can be effectively brought into view and resisted. It is the processes of social control and resistance (or "how things are put together" to use Smith's [1992, 88] formulation) that can be articulated through this multidimensional standpoint analysis, not a specifiable translocal political analysis or practice. I begin the next section with a brief description of the two research studies from which I draw examples to illustrate my approach, then shift to illustrate the three dimensions of my standpoint analytic approach.

Toward a Multidimensional Standpoint Framework

In the mid-1980s, I initiated a study to examine how gender, class, and race influenced the political consciousness and political practice of women from low-income communities in New York City and Philadelphia. This research was prompted by the question: how do people remain involved in community activism for social and economic justice over an extended period of time? To address this question, I explored the complex ways that women from different racial and class backgrounds became politically conscious of the relations of domination that shaped their lives and how their political analyses and political strategies changed with the shifting political and economic context. In the mid-1990s, I contacted a subset of the women originally interviewed in the mid-1980s to explore how their political praxis changed over time (see Appendix A for a more expanded description of the methodology used for this research).[8]

Upon moving to Iowa in 1989, I began to investigate the ways in which women from rural communities viewed the wider political landscape that contoured their lives and informed their political practice (see Appendix B for further description of the methodology used in this study). Throughout the rural research, I became increasingly aware of how this differing community context provided the grounds for certain kinds of political consciousness and political practices that contrasted sharply with my findings from the urban-based study. Yet these political perspectives and practices were not fixed and immutable. As I had found among the urban community workers, political praxis changed over time and was further influenced by varying political and economic forces. Here I faced one of the central dilemmas that constrain the development of comparative standpoint analyses; namely, that dimensions upon which we might generate our comparisons are ever-shifting social dynamics that are difficult to specify even in one particular site. On the one hand, it might easily be argued that little basis exists for the comparison in these two cases regardless of theoretical position adopted. On the other hand, such a sharp analytic exercise can provide an illustrative model for the development of comparative standpoint analyses. I turn now to discuss the dilemmas encountered in conducting ethnographic work from differing feminist standpoint perspectives. Throughout the discussion, I make reference to findings from my research with community workers in urban and rural settings as a way to illustrate each of the dilemmas posed.

Dilemmas of the Embodied Standpoint

Many feminist theorists understand standpoint as embodied in specific actors who are located in less privileged positions within the social order and who, because of their social locations, are engaged in activities that differ from others who are not similarly situated. As discussed above, these theorists are often criticized for drawing upon an essentialized view of women and equating particular ways of knowing with their identities as women. Carol Gilligan's (1982) work is often identified as exemplifying the essentializing tendencies of this strand.[9] As noted earlier, Collins has also been faulted for failing to adequately incorporate class or sexuality into her analysis of "Afrocentric feminist consciousness" (see White 1990). While these criticisms must be taken into account when assessing the usefulness of an embodied construction of standpoint, it is also important to explore the methodological implications of this approach. Is failure to fully contextualize the standpoint of particular women inherent to the methodology or a consequence of the challenge in articulating the complexity of particular women's lives? In my view, the use of an embodied standpoint as one methodological starting point does not necessarily presume privileging or rendering invisible other aspects of women's experience or ignoring the fluidity of its construction. However, the difficulty in fully explicating the social construction of women's social location remains as a fundamental challenge to feminist researchers working from an embodied standpoint perspective.

For example, many feminist theorists who contribute to the embodied strand of standpoint theorizing argue that low-income women of color or others located in marginalized social positions develop a perspective on social life in the United States that differs markedly from that of middle- and upper-income people.[10] Collins (1990) explains that since working-class Black women are "much more inclined to be struck by the mismatch of [their] own experiences and the paradigms of sociology itself," they are more likely to identify "anomalies" between their experiences and those represented by normalized, yet distorted, sociological accounts (pp. 50–51). Here Collins is describing the advantages of "outsider within theorizing" for sociology. Smith (1993) describes her formulation as "insider sociology" (p. 190). The shifting use of the terms *insider/outsider* highlights a central contribution of embodied standpoint theorizing when recognized as social and relational achievements (see chapter 4). While extolling the benefits of "insider" knowledge for understanding and articulating the construction of domination, Collins and Smith also highlight the value of this knowledge for transforming the dominant practices of their field (hence, Collins's notion of the "outsider within").

Women activists I interviewed in both urban and rural settings expressed political analyses that correspond with "outsider within" as well "insider" constructions of "situated knowledges." Ann Robinson, an African American community worker in Harlem, discussed the difficulties she faced as a low-income woman of color and how her experiences influenced her analysis of racism, sexism, and class. Ann described how her experience with the welfare system increased her sensitivity to others forced to rely on public assistance. Further, she insisted, her personal experiences as a single mother on welfare enhanced her commitment to fighting injustice and economic inequality. White European American and rural resident Amy Grove, who lost her home and farm during the "farm crisis" of the early 1980s, said that she had "a lot more compassion and understanding of what other people go through" because of the foreclosure. Following the foreclosure, Amy accepted a job with the social services department. She believed this made her more effective as a government employee and community worker in rural Iowa. This perspective mirrors the narrative accounts of the urban community activists like Ann Robinson who believed that because they had "been there" and had experienced poverty and discrimination, they were more sensitive to other community members undergoing economic and emotional stress. Of course, narrations of one's privileged stance as an "indigenous" knower does not equate with one's actions and having "been there" does not necessarily produce corresponding political analyses.

Urban community activists, even those who shared similar backgrounds, were not always in agreement about the solutions to the problems of poverty and what political actions would help improve the lives of the poor. A few women felt that if an individual remained in school and worked hard on the job, he or she could leave the ranks of the poor—a perspective that mirrored dominant discourse on welfare reform (see chapter 7 in this volume). Others insisted that the society must provide the poor with better education and expanded employment opportunities to help them out of poverty—a more progressive construction but one still focused on individualist strategies. In contrast, other workers felt that the rich, who rule our society, are not interested in eliminating poverty; therefore, the poor must gain control of the major political, economic, and social service institutions in the United States. The contrast between urban community workers' analyses of how to counter poverty in their communities reveals how political perspectives can vary among those who share similar racial-ethnic and class positions. This analysis contests an essentialized definition of standpoint that equates particular ways of knowing with specific social identities. However, if we take this embodied construction as one angle of investigation, it is possible to explore the relationship between particular social locations and varying constructions of oppositional as well as dominant political analyses. This becomes more apparent when we shift from racial/class/gender constructions of an embodied standpoint to situational constructions as I illustrate with Barbara Drake's account.

White European American factory worker Barbara Drake also discussed her situated ability to see how power works in her small Iowa town and said that people who hold positions of "prestige" in her community can do and say things that others cannot. When I asked her to describe those with prestige, she pointed to members of the community who had lived in the town "forever," who came from families with a long history in the community. In this illustration, Barbara did not call on racial identity or class location as a way to explain her different understanding of power. She saw it through her "newcomer" status. Since the dynamics of whiteness and, to a less salient degree, class are not made explicit in Barbara's reported experience in her small rural town, her claim to a different form of knowledge poses a challenge to standpoint perspectives that exclusively center the processes of race, class, and gender in shaping differing standpoints. This is not to say that Barbara's gender, class, and race were not significant organizing frames through which she saw her differing location. However, these dimensions were not made self-evident in her narrative. Barbara's account further illustrates the challenge faced by ethnographers who define standpoint as embodied in the class, race, and gender position of particular knowers without locating these constructions in particular community contexts. However, it also highlights the difficulty in using spoken accounts of experience or an individual's viewpoint as an access to, or way to locate, a standpoint since these expressions capture dominant as well as alternative political analyses.

As I shifted my research to a rural context I was immediately aware of my own position as an "outsider" to the communities I studied. On the one hand, as a "native" New Yorker and former urban social worker, I was more familiar with the neighborhoods and broader community context in which the urban community workers I interviewed worked. On the other hand, as someone from a white working-class background, my racial-ethnic difference from the predominantly African American and Puerto Rican women was salient in most encounters. As I began to interview white European American women in rural Iowa, I recognized how the dynamics of regional familiarity positioned me differently with respect to white rural women despite our racial "similarity." Over time, my relationship to the women I met in both settings also changed as did my own perceptions of "outsiderness." As I demonstrated in chapter 4, this shifting insiderness/outsiderness was a source of important ethnographic information and continues to guide my ethnographic research strategies.

Heightened sensitivity to the multiplicity and contradictions of women's embodied standpoints as well as a researcher's own position in the field has made it difficult for feminist ethnographers to explicate the complex relationship between race, class, and gender. This unstable process of intersectionality is shaped by hegemonic constructions of race, class, and gender that pervade personal narratives and ethnographic encounters.[11] It is also contoured by regional discursive and material practices as illustrated in Barbara Drake's construction of her status as "newcomer." Further, since "insider" analysts do not develop their political perspectives outside the dominant discursive frames, their situated knowledges do not automatically contribute to an oppositional consciousness. The second approach to standpoint theorizing attempts to articulate the ways in which "different ways of knowing" (Belenky et al. 1986) or "situated knowledges" (Haraway 1988) are located in and derived from different types of communities, organized by, and, at times, in opposition to relations of domination.

Dilemmas of "Community"

In contrast to the first approach, some standpoint theorists define standpoint not as a property of disconnected knowers but as located within particular communities.[12] Through this strand of standpoint theorizing, we could better analyze Barbara Drake's conceptualization of her identity as "newcomer." Barbara locates her privileged standpoint in a relational community context rather than in her individual identity as a woman or working-class resident. Furthermore, from a relational standpoint perspective, the identity of "woman" or class or other embodied identities are constructed in community and therefore cannot be interpreted outside the shifting community context.

However, when we shift from the individual embodied definition of standpoint to a relational or community construction we face another challenging dilemma; namely, how do we define and locate community? Is community a geographic and identifiable site or a collective process through which individuals come to represent themselves in relation to others with whom they perceive share similar experiences and viewpoints? Collins (1990) draws on the later construction of community for her analysis of Black feminist thought. Collins (1997) argues that "the notion of a standpoint refers to historically shared, *group*-based experiences" (p. 375, emphasis in original). But how do we identify or define the boundaries of a group when it is not coterminous with a definable geographic area? Like the embodied approach to standpoint theorizing, group-based approaches have also been criticized for unproblematically using women's class and racial identities to define who is or is not part of a particular group. Yet, as my research in both rural and urban settings demonstrates, identity conceptions including those that are coterminous with racial-ethnic identities cannot be detached from geographic or other constructions of community.[13]

The concept of "community" brings with it a host of associations. As Raymond Williams (1976) demonstrates, the complexity of the term *community* also relates to the historically changing definitions of community and to the various historically specific forms of social organization of community. However, a conceptualization of community as coterminous with small town and rural life as in Ferdinand Tonnies's (1963) *gemeinschaft* construction remains a prime feature of agrarian ideology. This construction of rural community life has material consequences for the rural Iowa residents I interviewed. Many of the white rural community workers internalized this conservative definition of community and constructed their political activities accordingly. The social control features of the *gemeinschaft* construction of rural community life limited their effectiveness in challenging inequality and discrimination in their small towns. They recognized the sanctions they would face if they spoke out against the dominant view of economic development. From a relational standpoint perspective, however, accounts from the rural and urban community workers tended to turn the *gemeinschaft-gesellschaft* distinction on its head. Those who felt "outside" the dominant construction of insider felt marginalized in this "close-knit" community; while many of the urban women described close ties they had with neighbors and other community workers.

The dimension of time is also brought into the frame to shake up any firm continuity in any one location. White rural community worker Marlee Castle recalled: "It used to be that you could share equipment, you could ... trade labor and so forth [with your neighbors]. That's virtually nonexistent. You don't find very many farmers out there that will do that any longer. They go to the other farmer's landowner, and say, 'I can do a better job, or I can do this for you,' and ... it's a real different kind of mentality than what it was ten years ago." Of course, further analysis is required to assess the extent to which Marlee's construction of community mirrors other accounts and aligns with other ethnographic modes of analysis. However, the fact that she experienced a diminished sense of communion in her rural town informed the way she related to her neighbors and friends, and in turn, informed her political analyses and political engagement during the 1990s.[14]

While many of the rural women interviewed in the 1990s expressed similar concerns for the perceived loss of Gemeinschaft-like social relations in their small town, the urban community workers frequently mentioned how people in their embattled urban neighborhoods pulled together during difficult times. Wilma North of Philadelphia said that in the mid-1980s, "Everybody in the community is trying to work together, to serve, [to] do something as far as these needs are concerned. They realize that you have to hang together rather than separately. They realize it's going to take all of us, all of our efforts to try to do something—to eliminate some of this." On first read, it would seem that the sense of shared oppression in the poor urban neighborhoods contributed to a heightened sense of connection among women activists. However, once I adjusted for time and explored constructions of "communion" within the rural accounts, I did locate a similar perception; namely that the collective nature of economic distress during the so-called farm crisis of the mid-1980s seemed to counter the experience of alienation expressed by Marlee Castle. In fact, Marlee reported that "the crisis was kind of a tie, it bound a lot of people together." She contrasted that time with the 1990s:

> There was a time when it wasn't embarrassing to say I'm having financial difficulties. We had to severely restructure our farming. We went through a bankruptcy, my husband and I, on our farm. We've been lucky to be able to stay out here, though. . . . There were many of them not that lucky. But there was a time when I think there was a lot of cohesiveness. People stuck together. They had goals [like] "my neighbor's in trouble, we've got to help them out." And that's gone again. It's scary that that's gone again!

Among the most salient factors that Marlee believed contributed to the loss of communion was the perception that many low-income "newcomers" were moving into the community thus disrupting the sense of cohesiveness built on long-term residency. Marlee's analysis should not be read as evidence that such cohesiveness existed, but as an indication of how this construction informed her own (and possible other middle-class white residents') political engagement.

These excerpts from my research highlight different ways rural and urban residents responded to the declining economic conditions in their communities—defined primarily in geographic terms. In both locations, activists expressed a belief that shared oppression drew members of their communities together. Embedded in each geographic account of community were class and racial-ethnic, among other, components of identity and communion. In other words, not all members of the geographic community are called into the frame. Non-geographic constructions of community are infused throughout the narratives, although less visible from view than the more typical geographic usage. And, as I emphasized with regard to outsiderness/insiderness, constructions of community remain in flux as individual members are repositioned by social and economic processes. Here I find the long-term ethnographic lens most helpful for mapping these changes over time.

The geographic conception of community is also illustrated in African American urban community worker Othelia Carson's narrative. She emphasized the importance of her relationship to her neighborhood because "you know the people—you know the thieves, you know the crooks." Othelia's description of her relationship to her urban community evokes some of the sentiments offered by the women interviewed in Iowa, although the rural women never mentioned thieves and crooks as members of their communities. In contrast, they drew distinctions between "insiders" and "outsiders" and those with "status" or "privilege" and others. While these constructions also dovetailed with racial-ethnic identity, racial-ethnic and gendered constructions of community were less salient in the rural women's spoken accounts when compared with the urban women's political analyses. However, as the racial-ethnic composition changed within the small rural communities, the saliency of racial-ethnic identity constructions increased.

This brief exploration into the dilemmas of the relational construction of standpoint reveals the persistence of experience as spoken or otherwise recorded as a way to identify "collective subject positions" (Haraway 1988) or communal constructions of standpoint (p. 590). An ethnographic approach to standpoint analysis provides the long-term vision and relational context in which to interpret the expressions of those who occupy different positions within a specifiable context and, therefore, serves to temper, to a certain extent, the tendency toward essentialized or fragmented accounts associated with the embodied standpoint perspective. However, we are left with some of the same methodological challenges associated with reliance on individual expressions or other observations of experience. How do we treat contrasting experiences and analyses of the "partial views and halting voices" (Haraway 1988, 590) articulated within shifting community contexts? From a communal/relational standpoint perspective, do all individual constructions of experience constitute a standpoint? As ethnographers of women's political consciousness and practices, the problem of how to relate to and treat the testimony of individual knowers remains to haunt us.

Chéla Sandoval (1991) treats experience as simultaneously embodied and strategically created in community and concludes that this dynamic interaction affects the political practice of third world women. Sandoval's model of oppositional consciousness offers a methodological strategy that contests previously taken-for-granted categorization of women's political practice. Many feminist theorists who incorporate both the embodied and relational strands of standpoint epistemology emphasize that perspectives from the vantage point of the oppressed remain partial and incomplete. How partial the perspective remains a central problematic of feminist standpoint analyses. Furthermore, as Harding (1986) asks, "Can there be *a* feminist epistemological standpoint when so many women are embracing 'fractured identities' as Black women, Asian women, Native American women, professional, working-class women, lesbian?" (p. 163, emphasis in original). Constructions of community in and through which women experience and construct their perceived identities are "fractured," fluid, and shifting phenomena as well. The third strand of feminist standpoint epistemology provides a framework for capturing the interactive and fluid conceptualization of community and resists attaching standpoint to particular bodies, individual knowers, or specific communities or groups.

Dilemmas in Locating Standpoint

In the third construction of standpoint, standpoint is understood as a site from which to begin "a mode of inquiry" as in Dorothy Smith's "everyday world" institutional ethnographic approach to standpoint epistemology. Smith (1992) explains that her approach "does not privilege a knower" (or subject of research) whose expressions are disconnected from her social location and daily activities (p. 91). Rather, Smith starts inquiry "with the knower who is actually located: she is active; she is at work; she is connected with particular other people in various ways.... Activities, feelings, experiences, hook her into extended social relations linking her activities to those of other people and in ways beyond her knowing" (p. 91). This mode of inquiry calls for explicit attention to the social relations embedded in women's everyday activities. As Smith (1996) explains, her "everyday world" approach:

> aims at knowing the social as people actually bring it into being. Its objects would not be meaning but the actual ongoing ways in which people's activities are coordinated, particularly those forms of social organization and relations that connect up multiple and various sites of experience since these are what are ordinarily inaccessible to people. And unlike maps of lands, seas, and seacoasts, these have to be maps of relations in motion, the dynamic of which generates changes in how we are related, what we experience, and what we do and can do. (P. 24)

Smith's (1992) analysis "of 'standpoint' as 'a *method of inquiry*' " (88) offers a valuable methodological strategy for exploring how power dynamics are organized and experienced in a community context.

Racial formation theory provides another "method of inquiry" that articulates well with Smith's feminist standpoint approach. Although Michael Omi and Howard Winant (1986), the most prominent proponents of this framework, do not attend to gender and sexuality, their approach offers a conceptual tool for mapping the way racial meanings and racial identities infuse gender identities and institutional arrangements in a particular society (Winant 1994, 23). By drawing on the methodological and conceptual tools offered by institutional ethnography (Smith 1987) and racial formation theory (Omi and Winant 1986), we can broaden our approach to standpoint analysis to incorporate the discursive fields and material structural conditions that shape how different women's lives are organized by relations of ruling, how these experiences change over time, and how women resist, or reposition their relationship to, mechanisms of social control. Both approaches leave open the specific content of "how things are put together" (Smith 1992, 88). The challenge in articulating these daily practices and processes to form "maps of relations in motion" (Smith 1996, 24) is well illustrated with reference to the experiences of the Mexican and Mexican American residents who began moving in 1990 to rural southwest Iowa for work in an expanded food-processing plant. As the number of Latinos increased in the town, the perception of many white residents shifted from denying the permanency of the changing racial-ethnic composition in their town to active resistance to resentful acceptance and to, a lesser extent, supportive attitudes.

Despite the diversity among the Latinos (who had moved from rural towns in Mexico, small towns in the United States, as well as large cities like Chicago and Mexico City), white European American residents initially saw all Mexicans and Mexican Americans as illegal immigrants and transitory workers. However, white ethnic residents' perceptions of the Latinos shifted in response to outside intervention by the Immigration and Naturalization Service (INS). Racial-ethnic consciousness initially remained hidden from view within the predominantly white communities. By spring of 1992 when the Latino community had grown to form approximately 10 percent of the population in Midtown (the pseudonym for the town in which the expanded food-processing plant is located), a local resident called the INS who, in turn, conducted a massive raid in this town of 1,250 to identify and deport illegal workers and their families. Ironically, this action, born in anti-Latino sentiment, created the grounds for a redirection of racialization processes and racist attitudes. The INS raids, subsequent deportations, and ongoing investigation served to regulate the lives of all Mexicans and Mexican Americans living in the town. However, INS intervention also made visible the contradictions in the construction of the "outsider" as discussed in chapter 4. While INS activities confirmed white European American residents' fears that there were many undocumented Mexican workers in the plant; it also demonstrated that many Mexican and Mexican American residents were "legitimate" members of the community.

The community workers in rural Iowa have a different relationship to the interlocking of gender, race-ethnicity, class, and political action when compared with the urban community workers. To understand the differences between the individual, interpersonal, spatial, and historic contexts of their lives requires an analysis that is grounded in each community worker's varying perspectives and experiences as well as the organization of his or her everyday activities. By approaching standpoint as a site of inquiry as well as an embodied perspective and relational achievement, my multidimensional materialist feminist standpoint analysis leaves room for the fluidity of social, political, economic, and ideological manifestations of women's experiences as they shift over time and place.

Conclusion

A careful review of feminist standpoint theories reveals three dominant constructions of standpoint that offer different strategies for ethnographic investigation of women's political praxis. Multidimensional standpoint methodology for comparative ethnographic research must confront the dilemmas of experience at three junctures: at the level of the individual knower, in constructions of community, and within methodological strategies.

Knowledge generated from embodied standpoints of "subordinates" is powerful in that it can help transform traditional categories of analyses that originate from dominant groups.[15] However, as many feminist standpoint theorists argue, it remains only a partial perspective. By placing the analysis within a community context, we can better reveal the multiplicity of perspectives along with the dynamic structural dimensions of the social, political, and economic environment that shape the relations of ruling in a particular social space. The multidimensional feminist standpoint analysis explicated through the above discussion enhances our understanding of how community is constructed, sustained, and redefined by community members in different contexts and how conceptualizations of community also promote or inhibit political activism. By exposing "the arbitrariness and instability of positions within systems of oppression," we draw upon "a conception of power that refuses totalizations, and can therefore account for the possibility of resistance"—a central goal of feminist praxis (Martin and Mohanty 1986, 209).

The multidimensional feminist standpoint analytic model I propose is one that remains consistently relational, open to contestation, and designed to challenge taken-for-granted constructions that derive from either a view from above or a view from nowhere.[16] Ethnographers of women's political praxis also need to go beyond reliance on "experience, as spoken" or individually manifest (Smith 1996, 1). Smith's "everyday world" standpoint methodology provides a framework through which to use "experience, as spoken" to explore ruling relations manifest in the actualities of women's lives rather than an end in itself. Experience is itself organized through relations of ruling not visible to individual knowers and is therefore politically constituted. The content of women's spoken experience must remain open to exploration from a number of angles: first as constructed knowledge from individual knowers, next as an expression of a relationship to other knowers and multiple institutional sites of power, and finally, as a site of inquiry. Simultaneously, attention must be paid to how gendered processes of racialization inform the construction of experience within these three analytic dimensions. By utilizing the multiple dimensions of standpoint epistemology, it becomes possible to build a foundation for comparative materialist feminist analyses that remain sensitive to the partial and shifting nature of relationships under multiple and mutually constituting systems of oppression. The ethnographer is herself an actor in the field of study and must also reflect on the ways her relationship to the field and to local residents or community members is shaping the angle of vision.

In the next section, I shift the angle of vision from the practice of ethnography to the analysis of texts to demonstrate the value of a materialist feminist approach to discourse. The two chapters in Part III highlight the power of a materialist feminist discourse analysis for policy studies and social movement research. The discourse analysis I utilize resonates with the approaches that simultaneously incorporate discursive, cultural, and structural factors.[17] A materialist feminist approach to discourse analysis focuses attention on the social and political context, subject positions and power relations in and through which social movement frames or governing practices are generated, circulated, and reinscribed within different discursive and institutional sites as well as the shifting discursive fields surrounding the production of specific movement frames or social policy.[18]

PART III

Feminist Materialism, Discourse Analysis, and Policy Studies

CHAPTER **6**

Community Control
Mapping the Changing Context

On October 6, 2002, the *New York Times Magazine* published an article on the demise of "community control, or, as it came to be known, decentralization" (Traub 2002) that highlighted the problems parents and teachers have had with the implementation of community control in Ocean Hill-Brownsville (p. 70). This Brooklyn neighborhood was the center of the struggle for community control of schools in the 1960s. Black and Puerto Rican activists and white allies fought the New York City Board of Education for the right of the local neighborhoods to control the education of their children. In response to the demands for community control and in the context of the racial unrest of the late 1960s, New York State established a system of local school boards that was designed to give the local residents control over the elementary and middle schools in their communities. By all current accounts, community control of schools failed to improve the quality of the schools nor provide effective control for community residents. In fact, as *New York Times* reporter James Traub (2002) notes, even many of the early supporters of the movement were looking forward to the end of 2002, when Ocean Hill-Brownsville and other New York City neighborhoods would "be liberated from community control" (p. 75).

Examples of the process by which social movement frames achieve wide acceptance and become institutionalized in various social practices but lose the critical feminist or progressive intent can be found throughout feminist praxis, from the transformation of "battered women" into the "battered woman syndrome" to the depoliticization of "sexual harassment."[1] My goal in this chapter is to demonstrate the value of a materialist feminist discourse analysis for explicating how social movement frames gain wide appeal but over time lose the progressive formulation that incited their production or, more are used to counter progressive goals. To examine this process, I center the oral narratives of women community activists involved in the struggle for community control of schools in New York City during the late 1960s and early 1970s. The use of oral historic evidence to construct a history of "what happened" at certain points in time has been challenged effectively by historians, most notably Joan Scott (1992). Scott does not suggest we discard experience in historical research but that we contextualize and historicize its usage. My methodological solution to this challenge is to resist treating the oral narratives as fully accurate representations of specific events, although I do use individual testimony to capture moments that are significant to the women as they narrate the stories of their lives.[2] I explore their descriptions and analyses of their life stories as personally meaningful constructions that further shape their experience and interpretation of the world in which they are embedded. For this analysis, I also examined newspaper articles and archival data as well as secondary historical accounts of the period from the early 1960s to the 1990s to understand the shifts in constructions and implementation of community control.

Discourse limits what can be discussed or heard in a political context and is not tied necessarily to particular organizations. Gender, race, class, region, among other patterns of inequality, shape whose voices are represented and heard in a public policy debate as well as in a social movement context. I illustrate this process with reference to the community control frame popularized during the later 1960s. As Howard Hallman (1969) notes, the call for "community control emerged as a demand of black nationalists as a means of achieving 'black power,' a slogan that gained popularity during the Meredith Mississippi Freedom March of June, 1966" (p. 1). The community control frame continues to resonate for residents in communities across the United States and has been expanded from the 1960s usage by black power activists and urban minority parents to members of the religious right, residents of suburban communities, and community police. The call for community control resonated with civil rights activists as well as policymakers, for low-income women in poor neighborhoods as well as the religious right who now use the frame to justify demands for teaching creationism in the public schools and banning books such as *Heather Has Two Mommies* from the school library.[3] The diverse political constituencies who use the community control frame for contradictory purposes illustrates how movement actors lose control of a movement frame over time.[4] Analysis of this political, economic, and social context surrounding the development and the wide acceptance of the community control frame demonstrates the inherent contradictions in the discursive field from which it was drawn.

For this analysis, I draw on data from a case study of women community activists employed in community action agencies who struggled for community control of schools and other community-based institutions in New York City.[5] I gathered focused life histories from women who were employed by the community action programs in Harlem and the Lower East Side of Manhattan and Bedford-Stuyvesant in order to examine their motivation for community work, the political analyses and political strategies they developed over time, and the ways in which the changing political economy influenced their work.[6] In this chapter, I center the oral narratives of community activists involved in the community control of schools struggle in New York City during the late 1960s and early 1970s. I also draw on newspaper accounts and archival data, annual reports, and minutes from monthly board meetings, as well as relevant archival data and secondary research for this analysis.

Materialist Feminist Discourse Analysis

For this materialist feminist social movement analysis, I utilize Foucault's (1972) discourse analysis as a methodology to reveal how movement frames contest, reproduce, or participate in relations of ruling. While discourse organizes relations among and between movement actors and others, subject positions within the discourse are infused with gender, racial-ethnic, and class inequalities. In addition, despite continuity within discourse, certain significant shifts in interpretation are revealed when social movement frames are analyzed over time. As Patrick Mooney and Scott Hunt (1994, 188) conclude from their study of the U.S. agrarian movement, "movements are shaped by a repertoire of interpretations in which the alignment of master frames varies with changing socioeconomic and political contexts" (quoted in Benford 1997, 417).

From my materialist feminist theoretical perspective, movement frames are constituted in discourses that organize and are structured by ruling relations and are embedded in everyday activities. Ruling relations and resistance are evident in both the processes that generate a particular social movement frame as well as in the way the frame is circulated, interpreted, and reinscribed with alternative meanings, and taken up by potential allies as well as opponents. Collective action frames can also resist domination or at least demonstrate the cracks and fissures in the dominant discursive field.[7] In the analysis to follow, I illustrate how social movement framing and less visible discursive realms intersect, at times, creating contradictory constructions of political action as political context and constituency shift. I now turn to a discussion of the community control frame to illustrate the power of a materialist feminist discourse analysis.

The "Community Control" Frame

In 1990 in the suburban town of Joshua Gap, California, a group of residents called for the removal of *Impressions*, the multicultural reading series published by Harcourt Brace Jovanovich, from the local elementary school. The protesting citizens claimed that this series presented ideas and values that were at odds with the traditional values of their community. David Post (1992) found in his insightful analysis of this struggle "that in Joshua Gap the concept of the community, like that of the nation, was itself imagined and constructed by members," many of whom had only recently moved to the town (p. 676). Across the United States, numerous conservative and, in some cases, reactionary and racist calls for community control of schools are reported in news items and opinion columns as well as in scholarly accounts. This development may not seem strange if one took the call for "community control of schools" out of the context in which it was originally expressed. However, in many ways, the call for community control of schools in the second half of the 1960s contained within it the contradictions that are revealed in the protest by elementary school parents in Joshua Gap.

To understand the contradictions of this movement frame, I begin by discussing precursors of the community control of schools movement, then focus on the discursive, political, and social context in which it arose in New York City. Next, I shift to the standpoint of women living and working in low-income New York neighborhoods who participated in the movement for community control of schools. I conclude by illustrating how the discursive themes evident in its construction and political implementation laid the grounds for the cooptation of the frame for conservative, racist, sexism, and homophobic ends.

Precursors for Community Control of Schools

Alan Altshuler (1970), who chaired the Academic Advisory Committee on Decentralization in New York City in 1968, defined community control as "the exercise of authority by the democratically organized government of a neighborhood-sized jurisdiction" (p. 64). Altshuler's would entail continued accountability to "higher levels of government—just as are the charters of cities and suburbs today" (pp. 64–65). Community control in the sense that members of the low-income communities of color in New York City understood it included both political and administrative decentralization. However, few legislators or public officials who supported decentralization included political decentralization and community control in their vision.

In Altshuler's (1970) view, "neighborhood democracy has few precedents—that decentralization and widespread citizen participation have not been characteristic of American cities in earlier historical periods" (p. 12). As late as 1962, he notes, no obvious "demands for neighborhood government or community control" were observable. While calls for community control were absent in earlier periods, strategies for decentralizing large city bureaucracies like the public school system were begun much earlier.[8] The few early experiments designed to expand participation in public school governance emphasized administrative decentralization more than community control or political decentralization. In 1950 New York's city planning commission proposed the establishment of 66 districts to plan and coordinate schools, hospitals, recreation facilities, and streets (Cronin 1973, 190). The following year Manhattan Borough President Robert Wagner set up 12 planning districts in Manhattan. Only a few years later the Board of Education itself determined that some decentralized system of decision-making was needed to facilitate the administration of the public schools. As Melvin Zimet (1973) observes, "the concepts of administrative decentralization and community control gathered momentum and converged on a collision course" around 1967 when the Mayor's Advisory Panel on Decentralization of the New York City Schools (1969) released their

report (p. 9). While this discursive framing of the importance of local participation in planning and decision-making was a far cry from the radical call for
community control espoused by Black Power activists, the report did emphasize the link between civic participation and public education.

Mapping the Discursive, Political, and Social Context

In the context of the civil rights movement, which gained momentum following the 1954 court victory in *Brown v. Board of Education*, African American
parents and the wider African American community, were keenly disappointed
by the dismal failure of even the most sincere efforts to integrate the public
schools in urban neighborhoods.[9] With the passage of the Civil Rights Act in
1964, the federal government actively pressed for desegregation first in the
South, then in northern cities (Watras 1997). However, by 1967 more than half
of the African American and Puerto Rican children in New York City were
attending completely segregated schools, most of which were located in low-
income neighborhoods (Stein 1970, 21). Twenty-five percent of African Americans in urban areas lived in poverty while only 10 percent of urban white
residents lived at or below poverty in the mid-1960s. By the early 1970s, almost
50 percent of the parents of public school children in the 10 major U.S. cities
were living in poverty (Tyack 1974, 278). Not surprisingly, a disproportionate
number of these parents were African American and Latino.

With the failure of integration efforts, many Black leaders and Black parents recognized the need to reconceptualize how to improve the quality of education for African American children in urban neighborhoods (see Watras
1997). While Black Power activists articulated a radical vision of Black self-determination, liberal organizations such as the NAACP and the Urban League
supported a more circumscribed version of community control. The NAACP
and the Urban League both passed a resolution supporting community control of schools in 1969, however, that was more in keeping with liberal reform
than radical separatism.[10] When the struggle for community control erupted
in New York City, liberal Black organizations like the NAACP were reported to
support "community control so long as it did not prevent integration" (Ornstein 1974, 244). According to educational analyst Allan Ornstein, this left
these groups and their leaders "without a practical strategy and they eventually
fell into the background." In addition, Ornstein reports, "A. Philip Randolph
and Bayard Rustin and a large group of trade unionists publicly denounced
community control" (p. 244).[11]

African American leadership in urban communities recognized "that white
America is much more likely (though still not very) to concede a large measure
of ghetto self-determination than to accept large numbers of blacks into its
neighborhoods" (Altshuler 1970, 24). Altshuler (1970) discusses the Black residents' call for community control as a pragmatic response to white resistance
to integration (p. 23). Within the context of growing tensions and riots erupt-

ing in minority urban neighborhoods across the United States and the apparent insurmountable difficulties in achieving integration, it is not surprising that school and city officials began to see the benefits of community control. After all, as Diane Ravitch (1974) writes in her historical overview of public education in New York: "If the parents assumed control, they would have only themselves and their appointees to blame for failure" (p. 305).

Mayor Robert Wagner became interested in decentralization when he recognized the fiscal benefits that could accrue to New York City as a result. He did not frame his support for decentralization as a way to encourage democratic participation of local communities in the management of public schools (Zimet 1973). During his administration, a temporary commission was established to evaluate city finances. They concluded that it would benefit the city financially if the school system was reorganized into five separate school districts. When John Lindsay became mayor in 1966 he latched onto this idea as a way to bring more state money into the city (Zimet 1973, 9). Another discursive theme woven into arguments supporting community control related to increasing "competition" through enhancing parental choice. Contrasting the monopolistic approach of large centralized bureaucracies with more decentralized strategies, Anthony Downs of the Real Estate Research Corporation (1970) argues that: "Since consumers can shift their trade from suppliers who do not please them, suppliers have a strong incentive to provide what the consumers want. . . . Clearly, if greater competition causes these results in general, it might produce some tremendous improvements in big-city school systems" (p. 219).

In contrast to the administrative, fiscal, and consumerist construction of decentralization, Alan Altshuler along with other observers of this policy period situate the origin of interest in community control in the liberal reform efforts of social scientists like Lloyd Ohlin and Richard Cloward, Ford Foundation social planners (notably Paul Ylvisaker), and progressive federal officials like David Hackett and other White House staff of President John F. Kennedy. With the passage of the Economic Opportunity Act of 1964, the state formally incorporated a feature that emphasized the maximum feasible participation of residents in poor neighborhoods, thus linking the struggle for community control with state funded community action centers. The 1965 Elementary and Secondary Education Act also included the establishment of citizen advisory councils to assess local education policies (Gittell 1970, 248). While the state's support for community activism and community decision-making was short lived [for example, by 1971 most community action programs were circumscribed by narrow definitions of service delivery that undercut the enactment of maximum feasible participation (see Naples 1998a)], local residents (a disproportionate number of whom were African American and Puerto Rican) seized this window of opportunity to support their struggle to improve the services and quality of life in their neighborhoods. The schools became a central focus of their efforts.

The call for community control of schools was made in the context of a variety of competing political goals and discursive themes. Some actors drew on the frame of community control as a pragmatic response to institutional racism. Other actors articulated their call for community control with a liberal construction of social reform. A third group drew on a radical construction of community control to articulate separatist claims as found in the Black Power movement. Another set drew on the discursive theme of enhancing competition between school districts. City officials drew on the discursive theme of administrative efficiency to construct the fiscal and political advantage of decentralization in contrast to political decentralization. In addition to these competing discursive themes, other observers point to the racist subtext of white support for community control. Diane Ravitch (1974) writes that community control for "black schools appealed to a surprising cross-section of whites" for "black control of black schools implied white control of white schools, which they could comfortably support, for it guaranteed that black problems, black dissidence, and black pupils would be safely contained within the ghetto" (p. 105). While the fact that community control could be abstracted from the particular political, racial, and economic context and applied to other communities and other populations makes the concept appealing to a broader constituency, it also reveals how the concept could be appropriated and wielded by groups for racist and other reactionary goals.

Surprisingly, given the diversity of perspectives on community control, few participants in the controversy and subsequent legislative initiatives addressed the dimension of class and the economic constraints that inhibit the delivery of quality education in poor communities. Also missing in the discursive themes of the community control controversy was recognition of women's essential role in producing the public school itself. In fact, often unspoken within the daily practices of teachers and administrators are the expectations that much of the learning process depends upon parents, particularly mothers, labor in the homes (for example, supervising homework, assisting in school projects), in the schools (as volunteers in the classroom or for school trips), and in the community (fundraising and organizing school-community events) (Griffith and Smith 1990). Furthermore, mothers have consistently formed the constituents for political action designed to improve the quality of education for their children and other community members.[12] For mothers of children in low-income and minority communities, activism becomes an essential part of mother work (see Naples 1998a). Since mothers were often the ones to negotiate with the schools on their children's behalf, they were in the forefront of the battles for community control of schools. For example, Paula Sands became active in her Harlem community when she enrolled her child in an overcrowded public school in the late 1960s.[13] She was appalled by the conditions she witnessed in the school. She found the administrators and teachers insulting and unsympathetic. Her early activism against the racist and irresponsible school district led her into other struggles, against absentee landlords and police harassment, for welfare rights and bilingual education, to increase voter registration of low-income residents and expand library services. Through her activism, Sands developed a complex analysis of how power dynamics and relations of ruling in education and other spheres served to reproduce gender, race, and class inequality. By shifting to the perspective of low-income women living and working in poor communities who were active in the struggle for community control of school, the relations of gender and class that were missing from the recorded discursive themes and history are rendered visible. This feminist materialist perspective highlights the intersection of race, class, and gender in the struggle for community control of schools as well as provides the basis for explicating the co-optation of the frame for conservative, racist, sexist, and homophobic political goals.

The People's Board of Education

Community control of schools' activist Sukie Ports (1970) explains that attempts to integrate the public schools began in 1962 "when local school boards were asked to submit ideas for achieving integration within their own boundaries" (p. 65). Since her Harlem district was totally segregated at the time, there were no strategies that could effectively integrate the neighborhood schools. Local parents also recognized many problems with the "Open Enrollment" and "Free Transfer" plans that permitted students to register for schools outside their district (for example, "creaming" the better prepared students from the local schools). Their district (District 10–11) was the first to defy the Board of Education's "desegregation" policy and to demonstrate that the "policy could not be handed down city-wide and implemented systematically or effectively without the participation of the local staff and parents involved" (p. 68).

In the beginning of the 1965 school year, the Board of Education redrew the boundaries between districts breaking up Harlem District 10–11 and consequently disqualifying several members of the oppositional school board from membership on the board. The redistricting also removed virtually all of the white and middle-income children in East Harlem (Ports 1970). Part of the justification for the redistricting plan was to merge the predominantly African American area with the adjacent community that was predominantly Puerto Rican, thus achieving "integration" by serving African American and Puerto Rican children, rather than devise a plan that would incorporate white students as well.[14] Along with the redistricting plan came the announcement that a new junior high school (Intermediate School 201) would be established in the redrawn district to be located at 127th Street and Madison Avenue in Harlem. As the beginning of the new school year drew near, parents and other local activists decided to shift their focus from integration of the school to the establishment of a quality segregated school under the leadership of a Black principal and local community control of staffing and other decisions. In contrast, the Board of Education's plan for I.S. 201 did not reflect this community-based vision. On the first day of the 1966 school year, parents in Harlem boycotted IS 201. Boycotts against other public schools erupted across the city, "and the concept of community control spread with them" (Berube and Gittell 1969, 13).

When the Board of Education proposed opening IS 201 in East Harlem, a group of local leaders and parents formed an Ad Hoc Parent Council to oppose the board's plan. A central actor in the Ad Hoc Parent Council was Preston R. Wilcox, then the director of the East Harlem Project, the community action program linked to two settlement houses. When the Economic Opportunity Act was passed in 1964, Wilcox, now professor at Columbia University School of Social Work, wrote a proposal for a coalition of East Harlem community organizations to establish a community action agency in East Harlem called MEND (Massive Economic Neighborhood Development). He followed the approach developed by Richard Cloward, a fellow professor at Columbia, "which held that powerlessness was itself a major cause of poverty" and "that the process of organizing and participation would help to overcome the neighborhood's sense of powerlessness" (Ravitch 1974, 294). Wilcox circulated a paper he titled "To Be Black and To Be Successful" proposing that IS 201 be designed as an experiment in community control. At a community meeting with Mayor Lindsay and School Superintendent Donovan in March 1966, Wilcox argued that "if the school system can do no more than it is already doing, then the communities of the poor must be prepared to act for themselves . . . just as they must become involved in the direction of all programs set up to serve their needs" (quoted in Ravitch 1974, 296). In December 1966, the 201 protest group joined with other parent activists and their allies in a three-day sit-in at the Board of Education, declaring themselves the People's Board of Education. These events forced the school superintendent to meet with teacher union representatives, community leaders, and Ford Foundation staff to develop a plan that would give parents of public school children a role in educational policy-making (Ravitch 1974).

A key organization that helped to coordinate parents efforts to reform their children's schools was Bronx Parents United.[15] Bronx Parents United originated when parents in a Bronx elementary school joined to protest their children's expulsion from kindergarten. Jewish community worker and parent advocate Teresa Fraser, an active member of Bronx Parents United, explained that the children were "suspended from kindergarten for some very silly, minor infraction." Bronx Parents United then became the vehicle for expanded parent organizing following the sit-in by the People's Board of Education.

Fraser described how the People's Board of Education developed spontaneously from the dismissive behavior of formal Board members:

> There was a finance hearing at the Board of Education and it was one of these typical things where nothing—I know because I was really involved in it—nothing special was planned. . . . We went down and carried on about where the money was going. Some lady from Brownsville asked if she could speak earlier than her time because she had to go pick up her kids, and they said: "No." And the person who was at the microphone, whoever's turn it was, said: "She can have my time." . . . And whoever it was running the meeting said: "No way!" And people got pissed and said: "Let her talk!" And . . . I swear to god this was not a planned thing. And they got up and recessed. And people were just furious. And they came back and they called off the hearing on the Board of Education budget because some lady from Brownsville wanted to speak so she could go pick up her children. And . . . a couple of other people were in the audience, said if they're not going to listen, we will listen. And that became the People's Board of Education. [Interview with author 1984]

The parents and their allies stayed in the building for three days and three nights. Fraser recalled with amazement that the Board of Education officials "tried to freeze" the parents out of the building by turning on the air blowers.

After three days the members of the People's Board of Education were arrested. Their arrest was followed by the Board of Education's release of reading scores for each school in the city, which revealed that 20 percent of the city's school children were falling two years behind their grade level. Not surprisingly, poor neighborhoods had the lowest reported reading scores, "well-to-do" neighborhoods had the highest scores (Ravitch 1974, 309). With these data, advocates of community control had empirical evidence that the public school system systematically failed to educate low-income and minority children. Parent advocates viewed gaining access to the reading scores as one of their most important and successful achievements. Once parents came to realize the collective nature of the reading problem, they were in a much better position to push for changes in the school system.[16]

Decentralization versus Community Control

In 1967 Mayor Lindsay appointed Ford Foundation President McGeorge Bundy to chair the Advisory Panel on Decentralization.[17] Their report asserted that local public schools should become community institutions "that will liberate the talents, energies and interests of parents, students, teachers, and others to make common cause toward the goal of educational excellence" (Mayor's Advisory Panel on Decentralization of the New York City Schools 1969, 119). In this way, the schools would become "responsive to the needs and sensitive to the desires of groups that are in a minority in a particular locality" (p. 119).

The Advisory Panel believed that the decentralization of the schools would "couple the advantages of urban bigness with the intimacy, flexibility, and accessibility associated with innovative suburban school systems" (p. 120).

The report recommended "the creation of a Community School System, to consist of a federation of largely autonomous school districts and a central education agency" (p. 120). They envisioned the Community School Districts as "governed by boards of residents chosen jointly by the Mayor (on the advice of the central education agency), and by parents of children attending district schools" (p. 120). According to Ravitch (1974), "all the major organizations of education professionals in the system attacked the report" (p. 334). Parent advocates and many community organizations saw it as offering local communities less autonomy and power than they desired. The Combined Action Committee, a joint committee of the Council of Supervisory Associations of the Public Schools of New York City and the United Federation of Teachers, argued against the report fearing that it established " 'community control' as a new civil liberty" (Stone 1969, 353).

In the midst of heated arguments between and among proponents and opponents of community control, the State Board of Regents cosponsored another decentralization bill with the New York State Commissioner of Education. The Regents bill emerged as the preferred form of decentralization legislation even as other groups were promoting their alternative visions of community control. The Regents bill was gaining support when tensions erupted in Ocean Hill-Brownsville. According to Ravitch (1974) these events caused the legislators to be more cautious in their attitudes toward decentralization (p. 360). They passed a bill that added another year to the deliberation process. Among other features, this Marchi Bill "empowered the Board of Education to delegate to local school boards 'any or all of its functions, powers, obligations and duties'; and recognized the three demonstration districts as equivalent to regular local school boards" (p. 360). After heated discussion, a law was passed that emphasized administrative decentralization rather than community control (Zimet 1973).

Evaluation of the law reveals at best only modest achievements. Many critics as well as allies saw little improvement in the quality of education for the children in low-income and minority urban neighborhoods in New York City. Furthermore, resident participation in school board elections declined greatly from a disappointing high of 15 percent in the first elections in 1970.[18] Fewer eligible voters participated in the second elections in 1973. By 1986, only 7.5 percent of the eligible voters participated in the triennial school board elections. The composition of the school boards also became less representative of the local community over time. By 1988 "employees of the school system, including 27 members of the teachers' union filled 70 of the 288 seats on local boards" (Buder 1988:E6). *New York Times* reporter Leonard Buder pointed out that "in one Brooklyn district where 85 percent of the pupils are black or Hispanic, eight of the nine school board members are white" (p. E6).

A number of factors contributed to the difficulties faced in implementing the decentralization plan in the low-income neighborhoods. Those living in poverty are hard pressed to find the time and resources (such as money for transportation and child care) that are required of community board members (Gittell 1970). Many do not have the kinds of jobs that permit them to take time off, and many working mothers cannot afford to take time away from their families after work without alternative child care or household help (Zimet 1973, 34).[19] Time constraints and financial difficulties coupled with organized campaigns by groups like the teachers' union and the Catholic Church placed low-income parents in a relatively weak position in vying for seats on the school boards and participating in school board politics over time. However, participation in the struggle for community control of schools did encourage many mothers to broaden their activism on behalf of their children and communities.

Limits and Unintended Consequences of the Community Control Frame

For some movement participants, " 'community control' came to symbolize the struggle for democratic power just as 'no taxation without representation' symbolized a similar struggle by the founders of the American republic" (New York CLU 1969, 340). According to Frank Lutz and Carol Merz (1992), "The *local* governance of public education has its roots in the basic idea of American democracy" (p. 33, emphasis in original). Citing de Tocqueville, they argue that "school boards are the 'grassroots of American democracy' "where people gain "hands-on experience in the political process. . . . This is what grassroots democracy is about and why local school governance is democratic in the unique sense of American democracy" (Lutz and Merz 1992, 63). While many of the women I interviewed drew on this discursive theme in their discussion of the community control of schools movement, they also emphasized that community control was necessary to ensure the survival of their communities and to promote the empowerment of community members. Their narratives contained a complex analysis of the intersection of race, class, and gender and emphasized the significance of participatory democracy for social justice. My materialist feminist analysis of their discourse on the community control of schools movement revealed a "critical praxis" (Lemke 1995, 131), one that stressed the dialectical relation between activism and democratic theory, between experience and reflection. The community workers did not separate their politics from their social locations and personal commitment to improve the conditions of neighborhood schools and other community-based institutions. Furthermore, they explained, their participation in the movement changed them and changed how they viewed the role of American institutions in poor urban neighborhoods.

Mario Fantini (1969), who helped write the Advisory Panel's report on decentralization, observed that through the process of participation in the community control of school movement, East Harlem parents "became more engaged in the education process" and as a result, the call for " 'quality education' replaced 'Black Power' as the slogan" for the movement (p. 333). His findings seem to support the fear expressed by some critics that decentralization and community control channel social protest into less radical challenges to the status quo (p. 335). Seymour Martin Lipset (1970) argues that "local control can be a very conservatizing influence," diverting attention from the issue of class inequality which is at the core of the problems faced by inner-city residents (p. 32). He contends that: "To encourage those in the lower class to believe the problem is largely one of community control rather than of class structure must simply lead to a further sense of defeat, will reinforce the basic inferiority feelings which class-linked values impose on those at the bottom" (p. 32). The women I interviewed also recognized the limits of community control for communities with little financial resources and for children whose families are grappling with a host of problems related to poverty, poor housing and health care, and drug addiction. Yet they remained convinced that those educators who do not live in the community "don't have a stake in making the school good." So while community control may not be the answer to the educational problems of poor neighborhoods, they argued, it is a necessary foundation for improving the quality of education for minority and low-income students.

Community control can contribute to empowerment of local residents as well as provide the grounds for local interests to wield power over others in the community. In fact, one of the most fascinating findings in my materialist feminist analysis of the community control of schools movement is who participated in the debate; passionate supporters as well as ardent critics treated the content of the "community" as a given. Few advocates or opponents discussed who comprised the community or pointed to the fluidity of its construction over time. While there were heated deliberations on how to draw geographic boundaries to define community districts, how to achieve local control of schools, and what mechanisms would contribute to effective community representation on local school boards, none of the written accounts or oral narratives I gathered mentioned the instability of the construct "community." In contrast to this view of community, a materialist feminist perspective emphasizes the diversity of perspectives and needs as well as how inequalities of power and resources are woven in and throughout different locales. Relations of ruling are embedded in local interactions in ways that privilege some residents, some members of the defined polity, over others. Dimensions such as age, race, gender, class, length of time in the locale, marital status, caretaking responsibilities, language facility, level of literacy, type of occupation, religion, cultural background, immigrant status, and others features too numerous to list contribute to inequalities among community members. Furthermore, many who might be physical and legal members of a certain locale may not feel part of the community in which they live and work and therefore will not make claims on the polity. I turn now to the contemporary context in which the call for community control has been mobilized in order to reveal the complex relations of ruling embedded in the frame.

Community Control in Contemporary Perspective

Following the death of United Federation of Teachers President Albert Shanker, Nathan Glazer (1997) revisited the community control of school movement in New York City in his column in *New Republic*. He noted that the system of local community control initiated in 1968 ended just before Shanker died.[20] He points out that in contrast to the community control struggles of the late 1960s, the contemporary "attack on school bureaucracies comes from the right (p. 25)." Nathan sees many parallels between the community control of school movement and conservative support for charter schools. Charter schools are "funded by the government," "free of local bureaucratic controls," and can be run by private entrepreneurs as well as public and not-for-profit entities. Conservative policy analysts as well as corporate interests argue that charter schools will "improve the achievement of minority and low-income students" (Glazer 1997, 25). In addition to a number of similarities in the discursive support for community control and for charter school movements, Glazer (1997, 25) also sees a parallel in the nature of concerns raised against both policy initiatives, i.e., whether local boards "run schools independent of centralized bureaucracies." Glazer's defense of charter schools includes many of the discursive themes evident in the earlier community of control movement—for example, charter schools will increase competition between schools by enhancing parental choice and as a result improve the quality of education, and, even if educational quality does not result, charter schools can produce informed parents who are better prepared to advocate for their children's education.

While the community control of schools movement did focus on who had the legitimate right to teach minority children (i.e., white teachers were often criticized for not understanding the needs of minority children), contemporary attacks on public schools by parents and religious groups also include protests against teaching materials, novels such as *Of Mice and Men* by John Steinbeck, *Catcher in the Rye* by J.D. Salinger, *The Color Purple* by Alice Walker, and sex education, and evolutionary biology as well as gay and lesbian student clubs and even self-esteem programs.[21] Conservative parents who are active in these struggles complain that "schools are subverting the values that children learn at home" (Boyer 1984, 14). Resistance to textbooks said to promote "secular humanism" have received support from conservative judges like Alabama District Court Judge W. Brevard Hand, a Nixon appointee, who banned more than 40 textbooks from Alabama public schools in 1987. In explaining his decision,

Hand stated "that the books ignored the history of the Puritans and presented colonial missionaries as oppressors of native Americans (Vobejda 1987, p. A19). The "conflict over parents' rights to restrict what their children hear" (Thomas 1987) includes parents' demands "to allow students to 'opt out' of being subjected to material that offends their parents' religious beliefs" (Thomas 1987, 16).

These challenges come from progressive as well as conservative corners. For example, Fred Hechinger (1986) reports that an Arizona chapter of the NAACP "objected to Harper Lee's novel *To Kill a Mockingbird* because it contained 'derogatory terms for blacks' " (pp. C1, 14) However, People for the American Way, a Washington-based group concerned with the separation of church and state among other constitutional issues, found that only "5% of the protests were launched by liberal groups seeking to ban material they deemed politically incorrect" (Warren 1991, A3). Many of the protests waged under the banner of local control are fueled by conservative organizations like the Rev. Pat Robertson's National Legal Foundation, Beverly LaHaye's Concerned Women for America, National Association of Christian Educators, and Phyllis Shafley's Eagle Forum, all located far from the local scene.[22]

Representatives of two organizations that are promoting "censorship" of certain reading materials in California schools have been reported to argue "that they are merely exercising their right to have a hand in what their children learn" (Warren 1991, A3). The religious right formulates the struggle in terms of parental control over their students' education, which parallels a central discursive theme of the 1960s debates over community control of schools. Not surprisingly, there is a fundamental difference in the content of their interpretation of who has "superior vested interest in the future of the children" (p. A30). The issues at the forefront of these battles include attacks against gays and lesbians, ethnic diversity, and sex education. When students in an Orange County school started a Gay-Straight Club in 1999 the school district voted to prohibit all student clubs rather than allow this club to continue. Parents and other "anti-gay protesters who traveled from Kansas to picket the school" (Katz 2000, B12). In settling a federal law suit initiated by the students and their parents who supported the club, the school district trustees voted to allow the club to meet on school grounds, but ruled that "no student clubs may use meetings to talk about sexual activity, defined as 'explicit discussion of sex acts or sexual organs' " (Katz 2000, B12).

Conservative parents and religious groups wage war against any curriculum that they believe "promotes homosexuality and teen-age sexual activity" (Trombley 1992, A3). Their emphasis on the "family ethic" (Abramovitz 1988) reveals the invisible heteronormative dimensions of community control that did not find direct expression in the 1960s. At that time, given the historical and political context, race was in the forefront of the discursive staging for the community control of schools movement. The dimensions of class and gender were close to the surface and were revealed when I shifted the standpoint of inquiry to women who were active in the movement. However, as the frame was mobilized in different contexts and under different historical conditions, the taken-for-granted heteronormativity of the "community" also included the possibility for social regulation of individuals and groups who do not fit into the normative "American" family as contemporary discursive themes reveal.

Bitter fights have erupted across the country against course materials like the "Rainbow Curriculum" designed for New York City public schools, which included discussion of alternative family forms and gay and lesbian issues. Not surprisingly, the challengers do not always represent community concerns. In 1997 Seattle Councilwoman Tina Podlodowski and her lesbian partner Chelle Mileur, a vice president for gay and lesbian Internet service PlanetOut, gave $6,000 to support the Seattle Public Schools' purchase of children's books about gay families in the Seattle Public Schools (*New York Times* 1997, N20). A *New York Times* article noted that "purchases were approved by most city schools through committees that included parents" (p. N20). In this case, the majority of parents did not oppose the purchase of such books as *Heather Has Two Mommies* and *Daddy's Roommate*. Instead, resistance came from organized conservative and religious groups. Therefore, given the instability of the term *community,* a diversity of groups and individuals can claim that they are speaking on behalf of the community.

Ironically, in discussing her objection to Seattle's public schools' decision to purchase the books, Linda Jordan, president of Parents and Teachers for Responsible Schools, stated that her group was preparing a "parental-rights form" as part of a campaign to mobilize parents against the school system. She feared that "the school district was not going to respect the diversity within their district and was not going to let parents be the moral authority" (*New York Times* 1997, N20). The notion of diversity Jordan narrates is a far cry from that described by the Puerto Rican and African American parents who felt that the white-dominated school system did not understand and respond to their children's different needs.

Despite the numerous criticisms leveled against decentralization, decentralized institutional strategies did open up avenues of participation for the community workers I interviewed that increased their political efficacy, at least in the short run, as well as their politicization. Concern for their children's education and the activism they undertook on their behalf led them into other avenues of protest and enhanced their understanding of the ways in which relations of domination circumscribed the lives of the poor. For a number of years parents were successful in gaining some control of the school system, in hiring African American and bilingual teachers, and in establishing local school boards that were, at one point in time, community led and community controlled. However, as with other community-based struggles to gain control of local institutions, changes within the wider political economy and backlash from powerful interest groups quickly coopted these efforts. Supporters of state-sponsored educational vouchers justify their support for "off loading" of public education through a rhetoric of parental choice, an individualistic variant of community control.

Ironically, the interests of many minority parents and conservative groups converge in support for vouchers as a way to provide "parental choice" and to ensure a better education for minority children. With the failure first of integration of schools, and subsequently of the community control of public schools, to improve the quality of education offered to low-income students of color, frustrated minority parents are joining conservative groups in advocating for a system of charter schools and educational vouchers that would enable them to use state money for different educational options. An episode of CNN's (2000) *Democracy in America* featured the 10-year-old Milwaukee Parental Choice Program, which was first funded by the state of Wisconsin in 1990 and expanded in 1995 to include religious schools among the educational choices. In 1998 Wisconsin Supreme Court upheld the state's decision to include religious schools in the program. As of fall 2000, 63 of the 91 schools in Milwaukee that participate in the choice program as religious schools, most of which are Catholic (CNN 2000).

Annette Williams, the African American state legislator who promoted this program, saw it as a way to give low-income parents access to private schools, which offered a better education than the Milwaukee public schools. She argued that "if the state was going to pay for the miseducation of children in the public schools, surely they would not object to paying a small portion to allow parents then to pick a school outside of the public schools" (CNN 2000). Ten years later she is involved in a battle to restrict the program to the low-income constituency for which it was designed. Drawing on the democratic frame of "freedom of choice," parents and conservatives groups insist that the program should be expanded so that all parents regardless of income can take advantage of it. In explaining his support for educational vouchers, Clint Bolick, legislative director for Institute of Justice, writes: "The same constitution that guarantees an equal educational opportunity to every child—black, white, rich or poor—will not be subverted to deny children that very opportunity" (CNN 2000).

In producing specific frames, social movement actors draw on existing popular constructions of social justice, democracy, or other discursive formulations that will have resonance for potential constituents.[23] In this way, frames like community control of schools are infused with "a repertoire of interpretations" (Mooney and Hunt 1994) that leave open the possibility for diverse political actors to mobilize the frame for different goals. Furthermore, as frames are incorporated into practice, they "descend to a lesser level of generality" (Fraser 1989, 164), where the contradictions embedded in the frame become more visible and the extent to which certain interpretations "are skewed in favor of the self-interpretations and interests of dominant social groups" (p. 154).

Conclusion

As emphasized throughout this analysis, discourse is not the property of individual actors or social movement organizations but is "a practice, it is structured, and it has real effects" (J. Ferguson 1994, 18).[24] The materialist feminist approach to critical praxis I recommend situates the construction and interpretation of frames within the broader discursive and institutional context of mobilization and attends to relations of ruling and structural inequalities within the framing process. Furthermore, a materialist feminist analysis of discourse attends to the historical and structural patterns of domination and resistance to render visible the features of everyday life that are unspoken or unrepresentated in discursive frames.

Discourse has material consequences for social movement actors. In order for movement frames to gain wide acceptance, they need to resonate with prevailing cultural constructions. Because master frames frequently draw on recognizable symbols and values to mobilize and effect social change, I argue, they have the potential of incorporation into the wider political environment in ways that originators might not have intended. Rather than the self-conscious product of social movement organizations, a materialist feminist analysis explores the processes by which movement organizations and movement actors are constrained in constructing their political identities, or when they successfully produce oppositional frames can lose control over how these frames are taken up and reinscribed over time. Furthermore, the social relations within movement organizations, as well as the structure and material practices of institutions and communities in which these organizations are located, shape the ways in which movement frames are produced, circulated, and taken up by potential allies as well as opponents.

This materialist feminist discourse analysis of the movement for community control of schools illustrates the social structural and material social relations that infuse as well as shape discursive fields which infuse the framing process. In addition, this materialist feminist approach reveals how movement frames contest as well as reinforce relations of ruling. The community control of schools frame was produced in the context of a heightened awareness of racial inequality as well as organized resistance to integration. It was mobilized within an environment that privileged, to a great extent, administrative decentralization over political decentralization and therefore contributed to deradicalization of the movement for local control. Different political and social actors brought contrasting visions of community control into their negotiations and those who held greater power in the process of implementation successfully gained control over the interpretation of the frame and the decentralization plan that derived from these negotiations.

Finally, this materialist feminist analytic strategy offers a powerful tool for social movement research as well as critical praxis. My approach provides an epistemology for examining how racism, class, sexism, and other dimensions of social inequalities are inevitably woven in and through even the most radical political projects. With this heightened analytic sensitivity to the dynamics of power within social movement organizations and across different arenas of social activism, movement actors may become more effective in resisting the depoliticization and cooptation of movement frames. In the next chapter, I analyze the broad discursive frames that infused the congressional hearings that led to the passage of the Family Support Act of 1988 and demonstrate how attention to gender, racial, and class subtexts of social policy formation and implementation advances our understanding of the relations of ruling that are woven through and reinscribed in legislative activities. While discursive frames have shifted from the late 1980s, the analysis in the next chapter demonstrates the value of a materialist feminist approach to social policy research that can be applied to contemporary policy debates.[25]

CHAPTER 7

The Gendered Social Contract
Constructing the "New Consensus"

Analysis of the 1987–88 U.S. congressional hearings on welfare reform that led to the passage of the Family Support Act of 1988—the legislation that instituted mandatory work for women receiving Aid to Families with Dependent Children (AFDC)—reveals the powerful discursive frames that continue to shape contemporary welfare policy. These hearings took place within an assertion of a new consensus between conservatives and liberals summarized by Senator Daniel Patrick Moynihan (D-N.Y.) during the hearings: "Simply put, poor adults who are able should be helped to work" (U.S. Senate 1987c, 6).[1] Moynihan went on to explain that "conservatives have persuaded liberals that there is nothing wrong with obligating able-bodied adults to work. Liberals have persuaded conservatives that most adults want to work and need some help to do so" (U.S. Congress, Senate 1987c, 6). In these debates, the concept of the social contract was used to illustrate the so-called new consensus between the Democrats and Republicans. The shift from the construction of a social contract as illustrative of a new consensus to a notion of contract that adheres only to the Republican position and is articulated through the Contract with America (Gingrich et al. 1994) may be explained simply by the fact that the Republicans were angling to capture a majority in Congress in the 1994 elections.[2] Yet such an explanation would mask the complex processes by which certain frames used in policy debates employ themes that resonate with popular ideology and are woven in and through the everyday practices of policy construction.[3]

Drawing upon a materialist feminist analysis of discourse, I demonstrate how the assertion of a new consensus on a redefined social contract participated in a broad discursive framing that privileged individualist and coercive behavioral strategies such as workfare and inhibited the incorporation of structural analyses into the resultant welfare policy.[4]

This analysis accents the social regulatory role of social welfare policy and specifically explores the discursive restructuring of a social contract as it applies to the state's defined obligation to low-income women and their families.[5] The welfare state's restructuring is part of the broader economic restructuring of Fordist productive processes that is also evidenced by, among other features, increased flexibility and "internationalization" of capital, labor, and production; decline in support for unionization in Western nation-states; and shifts in the nature and content of women's work in all regions.[6] The restructuring of the welfare state involves changes both in material practices of state distributive policies and in the discursive strategies used to justify such changes.[7] It is historically situated within a wider shift begun in the late 1970s when the terms of the Keynesian social contract established in the late 1930s were rearticulated to center so-called free market processes, privatization, and a diminished conception of the government's role in social provisioning.[8]

Under the Keynesian conception of the social contract, the government's part of the bargain included the use of fiscal and monetary policies to guarantee steady economic growth and, for workers and their families, the provision of economic safeguards such as unemployment insurance, retirement income, and aid to widows and their children to increase consumers' purchasing power (Bello 1994). These policies were themselves articulated within a discursive framework that privileged the two-parent, male-breadwinner and female-caretaker family form embodied in notions of the work ethic and family ethic, two of the central themes that continue to contour legislative discourse on the social contract.[9]

The discursive formation[10] of social welfare is also shaped by longstanding and historically shifting negative conceptions of "dependence" that value women differentially on the basis of marital status, age, and race-ethnicity.[11] In fact, Nancy Fraser and Linda Gordon (1994a) assert that "dependence is the single most crucial term in the current U.S. debate about welfare reform" (p. 4). Within contemporary social welfare discourse, welfare dependence, not poverty or unemployment, is viewed as the social ill that is the appropriate target for state action (see Amott 1990). Despite continuity within social welfare discourse, certain significant shifts are revealed when the discursive frames embedded in welfare policy are analyzed over time. For example, Fraser and Gordon (1994) also demonstrate how the concept of dependency has developed increasingly negative connotations especially as moral and psychological dependency began to replace social relations of dependency as the primary definition. Yet, as I argue, these shifts are rendered unproblematic through their incorporation into the notion of the social contract that discursively ties together the institutions of the economy, family, and state. However, analysis of the discursive processes through which the social contract was redefined during the 1987–88 legislative hearings reveals multiple contradictions that lay the grounds for further contestation.

Dynamics of Gender, Race, and Class in Welfare Policy

Feminist analyses of U.S. welfare policy reveal the extent to which gendered and racialized conceptions of family and work have limited who could make claims on the state.[12] The Social Security Act passed in 1935, which instituted the federal Aid to Dependent Children program, discriminated against women of color and women who did not adopt the marital and child-rearing norms of the dominant class. Widows were defined as "deserving" while divorced and unmarried women were treated as "undeserving" of state support. African American women were generally defined as undeserving regardless of marital status. In fact, 96 percent of the widows receiving aid during this period were white (Abramovitz 1988).

The criteria of deservingness included an assessment of the poor's morality. For example, amendments to the Social Security Act in 1940 incorporated the notion of the suitable home to control low-income women's sexual behavior and commitment to work. Public assistance could be withheld if women were not performing in ways acceptable to local welfare officials. State sanctioning of low-income women's behavior continues in the current legislation where women lose welfare benefits if they fail to participate in the required work, education, or training.

Social welfare policy has also been shaped by competing frames—to provide for those unable to provide for themselves while ensuring that the able-bodied not take advantage of assistance.[13] Able-bodied mothers of young children have always posed a problem for social welfare policy: are they deserving or undeserving of public assistance? The new consensus on welfare reform ruled that women with young children are now considered unworthy of aid. Furthermore, social policy continues to incorporate racist practices despite seemingly race-neutral provisions. Contemporary discourse on welfare reform unmasks this dynamic in the passage of the Personal Responsibility and Work Opportunity Reconciliation Act of 1996, which initially eliminated legal immigrants from eligibility. This bill's block grant approach to welfare also harkens back to widows' aid programs of the early 1900s that were designed and administered differently by individual states, which were not accountable to any federal entity for their racist and other discriminatory practices (Katz 1986). The return to moralism as a criterion for eligibility (for example, as in Wisconsin's Learnfare program) also turns back the clock to welfare practices challenged by the National Welfare Rights Movement in the late 1960s and subsequently ruled illegal.[14]

The Family Support Act echoed many of the themes underlying contemporary welfare reform initiatives. This act instituted mandatory welfare-to-work (workfare) provisions and strengthened paternity establishment provisions and child support enforcement, all of which were discussed within the context of the frames "personal responsibility" and "reducing dependency" on the government (Library of Congress 1988). Underlying the new consensus articulated through the 1987–88 welfare reform hearings were a series of interlocking frames that formed the discursive grounds for the Family Support Act. These frames are contemporary elaborations of themes that have long been dominant within the discourse on social welfare: fear that receipt of public assistance (1) fosters an intergenerational culture of poverty, (2) undermines the work ethic of the poor, (3) contributes to family breakup, and (4) encourages fathers' failure to support their children.[15]

The complex task of unraveling and analyzing the various incarnations of the social contract and the relations of ruling woven through them is beyond the scope of this chapter, although it will be useful to identify themes within the discourse on the social contract that resonate with earlier conceptualizations. What I offer here is an excavation of the powerful discursive frames related to the social contract that were infused throughout the welfare reform hearings of 1987–88. I use Michel Foucault's discourse analysis as a tool to examine the discursive frames that contoured the hearings. While I draw on Foucault's methodology, I do so within a materialist feminist framework, which highlights gender, racial-ethnic, and class inequalities that organize social relations within the legislative arena.[16]

Toward a Materialist Feminist Framework for Policy Analysis

Most researchers who explore welfare policy in the United States adopt conventional approaches to policy analysis that typically take one of three forms: (1) institutional policy studies that explore the social, political, and economic origins, assumptions, and implementation outcomes of specific policies typically from a macrosociological perspective;[17] (2) studies of the legislative process itself, including the influence achieved by varying groups and individuals;[18] and (3) evaluation studies that explore the effectiveness and different results of policies through an analysis of implementation procedures and outcome measures.[19] Discourse analysis of the frames that operate within policy debates and organize implementation strategies is a relatively new approach to policy analysis that, I argue, offers much to our understanding of how power operates in and through the welfare state.[20]

Researchers who conduct evaluation studies of policy outcomes are limited in their efforts by the unproblematic use of categories of analysis taken directly from the specific policy or policy arena and incorporated into the instruments designed to assess the policy outcomes (Oliker 1994). Assumptions about women, the poor, the family, work, and mothering go unchallenged. Consequently, conventional policy analyses serve to reproduce the power of the discursive frames that shape the policy and implementation processes (Schram 1995).

While policymakers are not free to choose the discursive frames through which to debate welfare policy, they are in a position of power to control whose voices will be represented in the legislative hearings. The organization of congressional hearings establishes spaces for certain actors to perform on the discursive stage, inhibits others from participating, and renders silent the voices of those whose perspectives do not fit within the individualist discursive framework. In fact, Margaret Prescod of Black Women for Wages for Housework was initially denied the opportunity to speak at the hearings. However, after repeated and unsuccessful attempts to present her testimony, she made herself visible by assertively gaining Senator Moynihan's attention during the hearings and forcing her way onto the stage.[21] Her experience illustrates that the coherence of the discursive frame, the new consensus, is maintained through organizational practices of exclusion that are part of the discursive strategies employed by the Congress members. When she was able to offer her analysis on the significance of women's work in the home, the discursive field did not grant her statements status or authority to be heard.[22] Prescod's experience demonstrates how "the *prohibitions* on what we can speak about, on who may speak and when, which interact in complex ways to form what Foucault calls a grid, . . . teach us that discourse is not simply a translation of domination into language but is itself a *power* to be seized" (Barrett 1991, 142; emphasis in original; also see Jones 1988).

Many feminists who explore the usefulness of Foucault's methodology for revealing how power organizes women's lives are ambivalent about numerous aspects of his approach, not least of which is his understanding of the subject.[23] Sociologist Caroline Ramazanoglu explains: "Analyses of women's experience of men's power underlie feminist criticisms of Foucault. They lead feminists to suggest two aspects of power which can conflict with Foucault's understanding. First, women's experiences suggest that men can *have* power and their power is in some sense a form of domination, backed by force. Secondly, this domination cannot be seen simply as a product of discourse, because it must also be understood as 'extra-discursive' or relating to wider realities than those of discourse" (1993, 22; emphasis in original). While other analysts would argue that Foucault does not negate coercive and nondiscursive features of power, he does neglect the way in which gendered patterns of power operate so that women's experiences might differ from men's (see Barrett 1991).

From a materialist feminist framework, it is important to acknowledge the gender, racial-ethnic, and class subtext of the legislative hearings.[24] While discourse organizes relations among and between legislative actors, subject positions within the discourse are infused with gender, racial-ethnic, and class inequities. This materialist feminist analysis uses Foucault's discourse analysis as a methodology to reveal how the discursive practices of the hearings organize relations of ruling in an explicit attempt to understand how domination and resistance operate in this legislative process.

Redefining the Keynesian Social Contract

Contemporary discussions of social contract evoke a tradition of rugged individualism[25] and liberal economic theory that is based on supposed equal relationships between two parties who are said to be free to enter into the contract (Pateman 1988; MacKinnon 1989). The state is typically viewed as the institution through which contracts are legally drawn and enforced.[26] Evoking this tradition and instituting the state as both a party to the contract and the contract's enforcer further demonstrate the dynamics of power embedded in this discursive frame.

A rearticulation of the social contract in the legislative hearings on welfare reform must also be viewed alongside the strategic shift in funds away from social needs. Since Congress is charged with the responsibility for approving legislation that reallocates federal spending, legislative hearings offer a significant vantage point from which to view this process of rearticulation. As the "democratic" state withdraws its support for social provisioning, it must justify its legislative actions. The process of justification includes articulating a framework within which to redefine the social contract. An important component of this process is the development of an individualist formulation of the problem that lends itself to state intervention without challenging the basic assumption of the social contract framework. This framework limits what is considered legitimate for congressional action and privileges individualistic solutions over structural ones. The assertion of a new consensus on welfare reform provided the discursive context through which a renegotiated social contract between the state and low-income citizens could be accomplished.

Despite the lack of representation by those who would be most affected by the legislative outcome (only one of the 246 witnesses had been a recipient of welfare), oppositional claims were evident within the congressional hearings. The analysis that follows began with the finding that, despite the existence of oppositional claims, the legislators constructed a bill that neglected the alternative structural analyses (see Peattie and Rein 1983). Key authors of the legislation such as Senator Moynihan, chair of the Subcommittee on Social Security and Family Policy of the Senate Committee on Finance, as well as progressive groups who testified in the hearings, identified problems such as racism in social policy and limited economic prospects for the working poor. Despite these challenges, the legislators proceeded to reaffirm the individualist and behavioral/moral frames of the work ethic and family ethic rather than address the structural barriers to women's economic security. The construction of the new consensus on welfare reform required a discursive strategy that excluded alternative perspectives and approaches and, as I illustrate, was accomplished through a process that linked assumptions about the work ethic and family ethic through the discourse of the social contract. Such discursive strategies are not the conscious property of autonomous individual actors. In fact, the actors themselves were caught in the web of individualist and behavioral/moral discourse on welfare, and, despite the professed intentions of many legislators to improve the lives of those in poverty, they proceeded to construct the poor single mother as an ongoing object for state intervention.

The "welfare recipient" defined through welfare policy does not exist as a factual entity with clearly identifiable needs and desires. The discursive processes through which legislative outcomes such as the Family Support Act are achieved construct the welfare recipient as a bureaucratic target for social policy. This constructed target bears little resemblance to the women whose lives welfare policy is designed to regulate (see, for example, Oliver 1995). Processes of social regulation found in social welfare practices are manifest in other discursive formations as well. A parallel exists between workfare and other social regulatory strategies of the Family Support Act and Foucault's analysis of the gaze in disciplines such as criminology and psychoanalysis. In all these examples, individuals are constructed as objects of inquiries and targets of power rather than as "members of social groups or participants in political movements" (Fraser 1989, 174). As Fraser explains, as a result of the "procedures for translating politicized needs into administrable needs" or "social service," "the people whose needs are in question are . . . rendered passive, positioned as potential recipients of predefined services rather than as agents involved in interpreting their needs and shaping their life conditions" (p. 174).

Establishing the Discursive Framework

The dominant contemporary discourse on welfare reform assumes that women's poverty is a consequence of their reluctance to train for and accept paid employment and that women on public assistance need sanctions and other coercive behavioral measures to ensure their cooperation in moving from welfare to work. These individualist and behavioral frames were incorporated in the first workfare program, Work Incentive (WIN), established in 1967 and furthered through the WIN Demonstration programs funded under President Ronald Reagan's 1981 budget.

On January 23, 1987, Senator Moynihan, acting as chair of the newly formed Senate Finance Committee's Subcommittee on Social Security and Family Policy, welcomed the committee to the hearings on "Welfare: Reform or Replacement? (Child Support Enforcement)," one of a total of 12 held during the One Hundredth Congress. The shape and focus were already established in the titles of the hearings (for example, "Child Support Enforcement," "Work and Welfare," and "Short-Term v. Long-Term Dependency") and press releases describing the goals. The press release announcing the hearings stated that the first hearings would include invited public officials and representatives from organizations who recently completed reports on "how to improve the existing family welfare system and how to promote the well-being of families with children" (U.S. Congress, Senate 1987a, 1). A key discursive framework for the hearings was the "enforcement of parental responsibility" through work and child support. The related frame, "strengthening families," was further tied to decreased economic dependency on the state. Welfare reform was narrowly defined as reducing receipt of welfare rather than reducing poverty.

Of the 246 witnesses at the 12 hearings, only five individuals spoke as citizens who would be directly or indirectly affected by the legislative action.[27] By pointing out the lack of participation in the hearings by women who were the targets of welfare reform, I do not want to suggest here that an increase in the number of women on public assistance who testified at the hearings would necessarily produce a different legislative outcome. By highlighting the power imbalance in who gets to testify at Congressional hearings, I am not implying that an increase in the sheer number of traditionally marginalized voices would inevitably "lead to more inclusive, democratic, and thus better social policy" (Campbell 2000, 47). While I recognize that early feminist analyses did hold out such hopes, this optimism cannot be sustained in the light of effective postmodern analyses of power, knowledge, and discourse. In contrast, I argue from a materialist feminist perspective that it remains important to assess who gets to speak in such settings and how these voices on incorporated into the policy process in order to understand how oppositional claims are coopted and heard within the dominant framework.

Voices of low-income people were represented by groups such as the Coalition of California Welfare Rights Organizations (U.S. Congress, Senate 1987d). Several other witnesses quoted from welfare recipients or low-income people they knew or who presented testimony in other hearings held by not-for-profit or religious organizations. However, only one ex-welfare recipient, Shirley Lawson, and another single mother, Carol E. Curtis, spoke at the Senate or House hearings. The relative absence of women on public assistance was organized by and through the discursive framing of the hearings. Their absence further marginalizes alternative perspectives and approaches to welfare reform.

The Discursive Frames of the New Consensus

Stephen B. Heinz, commissioner of Connecticut's Department of Income Maintenance, outlined in his testimony at the Senate Subcommittee hearings on February 23, 1987, what he saw as the three main points of consensus between Republicans and Democrats. The new consensus included "the idea of a contract between the welfare client and the agency—reflecting the mutual obligation that exists between poor families and society at large." Heinz also saw consensus on "the critical importance of self-sufficiency—usually through work: a good job" and the belief "that it should always benefit a family to work rather than to be dependent on welfare." Heinz outlined one last point of consensus: "the notion that parents are always responsible for their children—and that public policy should encourage, and when necessary, enforce, that responsibility" (U.S. Congress, Senate 1987c, 297).

Analysis of the dialogue between Shirley Lawson, the only witness who had been a recipient of AFDC, and Representative Henry Waxman (D-Ca.), chair of the Subcommittee on Health and the Environment of the House Energy and Commerce Committee, persuasively reveals how these discursive frames were woven together during the hearings (U.S. Congress, House 1987b).[28] Ms. Lawson wanted to testify at the House hearings on Medicaid issues (U.S. Congress, House 1987b) because, she said: "I want you [the Congressional members] to understand the problems people face when they lose public assistance" (p. 16).

She had recently finished a training course as a paralegal and was employed as a "community education specialist at the Marshall Heights Community Development Organization." Lawson reported that she was "on and off public assistance many times," participated "in different training programs which invariably did not teach me any useful skills, and in a variety of jobs, all of which led me nowhere but back on the public assistance program." She said that she "always wanted to work, but the jobs I could get never paid enough to support my family." Ms. Lawson had fulfilled her obligations under the "social contract" as defined during the legislative hearings. She describes the difficulty she faced once she ended public assistance. Housing subsidies were eliminated. She received Medicaid for four months as transitional coverage but does not know how she will manage health care coverage after this period is over. Her employer has a plan that costs $118 per month which she cannot afford.

Waxman thanked Lawson for her testimony and asked her a series of questions designed to determine the need and the amount of time necessary for transitional Medicaid coverage for families leaving public assistance. Key discursive frames underlying the dominant discourse of the legislative hearings informed Waxman's questions and led him to render invisible the structural implications of Lawson's testimony. A portion of this exchange follows:

Waxman   Would you be interested in buying Medicaid coverage for yourself and your family if it were available to you?
Lawson   Yes, I would if it would be in the realm that I could afford.
Waxman   If you could afford it. Now, how large a premium do you think you could afford?
Lawson   With the expenses that I have stated here today, at this point I just don't think I would be able to afford to pay a premium.
Waxman   So you would like to buy it but you don't see any price particularly that you could afford.
Lawson   At this point, no. I mean I would like to buy medical insurance. I believe it is a necessity. But as things are in priority, shelter and clothing and food are a little higher on the list, and by the time you get to medical coverage, there is nothing left.
Waxman   How long [sic] period do you think is fair to have Medicaid coverage? Six months? Nine months? What do you think is fair?
Lawson   I would like to say that I think 1 year to 1½ years would be fair, for the simple reason it would give a person a chance to become established in their job, and if they were going to get a promotion or even to better themselves once they enter the work world, it would give them a chance to just establish themselves and to see in which direction they are going. (P. 30)

Rather than explore the structural conditions that limited Lawson's ability to obtain adequate medical coverage such as the low pay she receives for her work, the high cost of medical insurance, and the fact that she as the employee is responsible for purchasing the insurance with her minimum-wage salary, Waxman set his questions within the frame of the "social contract." He asks: "How long [*sic*] period do you think is fair to have Medicaid coverage?" The question forces Lawson away from further discussion of the structural problems she faces that limit her ability to afford medical care for her family to one that assumes it is not the state's responsibility to provide such coverage. While Lawson's testimony was designed to show the problems with social policies that make it impossible for her to afford care, Waxman responds within the circumscribed frame of the social contract discourse. Yet Lawson has performed her obligation according to the social contract. She gained job training, found employment, and left welfare. The state, on the other hand, had not generated the economic or social context needed for Lawson to become economically self-sufficient. The social regulatory process comes into focus when we examine the remainder of the dialogue between Waxman and Lawson.

Waxman proceeded to ask Lawson about her previous employment. The question effectively shifted the discussion away from health care and appeared designed to demonstrate Lawson's inadequate work history. However, Lawson reported a long and varied job history. She answered that she was employed as a babysitter for three years. She also worked for the postal office for a short time and then in several work-study jobs while attending school. Ironically, she recalled that:

> The best job that I've ever had, . . . I worked for the Department of Human Services, and it was under a Government program. When they first started to RIF people out, I lost the job and had to go back on public assistance. If I could have kept that job, it would have cut me from the rolls, I'd say, 5 or 6 years earlier than now. (P. 31)

Waxman failed to comment on the obvious contradiction concerning the government's responsibility for Lawson's "dependency" on public assistance. His failure to acknowledge the relevance of Lawson's experience for the legislative hearings regarding workfare ignores the apparent contradictions in the legislative exercise to reform welfare. Waxman's interventions demonstrated his firm adherence to the individualistic frame guiding the hearings. More significantly, his questions clearly made salient the key discursive frames of the social regulatory role of the social contract when applied to low-income women.

Waxman next asked Lawson about her children. She told him that she has three children, ages 18, 15, and 13. Waxman wanted to know if they were in school or working. She answered his questions and tied it back to the importance of Medicaid since one of her daughters is in need of psychological counseling. Waxman did not comment on this point. He next asked Lawson: "Are any of the girls married or have children?" (p. 31). She responded: "No children, not married." Here Waxman draws upon the intergenerational theory of poverty in an attempt to construct Lawson as an illustrative case of the welfare mother who was breeding future welfare mothers. The fact that her adolescent children have no children of their own does not cancel out the implication of his question for reaffirming the dominant discourse on welfare mothers and the culture of poverty.

In the next part of the chapter, I further illustrate how the discursive frames of social contract, work ethic, and family ethic were embedded in the policy construction process. While I discuss each of these three frames in separate sections; they were, in fact, woven together throughout the hearings as the above exchange illustrates. The assertion of a new consensus legitimated the process by which the social contract between the state and low-income women was re-structured to privilege individualist and coercive behavioral strategies such as workfare and reinforced a limited notion of family.

Discursive Construction of the Social Contract

The social contract was a key discursive frame underlining the testimony of federal, state, and local legislators and conservative policy analysts who pre-sented at the hearings. The assertion of a new consensus on the social contract was privileged throughout. From the onset of the hearings, the alleged new consensus was given the status of a "natural occurrence" that led further to an assertion, by some officials, that the debate on welfare reform had achieved a level above politics. In the first hearing held by the Senate Finance Subcom-mittee on Social Security and Family Policy on January 23, 1987, Moynihan welcomed new committee members, especially ranking Republican leader Bob Dole, announcing, "A few weeks back many of us who watch television news came upon the term 'syzygy,' by which astronomers describe a rare alignment of the sun, the moon and the earth which causes all manner of natural won-ders. With Bob Dole coming on our Subcommittee, with the President calling for changes in our welfare system, with the governors and the mayors and the scholars coming forth with remarkably convergent proposals, we may just have one of those rare alignments that bring about genuine social change" (U.S. Congress, Senate 1987a, 3). The term *syzygy* was picked up again by then-governor of Arkansas Bill Clinton in his testimony on October 14, 1987. Clinton transformed the definition of the term from a natural, albeit rare, phe-nomenon to a "mystical alignment which has brought us all together in this moment in history, around this issue" (U.S. Congress, Senate 1987d, 30). With the defined new consensus framed as a rare occurrence analogous to a "natural wonder" or "mystical alignment," it was not surprising that some witnesses saw the major features of welfare reform as already agreed on in a bipartisan syzygy. For example, in describing the new consensus on the social contract, Richard Nathan of the Woodrow Wilson School of Public and International Studies, Princeton University, wrote in his testimony: "This 'new consensus' has detoxified welfare as a political issue at the state level in many states" (U.S.

Congress, Senate 1987c, 74). Since the dominant framework on the social contract was defined around an assertion of a rare new consensus among political factions considered to represent very different political interests, Nathan was able to declare that welfare was no longer a "political issue." This new consensus framework circumscribed what challenges could be brought forth by senators and other presenters. Yet analysis of the social contract discourse within the hearings reveals the highly contested political context in which such framing was accomplished.

One of the major internal contradictions of social contract discourse is that it is said to involve obligations on the part of two parties, the state and the welfare recipient. Witnesses in the hearings devoted disproportionately more time to the specific obligations of welfare recipients to the state and society than to the state's obligation to welfare recipients. However, reference to the state's part of the bargain appeared in various testimony. When such reference was made, however, little agreement existed on what the state was obliged to provide welfare recipients, nor was there any mechanism offered to enforce the state's side of the social contract.

The social regulatory role of the state regarding individual behavior took on a sharper focus as witnesses stressed the problems associated with "welfare dependence." Members of the Working Seminar on the Family and American Welfare Policy testified that "many people stay dependent on welfare through their own behaviors, such as dropping out of school, having children out of wedlock, and failing to work" (U.S. Congress, Senate 1987b, 87). The members of the Working Seminar stressed that public policy that does not impose standards of behavior and social obligations on the recipients of aid is patronizing. Only by forcing the poor to meet their "obligations" to society, they asserted, can we help improve their self-image and consequently reduce behavioral dependency.

Many of those who presented at the legislative hearings did acknowledge that the success of welfare reform depended on the strength of the economy. The testimony on this point was particularly poignant. In response to the testimony given by Governor Michael Castle of Delaware, chairman of the National Governors' Association Task Force on Welfare Prevention and Committee on Human Resources, Senator Moynihan summarized Harvard professor David Ellwood's (1988) research findings that "the rise in welfare dependency in the last four years has been more associated with unemployment than with the changing family structure" (U.S. Congress, Senate 1987a, 186). He reported that "when jobs go up, welfare dependency goes down." Mary Jo Bane, the former executive deputy commissioner of the New York State Department of Social Services representing New York State Governor's Task Force on Poverty and Welfare, argued that the key to the success of welfare reform "is a genuinely mutual effort among all of us—government, business, and private citizens—that recognizes our mutual obligations." She testified: "The initial step is to build a strong, inclusive economy that creates jobs at non-poverty wages for most workers, and that ensures that well-trained workers are available to fill them" (U.S. Congress, Senate 1987a, 94). Under Bane's formulation, the poor are expected to work and the economy is expected to be strong. But since the resulting legislation does not regulate the economy or provide for job creation, the social contract remains a contract between unequal parties.[29]

Governor Castle was among those presenters who did acknowledge the state's responsibility within the social contract framework. He explained: "We must embrace the notion of a social contract which embodies the principle that responsibility for reducing dependency flows in two directions—the individual to strive for self-sufficiency, and the society to remove the barriers to that achievement" (U.S. Congress, Senate 1987a, 183). It is not surprising that Castle and others who discussed the state's role within the redefined social contract understood "the barriers to that achievement" in very individualistic terms. They saw provision of job training or education and short-term transitional services as the chief means by which the state would remove the barriers. Castle believed that if the state did not "make the work programs better than welfare, then ultimately we are not going to succeed in what we want to do" (p. 184). In order to accomplish this goal, Castle argued for providing prenatal and primary health care, extending Medicaid coverage for those returning to work, and providing quality day care for welfare recipients to enter the paid labor market. By defining the state's obligation as provision of education, health care, child care, and job training, the larger inequitable context in which these services are made available is rendered outside the frame. For example, by viewing the provision of these services from within the individualist framework, structural problems such as sex discrimination and sexist and racist stereotyping of job training and educational programs as well as the limited availability of quality day care could not be incorporated as legitimate problems that the state must solve as part of its obligation to welfare recipients.

Witnesses representing research and advocacy organizations such as Food Research and Action Center and Wider Opportunities for Women offered specific recommendations that would address the structural problems welfare recipients face when they attempt to enter the paid labor market. For example, Cynthia Marano, executive director of Wider Opportunities for Women who also represented the National Coalition on Women, Work, and Welfare Reform, argued for a guaranteed minimum income and an increase in the minimum wage as two measures the government could take to fulfill part of its obligation to poor families. She was particularly concerned about the implementation of sanctions against welfare recipients who were unable to make the transition from welfare to work. She stressed that "we have to be absolutely positive that we don't penalize recipients for the failure of the private sector or for the failure of our not having the appropriate support services to make things happen" (U.S. Congress, Senate 1987a, 401). No member of the Senate Finance Subcommittee asked Marano questions following her testimony. Her testimony was affirmed by another panelist (David Liederman, executive director of the Child Welfare League), but no senator responded to Marano's major objection to enforcement of a one-sided social contract.

While Marano's testimony appeared to fall on deaf ears, at least in terms of legislative response, other new consensus critics were directly challenged, as the dialogue between Patrick Conovor and Representative Hank Brown (R-Col.) reported below demonstrates. Conover, policy advocate for the United Church of Christ Office for Church in Society, opposed mandatory workfare. He complained that the lack of jobs offering adequate income is a main factor contributing to poverty in America. Representative Brown challenged Conover's testimony on a number of dimensions, but Conover continued to assert a structural critique In fact, he finally attacked capitalism directly: "Representative Downey [D-N.Y.] thinks the dirty secret of welfare reform is that it is going to cost money. I think the dirty secret of welfare reform is that, as long as we have a private economic system which pays so poorly, we are not going to be able to provide the level of benefits and justify the level of benefits to those who are on welfare when we have a minimum wage that used to support, only 7 or 8 years ago, used to support a family of three above the level of poverty, and now a minimum-wage job falls $1,300 below what it would require" (U.S. Congress, House 1987c, 543). Brown next responded that the Reagan administration had "created more jobs than any country in the world . . . and that our standard of living is higher not only than any country in the world but any country in the history of the world" (p. 544). Conover continued his structural analysis, asserting "the problem before us, the problem that we are addressing, really is poverty. And when we think about it as the problem of welfare, I think we have just slipped a stitch, so to speak" (p. 544). Conover then complained about the difficulty of developing a coordinated approach to poverty as a consequence of the lack of coordination among different committees with different jurisdictions. Brown concluded his questioning by essentially dismissing the bulk of Conover's testimony: "I want to thank you for your comments. I agree with you on at least one thing; even the Lord would have difficulty sorting out and negotiating committee jurisdictions in the U.S. Congress" (p. 544).

Other witnesses also challenged the grounds on which the notion of a social contract could be drawn up and enforced since, they argued, the state could not live up to its side of the bargain. The alternative perspective presented by the Center on Social Welfare Policy and Law, among other policy groups and coalitions, did not alter the terms of the debate or the legislative outcome, but such critiques did effectively reveal the limits of the social contract framework. Since the structural arguments they posed fell outside the individualist and behavioral social regulatory focus of welfare reform, they could "not [be] treated as real" (Worrall 1990, 7) within the already established framework.

The individualist and behavioral framework of the discourse that shaped the legislative hearings effectively prevented larger structural considerations from entering center stage, or, if brought to the hearings, such perspectives were repositioned, ignored, or challenged. As a consequence of such framing and legislative practices, no provision could be made in the Family Support Act for expanding the number of available jobs or rectifying the inequities that exist in the labor market. Therefore, most of the obligation was placed on the recipients' side of the contract. Furthermore, these obligations were framed within a discourse designed to reaffirm both the work ethic and family ethic—ideal typical constructions that are contradictory when applied to women (see Gilman 1994).

How "Work, Not Welfare" Further Framed the Social Contract

Workfare was discursively tied to the concept of the social contract throughout the hearings. The redefinition of women's right to social support under the discursive frame of the new consensus placed low-income mothers in the category of the able-bodied and thus undeserving of state aid. The legislative hearings on work and welfare explicitly redefined able-bodied women on welfare as potential yet reluctant workers (U.S. Senate 1987c). Under this formulation, the state's role was to regulate poor women's entry into the paid labor market by focusing on them as able-bodied workers undeserving of state support. Since welfare recipients are viewed as reluctant to enter the labor market, the state must mandate their preparation for and entry into the paid labor market in order to meet their obligations under the social contract. However, the redefinition of single mothers as able-bodied workers remained caught in the contradiction between women's mothering role and their paid labor status. For example, at what stage a mother of young children entered the mandatory category was contested throughout the hearings. The final legislation defined pregnant women and women with children under the age of three (or, at a state's discretion, as young as one year) as exempt from the mandatory work requirement.

The topic of children's needs rarely held center stage in this round of welfare reform hearings. However, a number of presenters attempted to highlight the effect that mandating mothers' workforce participation would have on their young children. Father Bryan Hehir of the U.S. Catholic Conference spoke out against mandatory work for mothers of children under the age of six. He testified: "Our concern is really with the children rather than with the mothers. Our concern is with the impact on children, the most vulnerable resource a society has. And so we would particularly be concerned that mothers not be forced into the workforce until children reach school age. That seems to us to be a reasonable place to move from voluntary programs to mandatory programs" (U.S. Congress, Senate 1987a, 275–76). Father Hehir's testimony stands out as one of the few that addressed workfare's effect on young children; however, by decentering mothers, his formulation remained consistent with the dominant framework that shaped most other testimony.

Despite general agreement that children should not be placed at risk, the statistical fact of mothers' contemporary paid labor force participation was used to justify mandatory workfare for low-income mothers on welfare. Moynihan noted in his introduction to the welfare reform hearings on February 23, 1987, "Times have changed. Women with children have entered the labor force in record numbers. In 1986, 75% of mothers with children aged 6 through 17 were in the labor force, up from 55% in 1975. In 1986, 54% of mothers with children under the age of 6 were in the labor force, up from 39% in 1975. Although most of these mothers do not work full-time year round, the essential point is that a majority of all mothers, whether single or married, work at least part time. In 1985, only one-third of mothers did not work at all" (U.S. Congress, Senate 1987d, 5). Since "it is now the *normal* experience of mothers to work, at least part time," mothers receiving public assistance are now expected to work for pay outside the home and end their dependence on the state (p. 5; emphasis in original). Yet how women were to find and afford quality child care to replace their own labor in the home was never effectively addressed within the hearings.

Another contested feature of workfare was how the enforcement of the contract (elimination of mothers from receipt of public assistance if they failed to comply) would affect children in these families. Representative Fred Grandy (R-Iowa) was particularly concerned about this issue (U.S. Congress, House 1987a, 322). He questioned Governor Clinton repeatedly about how the state could protect children whose mothers were sanctioned. Clinton, speaking as a representative of the National Governors Association, finally concluded that individual caseworkers would have to assess the extent to which these mothers might be abusing or neglecting their children if they did not provide for their economic needs. He explained:

> I think you would have to wait and see if the children were neglected. Then obviously they would be subject to the laws of the State if they were neglected children, and I would think that the caseworker, having knowledge that this person has deliberately refused to comply with the terms of the contract which were reasonable, would at least sensitize the other people in the State Government to the possibility that the children might be abused by having the money misspent. And if that's true, then we have and every State has a rather elaborate procedure for dealing with that. I think that is about as far as we ought to go in that area. (U.S. Congress, Senate 1987a, 322)

Evident in this pass age are the contradictions women face when forced to work without the economic means to provide alternative care for their children. On the one hand, they could be found guilty of neglecting their children if they go to work without finding adequate care for their children. On the other hand, those who refuse to comply would also be viewed as suspect under the discourse on dependency.

Clinton refused to acknowledge a key aspect of Grandy's concern, namely, "isn't there a subclass beneath those employable individuals that will either have to be in some way maintained or supported or cut loose?" Clinton's reply rendered anyone "beneath those employable" invisible within the discourse. The new consensus so powerfully constructed the welfare recipient as reluctant worker that anyone who might not be employable (except pregnant women and mothers of very young children) disappeared from the frame. Despite his effort, Grandy could not reinsert them into the frame.

As a result of the separation of welfare policy from employment policies in the structure of federal legislative practice, many of the representatives from unions and other progressive groups who testified at the legislative hearings were concerned that AFDC recipients would be used to exploit low-waged laborers further. Union representatives and other advocacy groups were particularly concerned about the way workfare could be used to replace other workers. Morton H. Sklar, former director of Jobs Watch, described how workfare threatens existing civil service jobs (U.S. Congress, House 1987c). Gerald W. McEntee, international president of the American Federation of State, County, and Municipal Employees, noted that in addition to displacement of regular workers, "workfare creates a working underclass in the public sector" with "no rights, benefits or access to grievance procedures" (U.S. Congress, Senate 1987c, 320). This alternative discourse challenged the false separation between labor policy and welfare policy that shapes congressional practices. However, since policy formulation presumes such separation, no discursive space was available to incorporate this critique effectively in the welfare reform legislation.

The new consensus framed women on public assistance within a market model of the work ethic that made it possible for some witnesses to center the labor market needs of business over women's caretaking responsibilities, in absence of men who share this responsibility, or their economic security. For example, William Kolberg of the National Alliance of Business focused on the need to regulate the availability of women's labor. He explained: "We have a window of opportunity in the next few years. The demographics make it possible for us to do something. There are two-fifths less young people coming into the labor force over the next 10 years than ever; we have the smallest growth in our labor force that we have had since the Thirties. If our job creation can continue on even a moderate path over the next 10 years, we have a chance to find jobs, entry-level jobs, for people that are trained, willing, and able to work" (U.S. Congress, Senate 1987c, 193). Pierce Quinlan, executive vice president of the National Alliance of Business, affirmed Kolberg's perspective when he spoke in the Senate hearings the following year: "In sum, the training of welfare recipients to fill vacancies in the private sector is not only good social policy; it is good economic policy" (U.S. Congress, Senate 1988, 14–15). It is not surprising that, as representatives of business, Kolberg and Quinlan centered the needs of the labor market rather than the welfare recipient or the poor more generally. This focus on the labor market reverses the logic of the work ethic. Instead of stressing the value of work for its own sake for individuals receiving public assistance, this argument privileges the needs of the market and highlights the value of women's labor for the workforce. For example, Quinlan did not address the level of wages necessary to bring a family out of poverty, nor was he asked by Senate committee members how business could improve the economic lives of the working poor. Once again, the dominant framework of the social contract rendered unspeakable any suggestion that the capitalist market might contribute to poverty in the United States.[30]

Numerous presenters at the legislative hearings, however, did offer testimony that fell outside the asserted new consensus on workfare. For example, among the 18 presenters[31] who testified before the Subcommittee on Social Security and Family Policy of the Senate Finance Committee on January 23 and February 2, 1987, nine spoke out against mandatory workfare. Mayor Arthur Holland of Trenton, New Jersey, who represented the U.S. Conference of Mayors, asserted that "workfare as a punitive program can do more harm than good. Workfare jobs which are not properly supervised and do not lead anywhere do little to encourage or enable the recipient to become self-sufficient. Workfare participants often are denied the status of regular employees, not provided standard benefits or full worker protections, and in some cases are not paid at rates commensurate with the work performed" (U.S. Congress, Senate 1987c, 202). Within the alternative discourse, workfare was constructed as a punitive and discriminatory practice, one that simultaneously defined welfare recipients as workers and denied their rights as workers.

More damaging to the logic of the social contract frame was analysis of the loss of freedom that mandatory workfare denoted. Robert Fersh, executive director of Food Research and Action Center, remarked on this contradiction: "It seems to me we ought to start moving toward encouragement and recruitment and getting people's free will involved. After all, we are a country that very much believes in liberty and free will. And to the extent we have people come in voluntarily, I think we assure a greater measure of success, in that they have an investment in the outcome of whatever programs they participate in" (U.S. Congress, Senate 1987a, 376–77). This oppositional position revealed the fragile basis on which workfare was constructed. The individualist frame of free will needed for a position within the social contract stands in direct contradiction to the coercive behavioral frame of the new consensus.

Ironically, justification for coercive workfare strategies is located in the abstract and circumscribed construct of citizen. The new consensus constructed those living in poverty as "less than full citizens" (as members of the Working

Seminar described it) by virtue of their economic insecurity (see U.S. Congress, Senate 1987b, 87). An excerpt from the testimony of Michael Novak of the American Enterprise Institute illustrates this formulation:

> The problem then is in our society, it seemed to us, that there is a growing number of fellow citizens who are not coping very well for themselves or for those who are dependent on them. We found this particularly shocking in the country—in a free country such as ours—because a free country depends on citizens of independence. It depends on citizens able to fend for themselves and to make themselves a contribution to the common good. And if instead they solely take from the common good, they are not in a position to exercise the independence becoming free citizens. (U.S. Congress, Senate 1987b, 79)

Novak equates freedom with economic independence and conflates economic independence with one's ability to contribute to the common good. Economic self-sufficiency is the sole measure of one's ability to contribute. No other activity or measure is relevant. Moynihan agreed. Referring back to Novales point, Moynihan stated: "We are talking about citizenship here; and if we can make that our standard, we can't go all that wrong" (p. 110). According to this formulation of citizenship, to gain our freedom we must fulfill certain obligations that ensure our economic independence.[32] If someone is not economically independent, he or she is considered less than a full citizen and, therefore, not due the rights accorded to full citizens. Since this concept of citizenship is built on the assertion that "a free country such as ours . . . depends on citizens of independence," it is tied to the economic promise of capitalism. Low-income residents generally are a fundamental challenge to this construction of citizenship. Furthermore, women who are responsible for caretaking work and who are paid wages below poverty cannot make claims on the category of citizen. In the redefined social contract, women's ability to claim citizenship even through the secondary citizen-mother construction of the widows' pensions is further constrained. Here the discursive tie between the "scattered hegemonies" (Grewal and Kaplan 1994) of capitalism, patriarchy, and citizenship hidden in the frame of the social contract is made explicit. The contradiction in the construction of the free citizen as economically independent and the notion of the common good as based on a set of dependency relations goes unnoticed in this above formulation. As Pateman (1988) notes, the social contract framework requires citizens to give up some freedoms for the protection of the state (p. 2). Under the redefined social contract, low-income women have little or no freedom as a consequence of their gender and class status.

Enforcing Parental Responsibility and a New Family Ethic

Social regulation of the family ethic and work ethic was elaborated in the hearings through a revised, albeit unarticulated, construction of family wage. This revised family wage highlighted the breadwinning role and negated the nurturing role of both low-income parents. It also constructed "any job, even at first at minimum wage" (U.S. Congress, Senate 1987b, 88) as preferable to dependency on public assistance even if this wage does not bring a family out of poverty. Therefore, it differs fundamentally from the ideal-typical construction of the family wage as one designed for a male breadwinner to support his wife's in-home caretaking responsibilities. Furthermore, the distrust of poor women's nurturing ability is embedded historically in the discourse on the family ethic that regulates the families and family forms believed to provide the most suitable homes for young children.[33] In contradiction to the redefined new consensus, low-income African American women have long been constructed as inadequate mothers because of their labor force participation (D. Roberts 1993, 1995). Under the revised family ethic, mothers of all racial backgrounds on public assistance are defined as unable to provide suitable homes or positive role models for their children by the very fact of their economic dependence on the state. Of course, this formulation contradicts the premise on which the family ethic was built, namely, women's caretaking role and their economic dependence on men. Welfare dependency (counterpoised to the independent wage earner) immediately disqualifies women as effective child rearers (Fraser and Gordon 1994b). Yet the independent wage earner was built on the male-breadwinner model and remains problematic when applied to single women with children. The contemporary displacement of poor single mothers from both the family ethic and the work ethic is evident in the establishment of local state regulatory programs that limit funds to mothers on public assistance who have additional children and the welfare program adopted in 1994 by California, where recipients are awarded child-care and medical benefits for up to one year after marriage or reunification of the mother and father to encourage two-parent heterosexual family formation.

Members of the Working Seminar asserted that "the crucible for the next round at welfare reform must be the family" (U.S. Congress, Senate 1987c, 90). Their interest in reforming the family included "reducing the number of single-parent families with children under 18" and enforcing parental responsibility. Stephen Heintz, commissioner of Connecticut's Department of Income Maintenance and chair of the American Public Welfare Association, addressed this concern: "The first obligation of public policy is to reinforce—through both words and actions—the centrality of the family and the primacy of parental responsibility in American society. We and our colleagues want to make the case that parental responsibility for the care of children must be enforced. We do not believe that poverty somehow removes the rights and obligations of parents toward their children" (U.S. Congress, Senate 1987a, 6). The enforcement of parental responsibility included mandating the work ethic of poor mothers and the family ethic of fathers who have been delinquent in their breadwinner role. It also included regulating the age at which a poor woman could parent and under what conditions she could be allowed to form an autonomous household. Policymakers were especially distressed over the number of adolescent mothers and the rise in the rate of so-called illegitimate births. The provision for "unmarried minor parents" (i.e., teenaged mothers) was designed to discourage the formation of young families (see U.S. Congress, House 1986, 284).

The Family Support Act "authorizes States to condition an unmarried minor parent's receipt of AFDC payments on his or her residence with a parent, legal guardian or other adult relative, or in an adult-supervised supportive living arrangement" (Library of Congress 1988, 279). A teenaged mother can receive an exemption from the state if her parents or legal guardians are dead or she "is not allowed to live with such parent or legal guardian"; the teenaged mother or her child would be in danger if she or they lived with "such parent or legal guardian"; or the teenaged mother has been living on her own for one year before the birth of her child or before applying for AFDC benefits (p. 279). Under the redefined social contract, the state treats teenaged mothers as children who should remain dependent on their own mothers or other relative serving as guardians. No witness or legislator called into question the legal implications for such a mandate for either the teenaged mother or the guardian. Given the gender division of labor in the household, this formulation is likely to place other women in the category of extended caregivers. The contradiction in this formulation was pointed out in the testimony of Margaret Prescod, representing Black Women for Wages for Housework. She noted that the requirement for mothers under age 18 to live with their parents "would force women who have already raised a family to take on the work and responsibility of another, responsibility they may not want" and force a teenaged mother into another form of dependency that would interfere with her ability to make choices about her children's care (U.S. Congress, Senate 1988, 156). The alternative discourse on the family challenged the differential application of dependency and, by extension, the very notion of the social contract. By demonstrating that teenaged mothers are not legitimate parties to the social contract, those operating from within the oppositional discourse further exposed the contradictions of the revised family ethic. However, such a challenge could not be incorporated or negotiated within the discursive framework of the hearings since it fell outside of the categories set up within the social contract.

As pointed out above, who was to care for the children of those mandated to work for pay outside the home was never resolved. The legislation did include funding to pay for transitional child care, but within the defined legislative framework the need for expanding day-care availability could not be addressed in the final legislation. Among those who emphasized the lack of available and affordable child care was Marian Wright Edelman, president of the Children's Defense Fund. No congressperson challenged Edelman's formulation, nor did any policymaker question the analysis of others who pointed out the limits of the contemporary child-care system. Since it was outside the individualist and behavioral frameworks circumscribing the legislative arena, no action could be taken to deal with this problem. And, consequently, the responsibility of the state in providing the means for mothers to move from welfare to work was further circumscribed.

In contrast to expanding child-care programs, the emphasis on child support enforcement was consistent with the regulatory framework of the discursive frame of the social contract, although implementation of such policies had the contradictory effect of further elaborating the state's welfare bureaucracy. Social regulation as a central component of welfare reform becomes more visible when we examine the contradiction between the stated goal of child support enforcement (namely, to provide economic support for poor children) and the inadequacy of such support in many cases, as pointed out by numerous witnesses. For example, Commissioner Heintz believed that child support should be sought even when the father does not have the economic means to provide it. He explained: "Child support should be pursued even when cost benefits are not readily apparent as may be the case with teenage fathers and others only intermittently employed. This makes a strong statement about the primary responsibility of parents to care for their children. Public policy must encourage, and obligate, parents to assume this responsibility" (U.S. Congress, Senate 1987a, 87). Most presenters who acknowledged that child support enforcement does not guarantee an end to poverty for many families regard it as only one factor that should be pursued. Rather than construct child support enforcement exclusively as an economic strategy to decrease women's economic dependency on welfare, most discussed it as a way to enforce fathers' responsibility under the family ethic.

A number of presenters representing advocacy organizations challenged this dominant perspective on child support enforcement and the male-breadwinner/female-caretaker model. Jack Kammer, executive director of the National Congress for Men, asked legislators to explore the historic, social, and ideological factors that contribute to the low level of child support by fathers: "I would urge that we remember the messages we have been sending to men since the dawn of the industrial revolution: You are more important in the factory, we tell them, than in the family. If we can elevate fatherhood to the lofty position motherhood so rightly holds, men will be less likely to throw it away" (U.S. Congress, Senate 1987b, 138–39). David Levy, president of the National Council for Children's Rights, also challenged what he termed the "sexist view toward custody in this country" (p. 153). Moynihan responded: "I am going to have to say that this is an issue of great interest, but it is somewhat beyond the jurisdiction of the Subcommittee on Social Security and Family Policy" (p. 153). Such fundamental and ideological challenges to the male-breadwinner model embedded in the family ethic found no legislative hearing. By questioning the gendered ideological construction of the family ethic, Kammer and Levy were speaking outside the new consensus framework. However, since their critique took for granted the two-parent family form as the ideal one for children, their testimony reaffirmed the very model they challenged.

The alternative analyses that pointed to the limits of child support enforcement as a strategy to increase the economic well-being of low-income women and their children challenged the dominant discourse on the family ethic that stressed fathers' financial role. From her structural vantage point, Margaret Prescod pointed to the racist and sexist features of the child support provision. Because of stratification in the paid labor market, she argued, Black and immigrant women will not receive sufficient child support to lift them out of poverty. Consequently, "women from these communities will be required to work the longest hours" to support their families (U.S. Congress, Senate 1988, 155).

Senator Moynihan was one of the few federal legislators to discuss the economic limits of child support enforcement. He was particularly concerned with the fact that child support is court-awarded on a racially differentiated basis (U.S. Congress, Senate 1987a, 171–72). Moynihan argued that this factor limited the value of child support enforcement for increasing the economic well-being of families headed by African American women and Latinas, who, he testified, were less likely to receive court-awarded child support, although he did not comment on what factors would contribute to such an outcome.[34] He did explicitly observe the racism embedded in social policies. One significant explanation for Moynihan's failure to address this institutional bias in his policy recommendations on welfare reform could be found in the powerful salience of the three dominant discursive frames outlined above. The new consensus was a discursive frame that functioned to exclude alternative analyses. The powerful interaction between the discursive construction of the redefined social contract, work ethic, and family ethic displaced structural challenges. Individuals such as Moynihan might recognize the limits of certain policy strategies for fighting poverty, yet since the defined goal was to end dependency on welfare, Moynihan's more nuanced and structural insights could not find discursive space within the resulting welfare reform. Furthermore, by framing the hearings with individualist and behavioral analyses of poverty, no discursive space was available in which to address the complex interplay of racism, sexism, and capitalism.

The Racial Subtext of the Social Contract

Race formed a powerful subtext that undergirded the discursive formulation of the social contract as well as the work ethic and the family ethic. African American women were highly visible in the discursive frame of the welfare reform hearings, as a number of passages above illustrate. However, structural issues that specifically related to the experiences of low-income African

American women such as inadequate child support payments, lower wages, and racist social policies fell outside the framework of the new consensus. Since the relationship between structural factors such as institutional racism, underemployment, and unemployment could not be centered in the new consensus framework, poverty among African American families was reinterpreted through individualist and behavioral frames.

Under the alternative discourse on race, "Black poverty . . . is impacted by racial discrimination" as well as class (U.S. Congress, Senate 1987a, 251). Douglas Glasgow of the National Urban League drew upon a structural analysis that highlighted class as the primary explanation for the increase in poverty among Americans of all racial-ethnic backgrounds. He referred to testimony given by the American Federation of Labor and Congress of Industrial Organizations (AFL-CIO) to criticize economic policy that contributed to an increase in U.S. poverty. Glasgow contextualized the structural conditions that led to an increase in the rate of poverty among African Americans. He offered an analysis that related the unemployment rate to the disproportionate rate of poverty for African Americans (U.S. Congress, Senate 1987a, 240). Moynihan responded to Glasgow's testimony by initially acknowledging the structural issues in the economy that contribute to poverty in the United States. He then discussed the "long-term debilitated population" who "require more than a job market." Glasgow agreed with this reframing, thus blurring the distinction between the structural factors contributing to African Americans' impoverishment and the culture of poverty explanation that is more in line with the individualist and behavioral frame set by the new consensus.

Using demographic data to outline characteristics of those who remain on welfare for periods greater than the norm of two years, some presenters described African American women as coterminous with other features that would lead to "long-term" dependency (U.S. Congress, House 1987c, 292). For example, in her testimony, Susan Rees, executive director of the Coalition on Human Needs, described the difficulty in trying to target the " 'neediest' among the AFDC population" She stated: "David Ellwood's work, as recounted in the recent GAO [Government Accounting Office] publication, 'Work and Welfare,' identifies several factors characteristic of the long-term recipient (black, never married before receiving AFDC, high school dropout, no recent work experience, entered AFDC at a very young age or when their children were younger than three). Yet, some of these factors have no impact alone but only in combination. In our survey, it seemed that everyone had at least one of these characteristics" (U.S. Congress, House 1987c, 292). The inclusion of the racial identity "black" as "characteristic of the long-term recipient" displaced white women from the frame, and conversely implicated Black women further, in the culture of poverty framework. This formulation of long-term dependency on public assistance continues to position African American women as responsible generally for transmitting poverty from one generation to the next (see Mink 1995).

There were a number of ways that race operated as a less visible subtext for a variety of constructions used to justify the redefined new consensus. Once again, such constructions did not go unchallenged. Margaret Prescod offered one of the most powerful critiques of the racial subtext in the new consensus when she concluded "that housework [as] a job is not new" (U.S. Senate 1988, 66). She continued: "Black women have been paid for generations for doing housework in white people's houses. When we did that work for no pay, it was called slavery." Prescod was committed to centering the value of women's work in the home. In stressing Black women's contradictory position as paid domestic worker, Prescod revealed the fallacy in separating women's domestic work from other forms of labor. By equating unpaid domestic work and slavery, she directly challenged the contradiction between workfare and the free individual and between the behavioral and individualist dimensions of the new consensus.

The structural analysis offered within the alternative discourse on race further challenged the discourse that targeted single women's poverty to the neglect of men's poverty. As Glasgow argued: "Over-emphasis on the notion of feminized poverty 'dichotomizes the status of black males and females in poverty and feeds practices that separate their plight.' A central weakness of this concept 'may be that it diverts attention from the staggering dislocation and disconnection of Black males from the labor market, income, and concomitantly, from the family,' and does gross injustice to the historical role played by Black women in providing essential income for Black families when Black males were unemployed or underemployed" (U.S. Congress, Senate 1987a, 252). Furthermore, he noted, African American men could not provide for their families, not because of a lack of commitment to the work ethic, but as a consequence of the structural barriers of institutional racism, underemployment, and unemployment. This alternative analysis of the work ethic and family ethic revealed the inadequacy of dominant formulations as they applied to African American women and men.

Other nonwhite or non-English-speaking groups were rarely mentioned in the hearings. On the rare occasion they were discussed, their insertion directly revealed the racist subtext of the new consensus. At one point, Representative Grandy wondered how people who lacked facility with English would understand their obligations under the contract (U.S. Congress, House 1987a, 342). As mentioned earlier, Grandy was among those legislators most concerned with how the social contract would be constructed and enforced. Governor Clinton agreed "absolutely" that it would "affect the terms" (p. 342). Grandy then posed this as a growing problem "as the Nation becomes perhaps more of a polyglot society" (p. 342). He asked Clinton whether "that contract is going to be perhaps contingent upon the ability of the person to speak or at least understand English at a functional level" (p. 342). Clinton replied that such a problem would only occur at the "margins" and then reasserted the significance of the responsibilities people have who "are living in America" (p. 342). In response to Clinton's construction of the issue as a "marginal one," Grandy shifted his position from one that highlighted the potential growth in the numbers of people who would not have sufficient facility with English to enter freely into the contract to a construction of the problem as marginal. He concluded his questioning: "Well, I agree with you in concept. I am asking you these *marginal* questions because I think the notion is so good" (p. 343; emphasis added). Few presenters raised the issue of facility with English as a prerequisite for entering into the social contract, yet Grandy's queries and the subsequent decentering of it as an issue demonstrate clearly that English proficiency was presumed. Consequently, no provision need be made in the subsequent legislation to ensure that welfare recipients have access to translations of the rules and regulations governing the social contract or to translators who could interpret the proceedings for them.

Just how little attention was given to the specific concerns of non-English-speaking recipients and immigrant groups is revealed in the following brief interchange between the late Senator John Chafee (R.-R.I.), Judith Gueron of Manpower Demonstration Research Corporation (MDRC), and Senator Moynihan.[35] The exchange is especially significant given that MDRC was responsible for evaluating the WIN Demonstration programs, the program model for the welfare reform proposals. The findings from MDRC's studies were used as further justification for workfare, yet MDRC gathered no data on immigrants or Puerto Ricans. Chafee was interested in what information MDRC had on immigrant groups and asked whether they had separate analyses about "Southeast Asians, Hispanics, Puerto Ricans, and maybe other groups, South Americans as opposed to Central Americans" (U.S. Congress, Senate 1987d, 84). Gueron answered: "Unfortunately, Senator, I think we know less than we ought to know. Some of that is because programs have had difficulty with language issues. For example, the program we studied in California explicitly, did not have a multilingual job club workshop for non-English or Spanish speaking people. So, in that case, Southeast Asians—a large group in California—were not part of the program. In other cases, where Hispanics certainly have been, we have not had numbers large enough to distinguish impacts. So, I don't think there is good evidence of the effect of programs on immigrants" (pp. 84–85). In an interesting turn of events, Moynihan jumped in with a specific example from previous testimony. He explained: "We heard from an official from Merced County, California, who described their welfare caseload which includes a very large group of persons who are receiving AFDCU [Unemployed Parent Program]. They are Hmongs from Laos. They have settled there, and they are a preagricultural community; and learning the ways of modem life and so forth is going to take them some time. They need temporary assistance in the interim" (p. 85). The construction of the Hmong as "a preagricultural community" negates their agricultural background (Bays 1994) and, not surprising in terms of this analysis, did not reflect the testimony to which Moynihan referred. In fact, it even distorted his own reference to the Hmong several months earlier in the hearing process. Here Moynihan stated that for the "Hmong tribesmen," their "dependency" on AFDCU was "a question of employment problems. It was no more than that" (U.S. Congress, Senate 1987a, 294).[36] Constructing them as "preagricultural" and in need of employment training or employment more generally placed them far outside the frame of gendered and racialized intergenerational dependency on government assistance. These constructions of the Hmong were used to justify disregarding their specific circumstances.

With the marginalization of all other nonwhite and non-English-speaking welfare recipients, African American women remain firmly at the center of the new consensus discourse. Unspoken, but not far from the surface of the new consensus framework, was the broader popular discourse that supports racist constructions of welfare recipients as Black and undeserving (see Mink 1995). Sensitivity to the wider popular racist constructions was evident in much testimony. As Dorothy Roberts (1995) points out, "Most Americans see no value in supporting [African American mothers'] domestic care-taking" (p. 201).[37] She also notes that "many workfare advocates fail to see the benefit in poor black mothers' care for their young children" (p. 201). Once again, the contrast between the racist images of the "long-term dependent" and what is defined as normal for mothers of young children reaffirmed the racial and gender subtext for the new consensus framework. The racial subtext of all three frames (social contract, work ethic, and family ethic) is infused with racist constructions of Black men's inadequacy as breadwinners and Black women's deficiency as caretakers. Since both Black men and women are constructed as outside of the work ethic and the family ethic, they have no rights under the social contract.

Within new consensus discourse, poverty and so-called welfare dependence in the United States are constructed as direct consequences of individual behavioral factors such as out-of-wedlock births, reluctance on the part of women to enter the paid labor market, and unwillingness of biological fathers to support their children financially. African American poverty, when explained through these frames, is constructed as a consequence of Black men's personal inability to support their families economically and of Black women's transmitting dependency on public assistance to their children. Since Hmong men and others who do not fit within the racist frame of the long-term recipient are marginalized within the discourse, they also have no legitimate or recognizable position within the social contract. Alternative perspectives on the relationship between race, gender, and poverty posed a direct challenge to fundamental assumptions of the new consensus on welfare reform. However, the discursive frames of the social contract, work ethic, and family ethic effectively deflected all structural challenges.

Conclusion

Relations of ruling were embedded in and reproduced by the discursive strategies and the nondiscursive organizational activities that shaped the congressional hearings on welfare reform. As this analysis reveals, legislative policy-makers were limited by the narrow frames placed around the hearings. However, certain actors did wield more power within the policymaking process than others. The discursive strategies are performed in the context of material relations of ruling that are themselves further affirmed through discourse.

The new consensus disqualified the poor from the authority to speak or to be heard about their lives and about the conditions that contribute to and could alleviate poverty in America. Through the silencing of perspectives that fell outside the dominant discursive frames, the state constructed a policy that appeared to avoid the contradictions inherent in the social construction of class and of gender and racial inequality. The powerful salience of the key discursive frames said to constitute the new consensus tendered outside the discourse all counterclaims based on structural analysis of poverty. Despite the fact that the legislation focuses on women's labor force participation, it placed on employers no requirements that would help rectify the inequities in the labor force. While the legislation established firm expectations of AFDC recipients, it placed little or no requirements on other parties to the social contract.

Of course, where and when clarity exists about the state's responsibility, welfare recipients might have some recourse for enforcement of the state's obligation by filing grievances or legal suits. The Department of Health and Human Services (DHHS) is charged with the responsibility for overseeing federal welfare policies by local city, county, and state governments. However, the interests served by these different levels of government remain firmly intertwined, thus calling into question DHHS's neutrality as enforcer of the contract. In addition, the state still defines the terms of the agreement and the context in which these claims are made. Further, the extent to which women receiving public assistance can avail themselves of grievance procedures contrasts greatly with the resources and power that local city, county, and state governments have available to them for defense of their actions or inactions. Poor women's access to legal assistance has been further curtailed by the withdrawal of funding for legal aid (Finnie 1995). The move to restrict legal-services attorneys from lobbying further circumscribes the ways in which low-income women and their families can gain access to the legislative process. Finally, the target for welfare reform remains the welfare recipient, not the conditions that contribute to the impoverishment of many single women and their children and other working poor families. Welfare reform becomes part of an extensive process by which the lives of low-income women and their families are organized and regulated by agents of the state.

This chapter reveals the discursive nature of power as manifest in the legislative process. Since the policy outcome has material consequences for women and their children who are recipients of public assistance, discursive strategies serve to structure the lives of the poor. They also circumscribe the legislative activities of the policymakers themselves. This analysis of the 1987–88 congressional hearings on welfare reform highlights how the new consensus operated as a discursive strategy and demonstrates the limits of policy analyses that start from the perspective of autonomous actors who are viewed as outside the discursive framework that structures their activities. What is at stake here is the restructuring of the state's role in regulating or supporting the economic lives of low-income women and their families. A feminist materialist discourse analysis provides insight into how the socially regulatory and restructuring processes are gendered and racialized.

Despite the existence of counterclaims, the legislators constructed a bill that neglected the alternative discourse. The evidence presented by those who opposed mandatory workfare and who argued for other economic changes was "not treated as real" (Worrall 1990, 7) because it did not fit into the discursive frame of the new consensus presented at the outset of the welfare reform hearings. Further evidence of this process is revealed when the alternative perspectives on welfare reform offered by legislators and others representing governmental and policy groups are examined. In the discursive process of constructing and reproducing the new consensus on welfare reform, the legislators rendered invisible the deep-seated contradictions within the redefined social contract.

Discourse analysis makes visible the fragile terrain on which this so-called consensus was built. The organizing frames of the new consensus are themselves contradictory forces. Individualist strategies designed to promote welfare recipients' independence from the state are placed alongside coercive behavioral strategies such as workfare and stipulations on teenaged mothers' residency. When placed against one another in the discursive frame of the new consensus, individualist and behavioral strategies work to disenfranchise welfare recipients as citizens with rights within the social contract. With no legitimate position for low-income women within the social contract, the state can justify coercive strategies to organize their everyday lives.

The social contract with low-income women is undergoing further restructuring through contemporary federal-level welfare legislation as well as local government initiatives. The 1996 welfare legislation, the Personal Responsibility and Work Opportunity Reconciliation Act, eliminated any system of entitlement based on financial need. Aid to Families with Dependent Children was defined as an entitlement program; if one fell below a certain measure of poverty, one would qualify for assistance. The level of assistance varied from state to state, and rules for proving eligibility often made claiming state assistance difficult. But the assistance was available, at least theoretically. The 1996 legislation officially ended AFDC. It provided block grants to individual states with little federal oversight, disqualified legal immigrants from receiving food stamps and Supplemental Security Income, and gave states the option of not providing other forms of assistance to immigrants without U.S. citizenship. The 1996 legislation also required recipients to work within two years of receiving benefits, and limited lifetime receipt of public assistance to five years—no matter what financial needs remained.

A feminist materialist approach informed by Foucauldian discourse analysis offers a valuable framework through which to investigate how consensus on welfare reform, the Contract with America, the Personal Responsibility and Work Opportunity Reconciliation Act, and other social policy constructions are accomplished and maintained. Such an approach will enrich future policy analyses by contextualizing the means by which individualist, behavioral, and narrow familial frames inhibit the incorporation of structural analyses into the policy construction framework. Attention to gender, racial, and class subtexts of social policy formation and implementation advances our understanding of how relations of ruling are reinscribed in legislative activities. With this understanding, we may better devise strategies to undermine and expose the dominant discourse that, as Foucault (1978) argues, "renders it fragile and makes it possible to thwart it" (p. 101).

Yet, oppositional discursive strategies alone cannot undermine the powerful systems of gender, race, and class oppression that shape social life in the United States. Discursive strategies must be linked to an understanding of the historically contingent social, economic, and political processes that materially contour the terrain on which structural inequalities are built. Furthermore, as Rose Brewer (1994) emphasizes, "emancipatory strategies" must include the development of "alliances reflecting the multiple social locations of women, racial-ethnic groups, and working people" who together can create "shared agendas across differences" (pp. 125–26). This analysis of the 1987–88 welfare reform hearings demonstrates the limits of the legislative arena for emancipatory projects, at least in the present incarnation of the social contract. Moreover, it offers a powerful lens through which to view the contradictions in the dominant frames as they are called on to justify the dismantling of the welfare state. This deepened sensitivity to the spaces, cracks, and fissures in the dominant discursive frames can be drawn upon as a resource to help generate the political communities necessary for progressive social change.

By mapping the ways relations of ruling render invisible the gender, race, and class dynamics embedded in bureaucratic rules and procedures, assumptions about clients, consumers, or citizens, and organizational products and outcomes, a materialist feminist standpoint approach can reveal how inequality is produced and reproduced in everyday life. In chapter 8, I illustrate my approach to oral narrative analysis by highlighting the experiences of women on public assistance who are completing a four-year college degree. The study was conducted in collaboration with an undergraduate research assistant, Gina Battani, who as a student mother on public assistance, inspired me to design the study and assisted me in its implementation. I outline the creative ways the women on public assistance and in college manage their child-care and educational demands as they face the economic and other structural barriers to their success in college.

PART IV

Activism, Narrative, and Empowerment

CHAPTER 8

Bringing Everyday Life to Policy Analysis

In this chapter, I present a case study of women on welfare and in college that was designed to explore the contradictions of the welfare state from the standpoint of those who are targets of state intervention. The organization of the "everyday world" of the women in this study poses a challenge to the dominant discourse and practices of both higher education and welfare policy. Drawing on Dorothy Smith's (1987, 1990a, 1990b) materialist feminist standpoint theory, I demonstrate the value of an "everyday world" analysis of policy implementation for uncovering hidden dimensions of state regulations as they are manifest in the daily experiences of women whose lives are organized in relationship to specific features of welfare policy. This study contributes to the ongoing analyses of women on welfare that contest the constructions of welfare recipients as "dependent" and lacking "work motivation."[1] The women in college who participated in this study demonstrated their courage and strength as they managed the pressures that shaped their daily lives. Their growth in self-esteem and personal power that occurred as a result of their experiences in college enhanced their resistance to and critique of the public patriarchal strategies embodied in welfare and educational policy.

This analysis draws on the experiences of 17 white European American women receiving Aid to Families with Dependent Children (AFDC) who between 1989 and 1992 were enrolled in the **PROM**oting Independence and Self-sufficiency through Employment and Jobs Opportunity and Basic Skills (PROMISE JOBS) Training Program, Iowa's response to the Family Support Act (FSA) of 1988. With the passage of the FSA, women on public assistance who lived in states that choose to implement the so-called college option (see Gittell 1990) were formally provided resources to advance toward a four-year college degree.[2] Title II, section 201(F) states that a recipient may attend an institution of higher education in order to fulfill their so-called contract with the state, namely, to make the transition from welfare to work. The FSA was the first welfare reform measure in the United States to support AFDC recipients who choose to study at the four-year college level.[3]

Limits and Possibilities of the College Option

Contemporary welfare reform measures continue to stress many of the themes embedded in the FSA, although none of the recent proposals include support four years of college education.[4] The themes of "ending dependency" and "mandatory work" are two of the most salient.[5] Fortunately, for a number of women receiving AFDC during the later part of the 1980s and the beginning of the 1990s, FSA included college as a form of classroom training that would fulfill their obligation under the mandated program.

As discussed in chapter 7, the principal stated goal of the FSA was to end long-term dependence on public assistance. Recipients with children aged three years (or as young as one year, at individual states' discretion) and older, were mandated to participate in job training, work experience, or educational courses that will increase their employability and contribute to self sufficiency. The legislation also included measures to establish paternity and for mandatory payroll deductions from noncustodial fathers to increase the financial resources available to single mothers on AFDC.[6] Transitional medical benefits and child care could be provided for up to one year following employment (Public Law 100-485, 2358, 1988). Iowa included the college option in PROMISE JOBS, which was initiated in October 1989.

The paid labor market is organized around a gender, racial, and regional division of labor (Amott and Matthaei 1991). Moreover, there is a high rate of unemployment and regional disparity in job availability (requiring some women who have trained in specific areas to relocate for employment in their profession). However, the college option did increase the employment opportunities for some women on public assistance.[7] Inclusion of the college option in Title II of the FSA was especially meaningful given the fact that "an estimated ⅓ to ½ of AFDC recipients already have earned high school diplomas or a GED; thus, they are eligible, at least in educational terms, to consider higher education as an option" (Kates 1991, 183). In Iowa the figures were higher than for the nation as a whole. In a 1990 survey of AFDC recipients in Iowa, researchers found that 66 percent of recipients had a high school diploma and 23 percent had a GED (Fisher 1991). On the other hand, contradictions between mandatory work-to-welfare approaches or "workfare" and college combined with the sexism, racism, class, and regional discrimination embedded in higher education act as constraints upon the academic success of women on welfare.[8] Such constraints contribute to the gendered reproduction of class that is captured in Diana Pearce's (1978, 1990) analysis of "the feminization of poverty."

To explore the limits as well as the possibilities of the college option for women on welfare, I shifted the standpoint of analysis to the "everyday world" of those whose lives are regulated through welfare policy. Feminist materialist standpoint methodology offers something very few policy approaches offer; namely, "situated knowledges" (Haraway 1988) on hidden dimensions of state activity as experienced by women who must negotiate the multiple policy arenas throughout their daily lives. Both Dorothy Smith and Donna Haraway argue that certain standpoints can provide a more reliable vantage point from which to assess how power is woven in institutions that contour women's daily activities. Smith's (1987) approach is particularly useful as it situates women's experiences within the local institutional practices that organize their lives. By utilizing this "everyday world" perspective, I could remain sensitive to women's experiences while also exploring how varying institutional practices of welfare policy implementation and higher education organize their lives. Through this approach, I uncovered conflicts between the everyday lives of women on AFDC in college and the demands placed on them by college and welfare policy implementation criteria.

Advantages of an "Everyday World" Approach to Policy Analysis

The categories used to organize and implement social welfare policy render invisible the specific needs and experiences of women who are the target of welfare policies. Smith's materialist feminist institutional ethnographic approach helps us link analysis of a specific policy to the broader social context in which it is embedded. For example, Alison Griffith and Dorothy Smith (1990) apply Smith's approach to their study of mothering, school, and social class. They illustrate how women's mothering work "knits together the organization of an economy and the paid work of family members with the organization of the school" (p. 8). Neither the paid labor force nor the educational system recognizes the work women do to maintain both institutions and how these gendered activities affect women's daily lives. Only by shifting the standpoint to mothers' daily lives do these activities come into view.

Undergirding much of the tension women face in negotiating divergent institutional expectations is the simultaneous differentiation between women's "productive" and "reproductive" lives in public policy and the failure to reconcile this false division (Sarvasy 1988). This problem is made visible when we ground our analysis in women's concrete negotiations across these multiple arenas and conflicting policy prescriptions. In fact, as Griffith and Smith (1990) argue, the bipolar construction of productive and reproductive labor fails to capture the "actual organization of women's work" (p. 6). Such a dualistic formulation misses "the actual work processes, the ways in which they are coordinated, the ways in which people are active and inventive in the specific local conditions of their lives" (p. 6). In contrast, Smith's institutional ethnographic approach provides a methodology through which to explore how relations between and across institutions "are accomplished in active work processes" (p. 7) and negotiated by women throughout their daily lives.

Methodological Considerations

This chapter highlights one aspect of a larger study of the implementation of the FSA in Iowa. This multilevel study includes discourse analysis of the congressional hearings leading up to the passage of the FSA (see chapter 7); six-month participant observation of the state task force charged with developing guidelines to implement the FSA in Iowa; in-depth interviews with members of the task force; attendance at periodic training sessions for local implementation staff; and participant observation and interviews with welfare caseworkers, administrators, and other "street level bureaucrats" (Lipsky 1980) in the service delivery areas designated to directly implement the policy. The study of women on public assistance in college was inspired by the experiences of an undergraduate student at Iowa State University, Gina Battani, who supported herself and her young child on public assistance. While taking a course with me on the sociology of gender, Ms. Battani complained about the lack of sensitivity toward women on public assistance expressed by other students in the class. She made the point that "they don't even realize that someone on welfare could be sitting in the seat next to them." Together we decided to design a study to identify and interview other students on public assistance. Ms. Battani assisted me in conducting the interviews and responded to earlier drafts of the chapter.

The primary data used for the analysis presented in this chapter are drawn from in-depth interviews, focus groups, and ongoing contact with 17 white European American women from rural communities in the Midwest who were enrolled in PROMISE JOBS. The women were identified through personal contact, referrals from those interviewed, and an advertisement in the newsletter of the Adult Students Information Office at Iowa State University (ISU). Of the 17 students, 12 students attended ISU and 5 were enrolled in three different community colleges and planned to continue their education in a four-year college. While the sample size is small, the in-depth data gathered on their daily experiences as mothers, students, and welfare recipients offers one corrective. More importantly, however, the goal of this analysis is not to explore how these women's individual experiences are generalizable to a larger population, but to highlight some of the inconsistencies, limits, and contradictions, as well as possibilities of the "college option" for women on AFDC.

Although all interviewed were white single mothers from rural communities and small towns in the Midwest, they do form a diverse group on other dimensions. Two were lesbian mothers, a group much neglected in the literature on low-income women. The students ranged in age from 23 to 42. They had between one and five children. Four of the women had graduated at the time of the follow-up interview in 1991. Two of the four had been unable to find employment that would pay a sufficient wage to move them off AFDC as of one year following their final interview. One found professional employment. Another subsequently enrolled in graduate school. One of these women dropped out of college toward the end of her freshman year. The remaining nine women were still enrolled in college as of December 1991, when the study was completed. Only pseudonyms are used in reporting findings from the study.

The interview schedule was open-ended and designed to elicit women's oral historical narrative[9] of their early childhood background including economic position; changes in economic status over time and coping strategies; childbearing, child rearing and child-care experiences; experiences with divorce, family court, child services, education, and welfare among other policy arenas; and their particular experiences with PROMISE JOBS and college. We gathered information on how each woman negotiated the different policy expectations, the multiple demands on her time, her support network, and the strategies she adopted to manage her household economy. While interview data did not provide the vivid material that a more broadly ethnographic approach generates, the oral narratives served as a powerful text for uncovering the tensions between the women's everyday lives and the demands placed on them by policy implementation criteria.[10] Furthermore, I adopted three strategies to supplement interview data: analysis of the PROMISE JOBS and college policies and practices as they specifically related to the women in this study; use of focus groups that brought several women in the study together to discuss their experiences in a collective context; and ongoing meetings with 6 of the 17 women that included numerous opportunities to work with them as they negotiated daily life crises and opportunities. These discussions occurred in person and on the phone and included topics such as problems they were having in classes, with public assistance, and with their children or ex-husbands. The contacts ranged from 20 minutes to several hours. I also served as academic advisor for four of the six women. On numerous occasions, I joined these women in family events, dinners, and other outings over the course of two academic years.

Each interview was tape recorded. The transcriptions of the tapes were reviewed for recurring patterns as well as unique themes. I was interested in commonalities as well as unique experiences—both offering important illustrations of gaps between daily life activities and individual needs as they conflicted or contrasted with the demands of welfare and higher education policy and practices. Focus group meetings were held to provide the context to further explore key issues identified in the individual interviews. The focus groups were also audiotaped and transcribed and, subsequently, analyzed using content analytic techniques. A similar process was utilized to analyze notes taken following the informal conversations.

Analysis of the experiences reported by the women in this study reveal major sets of contradictions in the FSA that constrained the educational attainment of these women on welfare and highlight the gap between policy constructions of "welfare mother," college student, and women's everyday lives. In the first section, I describe how constructions of welfare mothers' risk of "welfare dependency" in the FSA led to lowered priority given to those defined as "self-initiated" and "voluntary," which in turn posed particular difficulties for the women in this study. While such a construction is often tied to bureaucratic decisions designed to limit expenditures to welfare recipients said to exhibit low levels of self-motivation, those women in this study who were motivated to pursue their education did not receive sufficient and consistent resources to support their educational attainment. These resource limitations generated additional stress and time commitments that interfered with their educational goals. Next, I illustrate how mandatory workfare practices directly contradict practices associated with higher education as evident in policies toward child-care reimbursement, work study, and academic awards and achievements. In the third section, I detail some of the work these women do to make sense of and weave together the conflicting policy arenas through their everyday mothering, economic, and educational activities.

Constructions of Dependency and the College Option

One feature that characterizes the dominant discourse on welfare is a belief that women on public assistance have become overly "dependent" upon state support and require incentives and sanctions to encourage them to move from "welfare to work" (see Fraser and Gordon 1994a, 1994b). Furthermore, such assumptions of women's "welfare dependency" leads to a differentiation among those receiving public assistance. Terminology such as "at risk" and "nontargeted" or "self-initiated" are incorporated into implementation guidelines in an effort to target those most likely to suffer so-called welfare dependency and to conserve state funds by denying support to those presumed to make the required transition from welfare to work without additional state resources. With low priority placed on those who exhibit the motivation to work and gain classroom training, women who take steps to move from welfare to work may be undermined in their efforts.

The state of Iowa notified recipients who were mandated for participation in PROMISE JOBS through a letter and placed them on a waiting list. The PROMISE JOBS Provider Manual explained that: "Services of the program are prioritized in behalf of those clients who are considered 'at risk'. The 'at risk' population includes potential and actual long-term recipients as well as recipients who are soon to be ineligible for ADC assistance" (State of Iowa, Department of Human Services 1991, 1).[11] At least 55 percent of the FSA funds were designated for targeted recipients. Due to the lack of funding, a large percentage of "nontargeted" AFDC recipients who wished to return to school were placed on waiting lists. There were 1,856 targeted, other mandatory, and nonmandatory AFDC recipients on waiting lists for PROMISE JOBS by December 18, 1990, only a year after the start of the program (Fisher 1991, 6).

When someone was accepted for PROMISE JOBS an employability plan was developed and, if college was indicated, the state paid for child care while the student was in class as well as paid for their transportation to and from school. If an AFDC recipient started classes before they were called for PROMISE JOBS, the state defined them as "self-initiated" and did not cover the costs of the "classroom training." If an AFDC recipient was "nontargeted" for participation (for example, if she was pregnant or had a child under three) and chose to begin classroom training, the state could also decline to pay for her child care and transportation.[12]

To ensure that "at risk" women on public assistance moved from welfare to work, those who were mandated to participate were threatened with loss of financial support if they failed to fulfill their so-called contract with the state (Glazer 1988). This punitive approach included ongoing surveillance practices that took different forms in different local state programs.[13] While limited analysis of women's impoverishment narrows the scope of policy innovation, policing practices of welfare reform measures widened it greatly. Identified as agents of the state were a growing number of professionals including, in this case, college professors, librarians, and school administrators.

All the women interviewed criticized the requirement that they show proof of attendance in class by having instructors sign a daily attendance sheet.[14] Barbara Stern was in her late 30s, had two children, and was a junior when first interviewed for the study. She explained why she was offended by the attendance sheet requirement: "You're an adult student going to school. You're managing the home. You're managing school. You're trying to manage your life. You're trying to make all these ends meet and work out, and as far as I'm concerned, for them to bring you down because, I'm not saying all, but there are some teachers that look at you different because you're on ADC." She resented having to tell professors that she was on AFDC when no one else was expected to reveal how they were paying for college:

> Because otherwise you look out at that classroom and you don't know if that student's working their way to school. You don't know if Mommy and Daddy's paying for it. You don't know if Voc Rehab [the Department of Vocational Rehabilitation] is paying for it. You don't know if they're just taking out student loans and grants to get through school. But I have to fill out this piece of paper saying: "Hey, I'm on ADC," and you have to sign this paper saying: "I was in class.". . . It's like putting somebody back in second grade.

Barbara believed that "if you get a grade out of the class, you won't flunk it, this shows that you were there or that you did what you were supposed to do." She did not complete the forms the preceding semester and, she reported, "now I'm in trouble over this." Barbara's struggle against the attendance sheet requirement further demonstrates the contradictions of the mandatory workfare program that was ideologically designed to promote self-sufficiency.[15] In an effort to retain her autonomy and self-respect, Barbara challenged one of the dimensions of social control embedded in the FSA. Her act of resistance posed a threat to her family's financial security, but her continued acquiescence to the attendance sheet requirement was undermining her self-esteem.

Ironically, it is those who argue that long-term dependence on welfare undermines a recipient's self-esteem who also stress the need for close state supervision of welfare recipients participating in workfare (see Murray 1984).

The construction of "mandatory" participant was directly related to narrow assumptions about women's childbearing and child-rearing responsibilities. Pregnant women and mothers of children under age three (due to funding constraints, no state chose to mandate participation for women with children as young as one) were exempt from mandatory participation. However, this guideline failed to acknowledge the perspective of women who might wish to continue their classroom training while pregnant or parenting very young children. Karen Janson complained about the low priority given to voluntary participants in PROMISE JOBS. She was notified by letter that she was a mandatory recipient but was pregnant at the time. Consequently, "that was scratched off. They just wrote it off—it was canceled." But, she thought:

> You know, if I don't have to work until the baby's three years old, don't have to work or go to school [that's too long to wait]. I thought, why be dependent on assistance for another three years, I'll still be dependent on it. . . . [So] then I got a hold of them and said I was interested in PROMISE JOBS, went and talked to these people, and they said: "Well, you have no business going to school. You're six months pregnant. There's no way you can handle that."

Karen felt that her caseworker, who she described as a "stereotypical man," did not understand why she wanted to go back to school even though she was expecting another child. She got the message from him that she "should be home with my kids"—a message that directly contradicts the "welfare-to-work" thrust of the FSA. But Karen was adamant about her decision to go to college and got her caseworker's reluctant support. Karen's experience mirrors that of women who become pregnant while employed, namely, for a brief period of time their reproductive work is visible and their status as productive workers is questioned; although, as many feminist scholars argue, women workers are, in fact, treated as potential mothers and therefore their commitment to the paid labor force always remains in question (Sokoloff 1980). When incorporated into the sphere of welfare—an institution originally created to support "deserving" women's reproductive work (Abramovitz 1988)—the contradictions between women's so-called paid labor and unpaid nurturing work become even more apparent. Construction of "dependency risk" was further challenged by Karen's persistent demands for participation in PROMISE JOBS.

Street-level bureaucrats do have some latitude to reinterpret guidelines and make exceptions for certain clients as Karen's case illustrates. Despite the bureaucratic guideline that Karen should not advance her education while pregnant, her caseworker gave in to her definition of the situation. Everything was in place for Karen to receive the support from PROMISE JOBS when funding was cut and a priority list was established. She waited "just on the skin of [her] teeth, waiting for them to say that they got the money in." A couple of weeks before school began she received word that the money was available.

Melissa Kramer experienced a related problem—namely, the denial of PROMISE JOBS assistance to students who initiated college study on their own. The policy on self-initiated training reads: "When a self-initiated training program meets program standards, . . . the client may be enrolled in the classroom training component in order to be eligible for child care and transportation financial assistance. Clients enrolled in self-initiated training at the time application is made for PROMISE JOBS services are not eligible for financial assistance to cover tuition, fees, books, or supplies" (State of Iowa, Department of Human Services 1991). As a self-initiated student, Melissa was denied the support of PROMISE JOBS when she first applied. She went to the Office of Financial Aid for further assistance and was given a work-study position. But the additional income from work-study turned out to be "a total disaster" for her AFDC eligibility. She recalled:

> I applied [to Social Services] and I got denied. The amount of the money that I was bringing home from work-study was the amount of money that I was over. . . And I said, "I'm in work study," and he goes, "That's a job. Your job is to be a student." So I ended up being penalized. Here I was trying to make it so we could live and I got penalized for being on work-study and so I lost everything. So I ended up having to quit my work-study so I could qualify for food stamps and then qualify for day-care assistance.

Melissa's narrative highlights a major ongoing contradiction embedded in the "college option." Work-study would provide additional experiences to increase her future employment opportunities as well as enhance her family's present financial security. Yet, she was penalized for her work experience by the same social policy that was designed ideologically to increase her employability.

Incompatibility of Funding Rules, Employability Plans, and Measures of Success

The definition of work incorporated into the FSA and its implementation inadequately assessed women's mothering work as well as the time commitments and extra-classroom activities required for success in college. Three interrelated problems arose as a consequence of the narrow view of acceptable work for welfare recipients. First, since academic awards such as fellowships, scholarships, and work-study were counted against their AFDC payment, the students were often penalized for their success in college. Second, since child care was provided only during classroom hours, students could not attend special lectures or other academic activities required for college credit. Third, given the definition of full-time participation and the limited number of months for which state support was made available to PROMISE JOBS participants, little flexibility existed to counter the limitations of transferring from a two-year to a four-year college.

The women interviewed identified three key practices that limited their participation in college: (1) their removal from PROMISE JOBS if they were temporarily denied AFDC when work-study exceeded the allowable amount and the financial penalties for receipt of work-study, research assistanceships, and scholarships; (2) lack of funding for child care for lectures, study groups, or library research; which applied to all of the women in this study; and (3) constraints on transfer from a two-year to four-year college, which is a particularly important concern for women from rural communities who often live at great distances from four-year colleges.

Success in higher education is often measured by academic awards such as scholarships and research assistant activities. Work-study, evening lectures, and study groups also provide relevant experiences that could enhance an individual's academic mastery. Such activities may also be a requirement for certain classes. However, the implementation of PROMISE JOBS interfered with the women's full participation in college life. Melissa Kramer is a single mother of four children who had always wanted to attend college; but when she finally was accepted into the PROMISE JOBS program, she was "very disappointed with the government" because any scholarship or research assistanceship that she was offered due to her successful performance in college counted against her financial eligibility.

PROMISE JOBS initially provided funds for child-care reimbursement equal to the time devoted to attending classes and traveling to and from school. As Melissa reported: "Because I was doing my work study from 2:00 P.M. to 5:00 P.M. they would not cover my day-care assistance, and so my day care just jumped right back up because you only get day care for when you are in class, which means I would have to have all 8:00 classes and all 4:00 classes for [the child care director at the DHS] to pay my before- and after-school child care." Neglected in the assessment for child-care funds was support for study time, group projects, evening lectures, and laboratory exercises. Julie Mart felt frustrated when she could not attend meetings or lectures on campus in the evening. She did not think it "fair to my kids [to be] dragged down to everything." She explained: "They've been cooped up in school all day and I don't need to make them sit quiet and sit still all evening. And so I feel like I've missed out on some things." Due to the expense of child care, Julie did not spend much time in the library. She said: "I've gotten used to studying at home with a lot of noise and a lot of activity going on."

Another frequently mentioned difficulty arose when their children became ill. Norma Styles described taking her child to school when he was ill. Her narrative highlights the dilemma that all the women experienced as they negotiated the competing demands of mothering and academia.

It's either you stay home with them or you take a sick child to class. . . . But unless you have a friend or someone to leave him with, then you have to stay home and then you are penalized from your classes because you stay home with your sick child. But if you bring that child with you, you will also be scrutinized by your classmates because you're bringing a kid who's puking in class. So, you don't know where to go, what to do. So, I stayed home and I missed a mid-term and a quiz due to this and I can't make them up. And I don't think that's fair either.

Testing and attendance policies rarely incorporated the practical demands of mothering such as sick-child care or the consequent limited time for study and attendance at extracurricular activities. In addition, the overall lack of child care before and after school inhibited the women from integrating into the academic environment more effectively.

A third feature of implementation of the FSA in Iowa that posed a particular difficulty for rural residents was the problem they faced finding a four-year college within reasonable driving distance. Even two-year colleges were often located some distance from their homes. Rarely did they have access to public transportation. As a consequence, all of the women we interviewed who lived in rural towns needed to provide their own means of transport to and from school. One consistent concern mentioned by the women in this study was the cost of repairing their cars. Since the state does not permit recipients to own vehicles that are worth more than $1,500, the women who have cars usually experience great difficulties with their all-too-often unreliable vehicles. Melissa Kramer reported that her car "has 130,000 miles on it, and so everything has been going wrong with it. A year ago everything started to fall apart. . . . I mean the brakes, the fuel pump, it's just a lot of major repairs." Karen Janson travels 45 miles to the university in a car that is in "terrible condition." It has over 200,000 miles on it and she can't afford to pay for the repairs that are needed. She was forced to put $500 from her student loan into repairs.

Since most of those interviewed were living in a rural region before returning to college, all but four of the women had attended or were attending a two-year college. Unfortunately, entrance into a community college may interfere with the successful completion of a four-year college degree.[16] For example, in his evaluation of the effects of community college on students' "socioeconomic attainment," Kevin Dougherty (1987) found that students who were seeking a baccalaureate degree who started at a community college "attain less educationally and economically than comparable students entering four-year colleges" (p. 86).

The women in this study faced an additional complication when the original employability plan drawn up with their PROMISE JOBS' worker did not include a four-year degree program. In such a case, a participant could be prevented from continuing on in college. This applied particularly to those enrolled in two-year degree programs that are considered terminal degrees, namely, degrees for computer technician or nurses' aide, for example, for which employment could be sought upon completion of an AA degree. Many women reported that they initially set their sights on a two-year college program. Some who expressed interest in a four-year degree were often counseled into a two-year program. However, their educational horizons were raised once they entered college and experienced success or discovered other career paths that required a four-year degree. Fortunately, some street-level bureaucrats played a crucial role in interpreting the rules and regulations of workfare in such a way to permit the continued education of women who expressed an interest in pursuing a four-year college degree.

Further complications arose when they tried to transfer credits. Norma Styles graduated from a two-year school and transferred to complete a bachelor's degree. It will take her an additional four years to complete college because of the lack of comparability in the courses she took at the community college. Since Iowa placed a limit on the length of time it provided funding for women on AFDC to continue their college education (48 months or four years), women like Norma who transferred and must complete more than two additional years of college would not qualify for funds to complete their education. Norma was obviously disappointed by the "administrative" decision. She explained: "You get depressed because you come here and they go: 'Well, you've got four more years.' . . . And that's sad to lose all that money, training, time, efforts." Under contemporary welfare reform proposals that limit receipt of public assistance to two years, most women on public assistance will have little chance of attaining a four-year college degree even if such classroom training is acceptable under new guidelines.

Negotiating Gaps Between Policy Constructions and Everyday Life: Making Visible the Work Women Do

By shifting to the standpoint of the women in this study, we can identify certain significant gaps between their individual needs, daily life activities, and the demands of welfare and higher education policies. When we make these gaps visible, we also reveal hidden work women perform to negotiate the contradictions and competing demands. The previously invisible work they perform includes creative budgeting to "make ends meet" (see Edin and Lein 1997); supportive and unpaid child-care arrangements with other mothers; negotiating transport for school and child care; and managing multiple demands on their time. Even less visible is the informal work these women perform to support each other as well as younger students who construct the older woman student as mentor or surrogate mother. Such invisible work serves to link the policy-isolated arenas of home, welfare, education, and the economy.[17]

And, unfortunately, not all women succeeded in managing such complex negotiations.

A major feature of child support enforcement, Title I of the FSA, was that a woman would be dismissed from AFDC if the child support payment exceeded the AFDC payment. Implementation of the campaign to collect child support, in some cases, led to a temporary loss of welfare and a subsequent removal from the college supported program. Both Martha and Julie expressed their anxiety when they had no income for two months in a row as a result of this regulation. In each instance, the payment was a combination of several months of support due that Social Service account managers had applied as income for one month. Since the amount credited was above AFDC financial eligibility, they were removed from the program. When they realized they had been terminated, neither understood the grounds for their removal. After some delay, they reapplied and were reinstated. However, the process took two months to complete and both Martha and Julie had no other source of income during this period. Not surprisingly, they reported these experiences as extremely stressful. Further, when they lost eligibility for AFDC, they could not qualify for PROMISE JOBS.

Julie's elimination from AFDC meant that she had to reapply for PROMISE JOBS and was placed on the waiting list. She could not enroll in college until a place opened up for her on the list. She waited several months before she could continue her education. If this situation occurred during a semester in which she was enrolled, Julie would have been forced to drop out of school and lose the credits for the entire term. Since the weeks in which she was enrolled would be counted against her total eligibility, Julie (or anyone else in her situation) would be sanctioned further by the bureaucratic contradictions between child support, AFDC financial eligibility guidelines, and academic practices.

All the women described extremely imaginative ways they managed to get through each month on the tight and fluctuating budgets. Norma Styles and her two children, like the other families in this study, lived on a break-even budget. Norma described in detail how she made ends meet. She diligently collected coupons for use in the food store. She was able to turn $200 worth of food stamps into $400 worth of groceries. However, food stamps cannot be used to cover the cost of paper goods and hygiene products. Luckily, she had family and friends who would bring "care packages" with paper goods. She also used double couponing to stock up on paper goods and hygiene products. But, she reported: "You just never have enough Kleenex or paper towels. . . . [I] have to put back a little bit of money, change I get from my food stamps, I put back in my envelope and with that, I go and buy paper products. Because sometimes, that's the only place it is."

In addition to savings from these inventive budgeting measures, many of the women also engaged in bartering and sharing child care in order to meet their daily needs. For example, Norma Styles described the child-care cooperative she used to help her during her first two years in college. Jean Marks also organized a cooperative child-care exchange with her neighbor. She explained:

> So she watched all my kids for an hour every day while I was at class and then I would watch her child while she went to a class. . . . And I would meet her on the bus system and get the baby. . . . She was just coming on campus when I was going off. So just as I was getting on a bus, she'd be getting off and I'd grab [my] baby and get on the bus, and then I'd go get her child and take him to my house until she was done with her classes, and then she'd ride the bus over to my house. It was really a pretty complicated thing but we did it. We did it every single day!

The babysitting arrangement was highly dependent upon the regularity of the bus schedule. When the bus was late, Jean explained: "Then I would have to not get on my bus and wait, and then that would mean I would be a little bit late over to her house and her little boy would have to sit there and wait for me. And that was always a scary thing [because] he was in first grade."

All the women described the anxiety they felt juggling parenting and course work responsibilities. When asked to describe how she managed full-time school plus parenting, Melissa Kramer responded that she studied between midnight and one A.M. She said that: "Most nights I don't get to bed until about 1:00 or 2:00 because I have to go through their homework and do all of that and get baths and do laundry." The description of Melissa's everyday life differed drastically from the hegemonic constructions of the "welfare mother" who is defined as either dysfunctional and unable to cope or who needs external pressure to improve her educational skills and economic circumstances.[18] On the other hand, such balancing took its toll on their learning as well as their emotional well-being. Margaret Salmon explained: "It got to the point where I couldn't even do my homework. I was so far behind in all the readings that I just felt like why bother to do any of them. . . . But, I like the classes. I like learning what I'm learning. But I think it got to the point where I was just trying to do too much." Margaret contrasted her life as a student with a younger male student who does not have the same responsibilities. When she comes home she has to prepare dinner, do the dishes, spend time with her child, and it's only after he goes to bed that she can get to work on her homework assignments.

In an effort to serve nontraditional students, ISU established an Adult Students Center where older students could meet, gain support, and access resources such as a typewriter, computer, and tutoring. Barbara Stern and other ISU students all reported that they utilized the Adult Students Center at one point or another for information, support, or the computer. However, the center did not have the resources to deal with the more complex material needs of the women students on AFDC. No child care, emergency loans, or personal computers for home use were available. However, the opportunity to meet with other mothers in college did counter some of the isolation and stress they experienced. Barbara Stern was especially enthusiastic above the support she gained through the Adult Students Center. At the time of the interview, she served as a peer advisor for new adult students. Among the many activities made possible through the volunteer efforts of the women themselves, the center sponsored one especially crucial service. Barbara described this telephone message and contact service:

> There is a telephone [in the center]. We have little cards that you fill out and it gives your class schedule, what room you're in, from what time, and all this kind of stuff. And if something happens to one of your kids, or some kind of an emergency comes up, someone will take that message, and pull you out of class.
>
> While Barbara and other students in the study expressed appreciation for the center, their work to make the center services available to other students generated additional time commitment and responsibilities for them.
>
> Another dimension of women's hidden work is found in several women's narratives describing their role as mentors or surrogate mothers to younger students. Melissa, who is in her mid-30s, reported that the younger students "seem to seek me out, to sit next to me, to talk to me, I feel like I'm a counselor for a lot of students, that I'm there for a lot of students."

Not all the women successfully negotiated the complicated demands of mothering, poverty, and college. Audrey Bonds dropped out three-quarters of the way through her first year. She had taken fifteen credits her first semester and found that the amount of work coupled with the difficulty she had with two science courses was more than she could manage. She dropped two courses toward the end of the semester, changed her major, and enrolled for a lighter load the second semester. Toward the middle of the second semester her daughter experienced a series of medical problems. Audrey tried to manage the increasingly stressful demands but decided to drop out. She subsequently took a full-time job at minimum wage and has since quit the job to devote more time to her daughter's health care needs. She had no plans to return to college nor to return to work at the time of our last contact. The bureaucratic expectation that Audrey maintain a full college load to quality as a participant in PROMISE JOBS interfered with the flexibility she needed, first to adapt to the college environment, change her major (a common action taken by many first- and second-year college students), and then to care for her child.

Self-Esteem and the College Option

One significant progressive feature of the college option is found in the women's reported enhanced self-esteem. Reflecting on her years in college, balancing school work, work-study, community work, and mothering, Jean Marks said: "I don't understand it myself. It's like [the energy just] comes into me from someplace else and suddenly I'm doing this and it's just gonna happen and that's it. I have a real high energy level. It's pretty amazing!" The energy Jean described arose from a deeply personal desire to improve her life and fulfill some lifelong dreams. Returning to college was a long-held goal for all of the women interviewed. The increased sense of personal efficacy they experienced through their return to college contributed further to achievement motivation.[19] Not surprisingly, the women in this study broadened their educational and career goals as their self-esteem grew. The hunger for higher education that led them back to college in the first place was also enhanced by their experiences in college. For some, these experiences led to a desire for graduate education. Those who wanted to continue in graduate school recognized the economic advantage that a graduate degree would offer. A student's decision to attend graduate school is seen as a measure of success within higher education. In contrast, the women who wished to continue their education believed that welfare administrators and caseworkers viewed this as a luxury that poor women could not afford, that under the so-called social contract they should find employment immediately following completion of classroom training (see U.S. Congress, Senate 1987). The limited conception of appropriate work for women on public assistance renders invisible many women's aspirations and aptitudes for higher status careers and educational advancement.

Conclusion

From the standpoint of college women on AFDC we clearly see that the constructed target of social welfare policy, the "welfare mother," bears little resemblance those whose lives welfare policy seeks to regulate. Since welfare policy does not construct the poor single mother as college student, regulations for implementation of the FSA frequently conflict with the regulations and assumptions of higher education, which, in turn, does not construct the college student as single mother. Furthermore, constructions of gradations of dependency among welfare recipients led to implementation criteria that inhibited women who were motivated from obtaining sufficient resources to continue their educations. A narrow definition of appropriate work for women on welfare also constrained their access to training and higher education that would lead them to more secure economic futures.[20] Bureaucratic procedures adopted to assess and collect child support as a strategy to enhance the income of low-income women were found, in some cases, to interfere both with consistent receipt of AFDC as well as eligibility for PROMISE JOBS. When we shift to low-income women's standpoint, we also recognize how they resist oppressive features of social policies and utilize state provided resources to improve their lives. The women in this study worked more than the so-called double day to make sense of policy inconsistencies and compensate for the inadequate funding made available to them. Such features of women's daily lives and resistance strategies are invisible when viewed from the top-down angle of traditional policy analysis.

Neither welfare policy nor higher educational policy recognizes the actual everyday activities of low-income women nor acknowledges the additional work women must perform as a consequence of the gap between policy expectations and their daily lives. Lack of fit between the "welfare mother" constructed in and through welfare policy and the everyday actualities of the women's lives generated ongoing conflicts for those who participated in this study. Furthermore, when we shift to the arena of higher education we find that college campuses and academic policies are built upon the assumption that students are young and unencumbered with caretaking responsibilities in the home. Consequently, single mothers are particularly disadvantaged as they negotiate the college environment. Women college students on public assistance must creatively fill in the gaps between the expectations of these conflicting policy arenas and their daily lives. Through creative strategies of interdependence they also assist other mothers in the process. The effort that such filling-in work entails is invisible to policy makers and college administrators. Oftentimes these efforts are met with sanctions or other forms of disapproval as they confront the competing demands and contradictions within and across the policy arenas.

As Griffith and Smith (1990) demonstrate, mothering work "mediates class relations" and "coordinates and is coordinated by the relations of the economy on the one hand and on the other, by an educational system" (p. 5). Their case study focused on women's work as it articulated with their children's education, husband's employment, and, for some, their own paid work. This study of women on welfare in college further reveals the hidden work women do to mediate class relations and demonstrates the gendered nature of class. Low-income women's structural location as caretakers circumscribes their access to educational opportunities even when policy reform creates a small opening for them. The gender and class subtext of the state serves to confine their educational attainment as they attempt to negotiate the tensions between welfare and educational policy. On the other hand, while relations of ruling were embedded in local implementation regulations and practices, most women in this study resisted oppressive features of social welfare policies and utilized the college option to improve their lives.

Feminist state theorists demonstrate the "multitiered," class, gendered, and racial subtexts of the welfare state.[21] The subtexts include the division of labor within the state; the exclusion of women, low-income people, and people of color from the design of state policy; gendered assumptions about women's and men's unpaid and paid work; class, gender, and race policy outcomes such as the "feminization of poverty" (Pearce 1990); and gender, race, and class-differentiated social policies (for example, Widow's Pensions or Mother's Aid, Workmen's Compensation, and protective labor legislation). For example,

Barbara Nelson (1990, 124) demonstrates how the welfare state developed "two channels, one originally designed for white industrial [predominantly male] workers and the other designed for impoverished, white, working-class widows with young children" (p. 124).[22] While this study does not have the racial diversity to demonstrate how the racial subtext operates in practice, it does highlight the gendered class process. The Servicemen's Readjustment of 1944 (G.I. Bill) helped broaden the constituency of working-class men who could access higher education (Pulliam 1982). The G.I. Bill provided sufficient funding for working-class men to attend public as well as private universities at both the undergraduate and graduate levels. With the ethos of the time supporting their efforts, no daily surveillance was required to document their attendance or academic performance. Many of these men were married and had wives who supported their education through their own labor in and outside the home. In contrast, women on public assistance were treated very differently in the implementation of the college option in Iowa. The processes of surveillance undermined their autonomy. The lack of funding for child care and to support the real costs of higher education increased the labor time necessary for them to succeed in college. This study adds to the growing evidence that the state participates actively in gendering class relations. Such relations of ruling are woven in and through the legislative process, fixed in legislation, and further elaborated in local implementation regulations and practices.

The fragmentation of policies and decentralization of implementation contribute to contradictory expectations and the incorporation of unintended actors and policy arenas into the fluid state apparatus. The "situated knowledges" (Haraway 1988) of those affected by specific state policies can help uncover dimensions of state activity often hidden from view. When white rural women negotiate college and welfare their perspectives and experiences pose a challenge to the assumptions of both higher education and welfare policy and reveal the social-structural processes that contribute to women's impoverishment more generally. While women of color experience additional constraints as they negotiate the racial subtext of welfare policy implementation, they also have to navigate many of the same contradictions and bureaucratic demands highlighted by the women in this study.

While women are now mandated by welfare policy to engage in the so-called public sphere to a greater extent than in the past, they are encouraged to do so within certain limits.[23] These limitations continue to disadvantage women in the paid labor force and educational arena. They are mandated to accept low-paid jobs or, if given the opportunity to return to college, are prevented from fully participating in the academic environment. Work-study and research opportunities are closed to them since their participation interferes with their receipt of public assistance. Under contemporary welfare reform policy where recipients are limited to two years of support, caseworkers discourage women from enrolling in college courses that do not lead to a terminal two-year degree. For the women in this study, the state paid for child care while they were in class, but did not assist them in attending evening lectures or other related activities. The women who wanted to continue on to graduate school experienced disapproval from welfare caseworkers and administrators in publicly funded day-care programs who believed that the women should find work immediately after they graduate from college. What is viewed as a success in terms of the academy—namely, that a student chooses to continue her education—is discouraged in welfare policy.

The women in college who participated in this study demonstrated their courage and strength as they negotiated the private pressures that shaped their early lives. The growth in self-esteem and personal power that occurred as a result of their experiences in college enhanced their resistance to and critique of the coercive strategies embodied in welfare policy and the limits of educational policy for women with children. Despite the fact that they were pursuing a college education, their daily lives were more similar to other women on public assistance than they were to the other students in their classes. The complex daily lives of low-income women stand in stark contrast to the abstract existence of the "recipient" or "unmarried minor parent" who is the target of welfare policy.[24] Women's resistance to the oppressive features of the state serves as a challenge to "the form, the nature and objectives of welfare policy" (Williams 1989, 194) as well as to the cultural constructions of "welfare recipient." Institutional ethnography offers a tool for identifying the competing demands and contradictions faced by women on public assistance in college. The evidence gathered in the course of this research was designed to be used to advocate for more effective ways to support women in college who were receiving public assistance. By making visible the material practices and textual forces that contribute to women's difficulties in managing motherhood and college enrollment, it is possible to challenge the bureaucratic processes and sexist assumptions that contribute to women's impoverishment.

CHAPTER 9

Survivor Discourse
Narrative, Empowerment, and Resistance

In her now classic article, "Situated Knowledges: The Science Question in Feminism and the Privilege of the Partial Perspective," Donna Haraway (1988) argues that those subjugated by forces of oppression "are knowledgeable of modes of denial through repression, forgetting, and disappearing acts" (p. 584). Her argument for situating the social location and dynamics of power in the construction of knowledge raises important issues for the development and analysis of so-called survivor discourse that have yet to be explored. While those who have suffered abuse may be more likely than those who have not had such experiences to recognize the processes by which denial and repression contribute to the ongoing abuse of women and children in this society, their clearer vision is not an inevitable outcome of the experience of abuse. In fact, the term *survivor* is typically reserved for those who have self-consciously redefined their relationship to the experience from one of *victim*.[1] This redefinition can be accomplished through a combination of influences including personal reformulation of earlier experiences, therapeutic interventions, identification with cultural products such as "incest poetry" or survivor narratives and discussions with others who define themselves as survivors. Often incorporated as evidence for survivor status are presentations of public testimony or public claims that take the form of speaking out in the media or in other public forums. These forums and discursive formations often render invisible the "matrix of domination" (Collins 1990) embedded in and throughout their production and circulation. As Linda Alcoff and Laura Gray (1993) assert: "Before we speak we need to look at where the incitement to speak originates, what relations of power and domination may exist between those who incite and those who are asked to speak, as well as to whom the disclosure is directed" (p. 284).

Taking up the challenge posed by Alcoff and Gray to locate "where the incitement to speak originates," almost a decade ago I began charting the social and institutional locations from which—and the methodology through which— survivor discourse is generated to explore how "relations of ruling" (Smith 1987) are organized in and through these locations. I employ the term *relations of ruling* to help explore how the dynamics of gender, race, ethnicity, culture, and sexuality are infused throughout the institutional sites in which survivor discourse is produced. In this chapter, I offer a materialist feminist analysis of survivor discourse that attends to both the discursive and institutional practices that shape who gets to speak, who gets heard, and what the potential might be for challenging the depoliticization and reprivatization of survivor discourse.

I argue that with greater attention given to the material context in which survivors "come to voice" (Barringer 1992), go public with their experiences of childhood abuse (Naples with Clark 1996), or engage with each other in defining the meaning of these experiences in their lives, we might be better equipped to address two of the main problems faced within contemporary survivor politics: first, how to determine when and where certain strategies offer more effective challenges while others do not (for example, when speaking from "experience" is mediated, reprivatized, or oppositional in its effect); and second, how to remain sensitive to the myriad ways class, race, and sexuality, among other features of identity and history, differently affect survivors' experiences.

Materialist Feminism and Survivor Discourse

As emphasized throughout this text, materialist feminist scholars argue for an intersectional approach and resist abstracting gender from other dimensions of social identity.[2] The dynamics of gender, race, class, and sexuality are embedded in the diverse contexts through which survivor discourse is generated and challenged as well as woven into the discourse, yet few analyses provide an intersectional explication of how difference and institutional patterns of inequality shape the production and circulation of survivor discourse. According to Dorothy Smith (1989), we draw on the relevance established through "discourse institutionalized in relations and apparatuses of ruling" to interpret the world around us (p. 47). Much of the feminist work on survivor discourse emphasizes how social actors, including survivors of child sexual abuse, do not operate outside these interpretive processes and institutional practices.[3] While social actors are not free to choose the discursive frames through which to articulate political goals, some actors are situated in positions of power to control the production of discursive frames.[4]

Contemporary analyses of survivor discourse have yet to analyze intersectionally the multiple sites through which survivors of childhood sexual assault come to identify as survivors and interpret their experiences. Expert and otherwise mediated accounts, individual as well as group approaches, and structured as well as nonstructured dialogues among survivors all contribute to a multiplicity of social processes through which survivor discourse is generated.[5] Furthermore, talk shows, celebrity biographies, newspaper accounts, fiction, songs, poetry and dramatic presentations, survivor-generated newsletters, and research studies also inform the shape and content of survivor discourse.[6] Each of these diverse sites is further organized by social relations of class, race-ethnicity, culture, and sexuality, relations that change over time. Furthermore, those from different class backgrounds will have different access and relate differently to various productions or approaches within the complex construction of survivor discourse. In addition, as Janice Doane and Devon Hodges (2001) note, "Incest narratives produced under different historical conditions are distinguishable from one another, but even roughly contemporaneous stories that share generic similarities are not simple clones of one another" (p. 3).[7]

Some survivors of childhood sexual assault may not find it necessary to claim a public position within the discourse nor to enter the public discourse (although they are obviously implicated in survivor's discourse in significant ways).[8] Despite the pervasive belief in the importance of breaking the silence and speaking out about early childhood abuse in earlier accounts of survivor discourse,[9] not all of those who have experienced sexual abuse as children may find appropriate institutional sites in which, or sympathetic confidants with whom, to share their experiences. Furthermore, as Alcoff and Gray (1993) write, "The coercive stance that one must tell, must join a support group, or must go into therapy is justly deserving of the critique Foucault offers of the way in which the demand to speak involves dominating power and an imperialist theoretical structure" (p. 281).[10] One way to identity those who are left out of the discourse or who are coerced to speak is to clarify whose voices are surfacing within each institutional or local site through which survivor discourse is constructed and expressed. In this way we can identify the gaps, fissures, and silences as well as the voices and institutional locations that dominate the discourse.

The feminist movement to end violence against women was conceived in the consciousness-raising groups of the women's liberation movement during the late 1960s and early 1970s.[11] Within these groups women learned to move beyond discussion of privately experienced problems into political action. Feminist activists successfully raised public awareness of the privately experienced problem of wife abuse by naming the problem, then generating strategies to fight violence against women in all areas of social life. Activists worked with politicians to pass legislation that would protect women from abusive spouses and punish abusers. They negotiated with the police to develop effective community responses. They created hotlines and other services for battered women. They succeeded in earmarking public funds to support the development and expansion of battered women's shelters as a primary strategy to help women leave violent homes and relationships. Consciousness-raising strategies and feminist activism also led to a recognition of the extensive problem of sexual and physical abuse against children perpetrated by parents, primarily fathers, and other male relatives. Thus, feminists challenged the hegemonic myth of the nurturing nuclear family form and the long-held denial of childhood sexual abuse termed "a Freudian cover-up" by Florence Rush (1980).[12] The effective feminist challenge led to changes in law, a lengthening of the time frame for prosecution, a network of survivors groups, and an extensive recovery industry. It also prompted a backlash from powerful quarters, most prominently illustrated by the False Memory Syndrome Foundation founded in 1992 by parents accused of child sexual abuse. I examine the contours of the repressed memories/false memory debate in a subsequent section. In the next section, I discuss consciousness raising and the limits and possibilities of giving voice to survivors' experiences for an oppositional survivors' movement.

Giving Voice to Experience and the Limits of Survivor Discourse

In her assessment of consciousness raising (CR) processes, Deborah Gerson (1995) cautions that "the process of 'unlearning to not speak' does not solve the problematic of what is to be said, what is to be done" (p. 33). Her analysis raises questions about the efficacy of the call for survivors of childhood sexual abuse to "come to voice" (Barringer 1992) as grounds on which to build an oppositional survivors' movement. In her reflection on the potential for "insurgent collective" identities developed within CR groups to serve as the basis for collective social action, Gerson concludes: "The small group enabled women to forge an 'insurgent collective identity,' but the power to strategize and organize a movement to overcome the social conditions of that identity remained unrealized" (p. 29). The lack of a central organization to coordinate anti-institutional activity further inhibited collective political action (see Joreen 1973).[13] In addition, Gerson (1995) adds, "Speaking truth to power does not topple it, and the freeing of our voices has made it clear that women have many voices, many experiences, many truths" (pp. 33–34). While faith in the radical potential of consciousness raising has been shaken since the 1970s, contemporary feminists interested in developing an oppositional survivors' movement continue to promote consciousness raising as a vital political strategy.

Biddy Martin and Chandra Mohanty (1989) raise a concern that poses an even greater challenge to "speaking truth to power" and to working collectively with others who are coparticipants in struggles for social justice (p. 206). They point out that there is an "irreconcilable tension between the search for a secure place from which to speak, within which to act, and the awareness of the price at which secure places are bought, the awareness of the exclusions, the denials, the blindnesses on which they are predicated." Furthermore, as Patricia Hill Collins (1998) notes, "In the context of a new politics of containment in which visibility can bring increased surveillance, breaking silence by claiming the authority of experience has less oppositional impact than in the past" (p. 51). However, recognizing the limits of finding voice and speaking out need not result in an unwillingness to deal with the risks associated with such efforts. Rather, as Collins (1998) notes in her discussion of bell hooks's notion of self-reflective speech, "dialogues among individual women who share their individual angles of vision" can contribute to "the process of crafting a group-based point of view" that, in turn, can provide the grounds for collective action (p. 47).

The dilemmas of difference and depoliticization embedded in CR groups and other forums where survivors of child sexual abuse engage with one another can also be found in analyses of individual survivor accounts. As Louise Armstrong (1994) argues, the challenge for survivors is not only to have "the courage to think and to speak in one's own language" but "to make that language heard in the larger world" (p. 273). Yet how do we move from these local and limited sites of politicization to a more effective and broader movement? Doane and Hodges (2001) point out the tendency in early feminist accounts to construct the survivor as sexually innocent. In an effort to mobilize outrage against childhood sexual abuse, these narratives denied "all sexual feeling to the child" (p. 115). In contrast, they argue, authors Dorothy Allison (1992) and Sapphire (1996) offer complex fictionalized incest narratives grounded, respectively, in the world of poor rural whites and poor inner-city blacks that resist creating "a victim neither innocent nor blamable, neither passive nor free" (Doane and Hodges 2001, 117). In their assessment of the more complicated incest narratives produced by authors Allison and Sapphire, Doane and Hodges find "an alternative story that acknowledges asymmetries of power without sentimentalizing or desexualizing the female child" (p. 115). By challenging a reductive analysis of incest and complicating the construction of survivors to incorporate the intersection of gender, race, and class, writers such as Allison and Sapphire shift the standpoint of telling and foreground the ways race and class inequalities limit the opportunities for some women to come to voice about their experiences of childhood sexual abuse and to be heard when they do speak out.

British scholar Michele Crossley (2000) calls for narrative analyses that include attention to "the 'interchange of speakers' in a 'defining community' of which one forms a constituent part" (p. 73).[14] In this way, discourse analyses that fail to locate the material, contextual, and cultural context that surround and are woven through the production of diverse and overlapping narratives "tend to lose sight of human agency and personal subjectivity" (Crossley 2000, 73). The materialist feminist approach I recommend remains sensitive to the complex and shifting constellations of power in different locations, in CR groups as well as in self-help groups, in reading strategies and in processes of identification, in narrations of experience as well as in other modes of expression. While I agree that experience is a powerful basis on which to identify issues and create linkages with others, as a political strategy it remains limited, for it is necessarily bound up within particular social locations and discursive frames. The methodological challenge for an oppositional survivors' movement is to go beyond the local expressions of particular experiences to target the processes by which such experiences are organized.

Feminist activists and scholars of the 1970s contributed to the burgeoning literature on sexual violence against women that included exposing the "best-kept secret" of childhood sexual abuse (Rush 1980; Russell 1986).[15] Some of the earliest feminist accounts such as Louise Armstrong's *Kiss Daddy Goodnight* (1978) and Judith Herman's *Father-Daughter Incest* (1981) presented "telling" as the key to the politicization of survivors as well as to their mental health (Doane and Hodges 2001). A decade later feminist scholars foregrounded "the limits to the value of revealing secrets" in discussing the transformative potential of survivor's discourse (Cvetkovich 1995, 358). Many feminist writers recognize the importance of language for giving "voice—meaning—to our experiences" and shaping our subjectivity (Weedon 1987, 33).[16] However, the context in which "giving voice" takes place shapes the political and oppositional possibilities of such expression.[17] Furthermore, not all survivor accounts, even those generated without expert mediation (a strategy Alcoff and Gray recommend to abolish the separation "between experience and analysis embodied in the confessional's structure," offer similar political analyses [1993, 282]). What role do feminist "experts" play in legitimating or reprivatizing survivor discourse? What constitutes survivor discourse? What are the differences between survivor accounts that derive from individual narratives and those that result from collective CR strategies? When we shift to collectively generated survivor accounts, how do we treat the diversity of perspectives embedded within them? How do relations of ruling structure, in a materialist sense, what is possible to "know" within particular locations serving as the sites for CR groups and other forums that facilitate the production and circulation of survivor discourse?

My materialist feminist analysis of survivor discourse is grounded in the everyday practices of knowers who are differentially positioned within survivor discourse. This approach, drawn from Dorothy Smith's (1992, 91) "everyday world" sociology of knowledge, provides a strategy for locating survivor discourse in the material practices that give rise to diverse resistance strategies.[18] My approach is also influenced by the work of Nancy Fraser (1989). In her materialist feminist appropriation of Foucault, Fraser identifies three forms of "needs talk" used to make claims within the modern welfare state: "oppositional," "reprivatization," and "expert" discourses. Fraser explains the "plurality of competing ways of talking about needs" as follows: "(1) expert needs discourses of, for example, social workers and therapists, on the one hand, and welfare administrators, planners, and policy makers, on the other; (2) oppositional movement needs discourses of, for example, feminists, lesbians and gays, people of color, workers, and welfare clients; and (3) 'reprivatization' discourses of constituencies seeking to repatriate newly problematized needs to their former domestic or official economic enclave" (p. 157). Fraser argues that these discourses "compete with one another in addressing the fractured social identities of potential adherents" (p. 157). By attending to the relations of ruling embedded in the expert discourse on childhood sexual abuse as well as identifying the processes through which hegemonic assumptions of gender, race, class, and sexuality undergird dominant constructions, it is possible to highlight sites of resistance and contradictions posed by oppositional formations. This strategy is also useful for exploring the contradictions of reprivatization.[19]

Contemporary medical and psychiatric discourse on survivors of childhood sexual assault might obviously fall within the arena of expert discourse; yet upon further examination the line between expert and oppositional discourses appears shifting and murky especially when we insert the discursive and practical interventions of feminist psychotherapists.[20] Feminists who spoke as experts on childhood sexual assault contributed to an oppositional discourse that challenged the traditional psychoanalytic expert model.[21] Survivor discourse may appear to fall within the category of oppositional discourse. However, survivor discourse may also become reprivatized or reinscribed as expert discourse (Fraser 1989).

Feminist Experts and Survivor Discourse

Survivor discourse is often posed in contrast to expert discourse, which is legitimated through a distinction between different forms of knowledge production, one that derives from personal experience and emotional pain versus one grounded in more systematic and presumedly objective truth claims. Fraser (1989) includes "therapeutic discourses circulated in public and private medical and social service agencies" in her definition of "expert needs discourses" (pp. 173–74). She argues that while most expert needs discourses are "restricted to specialized publics," the "expert and rhetorics . . . are disseminated to a wider spectrum of educated laypersons, some of whom are participants in social movements" (p. 174). This is clearly the case in the psychotherapeutic constructions of childhood sexual abuse and the treatment needs of survivors.

Feminist challenges to psychoanalytic approaches that denied women's reports of childhood sexual abuse pointed out how the practice of psychoanalysis reproduced gender inequality as well as the abuse of women (Rush 1980; Herman 1981). Reports of sexual abuse committed by therapists, feminists argued, further illustrated how mental health professionals could misuse their power over women patients.[22] Feminist interventions into the medical/psychiatric discourse on childhood sexual abuse and incest included challenges from inside as well as outside the medical and psychiatric establishment. Feminists who were also psychotherapists spoke from their vantage point as trained professionals and experts on women's mental health needs.[23] While some may have experienced childhood sexual abuse or other forms of violence, their claims were typically supported through their experience treating women clients in need of mental health services.[24] More recently, feminists have raised concerns about the "trauma paradigm" that dominants contemporary psychotherapeutic approaches. Social work educator Mary Gilfus explains that the trauma paradigm, "renders trauma as an individual psychological response that is ultimately constructed and diagnosed as psychopathology" (1991, 1241). In contrast to the "trauma paradigm," Gilfus argues for "a survivor' centered epistemology that is oriented toward recognizing strengths as well as injuries, is culturally inclusive . . . and builds on the wisdom of victimization and survival that is part of women's lives" (1999, 1239). Since many feminist experts framed their analyses within the wider critiques offered by the feminist movement, their expert discourse can be viewed as a *bridge* discourse that helped link the feminist critiques with the wider social terrain (Fraser 1989, 174).[25] Feminist psychotherapists consequently contributed to the blurring between the expert construction of incest and survivor discourse.[26] Janice Haaken and Astrid Schlaps (1991), who make a point of distinguishing between their identities "as feminists and as psychoanalytic therapists, rather than as feminist therapists," recognize a "tension and theoretical divide between the personal and the political realms of experience" (p. 40). Drawing on feminist critiques of science, medicine, and psychoanalysis, feminist psychotherapists and researchers highlighted the role of social structural, particularly patriarchal, processes in shaping women's mental health; argued for a centering of women's perspectives in the therapeutic process; and emphasized the role of empowerment in healing from mental illness.[27] These major claims shaped the feminist expert stance on the treatment needs of adult survivors of childhood sexual abuse as follows: first, given the extent to which women are abused by men in this society, the experience of abuse is a common occurrence that typically goes unrecognized or unchallenged in therapeutic settings; second, centering women's standpoint means that women should be believed when they describe abusive experiences or, at the very least, women should be treated as credible representatives of their own experiences; and finally, empowerment as a form of healing can include confrontation with perpetrators of abuse through personal letters and other methods, including legal action as well as more collective public speakouts.

These claims were tied to oppositional discourse drawn from the feminist anti-violence movement. In recent years feminist clinicians have tempered the proscription to "believe women" with the recognition that "there is no singular woman's story" (Haaken 1998, 8). In a similar vein, feminist clinicians influenced by narrative approaches to psychology argue that "subjectivity as/in knowledge and power" should be understood "according to cultural discourses and cultural textuality" (Reavey and Gough 2000, 341). The narrative approach to therapeutic work with survivors also emphasizes the need to view people's accounts as situated rather than as either essentially true or false.[28] In this way, feminist and narrative therapeutic approaches directly contest what is at stake in the heated "repressed memory/false memory" debate.

Post-Traumatic Stress and Questions of Memory

The debate between proponents of "repressed memory" and "false memory syndrome" and, especially, the role of "recanters" (now termed *retractors—* those previously self-identified as survivors of childhood sexual abuse) in this debate further illustrate the need to deconstruct as well as locate the social and political context for survivor discourse.[29] As feminist practitioners Susan Contratto and M. Janice Gutfreund (1996) assert, "the 'recovered memory controversy' itself de-legitimizes survivors including (over the 'protests' of the anti-survivor movement) those whose abuse is corroborated by other evidence" (pp. 2–3).[30]

Reviewing the debate between supporters and opponents of "repressed" memories, I was struck by some similarity among critiques and a profound divergence among explanations.[31] Feminist and other survivor-oriented therapists who accept the phenomena of repressed memories are critical of the dominant therapeutic regime for denying the extent to which childhood sexual assault occurs and the complex post-traumatic symptoms that follow.[32] For the most part, they criticize the patriarchal and authoritarian structure of medical, psychiatric, and social work discourse and practices.[33] Supporters of the false memory position also critique the professional psychological community, but the content of their critique focuses on psychologists' role in planting false memories and promoting an irresponsible "hysteria" about the pervasiveness of childhood sexual abuse.[34]

Some feminist clinicians agree with critics of repressed memories that lists of generic symptoms such as those offered by E. Sue Bloom (1990) or Ellen Bass and Laura Davis (1988) misrepresent the complex experiences of survivors and presume observable and lifelong aftereffects.[35] Janice Haaken (1998) asserts that: "By ignoring the social context of memory retrieval and by treating memory as a sacral function that 'reveals' itself in an unmediated fashion, the authors [Bass amd Davis] suspend critical awareness of the various influences shaping how women's stories get told" (p. 197). Furthermore, Haaken argues, "While the trauma model may be mobilized to break through a deadening cultural insensitivity to human suffering, it also may be advanced defensively in countering scrutiny of therapeutic interventions in that suffering" (p. 76).

Those who challenge the existence or extent of repressed memories also criticize the organization of mental health and child abuse services, which, they argue, creates an institutional bias against accused parents. They argue that "memory work"[36] creates a context for, among other problematic outcomes, therapists implanting memories or validating false memories in their clients. Writers on both sides of the controversy are especially concerned with the additional harm done by the law enforcement and legal system when cases of childhood sexual abuse are investigated and subsequently brought into court.[37] Of course, proponents and opponents of repressed memories construct the victims of the legal system in contrasting ways: proponents concentrate on the further trauma suffered by survivors who are not believed or are constructed as complicit in their abuse while opponents center on the experiences of the "falsely accused" and the harm done to the family unit as a whole.[38]

An organization that has been central to the growing public attention to false memories is the False Memory Syndrome Foundation (FMSF). The FMSF was founded in 1992 by Pamela Freyd, the mother of psychologist Jennifer Freyd (1996), following Jennifer's accusation that her father sexually abused her. Pamela Freyd, who has a doctorate in education, has been a vocal critic of her daughter's account.[39] The FMSF has raised a large amount of money and attained public visibility and notoriety in a relatively short period of time when contrasted with the time that it took for the problems of childhood sexual abuse to reach a similar level of public discourse.[40] A contributing factor to the public receptivity achieved by FMSF is its appeal to family values and the construction of repressed memory advocates as undermining the nuclear family form.[41] According to FMSF, women who claim they were survivors of incest alienate themselves from their families and from the support that they require.[42] The FMSF inverts the construction of "victim" and "perpetrator," defining parents who are accused of sexually abusing their children as the victims and the adult daughters and their feminist therapists as "perpetrators" of false memories.[43]

False memory proponents are critical of the lack of "scientific" evidence developed to support the theory of repressed memories.[44] Some are especially vocal about the role of radical feminists and recovery books such as *The Courage to Heal* (Bass and Davis 1988) in creating an environment conducive to the development of false memories (see Wakefield and Underwager 1994). Repressed memory supporters, on the other hand, are concerned that the rise in attention to false memories undermines efforts by clinicians and survivors alike to demonstrate the extent to which children are sexually abused (although most false memory authors deny that is their intent [Loftus and Ketcham 1994; Yapko 1994]). Feminist clinicians concerned with the use of science to delegitimize survivor accounts, however, question the ways memory researchers remove the study of memory from "the context of other post-traumatic responses and study it in isolation as if there is no relationship between how people cope with trauma and how they recall it"(Brown 1996, 16).[45] Writers on both sides of the debate believe they are generating discourse in opposition to the dominant practices in the field of psychotherapy, although the contrasting standpoints—one rooted in the spoken experiences of women survivors, the other in the interests of the so-called falsely accused—profoundly shape the oppositional possibilities of their critiques.

Haaken and Schlaps (1991), as feminists and psychoanalytic therapists, articulate a divergent position within this debate on repressed memory of childhood sexual assault. Rather than focus on the truth or falsity of memories, they challenge therapeutic practices of "incest resolution therapy" and conclude that "incest resolution therapy risks over-objectifying incest in that incest becomes the unifying event around which the patient's symptomatology and difficulties are organized" (p. 39).[46] While they highlight the psychoanalytic dynamics between clinicians and their patients, they also explore the social and political context in which incest resolution therapy operates. Haaken and Schlaps make a strong argument for the power of the medical marketplace to push therapists toward short-term and "new and improved" methods of treatment (p. 45). They conclude with the feminist question: "Who decides the importance of sexual abuse in a woman's experience?" and highlight the dilemma of experience in their response: "The obvious answer is the woman herself, but we are concerned that many current applications of the literature on sexual abuse understate the clinical complexity of this question" (p. 46). Their solution to the dilemma lies in their commitment to "a broad-based psychodynamic approach" (p. 47). They make no mention of alternative settings for recovery nor do they address the broader debate on the role of self-help activities and mutual aid groups in the healing process. They do not discuss how the dynamics of race, class, gender, and sexual orientation shape the experience of survivors as well as shape the psychodynamic therapeutic context. Haaken and Schlaps do note that working-class and poor women and women of different cultural backgrounds may not have access to these therapeutic contexts and emphasize that poor women are treated with suspicion when their children are victims of child sexual abuse.

While Haaken and Schlaps begin their article "Incest Resolution Therapy and the Objectification of Sexual Abuse" by addressing the importance of feminist CR practices of the women's movement for "exposing the reality of women's abusive experiences within the family" (p. 40), they conclude with a reevaluation of the privatized psychotherapeutic setting. This should come as no surprise, for as therapists, Haaken and Schlaps are situated within this expert location. While they offer a sensitive critique of the practice of psychotherapy and sociopolitical constraints that might form the grounds for psychotherapeutic abuse, their goal does not include tackling a key issue of feminist praxis—namely, how women incest survivors might be empowered to determine the significance of childhood sexual abuse in their lives and to contribute to an oppositional movement. Yet when we shift to other sites in which survivors speak about their experiences of abuse, such as through the myriad texts and cultural products now defined as part of a so-called incest recovery movement, we confront other processes of reprivatization.

In the next section, I turn from the more privatized feminist therapeutic site in which survivors speak their experiences of abuse to a discussion of the multiple sites in which survivors speak to each other and in public in order to explore the possibilities for a more effective oppositional survivor discourse and diverse to identify sites of resistance. Since these sites are more dispersed and more easily accessed than the typically costly offices of feminist therapists, survivors from different and less privileged racial-ethnic, class, and cultural backgrounds may approach the process of healing through the so-called recovery enterprise.

The Recovery Enterprise and Reprivatization of Survivor Discourse

One of the recovery texts most vilified by the false memory advocates and one of the most widely read by survivors is *The Courage to Heal* by Ellen Bass and Laura Davis (1988). Laura Davis is an incest survivor. She shares her own experiences alongside those of other survivors in the book but notes that she did not originally identify as a survivor when she first started working on the book, that it took her a year before she could incorporate her own experiences of sexual abuse. Carol Barringer (1992) highlights the significance of this fear "to speak the truth" for other survivors as well. Barringer emphasizes that: "To speak of her abuse, the survivor must not only defy her perpetrator's threats and the societal taboo, but she must also give up the very protections that have enabled her to survive—the forgetting, the denial, the numbness" (p. 8). For Barringer, as for Bass and Davis, there are typical symptoms, identifiable patterns, and recommended strategies of healing for adults who were sexually victimized as children that act to construct the "incest survivor" as an identifiable "subject." Barringer, Bass, and Davis insist that the survivor knows best how to proceed through the healing process if given a nonjudgmental, safe place to explore her feelings, although they do offer a framework for healing. Further, they assert that: "If you don't remember your abuse, you are not alone. Many women don't have memories, and some never get memories. This doesn't mean you weren't abused" (quoted in Armstrong 1994, 212). This assertion is criticized by feminist writers such as Louise Armstrong (1994) and antifeminist writers as well as false memory proponents such as Wakefield and Underwager (1994), albeit for significantly different reasons.

Armstrong locates *The Courage to Heal* within a flurry of attention to incest in literature and TV that constitutes the incest recovery industry. In her provocative book, *Rocking the Cradle of Sexual Politics: What Happened When Women Said Incest* (1994), Armstrong notes with astonishment that since the publication of her book *Kiss Daddy Goodnight* in 1978, the public attention to incest has generated a lucrative incest recovery industry and a prime-time TV flood of celebrities going public with their experiences of childhood sexual abuse.[47] Armstrong (1994) writes:

> As a political story, it is a prime illustration of how it is now possible for the powers-that-be to use *noise* to achieve the same end that was once

served by repression. It is a story of how readily the solid feminist concept that "the personal is political" can be alchemistically transformed into "the *personal is the—public.*" It is, alas, the story as well of the power of the promise of "help" and the language of "treatment" to infantilize massive numbers of women, emphasizing their fragility, securing their helplessness, isolating them from the larger universe, so cementing their focus on the purely internal that it looms to fill their entire visual screen. All in the name of "empowerment." (P. 3, emphasis in original)

Rocking the Cradle of Sexual Politics offers a social history of, as well as Armstrong's personal response to, the transformation from "breaking the silence" as a political act to the more consumer-oriented and inward-turning recovery industry dominated by the media, psychiatry, and social work professions that now characterizes much of the discourse on incest and childhood sexual assault.[48] For Armstrong, the problem with the recovery-movement approach to incest is that it blurs significant distinctions between so-called symptoms such as alcoholism and eating disorders and the social structural dynamics of patriarchal power that provide the foundation for the persistence of incest and child sexual abuse in contemporary society. The recovery approach, she argues, also reduces the act of "breaking the silence" and "going public" to steps in the individual healing process. Such a formulation dilutes the original feminist thrust of the "personal as political" and undermines the collective empowerment process designed to effect more systemic social change.[49] To counter both the backlash against the survivors' movement as well as the depoliticized recovery movement, Armstrong (1994) argues: "There needs to be a greater awareness on the part of adult survivors that their experience is part of a greater social problem, and that they could play a role that can make a difference to children now" (p. 273). Further, "this would require that women reclaim their own experience, and adopt skepticism that one can find empowerment by turning power over to the 'experts.' "

However, when we turn to the process by which "adult survivors need to speak for themselves, out of certainty—not out of therapy" (p. 274), as Armstrong suggests, we face two thorny problems: first, what counts as "one's own language" or unmediated survivors discourse? and second, is unmediated survivor discourse inherently politically oppositional? These questions highlight the need to explore how survivors from different race, class, cultural backgrounds and sexual orientations are positioned differently within survivor discourse. For example, the power of what Doane and Hodges (2001) call "the official story" embedded in "middle-class discourse"—namely, "a family's private attempts to keep up appearances ... and celebrations of middle-class family life by the media, church, and state"—contributes to "self-silencing" and "internalization of the perpetrator's voice" and constrains middle-class survivors from speaking out (pp. 102–3). The presumption that working-class families have a greater propensity toward violence and inappropriate sexual behavior limits working-class survivors from speaking out for fear that their experiences will further fuel class reprisals. Lesbian survivors have expressed concern that the fact of their childhood sexual abuse has been used to explain their "divergent" sexuality. The heterosexism of many popular accounts of incest reaffirms this hegemonic construction.[50] Fortunately, lesbian survivors and others have generated oppositional discourse that challenges the heteronormativity of incest narratives to counter the hegemonic story.[51] For example, Ann Cvetkovich (1995) examines the queering of incest narratives performed by Margaret Randall's *This Is about Incest* (1987) and Dorothy Allison's *Bastard Out of Carolina* (1992) and emphasizes how "imaginative work . . . can ultimately be more 'healing' than an explicit rendering of the event" (p. 380).

Kimberly Crenshaw's (1993) intersectional approach also offers a strategy to contest essentializing narratives of women's experiences. In her discussion of violence against women of color, Crenshaw illustrates "how the experiences of women of color are frequently the product of intersecting patterns of racism and sexism" (p. 1243). This intersectional approach is evident in other work by feminists of color and antiracist scholars who examine the processes by which women of color have been marginalized within the contemporary battered women's movement.[52] I will turn now to address this last issue by focusing on a text that centers the concerns of Black women who are incest survivors. Some of the most powerful survivor narratives are written by African American and working-class authors. In fact, in their analysis of incest narratives Doane and Hodges (2001) highlight the work of authors Ralph Ellison (1952) and Toni Morrison (1994). Doane and Hodges argue that these authors effectively help reroute "the responsibility for incest from marginalized and poor people to those whose social status and authority allow them to commit acts of incestuous violence and to silence speech about them" (p. 5).

Locating Diverse Positions within the Discourse

In this section, I focus on *Crossing the Boundary: Black Women Survive Incest*, written by African American author Melba Wilson (1994). This book is simultaneously a personal narrative, a cultural and sociological analysis, and a self-help text. Wilson also offers guidance for "negotiating the professional incest industry" and for "survivors as professionals." The author starts from her experience as a Black woman, feminist, and incest survivor. Originally written for Black men and women in a British context, the U.S. edition includes two pages of resources listing U.S. psychotherapists, newsletters, health centers, and self-help groups. Wilson reviews and debunks myths about incest in Black communities, Black women's sexuality, and women loving women. Of particular interest is the attention she gives to the cultural productions of Black women. She devotes one of her seven chapters to the ways in which Black women writers have dealt with the topic of incest.[53] She recalls that she "began to realise that it is *only* in the work of these women that incest, and other forms of sexual abuse and violence against black women, appears consistently as a subject that concerns us as black people, and that ought to be on our agendas as communities" (p. 38, emphasis in original). Wilson expresses gratitude to "these women for having the courage to break the taboo of silence, an outgrowth of which was to reach out to women like me, who needed their stories in order to find the strength to tell our own" (p. 40).

Wilson highlights the significance of centering race and gender in an analysis of incest, something that few authors have accomplished, and of understanding different constraints. Wilson weaves her own story throughout the text and offers a sensitive articulation of the ways racism and sexism shape Black women's experience of incest more generally and places placing specific constraints on their speaking out about the abuse.[54] While her definition of "black feminism"—"maintaining a physical, mental, spiritual and emotional well-being, as well as economic, political and social opportunities on an equal basis with men" (p. 121)—does not seem to differentiate it from other forms of liberal feminism, she incorporates the ways sexism and homophobia are embedded in Black communities and therefore offers a more intersectional feminist analysis. She captures the challenge Black women face when reporting incest as follows: "If a woman does take action, and goes to the police for example, she is likely to be condemned by her own community for betrayal and to have her own sexuality called into question by the wider community, thus reinforcing the stereotypes. If she doesn't, she is left with maintaining the silence which gives tacit approval to the abuse, and thus undervalues her own worth as a participating and *equal* member of the community" (p. 133, emphasis in original).

Wilson's analysis underscores the importance of locating survivors and survivor discourse within diverse communities and of understanding the problems different survivors face as they attempt to "go public." She points out that "the experiences of white survivors are . . . automatically assumed to hold true for black survivors of incest and child sexual abuse" (p. 169). She also specifically addresses the concerns of lesbian incest survivors within a generally "homophobic" Black community (pp. 81–85). She reports: "Though no one I spoke with felt they were lesbian because of their experiences of incest, many raised the issue of an inability to trust men as a contributing factor" (p. 83). Wilson points out that heterosexual Black women she spoke with also expressed a lack of trust in men; however, she highlights the particular difficulty for Black lesbians who come out as incest survivors within the Black community. More often than not lesbians who come out as incest survivors must also face the inevitable question of whether one's lesbianism is a direct consequence of the abuse, that "if only we could somehow resolve our difficulties with men, we will no longer be lesbians" (p. 84).

While Wilson does not analyze how Black women from diverse class backgrounds might deal differently with the process of healing from and fighting against incest, she does begin to articulate how racism shapes when and how Black women might speak out against incest in their communities. She calls for "a dialogue about sexual abuse in black communities" (p. 159) that "must, should, start one-to-one in families, and spread outward" (p. 161). She concludes with two key recommendations that would increase sensitivity to Black women's experiences of incest: "(a) a closer look at social and cultural factors in child sexual abuse; and (b) more direct input by black women survivors into the therapeutic process for dealing with it" (p. 170). However, she does not offer specific strategies for accomplishing these broad-based goals.

For Wilson, as for many who write about healing from incest, the primary solution lies within the "therapeutic process." While she includes the names and addresses of self-help, mutual aid, and 12-step groups for incest survivors in her list of resources, her recommendations for healing center on professional, expert solutions. She calls for changes within the professional therapeutic establishment and the Black community, but fails to highlight more collective strategies for healing and challenging abuse in Black communities and beyond. As a consequence, her text is simultaneously critical of and supportive of expert models for intervention—albeit sensitized by attention to social and cultural factors. Wilson's text straddles both expert and survivor discourse in a complex presentation. On the one hand, by incorporating the ways in which sexism, racism, and homophobia circumscribe the lives of Black women, especially those who have experienced childhood sexual abuse, Wilson offers a more politicized analysis than is found in most self-help and personal narratives. On the other hand, by centering psychotherapy as the primary site in which survivors of incest and childhood sexual assault can find healing, Wilson also participates in the continued reprivatization of survivor discourse. However, as bell hooks (1993) stresses in *Sisters of the Yam: Black Women and Self-Recovery*, "the more black women work on our self-recovery, increasing our self-esteem, ridding our lives of debilitating stress, rejecting the learned impulse to try and meet everyone's needs, the less we will be seduced into co-dependency" (p. 76). Furthermore, hooks notes that no black woman she knows "is engaged in the process of self-recovery who is not also involved with rethinking the sexist attitudes towards women that are the norm in this society" (p. 157). This view resists positioning personal and collective empowerment as mutually exclusive. On the contrary, they are seen as interdependent processes of healing, politicization, and resistance. In fact, it can be argued that personal healing and individual competence building are necessary for achieving collective empowerment and therefore the two processes cannot be disentangled.

Negotiating Mediation when Going Public

The extent to which a survivor may choose to go public as a survivor is also infused with dynamics of race, gender, sexuality, culture, location, and personal history. What can be spoken and how it is framed are further influenced by the context in which the public disclosure takes place. Sociologist Norman Denzin (1990) points out that the very organization of public disclosure is subject to such "glossing" effects that there may be little hope for "pure" unmediated speech to survive. Again, the dominance of the recovery industry over the shape and content of survivor accounts greatly inhibits the development of an unmediated and oppositional survivor discourse.[55] As Elayne Rapping (1996) argues, "The new language [of 12-step groups and self-help books] is devoid of the kind of political inferences which colored the feminist and New Left ideas from which it ultimately sprung" (p. 107).

Despite the apparent value of the recovery discourse for survivors of numerous personal traumas, countless critics point out the limits of such discourse, especially when manipulated by the mass media. These critiques must be addressed if we are to effectively challenge the dominant discourse that shapes responses to adult survivors. For example, Norman Denzin (1990) maintains that in groups like Adult Children of Alcoholics (ACOA), Adult Children of Sex Addicts, and Adults Recovering from Incest, as participants "attempt to take back their lives and to make sense of the experiences" they had growing up, they risk turning themselves into "commodities sold in the public market place" (p. 13). Denzin asserts that: "We've entered an era where nothing is any longer hidden. The dividing line between public and private lives has dissolved; anyone's personal troubles can now serve as a front-page story, couched as a banal morality tale with a happy ending" (p. 13).

Linda Alcoff and Laura Gray (1993) also acknowledge the potential for cooptation that occurs when survivors speak out about their sexual abuse. Following Michel Foucault, Alcoff and Gray caution that the confessional mode of speech characteristic of survivor discourse "participates in the construction of domination" (p. 263). Yet, as they point out, Foucault also demonstrates in his work that "speech is an important site of struggle in which domination and resistance are played out" (p. 263). Discourse generated from the point of view of survivors has "paradoxically appeared to have empowering effects even while it has in some cases unwittingly facilitated the recuperation of dominant discourses" (pp. 262–63). To diminish the cooptation of survivor discourse, they argue that, in addition to eliminating the "expert mediator," we abolish the separation "between experience and analysis" (p. 282). They explain:

> A nonbifurcating ontology of experience and theory requires us to relinquish the idea that in reporting our experiences we are merely reporting

internal events without interpretation. To become the theorists of our own experience requires us to become aware of how our subjectivity will be constituted by our discourses and aware of the danger that even in our own confessionals within autonomous spaces we can construct ourselves as reified victims or as responsible for our own victimization. (P. 284)

In a postmodern attempt to counter such unself-conscious glossing of experience and to engage the reader more actively in the process—"thus projecting more of themselves into it, and taking more away from it" (Ronai 1995, 396), Carol Ronai presents her experiences of childhood sex abuse through a "layered account" that weaves personal memories with sociological analysis and statistical data. Ronai's creative text illustrates how survivor accounts can be infused with "the psychological literature on recovery" but that survivors can find that such "frames are useful" (1995, 396). As a sociologist, she is critical of the dominance of individualist recovery discourse; yet she admits that these narratives reflect her experience. She negotiates the tension between her experiences of incest, the comfort she finds in certain recovery literature, and her sociological training by challenging the form of producing and writing her account.[56]

In an effort to avoid the problem of expert mediation and such "glossing" effects, some survivors have turned to 12-step groups, a context in which all members share a common status. However, many critics argue that the recovery discourse generated by 12-step groups also shapes the subject and, therefore, glosses over the individual's experience.[57] For example, Denzin argues that in these groups, the lived experiences of the subject are reified in categories not of their own creation.[58] Contesting this reading of 12-step groups, incest survivor Judy Lincoln (1990) responds to an article in *Survivor Resource Chronicle* that criticized 12-step groups: "S.I.A. [Survivors of Incest Anonymous] is a 12-step program. It has all of the above recovery tools in it. It is run by survivors. Everything it has to offer is SUGGESTED! It doesn't say you have to forgive. Forgiveness is a choice! It speaks of a higher power and you interpret that for yourself. Your perception of God is up to you. . . . I am proud to be a 12-stepper. We do care, and we know what we are doing!" (p. 3). However, even if we appreciate that members experience their recovery through 12-step groups as personally empowering, the 12-step format explicitly discourages collective political engagement which is a foundational element for social change.[59] Such a stricture against social change efforts is especially troublesome to feminists who perceive 12-step groups as inhibiting the development of a survivors' movement.

After considering the 12 steps developed for Sexual Abuse Anonymous, Armstrong (1994) asks: "If this were a Twelve-Step program designed by rapists, could they have improved on this program of sin and redemption (sin, yours; redemption task, yours)?" (p. 220). Again, Armstrong considers such an approach to be highly depoliticized and one that poses no challenge to the abusive patriarchal order.[60] In opposition to the individual and apolitical solutions that mark the 12-step approach, survivor-generated organizations and feminist CR groups can pose explicitly political challenges to the dominant expert and recovery discourse on childhood sexual abuse. Not surprisingly, such approaches also present their own challenges and limitations.

No one is immune from internalized oppression. A central part of healing from childhood sexual abuse includes confronting the myriad ways survivors have been made to feel responsible for the abuse. However, discourse generated by those who have experienced childhood sexual abuse differs fundamentally from recovery discourse produced by medical experts or psychologists. The process by which such situated knowledge is generated contributes to the sense of empowerment experienced by survivors and others within the so-called recovery community. To ignore the process renders invisible the community context through which "recovery" takes place.

Survivor-Generated Sites for the Production of Discourse and Survivors' Praxis

Survivor-generated organizations and newsletters have the potential for creating a network among survivors that could broaden into a wider political movement. For example, VOICES (Victims of Incest Can Emerge Survivors) in Action, Inc. was founded in 1980 by Diane Carson and several survivors of child sexual abuse and their allies; the group sponsors conferences, publishes a newsletter, and provides referrals for self-help groups and therapists. However, these organizations frequently remain tied to the recovery enterprise or emphasize individual personal testimony and education over collective action. The July/August 2002 issue of "The Chorus," the newsletter published by VOICES in Action, included a number of articles on "sexual abuse by priests." Therapist Stephen Braveman called for "educating others about childhood sexual abuse" (p. 10). The issue also included a book review of *Set Us Free: What the Church Needs to Know from Survivors of Abuse* (Annis, Loyd-Paige, and Rice 2001), a study of 67 victims of abuse by priests. The reviewer emphasized one suggestion for change: "Pastors should speak out from the pulpit about abuse, about the denial of many churches to hear victim's complaints" (Blair 2002, 9). None of the articles encouraged a more activist response by church members or other interested parties.

The stated purpose of *Incest Survivor Information Exchange* (1990), another publication for survivors, "is to provide a forum for female and male survivors of incest to publish their thoughts, writings and art work and to exchange information. We encourage articles, poems, graphics, and one or two lines about who you are or how you are or what you think" (p. 23). Such a forum fosters individual expression and diverse perspectives on various issues that seldom coalesce into particular political strategies to attack abuse against women and children. In my survey of newsletters from both of these groups, I could find no discussion of the different challenges women of color and working-class women face in coming to voice as survivors or healing from incest. Little attention was given to the concerns of lesbian survivors of incest and child sexual abuse, although there were a number of columns devoted to male survivors. Given the lack of attention to issues of race, class, and sexual orientation and to political action, these survivor organizations fail to articulate a feminist political praxis to contest the deep-seated social problem of child sexual abuse and backlash against survivors who speak out. However, they provide important information and support for many survivors.

A somewhat different approach is evident in the more explicitly political representation of Looking Up, a Maine-based organization founded in 1983 by survivors Gayle Woodsum and Barbara Bostad. However, Looking Up describes itself as a nonprofit service organization with the philosophy:

> that each individual is already in possession of the qualities necessary to create a life filled with growth and satisfaction. The nontraditional programs offered through "Looking Up" provide survivors with opportunities that, according to Woodsum, "those who abused them made certain were not ever available to them. The most important of those opportunities are to speak the truth, be heard and believed; to be accepted without judgment; to know that isolation has been enforced and can now be broken; to understand that the abuse and its effects is the fault of offenders and not victims; to catch the first glimpse that life can be worth living." (*Survivor Resource Chronicle* 1990, 8)

In contrast to the individual recovery and service orientation of the statement of philosophy, the lead article by Lina Dunning in the same issue in which this statement appeared was titled "Fighting Back." According to editor Dunning (1990), survivors "must not lose sight of the enormous courage it takes to speak out to be a part of the movement against violence" (p. 1). Since the organization constructs itself primarily through the dominant social service and recovery approach that inhibits political action, it does not outline the political strategies needed to counter the social structural dimensions of violence against women and children, nor does it provide a forum in which such strategies could be articulated and debated.

If survivor narratives are easily coopted by expert mediation or inward-turning recovery solutions (even when these narratives are generated within survivor organizations), how can they form the basis of a more politically progressive and oppositional praxis? In her article "Talkin' 'Bout a Revelation: Feminist Popular Discourse on Sexual Abuse," Debi Brock (1990) argues that "women who reveal themselves to have been sexually abused when young risk having this become constructed as the crux of their identity—considered the formative experience of who they are" (p. 14). She then asks: "How then can women try to take control over their own lives by speaking about their experiences of sexual abuse?" This query mirrors concerns raised by Alcoff and Gray (1993) and Armstrong (1994).In the next section, I explore the processes through which survivors and feminist allies can contribute to a politically progressive and oppositional survivors' praxis, and highlight the challenges of such an endeavor.

Consciousness Raising and Oppositional Survivors' Praxis

Feminist theorists who support CR groups as a site for politicization of personal experiences highlight the ways in which consciousness-raising processes help contest dominant discourses (see Weedon 1987). However, as hooks (1984) points out, CR strategies do not necessarily provide the context through which participants can recognize how social structural dynamics such as capitalism, colonialism, or racism shape their experiences. Furthermore, since CR groups are developed in and through our local networks, members may not discover the diversity of experiences that organize women's lives and consequently marginalize women of different racial-ethnic, class, and cultural backgrounds. The lack of diversity within specific CR groups circumscribes their potential as sites through which to develop a broad-based survivors' movement.

With the lessons learned from past experiences with CR groups, with the growth of self-help and mutual aid models of engagement among survivors, and with greater sensitivity to dynamics of race, class, and sexuality in differentially shaping women's experiences, we can revision consciousness raising as a strategy for the development of oppositional survivor praxis. Consciousness raising as a product of a self-reflective dialogue between survivors of childhood sexual assault does not guarantee the development of a "higher" form of consciousness nor does it necessarily lead to political action. An engaged political struggle is required for survivors to theorize their own experience. Through such engaged collective struggle, individual expressions of experience are put up against others' expressions in the context of generating collective resistance strategies that further clarify how personal experiences are organized in and through relations of ruling. In this way, we are prevented from viewing personal experiences as particularist expressions and resist the tendency to generalize from them.[61] The materialist feminist approach I adopt is one that engages with concrete political struggles and in collective efforts to develop resistance strategies. It also requires collaboration of feminist allies as well as survivors in efforts to generate a diverse coalition politics such alliances can provide the basis for broad-based resistance to backlash against survivors who speak out and against the systems of oppression that contribute to the persistence of child sexual abuse.

The approach I recommend cannot be adopted in isolation. It requires a process of reflection embedded in engaged conversations or dialogues among survivors and allies, among those who claim the identity of survivor as well as those who do not. It is a process enacted in the world, in dynamic relationship with struggles of people who are "actually located; . . . active; . . . at work; [and] . . . connected with particular other people in various ways" (Smith 1992, 91). Self-help, CR, and therapy groups all provide the contexts in which survivors and allies can contest limited medical and psychiatric analyses of survivors, individualist theories of incest and childhood sexual abuse, and disempowering healing strategies. Proscriptions against explicitly political analyses and activism within certain self-help and 12-step groups need not deter survivors and allies from engaging in such activity. Survivor organizations need not be primarily vehicles for the reproduction of depoliticized recovery discourse or individualist analyses of survivors' experiences. In fact, I believe that any collective forum offers the potential for survivors to recognize each other and move beyond personal sharing that must, by necessity, form the basis for movement toward an oppositional stance. The materialist feminist strategy recommend takes the process of reflective dialogue as part of these ongoing political struggles in which survivors and their allies orient toward progressive social change.

Conclusion

Expanding the constituency of those who contribute to the construction of an oppositional survivor discourse is key to the political viability of a progressive survivors' movement. Feminist CR group strategies and reflective dialogue among survivors remain central to this process of reconceptualization. However, if we are to assess the limits as well as the possibilities of such activities for the development of oppositional discourse and political practice, we must explore how relations of ruling operate in and through these shifting and complex sites. Recognizing the diversity of ways survivors of child sexual abuse "come to voice" also expands the horizon of sites through which women engage in local conversations and "come to voice" about their experiences. In addition, it is important to recognize that allies as well as survivors of abuse can participate in creation of resistance strategies and oppositional politics.[62]

This dialogic materialist feminist approach retains the "process of reflective practice" (Alcoff 1988, 425) in the creation of survivors' narratives and makes evident the struggle for self-definition.[63] It also offers a strategy for broadening the voices and diversity of perspectives that can contribute to a politically oppositional survivor discourse. This approach counters the tendency toward the representation of "sexual abuse" as "a monolithic category and a totalizing discourse which blurs women's experiences" (Brock 1990, 14) and ignores the diversity of women's experiences across the intersectional terrain of race-ethnicity, class, sexualities, and culture. Such a political goal involves a commitment to ongoing dialogue among survivors as well as the creation of processes that are open to reconceptualization and contestation. The transformative possibilities of such dialogue are linked to explicitly political struggles. Survivor discourse need not be reified in individual survivor narratives nor coopted by apolitical recovery strategies nor limited by segregated and fragmented local contexts. By locating survivor discourse in the material as well as the discursive context, we can develop more effective strategies for a broad-based and politically oppositional survivors' movement. This strategy also facilitates linking the struggles against childhood sexual assault to broader feminist movements in such a way that new voices and new analyses can be inserted into the political process.

Feminist allies must continue to recognize the value of speaking out and of personal testimony by survivors for processes of personal empowerment. Personal empowerment is the necessary stepping stone toward building a more inclusive movement. Furthermore, going public forms the very grounds for collective dialogues among us.[64] Twelve-step groups and survivor-generated newsletters and organizations also provide an important context in which survivors can come to identify the collective and social structural conditions that shape individual experiences of childhood abuse. While we need to acknowledge the limits of such strategies, we should also honor the needs they fulfill for survivors who have long suffered with their memories and pain in silence and isolation. "Breaking the silence" endures as a foundational strategy through which survivors can challenge the continued denial of abuse that occurs within the patriarchal family and other institutions in contemporary society.

The processes through which survivor discourse is generated as well as the institutional and social location of survivors as authors of their own lives shape the extent to which survivor discourse stands in opposition to oppressive expert discourse. Furthermore, in some cases such a separation between expert and survivor sets up a false dichotomy. Not all discourse generated from the social and institutional location of experts is inevitably oppressive, especially if we acknowledge the value of feminist theoretical and political perspectives.[65] Feminist praxis remains central to the development of an oppositional survivors' movement and provides the grounds for linking this movement with other struggles to contest the dynamics of oppression in contemporary society.

CHAPTER 10

Survivors Going Public
Reflections on the Limits of Participatory Research

In 1996 I published a chapter cowritten with Emily Clark on "going public as survivors of childhood sexual abuse" in a book called *Feminism and Social Change: Bridging Theory and Practice,* edited by Heidi Gottfried. Emily and I are both survivors of childhood sexual abuse. The chapter was based on an ongoing dialogue we had between 1990 and 1992. Our dialogue ranged from discussions of our personal histories that included the stories of our abuse and recovery to reflections on contemporary events and dreams for the future. The published chapter focused on the motivation for and our experiences of "going public" as survivors. I was the primary author; Emily shaped the dialogue and commented on the numerous drafts. To a certain extent, we saw ourselves as collaborators, although the product was more an expression of my concerns than Emily's. Consequently, the written document of our dialogue was not jointly conceived nor evenly shaped. In this chapter, I revisit our dialogue and discuss the contradictions embedded in my attempt to generate a participatory research project.

Feminist activist researchers argue for a participatory approach to research as an important strategy for developing knowledge for advocacy and social change.[1] When I began this work in 1990, I was especially convinced that participatory research with adult survivors and other women who had experienced violence against them had the potential for generating survivor-centered discourses that could broaden our understanding of the myriad forces contributing to violence against women. I had also hoped that a reflective dialogic process would help illustrate how personal narrative and dialogue can form the grounds for the generation of oppositional consciousness and empowering strategies for fighting childhood sexual abuse. Finally, I also believed that by documenting our dialogue, Emily and I would generate situated knowledge about the coming out process.

The Satori Healing Collective

I first met Emily when I joined the Satori Healing Collective in early 1990. The Satori Healing Collective in Des Moines, Iowa, was formed in the spring of 1989 by survivors and supporters who were dissatisfied with the lack of treatment alternatives available for adult survivors of childhood sexual abuse. The dominance of apolitical and individualized medical and psychiatric approaches limits the options for adult survivors as well as the possibilities for an oppositional survivors' movement. Mental health workers are not immune to the societal pressure to deny the prevalence of childhood sexual abuse. As a consequence, many survivors who turn to mental health professionals for help do not receive the acceptance, safety, and trust needed for recovery. There is also evidence that a disproportionate number of health professionals and social service workers are themselves survivors of childhood sexual abuse (Rew 1989; M.B. Williams 1990). Therefore, the activist research project included the complicated goal of raising the awareness of mental health workers as well as reaching out to survivors themselves.

The primary goal of the collective was to help raise the consciousness of social service providers and health professionals about the effects of childhood sexual abuse and to generate survivor-centered approaches to recovery. In the course of our healing, Emily and I both chose to use our personal experiences as grounds for research, public education, and advocacy for and with other survivors. We began with the belief that healing from childhood sexual abuse occurs most effectively through collective group processes and mutual aid coupled with supportive counseling.[2] Both of us have benefited from the support of other survivors and counselors who helped us "name" our childhood experiences and examine how they affected all areas of our lives. Both of us became committed to transforming the treatment available for adult survivors through sharing our experiences with mental health professionals, students, and other community members.

The collective included a survivor who counsels other adult survivors and several women who had been in counseling with her. I was introduced to the group by one of my students who was a member of the group. Emily, a native Iowan, was one of the original members of the collective. Before I became involved with the collective, my work with adult survivors was personal rather than professional. When I moved from New York City to Iowa for a faculty position in Social Work and Sociology at Iowa State University, I began working with other survivors in Ames, Iowa, and helped organize three different weekly support groups in Ames. I had not spoken out in other public forums about my experiences as a survivor until I met Emily and the other collective members. Unfortunately, the collective was a short-lived effort. We last met formally in May 1990. At that time, for a variety of personal and structural reasons, individual members decided to pursue the goals of the collective in their different ways.

Reflections on the Dialogic Process for Participatory Research

When I met Emily, I was impressed by her willingness to speak out about her abuse in professional forums. Her courage inspired me in my desire to "go public." At my initiation, Emily agreed to reflectively explore our process of going public as survivors and consider what would constitute effective approaches to healing and empowerment for survivors of childhood sexual abuse. At that point, I was unclear exactly how we would use the dialogue, but thought it would be helpful to us as we continued to go public. Somewhat later I thought it would be useful to present a paper about our dialogue. This step eventually led me to suggest we publish it in the collection edited by Heidi Gottfried (1996).

Through reflective dialogue with Emily, I wanted to make self-conscious our process of going public as survivors of childhood sexual assault as well as the consequences of going public. We taped and transcribed our discussions and analyzed our previous dialogues as a basis for subsequent conversations. My desire to adopt this strategy followed from my belief that reflective practice—where we are "both observers (interpreters) and objects of observation (or interpretation)" (Morawski 1988, 189—can add to the wider efforts to transform the discourse on adult survivors of childhood sexual abuse as well as contribute to our personal empowerment as authors of our lives. Survivors experience abuse and recovery from a variety of different personal and social locations influenced by numerous social, cultural, and economic factors. Despite this recognition, I hoped that the product of our exchange might be used to encourage others to engage in dialogue about their experiences and document the challenges faced by going public.

In reflecting on the process we used to construct the chapter in *Feminism and Social Change*, Emily and I discussed the dilemma of interpretative authority and aired our different goals and frustrations. An earlier version of the chapter was first presented in a session on "Feminist Research Agendas: Conflicts and Dilemmas" at the Midwest Sociological Society (MSS) meetings held in Des Moines, Iowa, on April 13, 1991. When I approached Emily with the idea of discussing our ongoing conversations about going public in this session she was understandably less interested in addressing the "conflicts and dilemmas" in feminist research then in having the opportunity to participate in a public forum with sociologists, whom she viewed as professional educators who may meet adult survivors in the course of their work.

After the MSS session, when I proposed revising the paper for submission to *Feminism and Social Change*, she asked: "How will this help adult survivors? Isn't it just mental gymnastics?" She thought that a chapter in a book that did not target mental health providers or survivors themselves seemed frivolous. But over time two important shifts occurred. First, Emily reports, I softened my emphasis on feminist methodology. The shift in my perception of the project occurred as I responded to Emily's questions about why I found it necessary to develop an explicitly feminist model for going public. Emily challenged me to explain my terms and why the project of documenting the process of going public and its effect on us as survivors was so important to me. These clarifications helped her better understand my desire to contribute to debates in feminist research as well as my motives for going public. More importantly, our dialogue moved us both to rethink the overall project.

Second, Emily said she began to "realize the significance and need for what *you* are doing." The operative word here is *you*. She did not say *we*. In other words, the dialogic process changed each of us, enhanced our mutual understanding, and helped reshape the project itself; but it did not result in a more egalitarian product. Despite my theorizing about an alternative approach to knowledge construction and a commitment to feminist participatory research, the product clearly privileged my voice. Since many of the issues we dealt with in our conversations derived from my concerns as a feminist sociologist and since the project, as I defined it, was conceived in dialogue with others in the field attempting to develop alternative methodologies that are feminist, participatory and emancipatory, it inevitably privileged my concerns. But this recognition is one of hindsight and one that developed as a consequence of my dialogue with Emily, rather than something I could see clearly at the onset of our collaboration.

The Limits and Possibilities of Feminist Participatory Research

Emily and I were both interested in exploring the factors that led to our desire to go public with our childhood experiences. This theme ran through our on-going dialogue. Our struggles to survive the traumas of childhood sexual abuse led us to aggressively resist efforts of others to define us or to develop a totalizing image of "the incest survivor." In fact, it is this commitment that moved both of us to speak out and encouraged our collective dialogue. As we proceeded to discuss and reflect on our experiences, Emily and I recognized the shifting nature of going public; that is, as we told our story the salience of certain aspects of the story differed for each of us "in relation to shifting interpersonal and political contexts" (Martin and Mohanty 1986, 210).

While Emily and I agreed on the overall purpose of our work for and with other survivors, each of us had a different conceptualization of the purpose of this dialogue about the work. The difference can be partially understood in terms of our contrasting personal histories and social locations. The dialogue that became the backdrop for this chapter took place on numerous occasions from the winter of 1989 to the fall of 1992. Emily, a mother of three boys, worked full-time in the business she owned with her husband. While we both were born in the early 1950s, we grew up in different social milieus and had differing political histories. I, a native New Yorker, became politically active in the anti-Vietnam war movement and, later, the women's movement. I define myself as a feminist and view my recovery through a feminist lens. By contrast, Emily, a native of Iowa, regards both the women's movement and feminism as irrelevant to her work for and with adult survivors. Despite our different views on feminism, we both placed finding our voices and speaking out as central to our survival. It is this commonality in our survival strategies that made our dialogue possible.

At first, Emily felt frustrated with my focus on feminist methodology. Although she did not see how the development of a feminist methodology would directly help adult survivors she agreed to "help" me with my project. In explaining to Emily my commitment to adopting feminist participatory research strategies for our activist project, I discussed my take on the limits of traditional social science for understanding the experiences of adult survivors of childhood sexual abuse. I explained that feminists argue for a methodology designed to break the false separation between the subject of research and the researcher.[3] The objectification of research subjects limits our understanding of the social construction of meaning and experience as well as the process by which the relations of ruling organize consciousness and daily life. The dominant way to conduct research in sociology is one that stresses objectification, random sampling, control groups, standardized measurement, large sample sizes. This is why I found the feminist critiques of social science so important. I firmly believe that our positionality affects how we go about our work. Whether we are self-conscious about this phenomenon or not, our social location shapes the way we proceed to gather information and draw conclusions from that information. And as healers, as caretakers, health care workers, or as researchers, I believed that if someone had not dealt with his or her own issues or were unaware of one's limited angle of vision then it would get played out in some ways that could cause adult survivors of childhood sexual abuse further harm.

In response to Emily's questions, I explained my belief in the importance of identifying the consequences of speaking from our own experiences and my desire to avoid reproducing dominant ideology through the speaking-out process. I also shared my belief that one of the most effective ways to understand the experiences of adult survivors of childhood sexual abuse is through a dialogic process. Through dialogue, survivors can contribute to a new understanding of the healing process in order to define effective strategies for recovery, and, hopefully, to design more effective political activism against childhood sexual abuse.

While Emily and I agreed about the importance of speaking out or going public, we differed on what that process meant and how to generate a "survivor-centered" approach. Emily was especially skeptical about my desire to explore our methodology for going public and to contribute to debates about participatory research and feminist methodology At one point, Emily said that she thought the issues I raised regarding feminist methodology were "bullshit." Why then did she continue to work on the paper and the revisions for the chapter? At first, she said she did so as a act of friendship. Subsequently, she explained that through our ongoing dialogue she finally came to understand what

I saw as the significance of feminist methodology, i.e., the goal of challenging the limited ways that traditional researchers study childhood sexual assault and assess the needs of survivors. Although she did not see how the project addressed the immediate needs of survivors, she recognized that "if nothing else, it will focus changes. People will start questioning themselves, and that's not nothing."

Despite my theorizing about an alternative approach to knowledge construction and a commitment to feminist participatory research, the final product was inevitably more an extension of my concerns than of Emily's. Since the issues dealt with in the published chapter derived from my social location as a feminist sociologist and were conceived in more abstract dialogue with others in the field attempting to develop feminist methodologies that are feminist, participatory and emancipatory, the product clearly privileges my voice. Emily contributed her vision to the issues I raised, raised her own concerns, and challenged some of my unstated assumptions during our conversations as well as in response to drafts of the chapter. Through the dialogue, new issues were identified and new questions surfaced. As a consequence of her participation in the project, Emily said she developed a clearer understanding of feminism and a greater appreciation for the issues of methodology. I was, in turn, forced to explore the investment I had in debates on feminism and method and to revise my goals for the dialogue.

Conclusion

While I shaped the themes and overall structure of the chapter, Emily was a powerful presence throughout the process, challenging my presuppositions, questioning the validity of the project, helping me clarify my terms. In fact, much of my thinking about motivations for and the effects of going public is informed by Emily's sensitive and grounded analyses of her own experiences. Does this honest self-reflection on the imbalanced authoring process invalidate the value of reflective dialogue for survivors' discourse? I do not think so. However, it does highlight the difficulty in generating egalitarian feminist participatory research strategies.

Even when we jointly identified questions for further discussion, on reexamination we often interpreted the meaning of these questions differently. For example, Emily expressed concern that the critique of expert discourse would discourage survivors from seeking the support they need from professionals, whereas I thought it was important to distinguish between what survivors know and experience from what experts define for them. However, such positions did not emerge immediately. We contested a variety of issues before we recognized the source of our mutual misunderstanding. The dialogic process generated frustration and disappointment as we faced our differences in perception and understanding. However, when we were able to struggle through our frustration and clarify our positions to gain mutual understanding, we experienced a deepened level of communication in subsequent conversations. As a consequence of ongoing dialogue, we shifted our divergent interpretations and, to a certain extent and on certain occasions, adopted the other's point-of-view; and in other instances, we agreed to disagree.

A key strategy for me in contesting the limits of traditional social scientific research for social change has been to help generate alternative approaches informed by feminist praxis through continued dialogue and community work with those outside the academy. Emily, on the other hand, does not see the immediate relevance of academic discourse and feminist methodology for her goals. In fact, her personal history includes a negative experience in a college psychology course that turned her away from further higher education. She wants to create a text shaped by her autobiography that will appeal to a wider audience than the text in which our chapter appeared. However, through our reflective dialogue Emily and I learned a great deal from each other and take these lessons with us as we pursue the different avenues we have chosen to fight childhood sexual abuse.

PART **V**
Conclusion

CHAPTER 11

Negotiating the Politics of Method

Feminist researchers are neither immune to internalized oppression nor to the hegemonic constructions of research practice that insist on a distanced and objectifying angle of vision. Even when we adopt participatory and dialogic strategies, we cannot eliminate all power imbalances. By sifting the insights of feminist standpoint epistemologies through a materialist feminist lens informed by postmodern and postcolonial analyses of power, language, and subjectivity, I have been able to make visible the complex and shifting power relations that infuse ethnographic encounters. Throughout the book, I discussed the possibilities as well as the limits of reflective approaches for enriching ethnographic practice and activist research. As Biddy Martin and Chandra Mohanty (1986) point out, "a refusal to accept responsibility for one's implication in actual historical or social relations, . . . a denial that positionalities exist or that they matter, the denial of one's own personal history and the claim to a total separation from it" (p. 208), which contributes to the relations of ruling that pervade everyday life including academic discourse and practices.

Despite effective postmodern arguments against the utility of feminist standpoint theories, I have found a multidimensional approach to standpoint epistemology provides methodological guidance for analyses of women's political praxis. Postmodern and poststructural critics of standpoint theorizing are concerned that the notion of standpoint presumes a fixed and identifiable subject and retains a modernist approach to "knowledge," one that views certain social locations as more true or authentic than other standpoints. These critics typically refer to the embodied version of standpoint which is salient in some aspects of standpoint epistemology. In contrast, for my multidimensional approach, I conceptualize standpoint as embodied in individual knowers' spoken experiences and social identities and produced in communities as well as a site of inquiry.

An *embodied* perspective (one that is tied to particular social locations and particular positions in a community) emphasizes how researchers' social positions (not limited to one's gender, race, ethnicity, class, culture, and place or region of residence) influence what questions we ask, whom we approach in the field, how we make sense of our fieldwork experience, and how we analyze and report our findings. Feminist ethnographers drawing on this dimension of standpoint epistemology caution us to attend to our own social locations and remain sensitive to how our interactions in the field shape what we come to understand about social life in particular sites and among different groups. In my effort to utilize reflective practice in my research, I have also tried to recognize the agency of research subjects who also contribute to what can be seen and how to interpret what comes into view. As a consequence, I have had to acknowledge the limits of my control over what happens in the course of fieldwork. This is a humbling experience, to say the least, and often difficult to accept given that, as social scientists, we have frequently been trained to systematize fieldwork encounters and gain command of the fieldwork enterprise.

A second dimension of standpoint epistemology that is especially powerful for ethnographic investigation is one that conceptualizes standpoints as constructed through interactions between researchers and the persons researched in ever-changing social and political environments. This dimension of standpoint epistemology treats standpoints as *achieved in community* and as shifting over time and place. By locating the analysis of standpoint within community contexts and embedded in networks of relationships that shape different standpoints, I have been able to uncover the multiplicity of perspectives and the dynamic structural dimensions of the social, political, and economic environment that contour these differences. However, some perspectives will not surface during the course of a research study, therefore "findings" are always partial and unstable, and will most research efforts remain a work-in-progress.

The third dimension, as illustrated by Dorothy Smith's approach, treats standpoints as places in which to begin investigating the relations of ruling that shape everyday life. Smith's institutional ethnographic approach to standpoint offers more of a methodological guidepost for investigation than other dimensions of standpoint. While attending to the relations of ruling in everyday life, Smith's approach includes sensitivity to the power of discourse and textual bases of ruling as they organize daily life in ways that are not necessarily visible to the social actor.

As a consequence of recognizing the power of discourse in organizing everyday life as well as shaping policy innovations and political activism, my methodological approach has been further enriched by a materialist feminist appropriation of Foucauldian discourse analysis. As illustrated in chapter 4, a multidimensional standpoint epistemology informed by analysis of discourse revealed the fluidity of constructions of insiders and outsiders in the context of ethnographic investigation. As an outsider to the rural communities I studied in the 1990s, I was taken into confidence by others who themselves felt like outsiders. Because the local social construction of an "insider" was mythical, most residents perceived themselves as outsiders for one reason or another. The changeable nature of insider/outsider status in these rural towns was revealed with changes in the racial-ethnic composition as a result of economic and social restructuring. I also utilized a feminist materialist discourse analysis to examine how rural residents coped with and made sense of the changes within their communities and identified the contradictions in agrarian ideology that was evident through an analysis of the social dimensions of economic restructuring in rural Iowa (Naples 1994). The social and economic changes challenged residents' self-definitions, perspectives on rural community life and previously taken-for-granted notions of gender, racial, ethnic, and class relations. They viewed these changes through contradictory discourses on agrarianism and *gemeinschaft* that served as resources as well as impediments to social support and community development.[1]

My materialist feminist discourse analysis of the changes in conceptualization and implementation of community control and welfare policy uncovered the complex discursive, institutional, and historical factors that limit the effectiveness of social policy innovations, even with reference to the modest goals defined by decision-makers themselves. The separation of social life into various policies administered by separate divisions of government furthers the gender division of labor and enhances racial and gender inequality. Social movement actors are also implicated in the process by which progressive claims for justice are transformed and undermined over time. In the case of the claims by poor residents of African American urban communities to gain control over the programs serving their neighborhoods in the 1960s and 1970s, the initial success of the community control frame must also be understood as a consequence of its resonance with conservative forces who, in turn, were able to coopt the frame for reactionary purposes. My analysis of community control foregrounds how racism, class, sexism, and other dimensions of social inequalities are manifest even in the most radical political projects. With this heightened analytic sensitivity to the relations of ruling within progressive social movements and claims-making strategies, movement actors may become more effective in resisting the cooptation of movement frames for reactionary purposes.

Throughout my career as a researcher, I have tried to remain reflective of my own assumptions and interactions as an individual analyst of social life, as a disciplinary practitioner, and as a social activist. Donna Haraway persuasively analyzes "the *mediated* nature of all experience and of the ways that power differentials permeate those mediations" (Kruks 2001, 114, emphasis in original). I believe that reflective practice offers a resource to help make these mediations more visible and to increase the analytic complexity of ethnographic investigation. This approach to reflective practice helps make evident "the unmarked presences" (Burman 2001) in, and relational construction of, ethnographic accounts.

Attending to the role of emotions in the conduct and analysis of fieldwork is an important and undertheorized aspect of reflective practice. Anthropologist Susan Greenhalgh argues that emotions are "necessary features of all knowledge, influencing the values, observations, and thoughts that make up the process of intellectual inquiry" (Greenhalgh 2001, 55). Following Alison M. Jaggar (1989), Greenhalgh emphasizes "that emotional reactions that fall outside the bonds of convention—what she [Jaggar] calls 'outlaw emotions'— offer particular promise for feminist theory" (Greenhalgh 2001, 56). Furthermore, she argues, "atypical emotional responses, which are usually appropriate to the person's social situation of subordination, can facilitate the building of critical theory by motivating investigations into new issues and by enabling new versions of reality that challenge dominant views" (p. 56).[2]

Analyzing my emotional reactions as well as those with whom I interact in fieldwork and through texts has posed one of the greatest challenges for me. I have yet to fully incorporate the role of emotions in my assessment of different fieldwork experiences. However, in a recent autoethnography of the events leading up to my father's funeral, I foregrounded emotions as a strategy to analyze the processes by which family is constructed and maintained (Naples 2001). In this essay, I explored how, like other social phenomena, family must be achieved and constructed on a daily basis. How we perform family is shaped by material as well as cultural practices that are often invisible to us as we interact with family, friends, lovers, co-workers. In this autoenthographic effort, I benefited from dialogue and feedback from friends and co-participants. This dialogic strategy provided me with some analytic distance from the painful experiences described in this essay. Despite consulting with co-participants, my introspective ethnography by definition privileged my angle of vision. However, I argue, the practice of ongoing self-reflection provides one strategy to make visible how daily interactions are shaped by dominant constructions and structures of family.

It has been well-established in women's movement activism that language developed through collective dialogues and consciousness-raising processes can provide a basis upon which activists can identify and challenge oppressive practices in social institutions and in everyday life (Peattie and Rein 1983). Those who participated in the consciousness-raising groups of the women's movement learned the value of naming "the problem that has no name" (Friedan 1963). Once the problem was named as "patriarchy" or "sexual harassment" or "wife battering" or "acquaintance rape," we could politically challenge what previously had been defined as personal, private troubles. In my efforts to identify recovery discourses that are grounded in survivors' reflective understandings, I drew on the lessons of consciousness-raising in the hope that such a process could provide the basis for resistance to the medical/ psychiatric discourse and the limited treatment options that dominate in this area. In my view, the process of reflective dialogue among survivors of childhood sexual abuse goes beyond commonsense understandings to produce "theoretical knowledge grounded in lived experience" (Treicher 1989, 74) to reauthorize survivors' subjugated knowledges. However, this process is also limited by the ways in which hegemonic individualist and depoliticized thera-peutic discourse infuses "experience." Here I found a materialist feminist ap-propriation of Foucault's approach to discourse to be most helpful.

Another theme addressed in this book relates to the value of collaborative analysis and writing for broadening the perspectives represented in the final product of activist research. The consciousness-raising approach that served as a model for my dialogue and writing project with Emily Clark about going public as survivors of childhood sexual assault was premised on our defined identities as survivors (see chapter 10). However, as in other activist projects that utilize a dialogic approach, we experienced ourselves as both insiders and outsiders to each other's point of view at various moments throughout our di-alogue.³ Analysis of this activist project speaks to the limits of consciousness raising as the sole strategy for feminist praxis. As sociologist Deborah Gerson (1995) accurately notes: "Feminists, using similar bodies of experience can come to very different strategic answers" (p. 33). Our collaborative effort made self-evident how and where our views differed and the difficulties we had in negotiating our differences.

Despite the difficulties and limits of these resistance strategies, I continue to believe that processes of dialogue and consciousness raising remain central for the development of oppositional discourses and feminist praxis. Even though there are many dilemmas associated with these interrelated strategies, I have yet to discover effective alternatives for making visible the relations of ruling that shape research practice. I also believe that recognition of the limits of these ap-proaches can help temper expectations and claims made as a consequence of these efforts. While feminist ethnographic practice and activist research can be enriched by collective dialogue among co-participants, the personal relation-ships and political investments that are evident during the research process are ever changing and therefore provide an unstable ground for fixing, at any one point in time, how reflective dialogues should inform analysis. However, I re-main convinced through my myriad research endeavors that a reflective and dia-logic process can provide a rich context through which to critically assess how dominant discourses infuse our own understandings of what counts as data and whose voices are privileged in our ethnographic accounts. For example, a reflec-tive dialogic process can offer a context in which conflicts in interpretation are revealed and, more importantly, renegotiated in a more egalitarian fashion than is found in traditional social science methodology or in other approaches to activist research.⁴

Dialogue is offered as a strategy to enhance the reflective practice re-quired for deepened ethnographic understanding.⁵ One the one hand, this reflective approach implies the development of more egalitarian and partici-patory field methods than traditionally utilized in social scientific investiga-tions. On the other hand, dialogue can "easily elide questions of power" (Newton and Stacey 1996, 297). In recognition of this potential problem, educational theorist Elizabeth Ellsworth calls for the development of "multi-vocal alliances" that acknowledge how the dynamics of power are relational and not unidirectional. My approach to activist research is consistent with Ellsworth's call for "multivocal alliances." However, the development of effective strategies for initiating and nurturing such alliances offers one of the most difficult challenges for feminist praxis. At the National Women's Studies Conference in 1986, human rights activist Charlotte Bunch (1987) stressed the value of "diversity among feminists" as "a resource for gaining a broader understanding of the world" (p. 51). However, the process by which feminist activists generate coalition-building dialogues remains unclear in the context of the fragmented and contentious world we inhabit. Furthermore, as Bernice Johnson Reagon pointed out in 1981, coalition-building work can be a difficult and uncomfortable, even dangerous, endeavor.

With these challenges in mind, I remain optimistic that feminist praxis will continue to invigorate ethnographic investigation, narrative analysis, and activist research, among other methodological approaches. I view the relationship between feminism and method as a work-in-progress. Heeding calls for reflective practice, feminist researchers will continue to reformulate their epistemological frameworks and methodological strategies in response to different research experiences, shifting feminist theoretical debates, and personal reflections. By extending our repertoire of research strategies designed to minimize inequities in the knowledge production process, I believe we will be in a better position to generate knowledge that can support collective action for social, political, and economic justice. In sharing the lessons I have learned in my travels as a feminist and a methodologist, I hope to encourage others to join in this collective journey.

Appendices

A. Researching Urban Community Workers in New York City and Philadelphia

In order to situate their community work in a historical context and to examine the state's role in political socialization, I centered the experiences of community activists who were employed as community workers in the antipoverty community action programs in New York City and Philadelphia between 1964 and 1971 (see Naples 1998a). Follow-up interviews conducted in the mid-1990s focused on gathering an oral narrative of their work, community, political, and family activities since the mid-1980s; changes in political analyses and practices; when relevant, children's political analyses and practice; and personal and political visions for the future. The interviews ranged from one and a half to four hours and included one or more separate sessions.

The sampling techniques used to identify the women were designed in response to the different organizational structures of the antipoverty programs in each city. Philadelphia created a centralized commission to oversee the work of 12 area offices. A sample of 22 community workers were chosen from a central list of staff, representatives, and recently retired or laid-off workers. The decentralized structure of New York City's antipoverty programs required a different sampling procedure. The Lower East Side of Manhattan and neighborhoods in Harlem and the South Bronx were identified for their active antipoverty programs. Researchers and professional community workers who had been active in these communities during the early years of the community action programs were asked to identify women they had known in their own community work. I then contacted those who had been named and asked them for other recommendations. These women were contacted and asked for additional recommendations.

A total of 64 community workers were interviewed for this study. Forty-two of these women lived in the communities in which they worked; 11 were nonresidents. Of the 42 resident community workers identified for this study, 26 were African American, 11 were Puerto Rican, 4 were European American, and 1 was Japanese American. The women ranged in age from 36 to 72. Seventeen of the original 52 community workers women interviewed in 1984–85 were reinterviewed in 1995.

B. Studying Community Action in Rural Iowa

The rural data derive from an ethnographic study of two small towns in southwest Iowa designed to explore community-based responses to economic change with a special focus on the experiences and perspectives of low-income rural women. The ethnography highlighted the vibrant social processes and cultural beliefs that shaped responses as well as resistance to the economic and social changes. One of the two towns experienced a major demographic shift as a result of the expansion of a local food-processing plant. The proportion of nonwhite residents was negligible in 1990 when the study began. By 1996 over 10 percent of the population was Mexican and Mexican American.

The research reported in this book highlights one aspect of the findings from the 12-year study; namely, the efforts of community workers in these two towns who were in the social position that enabled them to act as bridgeworkers between the white European Americans and the Mexican and Mexican American residents who have moved to the town for employment in the expanded plant. This research also includes exploration of the racialization experiences of Mexican and Mexican American residents as well as their perception of the effectiveness of a wide array of community workers. Since there was only one community action program serving this town and only one worker employed in this program, it was necessary to develop a broader definition of community worker in order to explore the social action processes in this small town. As a consequence, community workers, who were identified through ethnographic observation and interviews with community residents, encompass a broad range of community members including paid and unpaid, full-time and part-time workers, and those who have willingly chosen to play a bridging role as well as those who have been thrust into this position as a consequence of their language skills, social position, or employment.

Data are drawn from both ethnographic and in-depth interviews. Ethnographic data included observation of numerous community events such as school board, city council, and economic development committee meetings, church and other community events, and informal gatherings. In addition, open-ended responses to in-depth interviews were used to identify the salient experiences of community workers and other relevant community residents. Data consist of: (1) interviews with a subset of Mexican, Mexican American, and white European American community workers; (2) interviews with other community residents who are well-placed to comment upon the effectiveness of the community workers including clergy, educators, public officials, and other community leaders; and (3) interviews with additional Mexican and Mexican American residents in order to assess their perspectives on race relations and what influence the community workers have had in their daily life experiences.

Two interview schedules were designed. The first, focused on the community workers, explored their motivation for community work, their varying perceptions of their role in the community, their goals, and their perceived effectiveness. The second, focused on assessing the wider community's reaction to their efforts, especially the Mexican and Mexican American residents, included a section on experiences with and perceptions of the community workers' bridging activities. The second interview schedule also gathered background family and demographic information, migration patterns, household survival strategies, family relationships, support network, evaluation of economic development and community process, and experiences of discrimination.

Notes

Chapter 1

1. See, for example, Abu-Lughod 1993; D. Bell 1993; Coffey 1999; Collins 1990; Mohanty 1991a, 1991b; Naples 1994; Stanley and Wise 1990; D. Wolf 1996a.

2. Education and human development scholar Mark Tappan (2001, 47) discusses "interpretive" approaches to social and psychological research as linked to "hermeneutics, the art and practice of textual exegesis or interpretation, is the methodology most appropriate for understanding 'recorded expressions' of human existence and experience." Drawing on Wilhelm Dilthey's philosophy Tappan cautions that "interpreters must be aware of the power that they hold to shape the understanding of others' lived experience" (p. 46).

3. As Leslie Bloom (1998, 35) further explains:

   > Power is situated and contextualized within particular intersubjective relationships. In accordance with Cotterill (1992, 605), I want to make a case that "issues of power and control which are fundamental to the research process shift and change, and within the interview situation the researcher as well as the researched is vulnerable. To deny that is to deny the subjective experience of the researcher as a woman."

   Also see Ristock and Pennell (1996).

4. Following Chéla Sandoval (2000), I do not capitalize the terms *first world* and *third world*. In her discussion of "differential social movements," Sandoval defines "U.S. third world feminism" as "the deliberate politics organized to point out the so-called third world *in* the first world" P. 191 n. 1, emphasis in original.

5. Examples of these texts in the area of qualitative research techniques are Hammersley and Atkinson 1995; Lofland and Lofland 1995; Strauss and Corbin 1990.

6. Two recent texts that do foreground epistemology or theoretical traditions include John Creswell's (1998) *Qualitative Inquiry and Research Design: Choosing Among Five Traditions*, and Jaber Gubrium and James Holstein's (1997) *The New Language of Qualitative Method*. Gubrium and Holstein attempt to blur the supposedly firm boundaries between such approaches like naturalism, ethnomethodology, or postmodernism—three of the four approaches they explore. To incorporate research strategies focused on "the affective, visceral, and subjective dimensions of experience" (p. 56), Gubrium and Holstein include a fourth approach they term "emotionalism." After describing how researchers within the four approaches "talk" about their methodological strategies, the authors highlight the special sensitivities of, and tensions within each approach and call for "interpretive practice" that combines elements of all four. For example, they argue that "postmodernism contributes most significantly to qualitative inquiry by spurring researchers to critically examine their methodological assumptions and choices with an eye to expanding their own epistemological and empirical horizons" (p. 97). Further, they assert that since "*what* is talked about [as in naturalist and emotionalist inquiry] can't be separated from *how* the talk is conducted [as in ethnomethodogy], the *whats* and *hows* of meaningful interaction are equally important to understanding whatever has interactionally transpired" (p.118, emphasis in original). [This discussion also appears in Naples 1998d.]

7. See, for example, Behar and Gordon 1995; Clifford 1986; Clifford and Marcus 1986; Hammersley 1992; Marcus 1998; Mascia-Lees, Sharpe, and Cohen 1989; Van Maanen 1988.

8. See, for example, Hurtado 1996.

9. See, for example, Campbell and Manicom 1995; Coffey 1999; Devault 1999; D. Wolf 1996.

10. See, for example, Prus 1996.

11. Standpoint theorists like Dorothy Smith, Nancy Hartsock, and Patricia Hill Collins (1998), find postmodern interventions suspect, given, as Collins (1998) asks: "Who might be most likely to care about decentering [the subject]—those in the centers of power or those on the margins?" (p. 127). Collins is concerned that "postmodern views of power that overempha-

size hegemony and local politics provide a seductive mix of appearing to challenge oppression while secretly believing that such efforts are doomed." She concludes that a "depoliticized decentering disempowers Black women as a group while providing the illusion of empowerment" (p. 137). See also Barrett and Phillips 1992; Butler and Scott 1992; Clough 1994; di Leonardo 1991; Hartsock 1987; McNay 1992; Nicholson 1990; Smith 1999; Visweswaran 1994.

12. Another dimension of critique involves the construction of standpoint epistemologies as "science" in search of "truth." For example, sociologist of law Carol Smart (1995, 11) criticizes "standpointism" for requiring "precise rules" for the production of knowledge and requiring that a feminist academic "act as interpreter and disseminator of this knowledge." Here Smart (1995) is referring primarily to criminologist Maureen Cain's (1990) analysis of standpoint epistemologies as a successor science, although she also finds fault with Harding's notion of "strong objectivity." Smart explains that this approach "participates in creating hierarchies of knowledge" that is supported by "the promise of a good political outcome." She contrasts this promise with postmodern/poststructuralist feminism that offers "no programmes of action and Utopian visions" (p. 11).

13. Kathy Ferguson (1991) recommends irony as "a vehicle for enabling political actions that resist the twin dangers of paralysis (nothing can be done because no final truth can be found) and totalization (there is one way to do things, the way reflecting the truth that has been found)" (p. 338).

14. This is illustrated by two of the most widely read ethnographic accounts of urban communities, Elliot Liebow's (1967) *Tally's Corner* and William F. Whyte's (1955) *Street Corner Society.*

15. For example, in *All Our Kin*, Carol Stack (1974) demonstrated how African American women's network building and kinship work helped the rural poor to survive the migration to northern cities during the 1960s.

16. See Fitchen 1981; Stack 1974.

17. Aldon Morris (1992, 363) defines oppositional consciousness as "that set of insurgent ideas and beliefs constructed and developed by an oppressed group for the purposes of guiding its struggle to undermine, reform, or overthrow a system of domination." The power of oppositional consciousness lies in its ability "to strip away the garments of universality from hegemonic consciousness, revealing its essentialist characteristics" (p. 370). See also Sandoval 1991; Mansbridge and Morris 2001.

18. See also Benford 1993.

19. See, for example, Oliker 1994.

20. Nancy Campbell (2000) defines "governing mentalities" as "epistemological frames, interpretive paradigms, standards of evidence and proof, and what drug scientist Normal Zinberg [1984] called 'set'—the personal, psychological, and emotional response to a deeply charged subject" (pp. 45–46).

21. See also Escobar 1984–85; J. Ferguson 1994; Loseke 1992.

22. Dorothy Smith (1987) defines "relations of ruling" as a term "that brings into view the intersection of the institutions organizing and regulating society with their gender subtext and their basis in a gender division of labor" (p. 2). The term *ruling* is used to identify "a complex of organized practices, including government, law, business and financial management, professional organization, and educational institutions as well as the discourse in texts that interpenetrate the multiple sites of power."

23. See Chew 1998; Mitchell and Morse 1998.

24. See Ellsworth (1992) for a fascinating discussion of the limits of "empowerment" in critical educational practice.

25. As critical education theorist Elizabeth Ellsworth (1992, 108) points out with reference to her efforts to create dialogue across differences in her classroom: "Because all voices within the classroom are not and cannot carry equal legitimacy, safety, and power in dialogue at this historical moment, there are times when the inequalities must be named and addressed by constructing alternative ground rules for communication."

26. Nancy Fraser's framework has also proven useful in my analysis of the diverse experiences and documents I examined in my long-term (1990–98) ethnographic research in the rural Midwest (Naples 1997). In this study, I found that the dominant approach to economic development seemed to fit Fraser's (1989, 163–64) "thin theory of need" as described in her discussion of the "politics of needs interpretation." As a consequence of the "thin theory of

need" approach, decision-makers render invisible the political dimensions of their activities. Residents of the small rural town I interviewed who were not authorized to contribute to the thick definitions that are necessary for action to proceed held a variety of alternative interpretations.

27. Foucault's discussion of "subjugated knowledges" differs somewhat from Haraway's (1988) concept of "situated knowledges," which she defines as the self-reflective analysis of those within a particular social location (p. 584). Haraway argues that "situated knowledges" generated from the point of view of "subjugates" will provide "more adequate, sustained, objective, transforming accounts of the world." She explains: "Many currents in feminism attempt to theorize grounds for trusting especially the vantage points of the subjugates; there is good reason to believe vision is better from below the brilliant space platforms of the powerful. Building on that suspicion, this essay is an argument for situated and embodied knowledges and an argument against various forms of unlocatable, and so irresponsible, knowledge claims" (p. 583).

28. See, for example, Barrett 1980; Eisenstein 1979; Hartmann 1981.

Chapter 2

1. Sandra Harding (1987) identifies five key dimensions of feminist analyses: (1) understanding social live from women's perspectives; (2) remaining sensitive to the multiplicity of women's lives across race, class, sexualities, culture; (3) breaking down the separation between objectivity and subjectivity; (4) revealing the relationship between politics and science; and (5) challenging the separation of context and justification.

2. See also hooks 1984; Collins 1990; Harding 1991.

3. See, for example, Collins 1990; Devault 1999, Fine 1992; Fonow and Cook 1991; Harding 1986, 1991; Ristock and Pennell 1996; H. Roberts 1981; Smith 1987, 1990a, 1990b; D. Wolf 1996a; M. Wolf 1992.

4. Drawing on Bruno Latour and Steve Woolgar's (1979) analysis in *Laboratory Life*, feminist theorist Katie King (1994, xvi) argues that "feminist objects of knowledge, theoretical objects, political identities are made and materialized over time in political production" (p. xvi). See also Sandoval 1991.

5. See, for example, Alexander and Mohanty (1997). King offers a powerful illustration of this process in her discussion of Alice Echol's (1989) historical and theoretical construction of "radical feminism" and "cultural feminism." As King (1994, 26) argues, "From her [Echols' 1989] vantage point in *Daring to Be Bad*'s introduction (at the end of the eighties) it is radical feminisms' 'theoretical deficiencies,' 'short comings, contradictions, and fuzziness' (10) that led to its degenerated successor cultural feminism."

6. The shifts included the consolidation of funding away from targeted programs to block grants, the devolution of the welfare state to the local city and state governments, and urban disinvestment. Also lost since the early 1970s is the commitment to maximum feasible participation of the poor that was emphasized during the War on Poverty and comprehensive, multiservice, community-based approaches to fighting poverty. Also diminished during this period were calls for local community control over the assessment of community needs and the design and implementation of antipoverty programs. Contemporary welfare reform shifts control over funds for social support to the individual states, but it does not require or invite the active participation of community residents and welfare recipients in program design, resource allocation, and implementation.

7. See, for example, Delphy 1975; Ehrenreich 1984; Ferguson and Folbre 1981; Folbre 1984; G. Joseph 1981; Vogel 1983; Young 1980.

8. See, for example, Barrett 1980; Ehrenreich 1976; Kuhn and Wolpe 1978; Vogel 1983; Young 1980.

9. See, for example, Offe 1984; Brown 1988.

10. The lives of low-income women, especially those who are Black or Latina, are disproportionately shaped by the contradictions of state policies. We need only examine the data on welfare recipients to recognize the racial and gender manifestations of social policy. See Mink 1998; Neubeck and Cazenave 2002, D. Roberts 1997.

11. See also Jones 1990; Sarvasy 1992.

12. See Bookman and Morgan 1988; Edin and Lien 1997; Naples 1998b.

13. The low level of support offered to female-headed families is one illustration of this dynamic. The "state organization of domestic life" has historically shaped women's daily lives as well as limited their future options (E. Wilson 1977, 9). Social security was tied to husband's earnings, thus penalizing women who worked full time in the home. Divorced women were often made ineligible for mother's pensions. Married women or those unmarried women living with a man were also denied support (see, for example, Abramovitz 1988; Katz 1986).

14. See, for example, Giddings 1984; Stack 1974. William Julius Wilson (1987), in his challenge to conservative views on poverty, identifies Black male joblessness as the primary factor contributing to poverty in the Black community. While his analysis does clarify some of the racial dynamics that operate to keep Black people poor, he accepts the two-parent male and female household as the most desired family form. But even in the two-parent family, people of color do not necessarily find a way out of poverty (Williams 1989). Focus on the deviations from the two-parent male and female household as an explanation for poverty diverts our attention from the structural conditions that keep many families of all constellations poor.

15. H.R. 4737 passed by the House in May 2002 earmarked $1.6 billion for marriage promotion.

16. Furthermore, the state's unwillingness to grant autonomy to teenaged mothers places other women in the category of extended caregivers. Even more problematic has been the feature of the 1996 Personal Responsibility and Work Reconciliation Act ([PRWORA) that supported abstinence-only programs (funded at $50 million per year). President Bush proposes to continue this provision in his TANF Reauthorization plan. TANF replaced Aid to Families with Dependent Children (AFDC) which was established through the Social Security Act of 1935 under the name Aid to Dependent Children (ADC).

17. For example, provisions included in versions of bills that preceded the passage of the PRWORA, signed by President Bill Clinton in 1996, gave states the option of denying aid to adolescent mothers who were not married.

18. See Abramovitz 1988; Brewer 1989; MacKinnon 1989; Pascall 1986; Sarvasy 1988; Williams 1989.

19. See Christensen et al. 1988; Smith and Griffith 1990. Gender neutral terms pervade the debate on social reform from the state's early attempts to deal with the existence of the poor in 17th century England to the present. For example, the Elizabethan Poor Law of 1601 distinguished between the "worthy" and "unworthy" poor (Katz 1986). Terms such as "deserving" or "single-parent family" conceal the gender and racial identity of the "recipient" (Pascall 1986; Sarvasy 1988). In the Family Support Act of 1988, abstract language of "participant's" and "family's needs" and "participant's spouse" are used in place of gendered descriptors. As a consequence, the concrete gendered relations within a family is rendered invisible.

20. See Brown 1988; Sarvasy 1988; Williams 1989.

21. Abramovitz 1988; Fraser and Gordon 1994a, 1994b; Mink 1994.

22. See Fraser and Gordon 1994a, 1994b; Mink 1998; Neubeck 2001. In 2002, civil rights, welfare rights, and immigrant rights groups joined in an effort to support a bill on Racial Equity and Fair Treatment that would strengthen due-process and antidiscrimination protections in welfare programs, restore benefits and translation services to immigrants, and use a "racial impact statement" to access state performance.

23. In the Family Support Act of 1988, if a "mandatory Program participant" did not have "good cause" for failing "to comply with any requirement imposed on his or her participation in such Program," her "needs shall not be taken into account in determining the family's need for AFDC Benefits" (Library of Congress 1988, 278). If a "participant" did not comply with the workfare requirements a second time, sanctions would continue for three months. A "subsequent noncompliance" led to a six-month sanction.

24. See, for example, Katz 1986, Mink 1995, 1998; Abramovitz 1988; Campbell 2000.

25. See, for example, Abramovitz 1988; Mink 1995, 1998; D. Roberts 1993, 1995; Sarvasy 1988. The 1996 Personal Responsibility and Work Reconciliation Act denied additional benefits to a mother for any additional children who were born while she was receiving welfare. As sociologists Ken Neubeck and Noel Cazenave (2001) demonstrate in their award winning book *Welfare Racism*, these provisions were a direct outgrowth of explicit discussions of "procreation-targeted race population control" designed to curtail the growth in the "black underclass" (p. 157).

26. See Vogel 1993; O'Connor, Orloff, and Shaver 1999.
27. See, for example, Abramovitz 1988; Gordon 1993; MacKinnon 1989; Mink 1994, 1998; Smart 1981.
28. Grewal and Kaplan (1994) define "scattered hegemonies" as "the effects of mobile capital as well as the multiple subjectivities that replace the European unitary subject" (p. 7).
29. See Cantú 1999; Bernstein and Reimann 2001.
30. My use of the term "state-in-action" parallels the argument in contemporary critical legal studies for analyses of the law in action, i.e., law viewed "as a practice that both constrains and enables action" (Chunn and Lacombe 2000, 13; also see Comaroff 1994) and the work of law in shaping consciousness and identities (see, for example, Merry 1995).
31. Chicano studies scholar Chéla Sandoval (1993) defines third world feminism as the coalition "between a generation of U.S. feminists of color who were separated by culture, race, class, sex or gender identifications but united through their similar responses to the experience of race oppression" (p. 53). She argues for "a 'coalitional consciousness' in cultural studies across racialized, sexualized, genderized theoretical domains: 'white male poststructuralism,' 'hegemonic feminism,' 'third world feminism,' 'postcolonial discourse theory,' and 'queer theory'" (p. 79).
32. Sandoval's (1991, 2) analysis of "oppositional consciousness" focuses on the development of third world feminism "as a model for the self-conscious production of political opposition." In challenging the separation of different political approaches, Sandoval demonstrates how political actors can function "within yet beyond the demands of dominant ideology" (p. 3). She emphasizes how "differential [oppositional] consciousness makes more clearly visible the equal rights, revolutionary, supremacist and separatist, forms of oppositional consciousness, which when kaleidescoped together comprise a new paradigm for understanding oppositional activity in general"(p. 16; see, also, Sandoval 1993, 2000).
33. Also see Harding 1986, 1991; Jaggar 1983; Mohanty 1991a, 1991b; H. Rose 1986.
34. See, also, Collins 1990; King 1994.
35. Political theorist Kathi Weeks (1998) also considers the conceptualization of feminist standpoint, "as an achieved, constructed collectivity" useful for "the feminist political project" (p. 8). She explains that this conceptualization of a feminist standpoint "can serve as an inspiring example of a collective subject, a subject that is neither modeled after the individual, and thus somehow unitary and homogeneous, nor conceived as spontaneous and natural community" (p. 8).
36. Sonia Kruks (2001) demonstrates how Sartre's notion of *praxis* is useful for establishing the process by which situated knowledges can become communicable to others and "systematically demonstrated, rather than, as in Haraway's work, rhetorically asserted" (pp. 118–19). She explains praxis as follows:

> the specific characteristics of human practical activity must be the point of departure in accounting for the possibility of human knowledge and reason. It is in *doing* (rather than in seeing, or contemplating) that we come (at least initially) to generate forms of knowledge. An adequate theory of situated knowledges, Sartre teaches us, cannot be developed primarily from Haraway's metaphor of vision. For although vision represents a way of accessing the world, it is not by itself a means to transform it. (P. 119)

> Kruks stresses that through "the study of one's own situated praxis, ever wider sets of social and historical processes may be made intelligible" (p. 119). While I do not follow Kruks's lead in exploring the value of the existential phenomenology of Sartre and Simone de Beauvoir, I share her goal of opening up to and understanding the experiences of others "whose worlds and experiences are not our own" in order to enhance the possibility "of respectful solidarity among otherwise different women" (p. 22).

37. See also Mohanty 1992a, 1992b.
38. See also Bookman and Morgen 1988; Gordon 1986; West 1981.
39. See, respectively, Chodorow 1978; Moynihan 1967. Also see Glenn, Chang, and Forcey (1994) and James and Busia (1993) for analyses that contest the traditional constructions of mothering based on white, middle-class nuclear family models.
40. Deborah Fink (1986) and Carolyn Sachs (1983, 1996), for example, challenge common notions of women as peripheral to men on family farms and in agriculture more generally.
41. See, for example, Maggard 1990; Naples 1994; Seitz 1998; D. Wolf 1996a.

42. See, for example, Harding 1986; Scott and Shah 1993; Smith 1987; Visweswaran 1994; M. Wolf 1992.
43. See, especially, Smith 1990a, 1990b, 1999.
44. See also Kondo 1990; Visweswaran 1994.
45. While recognizing the value of postmodern interventions in feminist thought, Kruks (2001, 14) is troubled by what she sees as the move to deny "any original interiority to the subject" as Joan Scott argues in her now classic essay on "experience." Scott (1992) asserts that "historical processes . . . through discourse position subjects and produce their experiences" (p. 25). Kruks (2001) sees Scott's theoretical move as a contradictory one, since Scott "still wants to insist that the subject has 'agency,' because it is positioned among conflicting discursive systems that 'enable choices' " (p. 34).
46. In describing their approach to qualitative method, what they term "interpretive practice," Jaber Gubrium and James Holstein (1997) highlight the ethnomethodological practice of "analytic bracketing" and explain that there are two aspects of interpretive practice: artfulness and substantial analysis (p. 121). They emphasize that analytic bracketing "allows us to set aside the 'constructedness' of contextual features in order to describe their apparent contours and substance" without abandoning the notion "the circumstantial phenomena under consideration are themselves constructed and subject to further constitutive analysis (including analysis of how the analyst comes to identify and represent them" (p. 120).
47. Alexander and Mohanty (1997) address this tension between feminist political goals and "postmodernist discourse [that] attempts to move beyond essentialism by pluralizing and dissolving the stability and analytic utility of the categories of race, gender, and sexuality. This strategy often forecloses any valid recuperation of these categories or the social relations through which they are constituted" (p. xvii). They caution that "the relations of domination and subordination that are named and articulated through the processes of racism and racialization still exist, and they still require analytic and political specification and engagement." Also see Fraser and Nicholson 1990.
48. See Bhabha 1994; Rajan 1993; Said 1978; Spivak 1988, 1999.
49. See Collins 1990; di Leonardo 1991; Mohanty 1991a, 1991b.
50. Mohanty is critical of Western feminist constructions of third world women as victims rather than as agents. By emphasizing these women's experiences of male violence, colonial processes, economic development, and religious oppression, Western feminists construct a totalizing image of "the" third world woman that masks the great diversity in such women's lives and their resistance to oppression. In addition, Mohanty argues, first world feminists gain power by distancing themselves from third world women's concerns and constructing themselves as liberated. See also Alexander and Mohanty 1997; Grewal and Caren 1994; Hurtado 1996; Kaplan, Alarcón, and Moallem, 1999; Lowe 1996; Minh-ha 1989; Mohanty Russo and Torres 1992; Narayan 1997; Shohat 1998.
51. See also Spivak 1988.
52. According to Chris Weedon (1987), poststructuralist "does not have one fixed meaning but is generally applied to a range of theoretical positions . . . [including] the apparently 'apolitical' deconstructive criticism, practised by American literary critics in which they are concerned with the 'free play' of meaning in literary texts, the radical-feminist rewriting of the meanings of gender and language in the work of some French feminist writers and the detailed historical analysis of discourse and power in the work of Foucault" (pp. 19–20).
53. See, for example, A. Ferguson 1991; Hennessy and Ingraham 1997; Weedon 1987.
54. See G. Joseph 1981; Mohanty 1991a, 1991b; Spivak 1987.
55. See also A. Ferguson 1991; Hennessy 1993.
56. Sandoval (2000) asserts that Moraga's "theory in the flesh" is "a theory that allows survival and more, that allows practitioners to live with faith, hope, and moral vision in spite of all else" (p. 7). Moraga's "theory of the flesh" and Anzaldúa's (1987) construction of *la conciencia de la mestiza* are built from "gut-wrenching struggle" as communication scholar Jacqueline Martinez explains (2000, 83). Martinez cautions that: "The attention to the embodied flesh that is the substance and methodology of much of Chicano feminist theorizing must not be theorized away in abstract language that allows for a distanced and removed engagement" (p. 84).
57. See Hennessy 1993; Landry and MacLean 1993. Philosopher Ann Ferguson (1991) defines "feminist-materialism" as follows. It "assumes that male power (a) is based on social prac-

tices rather than simply in biological sex differences; (b) connects to systematic inequalities in the exchange of work between men and women in meeting material needs; and (c) involves historically specific rather than universal systems of male dominance" (p. 1). While indebted to postmodern theories that reject "an essential and unitary theory of self," Ferguson (1991) argues that her approach retains "a totalist project in ways that many postmodernist approaches would reject" (pp. 25–26).

58. Sandoval (2000) defines her complex project in *Methodology of the Oppressed* as exploring "the mobile interchange between the sovereign, Marxist, and postmodern conceptions of power" in order to explicate the development and political potential of "differential consciousness" (p. 77).

59. See also Bell 1993; MacCannell and MacCannell 1993. Hennessy (1990, 254) argues that "to see feminism as inexorably bound to struggles against class exploitation, white supremacy, and compulsory heterosexuality requires an analytic that can attend to the interconnections among various modalities of oppression and exploitation at any one instance of the social and situate that instance in the reach of capitalist power relations" (p. 254). Although she finds that "Foucault's project *has* opened up productive avenues for developing materialist feminist theory," she argues for "an alternative post-Althusserian analytic" that is "more in keeping with a feminism that aims to come to terms with the materiality and politics of difference" (p. 254, emphasis in original). In contrast, I found in Foucault's approach to discourse a powerful methodological tool for materialist feminist analysis when grounded in a multidimensional standpoint epistemology that can explicate how "discursive and nondiscursive practices" relate to "the materiality of discourses and the materiality of institutions" (p. 266).

60. See also McNay 1992; Barrett 1991; Bell 1993; Grimshaw 1993; Hennessy 1990; McNay 1993; Ramazonoglu 1993.

61. Campbell (2000) contrasts "conventional policy analysis" with critical approaches that explore "the structures of political exclusion, social isolation, and economic marginalization" (p. 8).

62. Poststructuralists view language not as an abstract system of expression used to describe "a 'real' world" (Weedon 1987, 41) but "as a site of struggle where subjectivity and consciousness are produced" (Orner 1992, 80).

63. Timothy Diamond's (1992, 5) analysis of nursing-home care offers a vivid example of the power of materialist feminist institutional ethnography for making visible how "the work of caretaking becomes defined and gets reproduced day in and day out as a business." This rich ethnography is based on Diamond's work as a nursing assistant in two nursing homes in the Chicago area. By shifting to the everyday world of nursing-home staff and residents, Diamond demonstrates how "bureaucratic control continually expanded into the everyday setting as the various professionals, managers, and certifiers went about their work practices naming the everyday life in terms of their categories" (p. 211). His institutional ethnographic work revealed "two kinds of narratives on care giving: one formal, written, and shared by the professionals and administrators; another submerged, unwritten, and shared by the people who lived and worked on the floors" (p. 215). Other work that illustrates the power of institutional ethnography includes Marjorie Devault's (1991) *Feeding the Family* and the excellent case studies presented in Marie Campbell and Ann Manicom's (1995) edited collection *Knowledge, Experience, and Ruling Relations: Studies in the Social Organization of Knowledge*.

64. This discussion also appears in Naples 2002a, xxx.

65. These quotations are excerpted from the following web site: http://www.opdv.state.ny.us/coordination/safetyaudit.html.

66. See, for example, Cancian 1996; Fine 1992; Fine and Weiss 1996; Hale 1996; Reinharz 1992; Wolf 1996.

67. Maria Mies (1991) describes this process as "reciprocal research" (p. 71). Although she shared neither culture, class nor ethnic background with her "conversation partners" (to use Stern's term), Mies found this process enriched her work with Indian women.

68. Stern differentiates her framework from Freire's dialogic approach. Most who follow Freire's lead understand the process as one enhancing understanding between "insiders" and "outsiders." For example, Elden and Levin (1991) describe how participatory research can empower participants through the process of "cogenerative dialogue" (p. 134). They

point out that for Freire a dialogical relationship "is characterized by '*subjects* who meet to name the work in order to transform it'" (quoted in Elden and Levin 1991, 134; emphasis added); however, they focus on the dialogue between insiders and outsiders.

69. See also Code 1991; Hale 1996; S. Joseph 1996, for discussions of the complications associated with friendships with subjects of research.

Chapter 3

1. Like sociologist Laurel Richardson (1997), a number of authors writing on the theme of reflective practice use the term "reflexivity." I prefer to use the term "reflective practice" since it indicates a more thoughtful process and does not evoke the often-unconscious responses to stimuli associated with "reflex" (also see Lather 1992). However, I do use the term "reflexivity" in quoting these authors.

2. Thorne (1995) emphasizes that "gender extends beyond daily cultural performance, and it will take much more than doing drag and mocking naturalized conceptions to transform it. Gender—and race, class, and compulsory heterosexuality—extend deep into the unconscious and the shaping of emotions . . . and outward into social structure and material interests" (p. 499).

3. See Hertz 1997; D. Wolf 1996a.

4. For example, Alexander and Mohanty (1997) stress that: "We cannot overestimate the need for conscious self-reflexivity about the complicity of intellectual frameworks in politics, in the fact that something is at stake, in the very process of reauthorizing and mediating inequalities or regressive politics of different kinds" (p. xviii).

5. Feminist and critical education theorists have also explored the different approaches to reflectivity in the classroom. In discussing the features of "reflective teaching" that she finds more useful for her work, Jennifer Gore (1993) describes the three "levels of reflectivity" discussed by Max van Manen (1977), "the technical, the practical and the critical" (p. 149). Gore argues that "reflection on social and political conditions" has been more effectively adopted than reflection on the actions and discourses that undergird classroom practices (p. 148). She defines "reflective teaching" as: "teaching which attends, mindfully, to the social and political context of schooling, as well as to technical and practical aspects, and which also assesses classroom actions on the basis of their abilities to contribute toward greater equity and social justice, and more human conditions in schooling and society" (p. 149). Gore then cautions that without increasing awareness of "how it is that certain practices are taken for granted in classrooms" and how they create "a limited set of already-constituted management techniques" (p. 154), "the spaces for freedom" in the classroom will be further constrained (p. 156).

6. See, for example, Blee 1998, 2002; Ginsburg 1997.

7. See, for example, Luttrell 1997; Naples 1998a.

8. See, for example, de Castell and Bryson 1998; Personal Narratives Group 1989; Reay 1996; M. Wolf 1992, 1996.

9. See also Blee 2002; de Castell and Bryson 1998; Luttrell 1997; Poletta 1998.

10. This paragraph and the next are revised excerpts from Naples 2001 (pp. 35–36).

11. Linda Alcoff (1988) uses the concept "positionality" to describe "the subject as nonessentialized and emergent from a historical experience" (p. 433). This form of analysis and writing also helps "to reveal the role of emotions in the production of anthropological knowledge" (p. 55).

12. See also Abu-Lughod 1993; Behar 1993; Greenhalgh 2001; M. Wolf 1992.

13. See, for example, Patai 1994.

14. See, for example, Armstrong 1990 cited in Alcoff and Gray 1993; Kaminer 1995.

15. See Patai and Koertge 1994.

16. See Collins 1990; Hartsock 1983; Lugones 1992; Sandoval 1991, 2002; Smith 1987.

17. See, for example, Anzaldúa's 1987; Moraga 1981; Collins 1990.

18. See Aguilar 1981; Geertz 1983.

19. See also Enslin 1990, 1994.

20. See, for example, Alcoff 1991–92; Fine 1998. Over a decade ago, Michelle Fine wrote, "Qualitative researchers interested in self-consciously working the hyphen–that is, unpacking notions of scientific neutrality, universal truths, and researcher dispassion–will be invited

to imagine how we can braid critical and contextual struggle back into our texts" (p. 131). In responding to this call feminist scholars have developed an impressive body of work that provide creative approaches for "working the hyphen" (see, for example, Lather and Smithies 1997; Phalen 1989; Richardson 1997; M. Wolf 1992).

Chapter 4

1. See Aguilar 1981; Messerschmidt 1981; Pollner and Emerson 1983.
2. Simmel's (1921) analysis was based upon a rigid conception of social life which assumed an unchanging caste-like distinction between the "stranger" and the "insider," an inattention to power in encounters between the "stranger" and "insiders," and a belief in the stranger's greater "objectivity."
3. See also Wilson 1974.
4. See Bat-Ami Bar On (1993) for a critique of "epistemic privilege" claimed by feminists for socially marginalized groups.
5. William J. Wilson (1974) supports Merton's position and further argues that "although it may be safe to hypothesize a connection between one's race and one's approach to race-related matters today, no sharp lines can be drawn between the writing of black and white scholars, and there is no guarantee that what is taken to represent the black perspective today will not be rejected by a new group of Insiders tomorrow" (p. 333). He urges that "the field of race relations be free to develop like any other substantive area in sociology, with the discovery and codification of knowledge, with the search for truth, and with the absence of arbitrary barriers imposed by Insiders and Outsiders doctrines" (p. 334).
6. See also Collins 1991; Harding 1991.
7. See Acker, Barry and Esseveld 1991; Collins 1990; Harding 1991.
8. See Naples 1992; Lorber 1994.
9. See also Haraway 1988; Sandoval 1991.
10. W.E.B. DuBois (1903) used the term "double-consciousness" to describe the "twoness" of the American Negro "two souls, two thoughts, two reconciled strivings; two warring ideals in one dark body, whose dogged strength alone keeps it from being torn asunder" (p. 45).
11. A total of 175 residents, both men and women, were interviewed in the two towns. See Appendix B for more detailed discussion of the methodology.
12. See Harding 1991; D. Smith 1987, 1990a, 1990b.
13. See also Fink 1992; Salamon 1992.
14. See Naples 1994; Monney 1988.
15. See also Fitchen 1992.
16. Winant 1994, 23; see also Frankenberg 1993; Hyde 1995; Omi and Winant 1986.
17. Trust is only one dimension through which understanding proceeds, as Riessman (1987) demonstrates. Culturally specific experiences and narrative forms through which these experiences are expressed interfere with understanding between researchers and informants who share gender characteristics but differ according to class, culture, race, ethnicity, or generation.
18. See, for example, Elden and Levin, 1991; Light and Kleiber, 1988; Maguire 1987, 2001a, 2001b.
19. See Johnson 1983; Lugones and Spelman 1983; Stern 1994.
20. See also Ellis 1995; Stacey 1991.
21. See Coffey 1999; C. Smith and Kornblum 1989.
22. See Johnson 1983; Stacey 1991.
23. Kathleen Blee (1998) demonstrates the value of emotions as an analytic framework in her research on white supremacists. She found that: "Beyond probing my own emotional stance vis-à-vis my racist respondents, analyzing fear as a medium of interaction also allowed me to understand more clearly the ways in which fear operates within racist groups themselves" (p. 393).
24. Ellis 1991; also see Kleinman and Copp 1993.
25. See also Oakley 1981.
26. See, for example, Blee 1998, 2002.
27. Also see Ellis 1991; Krieger 1985; Williams 1990.
28. See chapter 5 for a more detailed discussion of the differences in their approaches.

29. Of interest here is the fact that Simmel (1921) equated the "stranger" with the European Jew who he then defined unproblematically as trader and "no landowner" (p. 323). Nowhere does Simmel explore the long history and processes of exclusion and anti-Semitism that constricted the European Jew's landowning and other economic and political claims to "rootedness."

Chapter 5

1. Among the many provocative questions Harding (1991) raises are: "What kinds of knowledge about the empirical world do we need in order to live at all, and to live more reasonable with one another on this planet from this moment on? Should improving the lives of the few or of the many take priority in answering this question?" (p. 192). She argues for "socially situated knowledge" that could provide a "strong objectivity" from which to construct feminist science. For Harding, "strong objectivity requires that we investigate the relation between subject and object rather than deny the existence of, or seek unilateral control over, this relation" (p. 152). Also see Haraway 1988.

2. Hennessy (1993) defines a "global social analytic" as follows:

    I use the metaphor of "globality" here in order to refer to two distinct yet interdetermined registers of social relations: the worldwide (global) reach of capital's markets, and a (global) mode of reading systemically. . . .
        A global analytic posits the social not as a fixed or unified structure, but as an ensemble of relations in which connections between cultural, economic, and political practices are overdetermined. Global analysis understands the social in terms of systems and structures of relations. (Pp. 15–16)

3. Some feminist theorists criticize this aspect of standpoint theorizing for granting "epistemological privilege" to certain marginalized groups over others. As Bat-Ami Bar On (1993) points out, given "the existence of multiple socially marginalized groups; is any one of these groups more epistemically privileged than the others, and if that is not so—if they are all equally epistemically privileged—does epistemic privilege matter?" (p. 89).

4. See hooks 1984, 1989; Hurtado 1996.

5. See, for example, Gilkes 1988; Kaplan 1982.

6. See also Moya 1997.

7. See Stacey 1991; M. Wolf 1996.

8. In both urban and rural studies, the data gathered were evaluated using content analytic techniques. Each interview was audiotaped, transcribed, and, subsequently, analyzed for recurring themes and patterns. These themes and patterns were compared across narratives. In some cases, when respondents preferred not to have their interviews taped, the interviewer reconstructed the information as soon as possible after the meeting. These data were treated in a fashion similar to the observational field notes taken during a field trip.

9. For example, feminists scholars who center the role of mothering practices in generating different "ways of knowing" (for examples, Belenky 1986; Ruddick 1989) who argue that there are gendered differences in moral perspective (Gilligan 1982) have been criticized for equating such gendered differences with an essentialized female identity or, as in Nancy Chodorow's (1978)] work, treating gender "independently of other variables such as race, class, and ethnicity" (Spelman 1988, 81).

10. See Hartsock 1983; Harding 1991; Mohanty 1991a. In describing Nancy Hartsock's (1983) feminist standpoint epistemology, Sandra Harding (1986) explains:

    The subjugation of women's sensuous, concrete, relational activity permits women to grasp aspects of nature and social life that are not accessible to inquiries grounded in men's characteristic activities. The vision based on men's activities is both partial and perverse—"perverse" because it systematically reverses the proper order of things: it substitutes abstract for concrete reality; for example it makes death-risking rather than the reproduction of our species form of life that paradigmatically human act. (P. 148)

11. Legal scholar Kimberly Crenshaw (1993) uses the concept of *intersectionality* to analyze "how the experiences of women of color are frequently the product of intersecting patterns of racism and sexism" (p. 1243).

12. See Harding 1986.
13. See also Katznelson 1981.
14. According to Werner Schmalenbach, the experience of communion "is formed by an actual experience of common feeling" (quoted in Kathleen McCourt 1977, 232).
15. See Harding 1987, 1991; Collins 1990, 1991; Naples 1986.
16. Haraway 1988, 585; also see Smith 1987. As Haraway explains: "The science question in feminism is about objectivity as positioned rationality. Its images are not the products of escape and transcendence of limits (the view from above) but the joining of partial views and halting voices into a collective subject position that promises a vision of the means of ongoing finite embodiment, of living within limits and contradictions of views from somewhere" (p. 590).
17. See, for example, Gamson 1988; McCarthy 1994; Taylor and Whittier 1995,185; and Steinberg 1999.
18. See Campbell 2000; Donati 1992; Landry and MacLean 1993; Ramazanoglu 1993.

Chapter 6

1. See, for example, Loseke 1992; Walker 1990.
2. See also Bloom 1998; Chase 1995; Kondo 1990.
3. See, for example, Berliner 1997.
4. See also Tarrow 1992.
5. This forms part of a larger study of New York City and Philadelphia community workers in the War on Poverty (see Naples 1998a). For this chapter, I focus on a subsample of the women interviewed who lived in New York City and were active in the movement for community control of the schools. This sample includes 16 women who were living in the low-income communities that were the target of the War on Poverty when they were hired by community action agencies and eleven who were not residing in these communities and consequently are defined as "nonresident" community workers. These communities include the Lower East Side of Manhattan, Harlem, the South Bronx, and Bedford-Stuyvesant.
6. The oral historical method permits analysis of political mobilization across different social movements and community mobilizations. Personal narratives from activists can be used to explore the interaction between shifting constructions of identity and construction of movement frames (see Naples 1998a).
7. See Katzenstein 1998.
8. See Cronin 1973.
9. See Cronin 1973; Maynard 1970; New York CLU 1969; Stein 1970.
10. See Wagner (1997) for a discussion of the contradictions of "the liberal discourse on poverty" (p. 23).
11. Michael Harrington also came out against community control in the context of the 1968 Ocean Hill-Brownsville struggle between the teachers' union and the local community leaders. Cronin (1973) reports that Harrington viewed this struggle "not a simple conflict of right and wrong, but an antagonism of two rights . . . effective community involvement in the educational process" and "academic freedom and due process when a professional is dismissed" (p. 193).
12. See, for example, Stern 1998.
13. See also Naples 1998c, 327.
14. See Cronin 1973; Ports 1970.
15. This discussion also appears in Naples 1998a, 133–34.
16. See also Stern 1998.
17. The Ford Foundation subsequently agreed to fund three experimental community control projects. The Board of Education in consultation with the teachers union announced that the three projects would include East Harlem's IS 201 district, the Ocean Hill-Brownsville district in Brooklyn, and the Two Bridges district in the Lower East Side of Manhattan.
18. This corresponds to the low voter turnout for the community action programs (see Ornstein 1974; also see Yates 1973).
19. Discussions about financial support for Community School Board members led to compensation for members that did not take effect until July 1972. Not surprisingly, the law provided "compensation for the members of the central Board of Education, even though no such recommendation had been made" (Zimet 1973, 153).

20. See also Berger 1989.
21. See, for example, Jackson 1992; Katz 2000; Warren 1991. The National Council of Teachers of English's Committee Against Censorship surveyed schools in 1977 and found that 34 percent "that responded to its questions had received challenges to materials in their libraries; by 1982, the figure had risen to 56 percent" (Hechinger 1986).
22. See, for example, Hechinger 1986.
23. See also Tarrow 1992.
24. See also Loseke 1992.
25. See Sanford Schram and Joe Soss's (2002, 58) discussion of how the construction of welfare reform success has been accomplished by positive rhetorical interpretations of "caseload decline and leaver outcomes." Instead, they argue, for the development of alternative criteria" that "might point to less sanguine evaluations of reform" (p. 59).

Chapter 7

1. The debate underlying the assertion of this consensus included disagreement over whether the state should expend money for poor women and their children. Further movement toward state disinvestment in social programs accelerated after the 1994 elections when the Republicans gained control over the House and Senate.
2. In February 1994, U.S. House Republicans developed the foundation for what was defined as the Contract with America. Five principles were said to characterize this contract: "individual liberty, economic opportunity, limited government, personal responsibility, and security at home and abroad" (Gingrich et al. 1994, 4). These principles set the stage for a barrage of legislative actions that took the Democrats by storm after they lost their majority position in Congress as the result of the 1994 elections. While touted as a new agenda for American government, the contract drew upon themes that have long held sway in U.S. legislative arenas at all levels of government as well as in popular constructions of the United States. While many of the specific initiatives put forth by the House Republicans failed, the dismantling of welfare is one initiative that continued to gain momentum through local state waivers granted by President Clinton's administration (see Pear 1996, 54) and culminated in the passage of the Personal Responsibility and Work Opportunity Reconciliation Act of 1996.
3. In my analysis, framing necessarily delimits action. One point of connection between Snow and Benford's (1992) articulation of "master frames" and my understanding of discursive frames relates to the issue of resonance; namely, certain statements within particular discursive frames achieve status and authority when tied to larger discourses that resonate with prevailing cultural constructions. I might further this comparison by examining the processes through which certain New Right organizations and conservative analysts such as Charles Murray (1984) captured the discursive stage in welfare reform discourse by drawing on popular frames such as those examined in this analysis. However, the focus here is on the discursive frames evident within the legislative hearings and not on specific organizational actors.
4. These two orienting dimensions (individualism and behaviorism) derive from liberal philosophy and behavioral psychology, respectively. Liberal philosophy centers a gender-neutral individual "citizen" as the key unit of democracy, assumes a distinction between so-called public and private spheres, and, in most variants, views the political sphere as separate from the economic sphere (see Pateman 1988, 54). As a consequence, liberal philosophy operates in support of (1) gender inequality by rendering women's work in the home invisible, and (2) capitalism by minimizing the state's intervention in the economy. In fact, as Birte Siim (1988, 162) argues, in liberalism "the ownership of property was taken to establish a sphere of autonomy around the individual and the family into which die state should not intrude." The second dimension of behaviorism derives from behavioral psychology, which argues that individuals change their behaviors in response to a system of rewards and sanctions. Coercive strategies are acceptable when behaviors are deemed harmful to the individual or to society.
5. See also Piven and Cloward [1971] 1993; West 1981.
6. See Kuhn and Bluestone 1987; Vickers 1991. Teresa Amott (1993) offers a useful account of the effects of global economic restructuring on workers' wages (for example, she notes that "the purchasing power of minimum-wage workers fell by nearly 40 percent during the

1980s" [41]); on women's employment ("by 1989, 3.5 times as many women were working two or more jobs as in 1973" [72]); and on the disproportionate disadvantage of women of color in relationship to white men and women (namely, "the ratio of African American women's wages to white women's wages actually *fell*, from 92 percent to 88 percent, as did the ratio of Latinas to whites" [77; emphasis in original]).

7. During the 1980s and under President Ronald Reagan's leadership, the government reduced funding for public assistance by lowering benefits, cutting people off from Aid to Families with Dependent Children (AFDC) (Amott [1993] reports that 444,000 recipients were cut from AFDC in 1981), and by increasing bureaucratic review of AFDC cases leading to gaps in coverage.

8. See Carnoy, Shearer, and Rumberger 1983; Bawden 1984; Amort 1990; Bello 1994.

9. Mimi Abramovitz (1938) defines the family ethic as a "preoccupation with the nuclear family unit featuring a male breadwinner and an economically dependent female homemaker" (p. 2). The family ethic also privileges the white middle-class family over working-class and nonwhite racial ethnic families.

10. Foucault (1972) defines *discursive formations* as rule-bound systems guiding the formation and dispersion of statements that are interpreted as a related series of signs integral to the discursive system (Gutting 1989), in this case, social welfare.

11. See also Abramovitz 1988; D. Roberts 1993, 1995; Mink 1995.

12. See D. Roberts 1993, 1995; Brewer 1994; Mink 1995.

13. The Elizabethan Poor Law of 1601 distinguished between the "worthy" and "unworthy" poor (Katz 1986). This distinction was transported to the colonies and continues to shape the formulation and implementation of social welfare policy in the United States.

14. See West 1981; Pear 1996. Before passage of the new welfare reform Personal Responsibility and Work Opportunity Reconciliation Act in August 1996, waivers had been granted to individual state governments designed to place further controls on the behavior of low-income women. Wisconsin, for example, under a program called Learnfare, withheld public assistance from families when their children did not regularly attend school, thus extending the arm of the state even further into the lives of the poor. Other strategies were adopted by states to withhold funds if a woman receiving AFDC had additional children, for example. The California State Assembly had already passed a measure to limit welfare for people disabled as a result of alcoholism or drug abuse. As of May 1996, a total of 37 states had been granted waivers to reduce benefits or place coercive behavioral requirements on welfare recipients (Noble 1996).

15. See Katz 1986; Abramovitz 1988; Brewer 1994; Fraser and Gordon 1994a, 1994b.

16. See also Smith 1987, 1990a, 1990b; Fraser 1989.

17. See Skocpol 1992; Orloff 1993; Quadagno 1994.

18. See, for example, Wiseman 1991; Oliker 1994.

19. See, for example, Gueron 1987; Friedlander 1988.

20. See also White 1994.

21. According to Phoebe Jones Schellenberg of Black Women for Wages for Housework (personal interview, National Women's Studies Conference, Ames, Iowa, June 18, 1994), Prescod raised her hand and Senator Moynihan called on her. She explained that she wanted to testify, and he invited her to do so. As Jones Schellenberg explained, "The Senator reverted to his old professor role and couldn't help but call on her." Once he recognized her, to deny her request would call the so-called open process into question. Moynihan recognized Prescod as follows: "Now, a young lady asked to be heard who was not regularly scheduled, which is not our regular routine; but we have some time. If that young lady would come forward and give her name and her organization or affiliation, we will be glad to hear her" (U.S. Congress, Senate 1988, 64). Prescod then moved forward with three other members of Black Women for Wages for Housework and introduced them to the senators. They were "Phoebe Jones, who is a full-time housewife and mother, . . . Pat Albright, who is a welfare recipient, . . . and "Mary Hriskeu, who is a career woman, a graduate of the Wharton School." However, only Prescod presented testimony.

22. See discussion of "enunciative modalities" in Foucault 1972. Enunciative modalities are "the lands of cognitive status and authority" held by different statements (Gutting 1989, 232).

23. See Weedon 1987; Fraser 1989.

24. See Smith 1987, 1990a, 1990b; Fraser 1989; Naples 1998b; Hennessy 1993; Landry and MacLean 1993.

25. See, for example, De Janvry 1980.
26. See Gough 1957; Bawden 1984; Lessnoff 1986; Medina 1990.
27. The criterion on which this figure is based is whether the individual was listed as a witness in the table of contents for each set of hearings. In some cases, individuals were accompanied by others who were not listed. These individuals were not counted in the total. In other cases, when more than one individual representing the same organization was listed in the table of contents, they were included in the count. Forty-six individuals appeared at more than one hearing; in other words, 200 individuals testified at the hearings, for a total of 246 appearances.
28. Nancy Campbell (2000) demonstrates a similar dynamic in her analysis of congressional hearings on drug policy. The senators were interested in demonstrating through the testimony of female addicts that prostitution was a direct outcome of drug abuse. Campbell presents how one witness, "Beverley Lee Roman," a convicted drug addict and prostitute, "skillfully deflected their attempts to use her testimony to establish their hazy theories, vague connections, and moral condemnations as the truth of drug addiction" (p. 127). Campbell concludes that: "The unburdening of Beverly Lee Roman represented the transmission of knowledge from a marginal position to the more social central positions the senators occupied. Her story gave the senators grounds to claim they 'knew' drug addiction. No other witness throughout the entire set of hearings was treated in quite this manner. The senators integrated her testimony with elements from their own truth" (p. 130).
29. See also Pateman 1988.
30. Moynihan introduced Lawrence Mead as a key architect of the redefined social contract. He stated that Mead's "seminal work on obligation appeared several years ago and obviously greatly influenced the course of the discussion in our nation—you hear it; every witness is talking about 'social contracts,' and out in California they are drawing them up" (U.S. Congress, Senate 1987d, 195–96). Mead and other conservative analysts unambiguously committed to the individualist and behavioral frames did not view lack of jobs or low wages as the central problem for people on welfare.
31. This count does not include the three witnesses who accompanied other presenters.
32. See also Marshall 1965.
33. See Abramovitz 1988; Gordon 1993; D. Roberts 1993, 1995; Mink 1995.
34. For example, structural factors said to explain the lower level of child support awarded to women of color include discrimination in court decisions and the lower level of income earned by men of color (Burnham 1986).
35. The relatively little attention paid to immigrant groups stands in stark contrast to the new discourse on welfare reform, as evident in the September 1995 Senate debates (see Chang 1994). However, discourse analysis of social welfare reveals discursive continuity in that these groups continue to have no legitimate place within the social contract framework.
36. It is significant to note here that the AFDCU program specifically targeted two-parent families and was more likely to provide employment training and other program services for unemployed fathers.
37. Gwendolyn Mink (1995) makes the same point when she writes: "I don't think the apparent popularity of work requirements for welfare mothers reflects a new social consensus that all mothers should work outside the home. The work requirements are rather a response to widespread resentment that 'those people' are allowed to stay at home through welfare while 50 percent of mothers with young children are to some degree or another connected to the labor market. This resentment conjures up old racial concerns of 'female loaferism' in the form of the contemporary welfare myth that mothers on welfare are 'unwilling' to work" (p. 177).

Chapter 8

1. See Edin 1991; Oliker 1995a, 1995b; Polakow 1993; Spalter-Roth, Hartmann, and Andrews 1992.
2. Michigan, Nevada, Oregon, and Texas provided no support for post-secondary education. Alabama, Arkansas, Colorado, District of Columbia, Florida, Georgia, Louisiana, New Hampshire, New York, Puerto Rico, South Carolina, Texas, and West Virginia limited support to two calendar years. Maryland supported only participants who were enrolled in a four-year program leading to a baccalaureate degree prior to April 1, 1990; all other partic-

ipants were limited to two-year programs. Alaska limited support for post-secondary education to 30 months. Idaho supported four years of post-secondary education but limited the support to a maximum of 70 clients in State Fiscal Year 1991 (Hagen and Lurie 1992).

3. Unfortunately, this option was short-lived. In 1996, the U.S. Congress passed the Personal Responsibility and Work Reconciliation Act (PRWORA) that limited continuous receipt of public assistance to two years with a lifetime cap of five years. This effectively contributed to the end of the college option for most women on public assistance.

4. PRWORA, signed into law by President Clinton in 1996, ended "entitlement" or financial need as a basis for claiming state assistance. Behavioral and racist measures were expanded, most notably illustrated in the denial of assistance to immigrants.

5. Contemporary welfare reform is now concerned with what contributes to leaving welfare (the term used is *leavers*), yet the frame of "dependency" continues to be applied to those who, for a variety of reasons have not left welfare. The imposition of time limits and the number of strictures put on those receiving public assistance may discourage women from applying for assistance or from continuing to receive assistance even if eligible. Thus, the terms of the debate have shifted since the 1990s given the change in the structural context for receipt of public assistance and legislative policy agenda.

6. The FSA also provides support for the training and employment assistance of men who are recipients of AFDC-UP (Unemployed Parent) program.

7. See Bose 1985; Felmlee 1988; Nettles 1991.

8. See Sadker and Sadker 1991; Wolin 1981.

9. See, for example, Geiger 1983; Gluck and Patai 1991.

10. See, for example, Griffith and Smith 1990; Smith and Griffith 1990.

11. Those "who are soon to be ineligible" include women whose youngest child is reaching age 18 (State of Iowa, Department of Human Services 1991, 1).

12. Target recipients were defined as: "1. Parents who are not yet aged 24 and who have not completed high school or have no work history during the past 12 calendar months. 2. Persons in households where the youngest child will become ineligible for ADC . . . within the next 24-month period. 3. Persons who have received ADC . . . for any 36 months during the most recent 60-month period. 4. Parents under the age of 20 who have a child under the age of 3 but have not completed high school" (State of Iowa, Department of Human Services, 1991, 8).

13. For example, "Learnfare" was implemented in Wisconsin to keep adolescents on ADC in school. The program proved costly to implement and little evidence was found to support the claims that Learnfare succeeded. Schools did not have accurate attendance reports and local social service agencies reported difficulty in processing the Learnfare program (State of Wisconsin Legislative Audit Bureau 1990; Corbett et al. 1989; Capital Comments 1990).

14. This practice relates to a series of "degradation rituals" (Piven and Cloward [1971] 1993, 397) long practiced by the state to control behavior and to stigmatize the poor. According to Piven and Cloward, through "degradation rituals," "the degraded welfare mother was thus made to serve as a warning to all Americans who were working more and earning less, if they were working at all. There is a fate worse, and a status lower, than hard and unrewarding work."

15. See, for example, Nathan 1987.

16. See Dougherty 1987; Velez 1985; Weis 1985. As indicated earlier, contemporary welfare policy limits the receipt of public assistance to two years. Workfare implementation further constrains women's educational attainment by mandating that the college credits they take must lead to a terminal degree. Recipients in their first two years of college are frequently prevented from taking courses that will facilitate their transfer to a four year college degree program. In February 2003, the U.S. House of Representatives approved a bill that increases the number of hours a welfare recipient is required to work from 30 to 40 hours a week. This bill cuts the number of months a recipient could enroll in college to 4 out of a 24-month period. The present legislation enables a recipient to enroll for up to 12 months out of a 24-month period.

17. See also Griffith and Smith 1990; Smith and Griffith 1990.

18. See, for example, Mead 1986.

19. See also Popkin 1990.

20. See also Oliker 1995a, 1995b.

21. See Abramovitz 1988; Gordon 1990a; Mink 1995; Naples 1998b; Nelson 1990; Smith 1987.

22. See also Skocpol 1992.
23. See Eisenstein 1986; Walby 1990.
24. See Bookman and Morgen 1988; Edin and Lien 1997; Naples 1998b.

Chapter 9

1. See Chew 1998; Mitchell and Morse 1998.
2. See, for example, Crenshaw 1993; Hennessy and Ingraham 1997b; Brenner 2000.
3. See, for example, Davies 1995; Haakan 1998; Reavey and Gough 2000.
4. See Bell 1995, Davies 1995.
5. See Champagne 1996; Crossley 2000; Haakan 1998.
6. See also Alleyne 1997; Armstrong 1994; Barringer 1992; Cvetkovich 1995; Derricotte 1989; Edell 1990; McLennan 1996; Rapping 1996; Wisechild 1991.
7. See also Smart 1999.
8. Furthermore, as Diana Meyers (2002) emphasizes, "Mandating oppositional politics as a prerequisite for the self-understanding needed to speak in one's own voice is insufficiently respectful of women's uniqueness as individuals, for many women have conflicting commitments or find other methods of getting in touch with themselves more in keeping with their personal style" (p. 20).
9. See Barringer 1992; Bass and Davis 1988; Butler 1978; Hall and Lloyd 1989.
10. See also McNay 1992; Meyers 2002; Wilson 1994.
11. See Dobash and Dobash 1992; Profitt 2000.
12. See also , for example, Butler 1978; Miller 1984; Ratner 1990; Stanko 1995.
13. Cited in Gerson 1995.
14. Crossley (1999, 2000) questions her earlier interpretation of the depoliticized therapeutic culture that pervades written incest narratives of the 1980s and 1990s. [Crossley published her previous publication under the name of Davies (1995).] In *Childhood Sexual Abuse and the Construction of Identity: Healing Sylvia* (Davies 199) she revisits her assessment of "the 'architecture of subjectivation' " by analyzing Sylvia Fraser's (1988) autobiography, *My Father's House: A Memoir of Incest and of Healing* (Davies 1995). Crossley explores the extent to which Fraser's incorporation of therapeutic discourse manifests "liberating and repressive potentials" (1999, 1694). Also see Clegg 1999; Doane and Hodges 2001.
15. See also Butler 1978. In Becky Thompson's (1994) excellent multiracial study of women's eating problems and the significance of childhood sexual abuse, she notes that the "combination of [feminist] activism and scholarship has also encouraged examination of the psychological and sociological dynamics of eating problems among surivivors of sexual abuse" (p. 65).
16. See also Armstrong 1994; Barringer 1992.
17. See Crossley 2000; Doane and Hodges 2001.
18. While Smith (1993) utilizes Foucault's notion of discourse, she differentiates her approach from Foucault and argues that "there are indeed matters to be spoken and spoken of that discourse does not yet encompass" (p. 183).
19. See, for example, Crossley 2000; Kitzinger and Perkins 1993.
20. See Marecek and Krazetz 1998; Mirkin 1994.
21. See, for example, Dinsmore 1991; Herman 1981.
22. See also Haaken 1998; McLellan 1995.
23. See Courtois 1988; Haaken and Schlaps 1991; McLellan 1995.
24. See, for example, Brickman 1984; Dinsmore 1991; Hyde 1986.
25. See, for example, Zerbe 1996.
26. See, for example, Enns 1996; McLellan 1995; Heenan and Seu 1998.
27. See, for example, Brown 1994; Dinsmore 1991; Walker 1998.
28. As Evans and Maines (1995) argue: "The significance of this contextual dimension cannot be under emphasized. Each context, viewed as a network of relations and as a site of conventionalized narrative practice, contains different interests, criteria for believability, and norms of reporting and storytelling. The recovered past of incest must flow through those contexts, which means that it is transacted in different terms that result in from slightly to very different versions of the past" (p. 319).
29. See for example, American Psychiatric Association 1993; Davis 2000; Pezdek and Banks 1996; Schuman and Glavez 1996.

30. See also Haaken 1995, 1998.
31. See also Beckett 1996; Davis 2000.
32. See, for example, Bloom 1990; Fredrickson 1992.
33. See, for example, Brown 1994.
34. See, for example, Goldstein and Farmer 1992.
35. See, for example, Armstrong 1994.
36. In her book of case studies, Annette Kuhn (1995) defines "memory work" as "a method and a practice of unearthing and making public untold stories, stories of 'lives lived out on the borderlands, lives for which the central interpretive devices of the culture don't quite work" (p. 8). She describes the process of memory work as "potentially interminable: at every turn, as further questions are raised, there is always something else to look into" (p. 5).
37. See, for example, Lowenstein 1990–91.
38. See Susan Estrich's (1987) account of how the law enforcement and court system victimizes women who are willing to report and proceed with criminal prosecution against the men who raped them. See also Armstrong 1994 and Feldman-Summers 1996. See Wakefield and Underwager 1994 for discussion of "falsely accused" dimension of the debate.
39. Janice Haaken (1998) provides a very interesting analysis of the mother/daughter dynamics at work in this case and explores the implications of it for the memory debate more broadly. See also Dolan 1996.
40. The extensive financial resources they have marshaled, along with a long list of professionals who support the foundation as members of the FMSF Scientific and Professional Advisory Board stands in stark contrast to the low-budget and predominantly volunteer-run survivors' groups facilitated through VOICES (Victims of Incest Can Emerge Survivors) in Action, Inc., founded in 1980 by survivors of child sexual abuse and their allies.
41. See Meyers 2002.
42. See Champagne 1996, 168.
43. The FMSF account of false memories and the proscription for reestablishing normalized family relations simultaneously challenges the validity of the sexual abuse charge by the daughter and "facilitate[s] the daughter's return to the family" (Davis 2000, 39).
44. See Loftus and Ketcham 1994; Ofshe and Waters 1994; Yapko 1994.
45. See also Reviere 1996.
46. According to Haaken and Schlaps (1991) incest resolution therapies foreground "the specific events surrounding the incest trauma, mobilizing of memories and affect associated with the incest experience, and encouraging catharsis as a means of resolving the trauma" (p. 39). The patient's contemporary "life difficulties and symptomatology" (p. 39) are viewed as a consequence of this traumatic early childhood experience. In the June 16, 1994, report of the Council on Scientific Affairs of the American Medical Association on "Memories of Childhood Abuse," the authors announced the adoption of a "new policy on memory enhancement methods," which asserts: "The AMA considers the technique of 'memory enhancement' in the area of childhood sexual abuse to be fraught with problems of potential misapplication" quote in Haaker and Schlaps.
47. See also Haaken 1998; Tavris 1993.
48. See also Davies 1995.
49. See also Tallen 1990.
50. See Blessing 1992; Champagne 1996; Wilson 1994.
51. See, for example, Dietz 2001.
52. See, for example, Lin and Tan 1994; Park 1998. In her multiracial study of women with eating problems, Becky Thompson (1994) argues that "taking into consideration women's multidimensional identities widens the range of psychological symptoms that may be attributed to sexual abuse" (p. 68). Furthermore, she points out, "since sexual abuse influences cultural/racial identities, responses to it are shaped by race and culture as well" (p. 68).
53. Wilson discusses *Gwendolen* by Buchi Emecheta (1990); *The Color Purple* by Alice Walker (1982); *I Know Why the Caged Bird Sings* by Maya Angelou (1969); *The Unbelonging* by Joan Riley (1985); and *Bake-Face and other Guava Stories* by Opal Palmer Adisa (1986).
54. Wilson acknowledges that she did not "know at the time (or, in fact, until much later) that" what her father did to her when she was 11 or 12 "was called incest; or that it was abuse; or that it was punishable by law; or that it was something you survived" (p. 26). As she takes us through the text, incorporating the events, writers, and coping strategies that helped her

identify and then heal from the incest, she reveals how she came to understand how her father's sexual abuse had a profound influence on her sexual development and personal life. Unlike exclusively personal narratives, however, her own story is used as a backdrop to her larger analysis, brought in almost as anecdotal evidence for the more general points she makes.

55. See Denzin 1990; Tallen 1990; Armstrong 1994.
56. Sociologist Norman Denzin (1990) provides a very different reading of recovery texts. He distrusts the entire recovery enterprise, which he finds typified by the sensationalism surrounding celebrities who go public with stories about their abusive childhoods, their alcoholism, and other personal difficulties. He examines the "coming out" stories of celebrities who are adult children of alcoholics or recovering alcoholics and concludes that texts that describe their experiences reflect the following levels of glossing: "first-hand, lived experience glosses; second-order, printed stories people tell others; and third-order glosses, those given in the daily news" (p. 14).
57. See also Denzin 1990; Rapping 1996; Reinarman 1995; Rice 1992.
58. Armstrong (1994) and other feminist writers (for example, Tallen 1990) are especially critical of 12-step approaches for incest survivors and other women-centered issues but for reasons that differ significantly from Denzin's. For Denzin (1990), the risk of taking our personal troubles into a public arena include entering a place where "nothing is any longer private or sacred" (p. 13). In contrast, the feminist formulation "the personal is political" insists that the personal is inherently and unavoidably political. The challenge for feminist praxis is to develop a collective process that contests how dominant discourse masks the way personal issues are politically constituted.
59. See, for example, Rapping 1996.
60. See also Tallen 1990.
61. Susan Friedman, quoting R. Radhakrishnan, also argues for the value of "relational narratives" for "a new kind of 'coalitional politics' based on 'relationality as a field-in-process' " (Radihakrishnan 1989, 311, cited in Friedman 1995, 40).
62. See also Champagne 1996.
63. See also Bernstein 1992.
64. See Love 1991.
65. See, for example, Brown 1994, 1996; Quirk and DePrince 1996.

Chapter 10

1. In her discussion of the androcentric threads within early participatory action approaches, Patricia Maguire (1996) explains that "feminism has taught me to pay attention to my vague annoyances, particularly in trying to grapple with the inconsistencies in attempting participatory research" (p. 111). Not surprisingly, a large percentage of this literature is devoted to work with women who have been battered or raped (see, for example, Light and Kleiber 1988; Maguire 1987).
2. E. Sue Bloom (1990) elaborates 35 "aftereffects" she identified in her work with adult survivors (also see Courtois 1988). We do not oppose the use of medical intervention such as medications and hospitalization when necessary but the exclusive reliance upon medical and psychiatric explanations and treatments for the "aftereffects" (Bloom 1990) of childhood sexual abuse often serve to pathologize the individual survivor and neglect to provide the context for long-term recovery.
3. See, for example, Gergen 1988.
4. In a recent article in *Women's Studies in Communications*, Liegh Ford and Robbin Crabtree (2002) detail their dialogue on disclosure of incest as interviewer and interviewee, as friends, and co-authors. Since both authors are academics, they shared an understanding of research strategies and methodological approaches that Emily and I did not. Despite this difference, I was struck by the similarity in their goals as participants in the dialogue. They also highlighted the value of feminist standpoint theory for their work. By adopting the method of layered account recommended by Ronai (1992), Ford and Crabtree (2002) argue that they "avoid the outmoded and essentialist notions of female experiences such as incest and sexual abuse while preserving the collective experience of oppression by and resistance to the patriarchy within which such abuse occurs" (p. 59). In addition, they ac-

knowledge the risk that re-tellings can contribute to the development of "a particular meta-narrative form" (p. 69) as well as recognized that "in some sense the inceest narrative is new in each re-telling" (p. 70).

Chapter 11

1. Agrarian ideology celebrates "farming and farmers as the heart of American society" (Fink 1992, xv). The independent male producer is defined as the farmer; women are viewed through their traditional role as homemaker, wife, and mother and in relationship to the male farmer (also see Sachs 1983). Agrarianism also emphasizes rugged individualism. Agrarian populists protested large corporate capitalism and government intervention and emphasized "grass-roots democracy" and "the rhetoric of justice and of a moral civil order that predated liberal capitalism" (Adams 1992, 368). Yet the growing diversity among those living in rural communities "worked against creating a program that included poor, 'backward' farmers and unpropertied laborers" (p. 370). Agrarian ideology also encompasses an emphasis on *gemeinschaft* that featured close-knit ties among community members who help each other through difficult economic and emotional crises (see Wilkinson 1991). Ongoing shifts in the rural economy enhance the diversification of perspectives and experiences among rural residents. The expansion of low-waged labor and the reshaping of women's work are also viewed as threats to traditional values and *gemeinschaft*.

2. Feminist educational theorist Berenice Malka Fisher (2001) emphasizes the significance of emotions for feminist pedagogy as well as theory-building. Referring to the work of John Dewey, Fisher writes that "feelings give coherence to experience. Stories told without feeling have an irritating, confusing, or comic effect" (p. 71). However, she notes:

   > there is nothing self-evident about the role of feelings in feminist discourse, either what they mean or how they should function. What is evident in the viewpoint I am developing is that attention to feelings broadens the opportunities for reflection. This type of reflection has a friendly quality, in the sense that it does not objectify a given feeling response as though it were an alien or dangerous specimen to be examined under a microscope. Rather, such reflection recognizes the kinship as well as the differences between thinking and feeling. Both involve ideas. Both presume and contribute to judgments. And both remain important elements of feminist discourse. (P. 71)

3. See also Joseph and Lewis 1981; Lugones and Spelman 1983; Stern 1998.
4. See also Borland 1991.
5. See also Burawoy 1991. See, for example, Borland 1991; Collins 1990; Tolman and Brydon-Miller 2001; Whyte 1991.

References

Abramovitz, Mimi. 1988. *Regulating the Lives of Women: Social Welfare Policy From Colonial Times to the Present.* Boston, Mass.: South End Press.

———. 1996. *Under Attack, Fighting Back: Women and Welfare in the United States.* New York: Monthly Review Press.

Abu-Lughod, Lila. 1993. *Writing Women's Worlds: Bedouin Stories.* Berkeley: University of California Press.

Acker, Joan, Kate Barry, and Johanna Esseveld. 1991. "Objectivity and Truth: Problems in Doing Feminist Research." Pp. 133–53 in *Beyond Methodology,* eds. Mary Margaret Fonow and Judith A. Cook. Bloomington: Indiana University Press.

Adams, Jane. 1992. "1870s Agrarian Activism in Southern Illinois: Mediator Between Two Eras." *Social Science History* 16(3):365–400.

Adisa, Opal Palmer. *Bake-Face and Other Guava Stories.* Berkeley: Kelsey St. Press.

Adler, Patricia A., and Peter Adler. 1987. *Membership Roles in Field Research.* Newbury Park, Calif.: Sage.

Aguilar, John L. 1981. "Insider Research: An Ethnography of a Debate." Pp. 133–49 in *Anthropologists at Home in North America: Methods and Issues in the Study of One's Own Society,* ed. Donald A. Messerschmidt. Cambridge, U.K.: Cambridge University Press.

Alcoff, Linda. 1988. "Cultural Feminism versus Post-Structuralism: The Identity Crisis in Feminist Theory." *Signs: Journal of Women in Culture and Society,* 13(3):405–36.

———. 1991–92. "The Problem of Speaking for Others." *Cultural Critique* 20:5–32.

———, and Laura Gray. 1993. "Survivor Discourse: Transgression or Recuperation?" *Signs: Journal of Women in Culture and Society* 18(2):260–90.

Alexander, M. Jacqui, and Chandra Talpade Mohanty. 1997. "Introduction: Genealogies, Legacies, Movements." Pp. xiii–xlii in *Feminist Genealogies, Colonial Legacies, Democratic Futures.* New York: Routledge.

Allen, Charlotte Vale. 1982. *Daddy's Girl.* New York: Berkeley Books.

Alleyne, Vanessa. 1997. *There Were Times I Thought I Was Crazy: A Black Woman's Story of Incest.* Toronto: Sister Vision: Black Women and Women of Colour Press.

Allison, Dorothy. 1992. *Bastard Out of Carolina.* New York: Penguin.

Altshuler, Alan A. 1970. *Community Control: The Black Demand for Participation in Large American Cities.* New York: Pegasus.

American Medical Association. 1994. "Report of the Council on Scientific Affairs." June 16.

American Psychiatric Association. 1993. "Statement on Memories of Sexual Abuse." December 12.

Amott, Theresa. L. 1990. "Black Women and AFDC: Making Entitlement out of Necessity." Pp. 280–98 in *Women, the State, and Welfare,* ed. Linda Gordon. Madison: University of Wisconsin.

———. 1993. *Caught in the Crisis: Women and the U.S. Economy Today.* New York: Monthly Review Press.

———, and Julia A. Matthaei. 1991. *Race, Gender & Work: A Multicultural Economic History of Women in the United States.* Boston: South End Press.

Anderson, Elijah. 1976. *A Place on the Corner.* Chicago: University of Chicago Press.

Angelou, Maya. 1969. *I Know Why the Caged Bird Sings.* Toronto: Bantom Books.

Annis, Ann W., Michelle Loyd-Paige, and Rodger R. Rice. 2001. *Set Us Free: What the Church Needs to Know from Survivors of Abuse.* Lanham, Md.: University Press of America.

Anzaldúa, Gloria. 1987. *Borderlands/La Frontera: The New Mestiza.* San Francisco: Spinsters/Aunt Lute.

Armstrong, Louise. 1978. *Kiss Daddy Goodnight: A Speak Out on Incest.* New York: Hawthorn Books.

———. 1990. "The Personal Is Apolitical." *Women's Review of Books* (March): 1–44.

———. 1994. *Rocking the Cradle of Sexual Politics: What Happened When Women Said Incest.* Reading, Mass.: Addison-Wesley Publishing.

Asad, Talal, ed. 1973. *Anthropology and the Colonial Encounter.* London: Ithaca Press.

Baca Zinn, Maxine. 1979. "Field Research in Minority Communities: Ethical, Methodological, and Political Observations by an Insider." *Social Problems* 27:209–19.

———. 1989. "Family, Race, and Poverty in the Eighties." *Signs: Journal of Women in Culture and Society* 14(4):856–74.

Bar On, Bat-Ami. 1993. "Marginality and Epistemic Privilege." Pp. 83–100 in *Feminist Epistemologies*, eds. Linda Alcoff and E. Potter. New York: Routledge.

Barrett, Michelle. 1980. *Women's Oppression Today.* London: Verso.

———. 1991. *The Politics of Truth: From Marx to Foucault.* Stanford, Calif.: Stanford University Press.

———, and Anne Phillips, eds. 1992. *Destabilizing Theory: Contemporary Feminist Debates.* Stanford, Calif.: Stanford University Press.

Barringer, Carol E. 1992. "The Survivor's Voice: Breaking The Incest Taboo." *NWSA Journal* 4.1: 4–22.

Bartlett, Peggy F. 1993. *American Dreams, Rural Realities: Family Farms in Crisis.* Chapel Hill: University of North Carolina Press.

Bass, Ellen, and Laura Davis. 1988. *The Courage to Heal: A Guide for Women Survivors of Child Sexual Abuse.* New York: Harper and Row.

———, and Louise Thornton. 1983. *I Never Told Anyone: Writings by Women Survivors of Child Sexual Abuse.* New York: Harper Colophon.

Basu, Amrita. 2000. "MillerComm Lecture. Mapping Transnational Women's Movements: Globalizing the Local, Localizing the Global." In *UIUC Area Centers Joint Symposium: Gender and Globalization.* University of Illinois, Urbana-Champaign.

Bawden, D. Lee, ed. 1984. *The Social Contract Revisited: Aims and Outcomes of President Reagan's Social Welfare Policy.* Washington, D.C.: Urban Institute Press.

Bays, Sharon. 1994. *Cultural Politics and Identity Formation In A San Joaquin Valley Hmong Community.* Ph.D. dissertation, Anthropology. UCLA.

Becker, Harold. A. 1963. *Outsiders.* New York: Free Press.

Beckett, Katherine. 1996. "Culture and the Politics of Signification: The Case of Sexual Abuse." *Social Problems* 43(1):57–76.

Behar, Ruth. 1993. *Translated Woman: Crossing the Border with Esperanza's Story.* Boston: Beacon Press.

———. 1995. *The Vulnerable Observer: Anthropology That Breaks Your Heart.* Boston: Beacon Press.

Belenky, Mary Field, Blythe McVicker Clincy, Nancy Rule Goldberger, Jill Matuck Tarule. 1986. *Women's Ways of Knowing.* New York: Basic Books.

Bell, Diane. 1993. *Gendered Fields: Women, Men and Ethnography.* New York: Routledge.

Bell, Michael. 1994. *Childerley: Nature and Morality in a Country Village.* Chicago: University of Chicago Press.

Bell, Vikki. 1993. *Interrogating Incest: Feminism, Foucault and the Law.* New York: Routledge.

Bello, Walden, with Shea Cunningham and Bill Rau. 1994. *Dark Victory: The United States, Structural Adjustment and Global Poverty.* London: Pluto.

Benford, Robert D. 1993. " 'You Could Be the Hundreth Monkey': Collective Action Frames and Vocabularies of Motive within the Nuclear Disarmament Movement." *Sociological Quarterly* 34(2):195–216.

———. 1997. "An Insider's Critique of Social Movement Framing Perspective." *Sociological Inquiry* 67(4):409–30.

Berger, Joseph. 1989. "Community Control Goes Awry in a City School Board." *New York Times* v139(Oct. 29):E5.

Berliner, David C. 1997. "Educational Psychology Meets the Christian Right: Differing Views of Children, Schooling, Teaching, and Learning." *Teachers College Record* 98:3381–85.

Bernstein, Mary, and Renate Reimann, eds. 2001. *Queer Families, Queer Politics: Challenging Culture and the State.* New York: Columbia University Press.

Bernstein, Susan David. 1992. "Confessing Feminist Theory: What's 'I' Got to Do with It?" *Hypatia* 7(2):120–47.

Berube, Maurice, and Marilyn Gittell, eds. 1969. *Confrontation at Ocean Hill-Brownsville.* New York: Praeger.

Bhabha, Homi K. 1994. *The Location of Culture.* New York: Routlege.

Blair, Norma Baker. 2002. "A Book Review of *Set Us Free: What the Church Needs to Know from Survivors of Abuse*." *The Chorus*, Voices in Action, Inc., XV(3):9.

Blee, Kathleen M. 1998. "White-Knuckle Research: Emotional Dynamics in Fieldwork with Racist Activists." *Qualitative Sociology* 21(4):381–99.

———. 2002. *Inside Organized Racism: Women in the Hate Movement*. Berkeley: University of California Press.

Blessing, Shana Rowen. 1992. "How to Be a Political Dyke and an Incest Survivor at the Same Time, or, Why are All the Dykes I Know Reading *The Courage to Heal*?" *Lesbian Ethics* 4(3):122–28.

Bloom, Leslie Rebecca. 1998. *Under the Sign of Hope: Feminist Methodology and Narrative Interpretation*. Albany, N.Y.: State University of New York Press.

Bloom, E. Sue. 1990. *Secret Survivors: Uncovering Incest and Its Aftereffects in Women*. New York: John Wiley and Sons.

Boelen, W.A. Marianne. 1990. "Street Corner Society: Cornerville Revisited." *Journal of Contemporary Ethnography* 21(1):11–51.

Bookman, Ann, and Sandra Morgen, eds. 1988. *Women and the Politics of Empowerment*. Philadelphia: Temple University Press.

Borland, Kathleen. 1991. " 'That's Not What I Said': Interpretive Conflict in Oral Narrative Research." Pp. 63–75 in *Women's Words: The Feminist Practice of Oral History*, eds. Sherna Berger Gluck and Daphne Patai. New York: Routledge.

Bose, Chris. E. 1985. *Jobs and Gender: A Study of Occupational Prestige*. New York: Praeger.

Boyer, Peter J. 1984. " 'Secular Humanism' Stirs School Censorship Furor." *Los Angeles Times* 103, sec. I (Nov. 11):1, 14–15.

Bradshaw, John. 1990. *Homecoming: Reclaiming and Championing Your Inner Child*. New York: Bantam Books.

Braveman, Stephen L. 2002. "Sexual Abuse by Priests." *The Chorus*, Voices in Action, Inc., XV(3):5, 10.

Brenner, Johanna. 2000. *Women and the Politics of Class*. New York: Monthly Review Press.

Brewer, Rose. M. 1988. "Black Women in Poverty: Some Comments on Female-Headed Families." *Signs: Journal of Women in Culture and Society* 13(2):331–39.

———. 1994. "Race, Class, Gender and U.S. State Welfare Policy: The Nexus of Inequality for African American Families." Pp. 115–27 in *Color, Class and Country: Experiences of Gender*, eds. Gay Young and Bette Dickerson. Atlantic Highlands, N.J.: Zed Books.

Brickman, Julie. 1984. "Feminist, Nonsexist, and Traditional Models of Therapy: Implications for Working with Incest." *Women and Therapy* 3(1):49–67.

Brock, Debi. 1990. "Talkin' Bout a Revelation: Feminist Popular Discourse on Sexual Abuse." *Canadian Woman Studies/Les Cahiers de la Femme* 12(1):12–15.

Brown, Laura S. 1994. *Subversive Dialogues: Theory in Feminist Therapy*. New York: Basic Books.

———. 1996. "Politics of Memory, Politics of Incest: Doing Therapy and Politics that Really Matter." Pp. 5–18 in *A Feminist Clinician's Guide to the Memory Debate*, eds. Susan Contratto and M. Janice Gutfreund. New York: Haworth Press.

Brown, Michael K. 1988. "The Segmented Welfare System: Distributive Conflict and Retrenchment in the United States, 1968–1984." Pp. 182–210 in *Remaking the Welfare State: Retrenchment and Social Policy in America and Europe*, ed. Michael K. Brown. Philadelphia: Temple University Press.

Buder, Leonard. 1988. "Decentralization of Schools Provides Painful Lessons: The Elusive Goal of Community Control." *New York Times* v138, sec.4 (Dec. 11):E6.

Bunch, Charlotte. 1987. "Making Common Cause: Diversity and Coalitions." Pp. 49–56 in *Passionate Politics*. New York: St. Martin's Press.

Burawoy, Michael. 1991. "Introduction." Pp. 1–7 in *Ethnography Unbound: Power and Resistance in the Modern Metropolis*, ed. M. Burawoy. Berkeley: University of California Press.

Burman, Erica. 2001. "Minding the Gap: Positivism, Psychology, and the Politics of Qualitative Methods." Pp. 259–75 in *From Subjects to Subjectivities: A Handbook of Interpretive and Participatory Methods*, eds. Deborah L. Tolman and Mary Brydon-Miller. New York: New York University Press.

Burnham, Linda. 1986. "Has Poverty Been Feminized in Black America?" Pp. 69–83 in *For Crying Out Loud: Women and Poverty in the United States*, eds. Rochelle Lefkowitz and Ann Withorn. New York: Pilgrim.

Butler, Judith, and Joan Scott, eds. 1992. *Feminists Theorize the Political.* New York: Routledge.

Butler, Sandra. 1978. *Conspiracy of Silence: The Trauma of Incest.* San Francisco: New Glide Publications.

Cain, Maureen. 1990. "Realist Philosophy and Standpoint Espistemologies or Feminist Criminology as a Successor Science." Pp. 120–40 in *Feminist Perspectives in Criminology,* eds. Louraine Gelsthorpe and Alison Morris. Milton Keynes: Open University Press.

Campbell, Marie L. 1998. "Institutional Ethnography and Experience as Data." *Qualitative Sociology* 21(1):55–73.

———, and Ann Manicom. 1995. "Introduction." Pp. 3–16 in *Knowledge, Experience, and Ruling Relations: Studies in the Social Organization of Knowledge.* Toronto: University of Toronto Press.

Campbell, Nancy D. 1999. "Regulating 'Maternal Instinct': Governing Mentalities of Late Twentieth-Century U.S. Illicit Drug Policy." *Signs: Journal of Women in Culture and Society* 24(4):895–923.

———. 2000. *Using Women: Gender, Drug Policy, and Social Justice.* New York: Routledge.

Cancian, Francesca. 1996. "Participatory Research and Alternative Strategies for Activist Sociology." Pp. 187–205 in *Feminism and Social Change: Bridging Theory and Practice,* ed. Heidi Gottfried. Urbana and Chicago: University of Illinois Press.

Canning, Kathleen. 1994. "Feminist History after the Linguistic Turn: Historicizing Discourse and Experience." *Signs: Journal of Women in Culture and Society* 19:368–404.

Cantú, Lionel. 1999. "Border Crossings: Mexican Men and the Sexuality of Migration." Ph.D. dissertation. University of California, Irvine.

Capital Comments. 1990. "The Learnfare Saga Continues." *Capital Comments* 8(6):3–5.

Carnoy, Martin, Derek Shearer, and Russell Rumberger. 1983. *A New Social Contract: The Economy and Government after Reagan.* New York: Harper and Row.

Chang, Grace. 1994. "Undocumented Latinas: Welfare Burdens or Beasts of Burden?" *Socialist Review* 93(3):151–85.

———. 2000. *Disposable Domestics: Immigrant Women Workers in the Global Economy.* Cambridge, Mass.: South End Press.

Chase, Susan E. 1995. *Ambiguous Empowerment: The Work Narratives of Women School Superintendents.* Amherst: University of Massachusetts Press.

Charmaz, Kathy. 1983. "The Grounded Theory Method: An Explication and Interpretation." Pp. 109–26 in *Contemporary Field Research: A Collection of Readings,* ed. Robert M. Emerson. Prospect Heights, Ill.: Waveland Press.

———, and Richard G. Mitchell, Jr. 1997. "The Myth of Silent Authorship: Self, Substance and Style in Ethnographic Writing." Pp. 193–215 in *Reflexivity and Voice,* ed. Rosanna Hertz. Thousand Oaks, Calif.: Sage.

Champagne, Rosaria. 1996. *The Politics of Survivorship: Incest, Women's Literature, and Feminist Theory.* New York: New York University Press.

Chew, Judy. 1998. *Women Survivors of Childhood Sexual Abuse: Healing through Group Work beyond Survival.* New York and London: Haworth Press.

Chodorow, Nancy. 1978. *The Reproduction of Mothering.* Berkeley: University of California Press.

Chow, Rey. 1993. *Writing Diaspora: Tactics of Intervention in Contemporary Cultural Studies.* Bloomington: Indiana University Press.

Christensen, Bryce, Allan Carlson, Maris Vinovckis, Richard Vedder, and Jean Bethke Elshtain. 1988. *The Family Wage: Work, Gender and Children in the Modern Economy.* Rockford, Ill.: The Rockford Institute.

Chunn, Dorothy E., and Dany Lacombe. 2000. "Introduction." Pp. 2–18 in *Law as a Gendering Practice,* eds. Dorothy E. Chunn and Dany Lacombe. New York: Oxford University Press.

Clark, Kenneth. 1965. *Dark Ghetto: Dilemmas of Social Power.* New York: Harper and Row.

Clegg, Christine. 1999. "Feminist Recoveries in *My Father's House.*" *Feminist Review* 61:67–82.

Clifford, James. 1986. "Introduction: Partial Truths." Pp. 1–26 in *Writing Culture: The Poetics and Politics of Ethnography,* eds. J. Clifford and G. Marcus. Berkeley: University of California Press.

———. 1990. *The Predicament of Culture: Twentieth Century Ethnography, Literature, and Art.* Ithaca, N.Y.: Cornell University Press.

———, and George E. Marcus. 1986. *Writing Culture: The Poetics and Politics of Ethnography.* Berkeley: University of California Press.

Clough, Patricia. Ticiento. 1993. "On the Brink of Deconstructing Sociology: Critical Reading of Dorothy Smith's Standpoint Epistemology." *Sociological Quarterly* 34(1):169–82.

———. 1994. *Feminist Thought.* Oxford, U.K., and Cambridge Mass.: Blackwell.

CNN. 2000. "Private Schools/Public Money." *Democracy in America* (Sept. 17). URL: wysiwyg://2http://www.cnn.com/SPECIALS/2000/democracy/

Coalition on Human Needs. 1996. "Welfare Watch." *Human Needs Report* (May 28):1.

Coffey, Amanda. 1999. *The Ethnographic Self: Fieldwork and the Representation of Identity.* Thousand Oaks, Calif.: Sage.

Collins, Patricia Hill. 1990. *Black Feminist Thought: Knowledge, Consciousness, and the Politics of Empowerment.* Boston: Unwin Hyman.

———. 1991. "Learning from the Outsider Within: The Sociological Significance of Black Feminist Thought." Pp. 35–59 in *Beyond Methodology: Feminist Scholarship as Lived Research,* eds. Mary Margaret Fonow and Judith A. Cook. Bloomington: Indiana University Press.

———. 1997. "Comment on Hekman's 'Truth and Method: Feminist Standpoint' Theory Revisited': Where's the Power?" *Signs: Journal of Women in Culture and Society* 22(2): 375–81.

———. 1998. *Fighting Words: Black Women and the Search for Justice.* New York: Routledge.

Comaroff, John. 1994. "Foreword." Pp. ix–xii in *Contested States: Law, Hegemony and Resistance* eds. Minnie Lazarus-Black and S.F. Hirch. New York: Routledge.

Contratto, Susan, and M. Janice Gutfreund, eds. 1996. *A Feminist Clinician's Guide to the Memory Debate.* New York: Haworth Press.

Coombe, Rosemary J. 1989. "Room for Manoeuver: Toward a Theory of Practice in Critical Legal Studies." *Law and Social Inquiry* 14(1).

Corbett, Thomas, Jeanette Deloya, Wendy Manning, and Liz Uhr. 1989. "Learnfare: The Wisconsin Experience." *Focus* 12(2):1–10. Madison: Institute for Research on Poverty, University of Wisconsin-Madison.

Cotterill, Pamela. 1992. "Interviewing Women: Issues of Friendship, Vulnerability, and Power." *Women's Studies International Forum* 15(5):593–606.

Courtois, Christine. 1988. *Healing the Incest Wound: Adult Survivors in Therapy.* New York: Norton.

Crenshaw, Kimberly. 1993. "Mapping the Margins: Intersectionality, Identity Politics, and Violence against Women of Color." *Stanford Law Review* 43:1241–99.

Creswell, John W. 1998. *Qualitative Inquiry and Research Design: Choosing among Five Traditions.* Thousand Oaks, Calif.: Sage.

———. 2002. *Research Design: Qualitative, Quantitative, and Mixed Methods Approaches.* Thousand Oaks, Calif.: Sage.

Cronin, Joseph M. 1973. *The Control of Urban Schools: Perspective on the Power of Educational Reformers.* New York: Free Press.

Crossley, Michele L. 1999. "Stories of Illness and Trauma Survival: Liberation or Repression?" *Social Science and Medicine* 48:1685–95.

———. 2000. "Deconstructing Autobiological Accounts of Childhood Sexual Abuse." *Feminism and Psychology* 10(1):73–90.

Cvetkovich, Ann. 1995. "Sexual Trauma/Queer Memory: Incest, Lesbianism, and Therapeutic Culture: Some Critical Reflections." *GLQ* 2(4):351–77.

Davies, Michele L. 1995. *Healing Sylvia: Childhood Sexual Abuse and the Construction of Identity.* London: Taylor and Francis.

Davis, Joseph E. 2000. "Accounts of False Memory Syndrome: Parents, 'Retractors,' and the Role of Institutions in Account Making." *Qualitative Sociology* 23(1):29–56.

Davis, Laura. 1990. *The Courage to Heal Workbook: For Women and Men Survivors of Child Sexual Abuse.* New York: Harper and Row.

de Castell, Suzanne, and Mary Bryson. 1998. "Queer Ethnography: Identity, Authority, Narrativity, and a Geopolitics of Text." Pp. 97–110 in *Inside the Academy and Out: Lesbian-Gay-Queer Studies and Social Action,* eds. Janice L. Ristock and Catherine Taylor. Toronto: University of Toronto Press.

De Janvry, Alain. 1980. "Social Differentiation in Agriculture and the Ideology of Neopopulism." Pp. 155–68 in *The Rural Sociology of the Advanced Societies: Critical Perspectives,* eds. Frederick H. Buttell and Howard Newby. Montclair, N.J.: Allanhed, Osmun.

Delphy, Christine. 1975. "For a Materialist Feminism." *Feminist Issues* 1(2).

Denzin, Norman K. 1990. "Presidential Address on *The Sociological Imagination* Revisted." *Sociological Quarterly* 31(1):1–22.

Derricotte, Toi. 1989. "Poem for My Father." Pp. 6–8 in *Captivity*. Pittsburgh, Penn.: University of Pittsburgh Press.

Desai, Manisha. 2002. "Globalization, Structural Adjustment and Women's Transnational Solidarities." Pp. 15–33 in *Women's Activism and Globalization: Linking Local Struggles with Transnational Politics*, eds. Nancy A. Naples and Manisha Desai. New York: Routledge.

DeVault, Marjorie. 1994. *Feeding the Family: The Social Organization of Caring as Gendered Work*. Chicago: University of Chicago Press.

———. 1999. *Liberating Method: Feminism and Social Research*. Philadelphia: Temple University Press.

———, and Liza McCoy. 2001. "Institutional Ethnography: Using Interviews to Investigate Ruling Relations." Pp. 751–76 in *Handbook of Interview Research: Context and Method*, eds. Jaber F. Gubrium and James A. Holstein. Thousand Oaks, Calif.: Sage.

Diamond, Timothy. 1992. *Making Gray Gold: Narratives of Nursing Home Care*. Chicago: University of Chicago Press.

Dietz, Christine. 2001. "Working with Lesbian, Gay, Bisexual and Transgendered Abuse Survivors." *Journal of Progressive Human Services* 12(2):27–49.

di Leonardo, Micaela., ed. 1991. *Gender at the Crossroads of Knowledge: Feminist Anthropology in the Postmodern Era*. Berkeley: University of California Press.

Dill, Bonnie Thornton. 1988. "Making Your Job Good Yourself: Domestic Service and the Construction of Personal Dignity." Pp. 33–52 in *Women and the Politics of Empowerment*, eds. Ann Bookman and Sandra Morgen. Philadelphia: Temple University Press.

Dinsmore, Christine. 1991. *From Surviving to Thriving: Incest, Feminism, and Recovery*. Albany, N.Y.: State University of New York Press.

Doane, Janice, and Devon Hodges. 2001. *Telling Incest: Narratives of Dangerous Remembering from Stein to Sapphire*. Ann Arbor: University of Michigan Press.

Dobash, R. Emerson and Russell P. Dobash. 1992. *Women, Violence and Social Change*. London and New York: Routledge.

Dolan, Maura. 1996. "Witness' 'Repressed Memories' Attacked," *Los Angeles Times* (Feb. 21):A16R.

Donati, Paolo R. 1992. "Political Discourse Analysis." Pp. 136–67 in *Studying Collective Action*, eds. Mario Diani and Ron Eyerman. London: Sage.

Dougherty, Kevin. 1987. "The Effects of Community Colleges: Aid or Hindrance to Socio-economic Attainment?" *Sociology of Education* 60:86–103.

Downs, Anthony. 1970. "Competition and Community Schools." Pp. 219–49 in *Community Control of Schools*, ed. Henry M. Levin. Washington, D.C.: Brookings Institution.

DuBois, William Edward B. 1903/1996. *Souls of Black Folk*. New York: Penguin Books.

Duncan, Cynthia M. 1999. *Worlds Apart: Why Poverty Persists in Rural America*. New Haven: Yale University Press.

Dunning, Lina. 1990. "Fighting Back." *The Survivor Resource Chronicle: Information For and About Survivors of Child Sexual Abuse* 5(3):1.

Ebron, Paulla, and Anna Lowenhaupt Tsing. 1995. "In Dialogue? Reading across Minority Discourses." Pp. 390–411 in *Women Writing Culture*, eds. Ruth Behar and Deborah A. Gordon. Berkeley: University of California Press.

Echols, Alice. 1989. *Daring to Be Bad: Radical Feminism in America, 1967–1995*. Minneapolis: University of Minnesota Press.

Edell, Therese. 1990. "Emma." *For Therese: The Music of Therese Edell: Various Artists*. Cincinnati, Ohio: Sea Friends Recordings.

Edin, Katherine. 1991. "Surviving the Welfare System: How AFDC Recipients Make Ends Meet in Chicago." *Social Problems* 38(4):462–74.

———, and Laura Lein. 1997. *Making Ends Meet: How Single Mothers Survive Welfare and Low-Wage Work*. New York: Russell Sage Foundation.

Ehrenreich, Barbara. 1984. "Life without Father: Reconsidering Socialist Feminist Theory." *Socialist Review* 14(1):48–57.

Eisenstein, Zillah. R., ed. 1979. *Capitalist Patriarchy and the Case for Socialist Feminism*. New York: Monthly Review Press.

———. 1986. "The Patriarchal Relations of the Reagan State." Pp. 181–89 in *Women and Poverty*, eds. B.C. Gelpi, N.C.M. Hartsock, C.C. Novak, and M.H. Strober. Chicago: University of Chicago Press.

Elden, Max, and Morten Levin. 1991. "Cogenerative Learning: Bringing Participation into Action Research." Pp. 127–42 in *Participatory Action Research*, ed. William Foote Whyte. New York: Sage.

Ellis, Carolyn. 1991. "Sociological Introspection and Emotional Experience." *Symbolic Interaction* 14(1):23–50.

———. 1995. "Emotional and Ethical Quagmires in Returning to the Field." *Journal of Contemporary Ethnography* 23(1):68–98.

Ellison, Ralph. 1952. *Invisible Man.* New York: New American Library.

Ellwood, David. 1988. *Poor Support: Poverty in the American Family.* New York: Basic Books.

El-Or, Tamar. 1997. "Do You Really Know How They Make Love? The Limits on Intimacy with Ethnographic Informants." Pp. 169–89 in *Reflexivity & Voice*, ed. R. Hertz. Thousands Oaks, Calif.: Sage.

Emecheta, Buchi. 1990. *Gwendolen.* New York: G. Braziller.

Engels, Frederick. 1972. *The Origin of the Family, Private Property, and the State.* New York: International Publishers.

Enns, Carolyn Zerbe. 1996. "The Feminist Therapy Institute Code of Ethics: Implications for Working with Survivors of Child Sexual Abuse. Pp. 79–91 in *A Feminist Clinician's Guide to the Memory Debate*, eds. Susan Contratto and M. Janice Gutfreund. New York: Haworth Press.

Enslin, Elizabeth. 1990. "The Dynamics of Gender, Class and Caste in a Women's Movement in Rural Nepal." Ph.D. dissertation. Department of Anthropology, Stanford University.

———. 1994. "Beyond Writing: Feminist Practice and the Limitations of Ethnography." *Cultural Anthropology* 9:537–68.

Epstein, Cynthia. 1981. *Women in Law.* Garden City, N.Y.: Doubleday and Anchor.

Escobar, Arturo. 1984–85. "Discourse and Power in Development: Michel Foucault and the Relevance of His Work to the Third World." *World Development* Winter:377–400.

Estrich, Susan. 1987. *Real Rape.* Cambridge, Mass.: Harvard University Press.

Evans, Wendy J., and David R. Maines. 1995. "Narrative Structures and the Analysis of Incest." *Symbolic Interaction* 18(3):303–22.

Fantini, Mario. 1969. "Community Participation." Pp. 323–37 in *The Politics of Urban Education*, eds. Marilyn Gittell and Alan G. Hevesi. New York: Frederick A. Praeger, Publishers.

Feldman-Summers, Shirley. 1996. "Litigation Pitfalls for the Psychotherapist Whose Client 'First Remembers' Childhood Sexual Abuse During Therapy." Pp. 109–22 in *A Feminist Clinician's Guide to the Memory Debate*, eds. Susan Contratto and M. Janice Gutfreund. New York: Haworth Press.

Feldman, Shelley, and R. Welsh. 1995. "Feminist Knowledge Claims, Local Knowledge, and Gender Divisions of Agricultural Labor: Constructing a Successor Science." *Rural Sociology* 60: 23–43.

Felmlee, Diane H. 1988. "Returning to School and Women's Occupational Attainment." *Sociology of Education* 61:29–41.

Ferguson, Ann. 1989. *Blood at the Root: Motherhood, Sexuality and Male Dominance.* Boston, Mass.: Unwin Hyman.

———. 1991. *Sexual Democracy: Women, Oppression, and Revolution.* Boulder, Colo.: Westview.

———, and Nancy Folbre. 1981. "The Unhappy Marriage of Patriarchy and Capitalism." Pp. 313–38 in *Women and Revolution*, ed. Lydia Sargent. Boston: South End Press.

Ferguson, Kathy E. 1991. "Interpretation and Genealogy in Feminism." *Signs: Journal of Women in Culture and Society* 16(2):322–39.

Ferguson, James. 1994. *The Anti-Politics Machine: "Development," Depoliticization, and Bureaucratic Power in Lesotho.* Minneapolis: University of Minnesota.

Fine, Gary. 1993. "Ten Lies of Ethnography: Moral Dilemmas of Field Research." *Journal of Contemporary Ethnography* 22(3):267–94.

Fine, Michelle. 1992. *Disruptive Voices: The Possibilities of Feminist Research.* Ann Arbor: University of Michigan Press.

———. 1998. "Working the Hyphen: Reinventing Self and Other in Qualitative Research." Pp. 130–55 in *The Landscape of Qualitative Research: Theories and Issues*, eds. Norman K. Denzin and Yvonna S. Lincoln. Thousand Oaks, Calif.: Sage.

Fink, Deborah. 1986. *Open Country, Iowa: Rural Women, Tradition and Change.* Albany: State University of New York Press.

———. 1992. *Agrarian Women: Wives and Mothers in Rural Nebraska 1880–1940.* Chapel Hill: University of North Carolina Press.

Finnie, Charles. 1995. "LSC Survives Another Bid for Closure: Legal Aid Backers Barely Consider Themselves Lucky." *Los Angeles Daily Journal* (Oct. 2):1.

Fisher, Berenice Malka. 2001. *No Angels in the Classroom: Teaching through Feminist Discourse.* Lanham, Md.: Rowman and Littlefield.

Fisher, Robert S. 1991. *A Profile of AFDC Recipients in Iowa: Results of a Survey. Final Report to the Iowa Department of Human Services.* Iowa City: School of Social Work and Public Policy Center, University of Iowa, February 1.

———, and Joseph M. Kling. 1990. "Leading the People: Two Approaches to the Role of Ideology in Community Organizing." Pp. 73–90 in *Dilemmas of Activism: Class, Community, and the Politics of Local Mobilization,* eds. Joseph M. King and Prudence Poser. Philadelphia: Temple University Press.

Fitchen, Janet M. 1981. *Poverty in Rural America: A Case Study.* Boulder, Colo. Westview.

———. 1992. *Enduring Spaces, Enduring Places: Change, Identity, and Survival in Rural America.* Boulder, Colo.: Westview.

Flax, Jane. 1990. *Thinking Fragments: Psychoanalysis, Feminism, and Postmodernism in the Contemporary West.* Berkeley: University of California Press.

Folbre, Nancy. 1984. "The Pauperization of Motherhood: Patriarchy and Public Policy in the United States." *Review of Radical Political Economics* 16(4):72–88.

Fonow, Mary Margaret, and Judith A. Cook. 1991a. "Back to the Future: A Look at the Second Wave of Feminist Epistemology and Methodology." Pp. 1–15 in *Beyond Methodology: Feminist Scholarship as Lived Research,* eds. Mary Margaret Fonow and Judith A. Cook. Bloomington: Indiana University Press.

———. and Judith A. Cook, eds. 1991b. *Beyond Methodology: Feminist Scholarship as Lived Research.* Bloomington: Indiana University Press.

Ford, Leigh Arden, and Robbin D. Crabtree. 2002. "Telling, Re-telling and Talking about Telling: Disclosure and/as Surviving Incest." *Women's Studies in Communication* 25(1):53–87.

Foucault, Michel. 1972. *The Archaeology of Knowledge and the Discourse on Language.* New York: Harper and Row.

———. 1975. *The Birth of a Clinic: An Archaeology of Medical Perception.* Trans. A.M. Sheridan Smith. New York: Vintage.

———. 1978. *The History of Sexuality: An Introduction, Vol. 1.* New York: Vintage.

———. 1979. "Governmentality." *Ideology and Consciousness* 6:5–22.

Frankenberg, Ruth. 1993. *White Women, Race Matters.* Minneapolis: University of Minnesota Press.

Fraser, Nancy. 1989. *Unruly Practices: Power, Discourse and Gender in Contemporary Social Theory.* Minneapolis: University of Minnesota Press.

———. 1993. "Beyond the Master/Subject Model: Reflections on Carole Pateman's *Sexual Contract.*" *Social Text* 37:173–81.

———. 1997. *Justice Interruptus: Critical Reflections on the "Postsocialist" Conditions.* New York: Routledge.

———, and Linda Gordon. 1994a. " 'Dependency' Demystified: Inscriptions of Power in a Keyword of the Welfare State." *Social Politics* 1(1):4–31.

———, and Linda Gordon. 1994b. "A Genealogy of Dependency: Tracing a Keyword of the U.S. Welfare State." *Signs: Journal of Women in Culture and Society* 19(2):309–36.

———, and Linda J. Nicholson. 1990. "Social Criticism without Philosophy: An Encounter between Feminism and Postmodernism." Pp. 19–38 in *Feminism/Postmodernism,* ed. Linda J. Nicholson. New York: Routledge.

Fraser, Sylvia. 1988. *My Father's House: A Memoir of Incest and of Healing.* New York: Ticknor and Fields.

Fredrickson, Renee. 1992. *Repressed Memories: A Journal to Recovery from Sexual Abuse.* New York: Simon and Schuster.

Freire, Paulo. 1968. *Pedagogy of the Oppressed.* Trans. Myra Bergman Ramos. New York: Seabury Press.

———. 1973. *Education for Critical Consciousness.* New York: Seabury Press.

Freyd, Jennifer. 1996. *Betrayal Trauma: The Logic of Forgetting Childhood Abuse.* Cambridge, Mass: Harvard University Press.

Friedan, Betty. 1963. *Feminine Mystique.* New York: Norton.

Friedlander, Daniel. 1988. *Subgroup Impacts and Performance Indicators for Selected Welfare Employment Programs.* New York: Manpower Demonstration Research Corporation.

Friedman, Susan Stanford. 1995. "Beyond White and Other: Relationality and Narratives of Race in Feminist Discourse." *Signs: Journal of Women in Culture and Society* 2(1):1–49.

Fuss, Diana. 1989. *Essentially Speaking: Feminism, Nature and Difference.* New York: Routledge.

Gallop, Jane. 1995. "The Teacher's Breasts." Pp. 79–89 in *Pedagogy: The Question of Impersonation.* Bloomington: Indiana University Press.

Gamson, William. A. 1988. "Political Discourse and Collective Action." Pp. 219–44 in *International Social Movement Research, vol. 1,* eds. Bert Klandermans, Hanspeter Kriesi, and Sidney Tarrow. Greenwich, Conn.: JAI Press.

Garfinkel, Harold. 1967. *Studies in Ethnomethodology.* Englewood Cliffs, N.J.: Prentice-Hall.

Gartner, Alison Fishman, and John Gartner. 1988. "Borderline Pathology in Post-Incest Female Adolescents: Diagnostic and Theoretical Considerations." *Bulletin of the Menninger Clinic* 52:101–13.

Geertz, Clifford. 1973. *The Interpretations of Cultures.* New York: Basic Books.

———. 1983. "Found in Translation: The Social History of the Moral Imagination." Pp. 36–54 in *Local Knowledge: Further Essays in Interpretive Anthropology,* ed. C. Geertz. New York: Basic Books.

Geiger, Susan N.G. 1986. "Women's Life Histories: Method and Content." *Signs: Journal of Women in Culture and Society* 11:334–51.

Gergen, Mary M. 1988. "Toward A Feminist Metatheory and Methodology in the Social Sciences." Pp. 87–104 in *Feminist Thought and the Structure of Knowledge,* ed. Mary McCanney Gergen. New York: New York University Press.

Gerson, Deborah A. 1995. "Practice From Pain: The Ambivalent Legacy of Consciousness Raising." Unpublished paper. Berkeley: University of California, Berkeley.

Giddens, Anthony. 1991. *Modernity and Self-Identity: Self and Society in the Late Modern Age.* Stanford, Calif.: Stanford University Press.

Giddings, Paula. 1984. *When and Where I Enter: The Impact of Black Women on Race and Sex in America.* New York: William Morrow.

Gilkes, Cheryl Townsend. 1988. "Building in Many Places: Multiple Commitments and Ideologies in Black Women's Community Work." Pp. 53–76 in *Women and the Politics of Empowerment,* eds. Ann Bookman and Sandra Morgen. Philadelphia, Penn.: Temple University Press.

Gilligan, Carol. 1982. *In a Different Voice: Psychological Theory and Women's Development.* Cambridge, Mass.: Harvard University Press.

Gilman, Susan Jane. 1994. "A Michigan Judge's Ruling Punishes Single Mothers." *Ms.* 5(3):92–93.

Gingrich, Rep. Newt, Rep. D. Armey, and the House Republicans. 1994. *Contract with America.* New York: Random House.

Ginsburg, Faye D. 1997. "The Case of Mistaken Identity: Problems in Representing Women on the Right." Pp. 283–99 in *Reflexivity and Voice,* ed. Rosanna Hertz. Newbury Park, Calif.: Sage.

Gittell, Marilyn. 1969. "Community Control of Education." Pp. 363–77 in *The Politics of Urban Education,* eds. Marilyn Gittell and Alan G. Halves. New York: Frederick A. Praeger, Publishers.

———. 1970. "The Balance of Power and the Community School." Pp. 115–37 in *Community Control of Schools,* ed. Henry M. Levin. Washington, D.C.: Brookings Institution.

———, with M. Schehl and C. Fareri. 1990. *From Welfare to Independence: The College Option. A Report to the Ford Foundation.* New York: Howard Samuels State Management and Policy Center, Graduate School and University Center, CUNY.

Glazer, Nathan. 1988. *The Limits of Social Policy.* Cambridge, Mass.: Harvard University Press.

———. 1997. "Homegrown." *New Republic* (May 12):25.

Glenn, Evelyn Nakano, Grace Chang, and Linda Rennie Forcey, eds. 1994. *Mothering: Ideology, Experience, and Agency.* New York: Routledge.

Gluck, Sherna Berger, and Daphne Patai, eds. 1991. *Women's Words: The Feminist Practice of Oral History.* New York: Routledge.

Goffman, Erving. 1976. "Gender Display." *Studies in the Anthropology of Visual Communication* 3:69–77.

Goldschmidt, Walter. 1947. *As You Sow.* New York: Harcourt and Brace.

Goldstein, Eleanor C., and Kevin Farmer, eds. 1992. *Confabulations: Creating False Memories, Destroying Families.* Boca Raton, Fla.: SirS.

Goodwin, Leonard. 1989. "The Work Incentive Program in Current Perspective: What Have We Learned? Where Do We Go From Here?" *Journal of Sociology and Social Welfare* 16(2): 45–65.

Gordon, Linda, ed. 1990a. *Women, the State, and Welfare.* Madison: University of Wisconsin Press.
————. 1990b. "The New Feminist Scholarship on the Welfare State." Pp. 9–35 in *Women, the State, and Welfare,* ed. Linda Gordon. Madison: University of Wisconsin Press.
————. 1993. *Pitied but Not Entitled: Single Mothers and the History of Welfare.* New York: Free Press.
Gore, Jennifer M. 1992. "What We Can Do for You! What Can "We" Do For "You"?: Struggling over Empowerment in Critical and Feminist Pedagogy." Pp. 54–73 in *Feminisms and Critical Pedagogy,* eds. Carmen Luke and Jennifer Gore. New York: Routledge.
————. 1993. *The Struggle for Pedagogies: Critical and Feminist Discourses as Regimes of Truth.* New York: Routledge.
Gottfried, Heidi, ed. 1996. *Feminism and Social Change: Bridging Theory and Practice.* Urbana: University of Illinois Press.
Gough, John W. 1957. *The Social Contract: A Critical Study of Its Development.* London: Oxford University Press.
Greenhalgh, Susan. 2001. *Under the Medical Gaze: Facts and Fictions of Chronic Pain.* Berkeley: University of California Press.
————, and Jiali Li. 1995. "Engendering Reproductive Policy and Practice in Peasant China; For a Feminist Demography of Reproduction." *Signs: Journal of Women in Culture and Society* 20(3):601–41.
Grewal, Inderpal, and Caren Kaplan, eds. 1994. *Scattered Hegemonies: Postmodernity and Transnational Feminist Practices.* Minneapolis: University of Minnesota Press.
Griffith, Alison I., and Dorothy E. Smith. 1990. "What Did You Do in School Today?: Mothering, Schooling, and Social Class." Pp. 3–24 in *Perspectives on Social Problems Vol. 2,* eds. G. Miller and J.A. Hostein. Greenwich, Conn.: JAI Press.
Grimshaw, Jonathan. 1993. "Practices of Freedom." Pp. 51–72 in *Up against Foucault: Explorations of Some Tensions between Foucault and Feminism,* ed. Caroline Ramazanoglu. New York: Routledge.
Gringeri, Christina. 1994. *Getting By: Women Homeworkers and Rural Economic Development.* Lawrence: University Press of Kansas.
Gubrium, Jaber F. and James A. Holstein. 1997. *The New Language of Qualitative Method.* New York: Oxford University Press.
Gueron, Judith. 1987. "Reforming Welfare with Work. Ford Foundation Project on Social Welfare and the American Future." Occasional Paper no. 2. New York: Ford Foundation.
Gutting, Gary. 1989. *Michel Foucault's Archaeology of Scientific Reasoning.* Cambridge, U.K.: Cambridge University Press.
Haaken, Janice. 1995. "The Debate over Recovered Memory of Sexual Abuse: A Feminist-Psychoanalytic Perspective." *Psychiatry: Interpersonal and Biological Processes* 58(2): 189–99.
————. 1998. *Pillar of Salt: Gender, Memory, and the Perils of Looking Back.* New Brunswick, N.J.: Rutgers University Press.
————, and Astrid Schlaps. 1991. "Incest Resolution Therapy and the Objectification of Sexual Abuse." *Psychotherapy* 28(1):39–47.
Hagen, Jan L., and Irene Lurie. 1992. *Implementing JOBS: Initial State Choices.* Albany: Nelson A. Rockefeller College of Public Affairs and Policy, University at Albany, State University of New York.
Hale, Sondra. 1991. "Feminist Method, Process, and Self-criticism: Interviewing Sudanese Women." Pp. 121–36 in *Women's Words,* eds. Sherna Berger Gluck and Daphne Patai. New York: Routledge.
————. 1996. *Gender Politics in Sudan: Islamism, Socialism, and the State.* Boulder, Colo.: Westview.
Hall, Liz, and Siobhan Lloyd. 1989. *Surviving Child Sexual Abuse: A Handbook for Helping Women Challenge Their Past.* New York: The Falmer Press.
Hallman, Howard W. 1969. *Community Control: A Study of Community Corporation and Neighborhood Boards.* Washington, D.C.: Washington Center for Metropolitan Studies.
Hammersley, Martyn. 1992. *What's Wrong with Ethnography? Methodological Explorations.* London and New York: Routledge.
————, and Paul Atkinson. 1995. *Ethnography: Principles in Practice.* London: Routledge.
Haraway, Donna. 1985. "A Manifesto for Cyborgs: Science, Technology, and Socialist Feminism in the 1980s." *Socialist Review* 80:65–105.

———. 1988. "Situated Knowledges: The Science Question in Feminism and the Privilege of Partial Perspective." *Feminist Studies* 14(3):575–99.

———. 1991. *Simians, Cyborgs, and Women: The Reinvention of Nature.* New York: Routledge.

Harding, Sandra. 1986. *The Science Question in Feminism.* Ithaca, N.Y.: Cornell University Press.

———. 1987. "Is There a Feminist Method?" Pp. 1–14 in *Feminist and Methodology*, ed. Sandra Harding. Bloomington: Indiana University Press.

———. 1991. *Whose Science? Whose Knowledge?* Ithaca, N.Y.: Cornell University Press.

———. 1997. "Comment on Hekman's 'Truth and Method: Feminist Standpoint Theory Revisited': Whose Standpoint Needs the Regimes of Truth and Reality?" *Signs: Journal of Women and Culture* 22(2):382–91.

———. 1998. *Is Science Multicultural? Postcolonialisms, Feminisms, and Epistemologies.* Bloomington: Indiana University Press.

Hartmann, Heidi. 1981. "The Unhappy Marriage of Marxism and Feminism: Toward a More Progressive Union." Pp. 1–41 in *Women and Revolution*, ed. Lydia Sargent. Boston: South End Press.

———, and Linda Andrews. 1992. *Combining Work and Welfare: An Alternative Anti-poverty Strategy.* Washington, D.C.: Institute for Women's Policy Research.

Hartsock, Nancy. 1983. *Money, Sex and Power: Toward a Feminist Historical Materialism.* New York: Longman.

———. 1987a. "The Feminist Standpoint: Developing the Ground for a Specifically Feminist Historical Materialism." Pp. 157–80 in *Feminism & Methodology*, ed. Sandra Harding. Bloomington: Indiana University Press.

———. 1987b. "Rethinking Modernism: Majority Theories." *Cultural Critique* 7:187–206.

———. 1996. "Theoretical Bases for Coalition Building: An Assessment of Postmodernism." Pp. 256–74 in *Feminism and Social Change: Bridging Theory and Practice*, ed. Heidi Gottfried. Urbana: University of Illinois Press.

———. 1997. "Comment on Hekman's 'Truth and Method: Feminist Standpoint Theory Revisited': Truth or Justice?" *Signs: Journal of Women in Culture and Society* 22(2):367–63.

Hawkesworth, Mary E. 1989. "Knowers, Knowing, Known: Feminist Theory and Claims of Truth. *Signs: Journal of Women in Culture and Society* 14(3):533–57.

———. 1990. *Beyond Oppression: Feminist Theory and Political Strategy.* New York: Continuum.

Haywoode, Terry. 1991. "Working Class Feminism: Creating a Politics of Community, Connection, and Concern." Ph.D. dissertation, The City University of New York.

———. 1992. "Working Class Feminism: Creating Community-Based Social Change." Paper presented at the Annual Meetings of the American Sociological Association, Pittsburgh, Penn., 1992.

Hechinger, Fred M. 1986. "Censorship Found on the Increase." *New York Times* v135(Sept. 16):C1, 14–15.

Heenan, M. Colleen, and I. Bruna Seu. 1998. "Conclusion: Questions, Answers and Absences in Feminist Psychotherapies." Pp. 219–27 in *Feminism and Psychotherapy: Reflections on Contemporary Theories and Practices*, eds. I. Bruna Seu and M. Colleen Heenan. Thousand Oaks, Calif.: Sage.

Hekman, Susan. 1997. "Truth and Method: Feminist Standpoint Theory Revisited. *Signs: Journal of Women in Culture and Society* 22(2):341–65.

Hennessy, Rosemary. 1990. "Materialist Feminism and Foucault: The Politics of Appropriation." *Rethinking Marxism* 3(3–4):252–74.

———. 1993. *Materialist Feminism and the Politics of Discourse.* New York: Routledge.

———, and Chrys Ingraham, eds. 1997a. *Materialist Feminism: A Reader in Class, Difference, and Women's Lives.* New York: Routledge.

———, and Chrys Ingraham. 1997b. "Introduction: Reclaiming Anticapitalist Feminism." Pp. 1–14 in *Materialist Feminism: A Reader in Class, Difference, and Women's Lives*, eds. Rosemary Hennessy and Chrys Ingraham. New York: Routledge.

———. 2000. *Profit and Pleasure: Sexual Identities in Late Capitalism.* New York: Routledge.

Herman, Judith L. 1992. *Trauma and Recovery.* New York: Basic Books.

Herman, Judith L., with Lisa Hirschman. 1981. *Father-Daughter Incest.* Cambridge, Mass.: Harvard University Press.

Hertz, Rosanna, ed. 1997. *Reflexivity and Voice.* Thousand Oaks, Calif.: Sage.

Hesford, Wendy S. 1999. *Framing Identities: Autobiography and the Politics of Pedagogy.* Minneapolis: University of Minnesota Press

Heyes, Cressida J. 2000. *Line Drawings: Defining Women through Feminist Practice.* Ithaca, N.Y.: Cornell University Press.

hooks, bell. 1984. *Feminist Theory: From Margin to Center.* Boston: South End Press.

———. 1989. *Talking Back: Thinking Feminist, Thinking Black.* Boston: South End Press.

———. 1990. *Yearning: Race, Gender, and Cultural Politics.* Boston: South End Press.

———. 1993. *Sisters of the Yam: Black Women and Self-Recovery.* Boston: South End Press.

———. 1994. *Teaching to Transgress: Education as the Practice of Freedom.* New York: Routledge.

Horowitz, Ruth. 1986. "Remaining an Outsider: Membership as a Threat to Research Rapport." *Urban Life* (14):409–30.

Hurtado, Aída. 1996. *The Color of Privilege: Three Blasphemies on Race and Feminism.* Ann Arbor: University of Michigan Press.

Hyde, Cheryl. 1995. "The Meaning of Whiteness." *Qualitative Sociology* 18(1):87–95.

Hyde, Naida D. 1986. "Covert Incest in Women's Lives" Dynamics and Directions for Healing." *Canadian Journal of Community Mental Health* 5(2):73–83.

Incest Survivor Information Exchange. 1990. *I.S.I.E. (Incest Survivor Information Exchange)* 10(4).

Jackson, Robert L. 1992. "Censorship Efforts in Schools Up 50% Last Year, Group Says." *Los Angeles Times* v111(Sept. 2):A16.

Jaggar, Alison. 1983. *Feminist Politics and Human Nature.* Totowa, N.J.: Rowman and Allanheld.

———. 1989. "Love and Knowledge: Emotion in Feminist Epistemology." Pp. 145–71 in *Gender/Body/Knowledge: Feminist Reconstructions of Being and Knowing,* eds. Alison M. Jaggar and Susan R. Bordo. New Brunswick, N.J.: Rutgers University Press.

James, Stanlie M., and Abena P.A. Busia, eds. 1993. *Theorizing Black Feminisms: The Visionary Pragmatism of Black Women.* New York: Routledge.

Johnson, John. M. 1983. "Trust and Personal Involvements in Fieldwork." Pp. 203–15 in *Contemporary Field Research,* ed. R.M. Emerson. Prospect Heights, Ill.: Waveland Press.

Johnson-Odim, Cheryl. 1992. "Common Themes, Different Contexts: Third World Women and Feminism." Pp. 314–27 in *Third World Women and the Politics of Feminism,* eds. Chandra Talpade Mohanty, Ann Russo, and Lourdes Torres. Bloomington and Indianapolis: Indiana University Press.

Jones, Kathleen. B. 1988. "On Authority: Or, Why Women Are Not Entitled to Speak." Pp. 119–33 in *Feminism and Foucault: Reflections on Resistance,* eds. Irene Diamond and Lee Quinby. Boston: Northeastern University Press.

———. 1990. "Citizenship in a Woman-Friendly Polity." *Signs: Journal of Women in Culture and Society* 15(4):781–812.

Joreen (a.k.a. Jo Freeman). 1973. "Tyranny of Structurelessness." *Ms.* 2(1):76–78, 86–89.

Joseph, Gloria. 1981. "The Incompatible Ménage à Trois: Marxism, Feminism, and Racism." Pp. 91–108 in *Women and Revolution,* ed. Lydia Sargent. Boston: South End Press.

———, and Jill Lewis. 1981. *Common Differences: Conflicts in Black and White Feminist Perspectives.* Garden City, N.Y.: Anchor Books.

Joseph, Suad. 1988. "Feminism, Familism, Self, and Politics: Rsearch as a Mughtaribi." Pp. 25–47 in *Arab Women in the Field: Studying Your Own Society,* eds. Soraya Altorki and Camillia Fawzi El-Solh. Syracuse: Syracuse University Press.

———. 1996. "Relationality and Ethnographic Subjectivity: Key Informants and the Construction of Personhood in Fieldwork." Pp. 107–21 in *Feminist Dilemmas in Fieldwork,* ed. Diane L. Wolf. Boulder, Colo.: Westview.

Kaminer, Wendy. 1995. "Review of *Voices From the Next Feminist Generation.*" *New York Times Book Review* (June 4).

Kanter, Rosabeth Moss. 1977. *Men and Women of the Corporation.* New York: Basic Books.

Kaplan, Caren, Norma Alarcón, and Minoo Moallem, eds. 1999. *Between Woman and Nation: Nationalisms, Transnational Feminisms, and the State.* Durham, N.C.: Duke University Press.

Kaplan, Temma. 1982. "Female Consciousness and Collective Action: The Case of Barcelona, 1910–1918." *Signs: Journal of Women in Culture and Society* 7(3):545–66.

Kates, Erika. 1991. "Transforming Rhetoric into Choice: Access to Higher Education for Low Income Women." Pp. 181–97 in *Women, Work, and School: Occupational Segregation and the Role of Education,* ed. Leslie R. Wolfe. Boulder, Colo.: Westview.

Katz, Alex. 2000. "Gay-Straight Club's Battle is Won." *Los Angeles Times* (Sept. 8):B1, B12.

Katz, Alfred H., and Eugene I. Bender, eds. 1976. *The Strength in Us: Self-Help Groups in the Modern World.* New York: New Viewpoints.

Katz, Michael B. 1986. *In the Shadow of the Poorhouse: A Social History of Welfare in America.* New York: Basic Books.

Katzenstein, Mary Fainsod. 1998. *Faithful and Fearless: Moving Feminist Protest inside the Church and Military.* Princeton, N.J.: Princeton University Press.

Katznelson, Ira. 1981. *City Trenches: Urban Politics and the Patterning of Class in the United States.* New York: Pantheon Books.

Kelly, Liz, Sheila Burton, and Linda Regan, eds. 1994. "Researching Women's Lives or Studying Women's Oppression? Reflections on What Constitutes Feminist Research." Pp. 27–48 in *Researching Women's Lives from a Feminist Perspective*, eds. Mary Maynard and June Purvis. London: Taylor and Francis.

Kendrick, Karen. 1998. "Producing the Battered Woman: Shelter Politics and the Power of the Feminist Voice." Pp. 151–73 in *Community Activism and Feminist Politics: Organizing Across Race, Class, and Gender*, ed. Nancy A. Naples. N.Y.: Routledge.

King, Katie. 1994. *Theory in its Feminist Travels: Conversations in U.S. Women's Movements.* Bloomington: Indiana University Press.

Kitzinger, Celia, and Rachel Perkins. 1993. *Changing Our Minds: Lesbian Feminism and Psychology.* New York: New York University Press.

Kleinman, Sherryl, and Martha A. Copp. 1990. *Emotions and Fieldwork.* Newbury Park, Calif.: Sage.

Kloppenburg, Jack. 1991. "Social Theory and the De/Reconstruction of Agricultural Science: Local Knowledge for an Alternative Agriculture." *Rural Sociology* 56:519–48.

Kondo, Dorinne K. 1990. *Crafting Selves: Power, Gender, and Discourses of Identity in a Japanese Workplace.* Chicago: University of Chicago Press.

Krieger, Susan. 1983. *The Mirror Dance: Identity in a Women's Community.* Philadelphia: Temple University Press.

———. 1991. *Social Science and the Self: Personal Essays on an Art Form.* New Brunswick, N.J.: Rutgers University Press.

Kruks, Sonia. 2001. *Retrieving Experience: Subjectivity and Recognition in Feminist Politics.* Ithaca, N.Y.: Cornell University Press.

Kuhn, Annette. 1995. *Family Secrets: Acts of Memory and Imagination.* London and New York: Verso.

———, and A.M. Wolpe. 1978. *Feminism and Materialism: Women and Modes of Production.* London: Routledge and Kegan Paul.

Kuhn, Sarah, and Barry Bluestone. 1987. "Economic Restructuring and the Female Labor Market: The Impact of Industrial Change on Women" Pp. 3–32 in *Women, Households and the Economy*, eds. L. Beneria and C.R. Stimpson. New Brunswick, N.J.: Rutgers University Press.

Laclau, Ernesto, and Chantal Mouffe. 1985. *Hegemony and Socialist Strategy: Towards a Radical Democratic Politics*, trans. Winston Moore and Paul Cammack. London: Verso.

Landry, Donna, and Gerald MacLean. 1993. *Materialist Feminism.* Oxford: Blackwell.

Lasch, Christopher. 1985. *The Minimal Self.* London: Picador.

Lather, Patti. 1986. "Research as Praxis." *Harvard Educational Review* 56 (August):257–77.

———. 1992. "Post-Critical Pedagogies: A Feminist Reading." Pp. 120–37 in *Feminisms and Critical Pedagogy*, eds. Carmen Luke and Jennifer Gore. New York: Routledge.

———, and Chris Smithies. 1997. *Troubling the Angels: Women Living with HIV/AIDS.* Boulder, Colo.: Westview.

Latour, Bruno, and Steve Woolgar. 1979. *Laboratory Life: The Social Construction of Scientific Facts.* Beverly Hills, Calif.: Sage.

Lemke, Jay L. 1995. *Textual Politics: Discourse and Social Dynamics.* London: Taylor and Francis.

Lessnoff, Michael. 1986. *Social Contract.* London: Macmillan.

Lewin, Ellen. 1993. "Lesbian and Gay Kinship: Kath Weston's *Families We Choose* and Contemporary Anthropology." In "Theorizing Lesbian Experience, Special Issue." *Signs: Journal of Women in Culture and Society* 18(4):974–89.

Library of Congress. 1988. "Digest of Public General Bills and Resolutions." Washington, D.C.: Congressional Research Service.

Liebow, Elliot. 1967. *Tally's Corner.* Boston: Little, Brown.

Light, Linda, and Nancy Kleiber. 1988. "Interactive Research in a Feminist Setting: The Vancouver Women's Health Collective." Pp. 185–201 in *Anthropologists at Home in North America: Methods and Issues in the Study of One's Own Society*, ed. D.A. Messerschmidt. New York: Cambridge University Press.

Lin, Margaretta Wan Ling, and Cheng Imm Tan. 1994. "Domestic Violence in Our Communities: A Call for Justice." Pp. 321–34 in *The State of Asian American Activism and Resistance in the 1990s*, ed. Karin Aguilar-San Juan. Boston: South End Press.

Lincoln, Judy. 1990. "Pride in 12-Step Programs." *The Survivor Resource Chronicle* 5(3):2–3.

Lipset, Seymour Martin. 1970. "The Ideology of Local Control." Pp. 21–42 in *Education and Social Policy: Local Control of Education*, eds. C.A. Bowers, Ian Housego, and Doris Dyke. New York: Random House.

Lipsky, Michael. 1980. *Street-Level Bureaucracy: Dilemmas of the Individual in Public Services*. New York: Russell Sage Foundation.

Lofland, John, and Lyn H. Lofland. 1995. *Analyzing Social Settings: A Guide to Qualitative Observation and Analysis*. Belmont, Calif.: Wadsworth.

Loftus, Elizabeth, and Katherine Ketcham. 1994. *The Myth of Repressed Memory: False Memories and Allegations of Sexual Abuse*. New York: St. Martin's Press.

Lorber, Judith. 1984. *Women Physicians: Careers, Status, and Power*. New York: Tavistock Publications.

———. 1987. "From the Editor." *Gender & Society* 1:123–24.

———. 1994. *Paradoxes of Gender*. New Haven: Yale University Press.

Loseke, Donileen. R. 1992. *The Battered Woman and Shelters: The Social Construction of Wife Abuse*. Albany: State University of New York Press.

Love, Nancy. S. 1991. "Politics and Voice(s): An Empowerment/Knowledge Regime." *differences: A Journal of Feminist Cultural Studies* 3(1):85–103.

Lowe, Lisa. 1996. *Immigrant Acts: On Asian American Cultural Politics*. Durham: Duke University Press.

Lowenstein, Sharon R. 1990–91. "Incest: Children Sexual Abuse and the Law: Representation on Behalf of Adult Survivors." *Journal of Family Law* 29(4):791–823.

Lugones, María. C., and Elizabeth V. Spelman. 1983. "Have We Got a Theory for You! Feminist Theory, Cultural Imperialism and the Demand for 'The Women's Voice.'" *Women's Studies International Forum* 6:573–81.

Luke, Carman. 1992. "Feminist Politics in Radical Pedagogy." Pp. 25–53 in *Feminisms and Critical Pedagogy*, eds. Carmen Luke and Jennifer Gore. New York: Routledge.

———, and Jennifer Gore, eds. 1992. *Feminisms and Critical Pedagogy*. New York: Routledge.

Luttrell, Wendy. 1997. *Schoolsmart and Motherwise: Working-Class Women's Identity and Schooling*. New York: Routledge.

Lutz, Frank W., and Carol Merz, eds. 1992. *The Politics of School/Community Relations*. New York: Teachers College Press.

Lynd, Robert Staught, and Helen M. Lynd. 1929. *Middletown*. New York: Harcourt, Brace and World.

MacCannell, Dean, and Juliet Flower MacCannell. 1993. "Violence, Power and Pleasure: A Revisionist Reading of Foucault from the Victim Perspective." Pp. 173–92 in *Up against Foucault: Explorations of Some Tensions between Foucault and Feminism*, ed. Caroline Ramazanoglu. New York: Routledge.

MacKinnon, Catherine A. 1989. *Toward a Feminist Theory of the State*. Cambridge, Mass.: Harvard University Press.

Maggard, Sally W. 1990. "Gender Contested: Women's Participation in the Brookside Coal Strike." Pp. 75–98 in *Women and Social Protest*, eds. Guida West and Rae L. Blumberg. New York: Oxford University Press.

Maguire, Patricia. 1987. *Doing Participatory Research: A Feminist Approach*. Amherst, Mass.: Center for International Education.

———. 1996. "Considering More Feminist Participatory Research: What's Congruency Got to Do With It?" *Qualitative Inquiry* 2(1):106–18.

———. 2001a. "The Congruency Thing: Transforming Psychological Research and Pedagogy." Pp. 276–89 in *From Subjects to Subjectivities: A Handbook of Interpretive and Participatory Methods*, eds. Deborah L. Tolman and Mary Bryudon-Miller. New York: New York University Press.

————. 2001b. "Uneven Ground: Feminisms and Action Research." Pp. 59–69 in *Handbook of Action Research: Participative Inquiry and Practice*, eds. Peter Reason and Hilary Bradbury. Thousand Oaks, Calif.: Sage.

Malone, Caroline, Linda Farthing, and Lorraine Marce, eds. 1997. *The Memory Bird: Survivors of Sexual Abuse*. Philadelphia: Temple University Press.

Mann, Susan A., and Lori R. Kelley. 1997. "Standing at the Crossroads of Modernist Thought: Collins, Smith, and the New Feminist Epistemologies." *Gender & Society* 11(4):391–419.

Mansbridge, Jane, and Aldon Morris, eds. 2001. *Oppositional Consciousness: The Subjective Roots of Social Protest*. Chicago: University of Chicago Press.

Marcus, George E. 1998. *Ethnography through Thick and Thin*. Princeton, N.J.: Princeton University Press.

Marecek, Jeanne, and Diane Krazetz. 1998. "Power and Agency in Feminist Therapy." Pp. 13–29 in *Feminism and Psychotherapy: Reflections on Contemporary Theories and Practices*, eds. I. Bruna Seu and M. Colleen Heenan. Thousand Oaks, Calif.: Sage.

Marshall, Thomas Humphrey. 1965. "Citizenship and Social Class." Pp. 71–134 in *Class Citizenship and Social Development: Essays by T.H. Marshall*. New York: Doubleday.

Martin, Biddy, and Chandra Talpade Mohanty. 1986. "Feminist Politics: What's Home Got to Do With It?" Pp. 191–212 in *Feminist Studies/Critical Studies*, ed. Teresa de Laurentis. Bloomington: Indiana University Press.

Martinez, Jacqueline. 2000. *Phenomenology of Chicana Experience and Identity: Communication and Transformation in Praxis*. Lanham, Md.: Rowman and Littlefield.

Mascia-Lees, Frances E., Patricia Sharpe, and Colleen Ballerino Cohen. 1989. "The Postmodernist Turn in Anthropology: Cautions From a Feminist Perspective." *Signs: Journal of Women in Culture and Society* 15(11):7–33.

Matthews, Nancy A. 1994. *Confronting Rape: The Feminist Anti-Rape Movement and the State*. London: Routledge.

————. 1995. "Feminist Clashes with the State: Tactical Choices by State-Funded Rape Crisis Centers." Pp. 291–305 in *Feminist Organizations: Harvest of the New Women's Movement*, eds. Myra Marx Ferree and Patricia Yancey Martin. Philadelphia: Temple University Press.

Maynard, Robert C. 1970. "Black Nationalism and Community Schools." Pp. 100–11 in *Community Control of Schools*, ed. Henry M. Levin. Washington, D.C.: Brookings Institution.

Mayor's Advisory Panel on Decentralization of the New York City Schools. 1969. "A Framework for Change [Reprinted from Reconnection for Learning: A Community School System for New York City, 1967]." Pp. 119–66 in *Citizen Participation in Urban Development Volume II—Cases and Programs*, ed. Hans Spiegel. Washington, D.C.: State Institute for Applied Behavioral Science.

McCarthy, John D. 1994. "Activists, Authorities and the Media Framing of Drunk Driving." Pp. 133–67 in *New Social Movements: From Ideology to Identity*, eds. Enrique Larana, Hank Johnston, and Joseph R. Gusfield. Philadelphia: Temple University Press.

McCourt, Kathleen. 1977. *Working Class Women and Grass Roots Politics*. Bloomington: Indiana University Press.

McLellan, Betty. 1995. *Beyond Psychoppression: A Feminist Alternative Therapy*. North Melbourne, Australia: Spinifex Press.

McLennan, Karen Jacobsen. 1996. *Women's Incest Literature*. Boston: Northeastern University Press.

McNay, Lois. 1992. *Foucault and Feminism: Power, Gender and the Self*. Boston: Northeastern University Press.

Mead, Lawrence. 1986. *Beyond Entitlement*. New York: Free Press.

Medina, Vicente. 1990. *Social Contract Theories: Political Obligation or Anarchy?* Savage, Md.: Rowman and Littlefield.

Merriam, Sharan B. 1997. *Qualitative Research and Case Study Applications in Education*. New York: Jossey-Bass.

Merry, Sally Engle. 1990. *Getting Justice and Getting Even: Legal Consciousness among Working-Class Americans*. Chicago: University of Chicago Press.

Merton, Robert K. 1968. *Social Theory and Social Structure*. New York: Free Press.

————. 1972. "Insiders and Outsiders: A Chapter in the Sociology of Knowledge." *American Journal of Sociology* 77:8–47.

Messerschmidt, Donald A., ed. 1981. *Anthropologists at Home in North America.* London: Cambridge University Press.

Messer-Davidow, Ellen. 2002. *Disciplining Feminism: From Social Activism to Academic Discourse.* Durham: Duke University Press.

Meyers, Diana Tietjens. 2002. *Gender in the Mirror: Cultural Imagery and Women's Agency.* New York: Oxford University Press.

Mies, Maria. 1982. *The Lace Makers of Narsapur: Indian Housewives Produce for the World Market.* London: Zed Books.

———. 1991. "Women's Research or Feminist Research? The Debate Surrounding Feminist Science and Methodology." Pp. 60–84 in *Beyond Methodology: Feminist Scholarship as Lived Research,* eds. Mary Margaret Fonow and Judith A. Cook. Bloomington: Indiana University Press.

Miller, Alice. 1984. *For Your Own Good: Hidden Cruelty in Child-Rearing and the Roots of Violence.* New York: Farrar, Straus, Giroux.

Miller, Dorothy. C. 1989. "Poor Women and Work Programs: Back to the Future." *Affilia: Journal of Women and Social Work* 4(1):9–22.

Minh-ha, Trinh T. 1989. *Woman, Native, Other: Writing Postcoloniality and Feminism.* Bloomington: Indiana University Press.

Mink, Gwendolyn. 1995. *The Wages of Motherhood: Inequality in the Welfare State, 1917–1942.* Ithaca, N.Y.: Cornell University Press.

———. 1998. *Welfare's End.* Ithaca, N.Y.: Cornell University Press.

Mirkin, Marsha Pravder, ed. 1994. *Women in Context: Toward a Feminist Reconstruction of Psychotherapy.* New York: Guilford Press.

Mitchell, Juliann, and Jill Morse. 1998. *From Victims to Survivors: Reclaimed Voices of Women Sexually Abused in Childhood by Females.* Washington, D.C.: Accelerated Development, Taylor and Francis Group.

Mohanty, Chandra Talpede. 1991a. "Under Western Eyes: Feminist Scholarship and Colonial Discourses." Pp. 51–80 in *Third World Women and the Politics of Feminism,* eds. Chandra Talpade Mohanty, Ann Russo, and Lourdes Torres. Bloomington and Indianapolis: Indiana University Press.

———. 1991b. "Cartographies of Struggle: Third World Women and the Politics of Feminism." Pp. 1–50 in *Third World Women and the Politics of Feminism,* eds. Chandra Talpade Mohanty, Ann Russo, and Lourdes Torres. Bloomington and Indianapolis: Indiana University Press.

———. 1995. "Feminist Encounters: Locating the Politics of Experience." Pp. 68–86 in *Social Postmodernism: Beyond Identity Politics.* Cambridge: Cambridge University Press.

———. 1997. "Women Workers and Capitalist Scripts: Ideologies of Domination, Common Interests, and the Politics of Solidarity." Pp. 3–29 in *Feminist Genealogies, Colonial Legacies, Democratic Futures,* eds. M. Jacqui Alexander and Chandra Talpade Mohanty. New York: Routledge.

———, Ann Russo, and Lourdes Torres, eds. 1992. *Third World Women and the Politics of Feminism.* Bloomington and Indianapolis: Indiana University Press.

Monney, Patrick H. 1986. "Class Relations and Class Structure in the Midwest." Pp. 206–51 in *Studies in the Transformation of United States Agriculture,* ed. A. Eugene Havens, with Gregory Hooks, Patrick H. Mooney, and Max J. Pfeffer. Boulder, Colo.: Westview.

Mooney, Patrick J., and Scott A. Hunt. 1994. "A Repertoire of Interpretations: Master Frames Ideological Continuity in U.S. Agrarian Mobilization." *Sociological Quarterley* 37:177–97.

Moraga, Cherríe. 1981. "Introduction." Pp. xiii–xix in *This Bridge Called My Back: Writings by Radical Women of Color,* eds. Cherríe Moraga and Gloria Anzaldúa. Watertown, Mass.: Persephone Press.

Morawski, Jill G. 1988. "Impasse in Feminist Thought?" Pp. 182–94 in Mary McCanney Gergen, *Feminist Thought and the Structure of Knowledge.* New York: New York University Press.

Morris, Aldon D. 1992. "Political Consciousness and Collective Action." Pp. 351–73 in *Frontiers in Social Movement Theory,* eds. Aldon D. Morris and Carol McClurg Mueller. New Haven: Yale University Press.

Morrison, Toni. 1994. *The Bluest Eye.* New York: Plume Books.

Moya, Paula M. L. 1997. "Postmodernism, 'Realism,' and the Politics of Identity: Cherríe Moraga and Chicana Feminism." Pp. 125–50 in *Feminist Genealogies, Colonial Legacies, Democratic Futures,* eds. M. Jacqui Alexander and Chandra Talpade Mohanty. New York: Routledge.

Moynihan, Daniel Patrick. 1967. *The Negro Family: The Case for National Action.* Washington, D.C.: Government Printing Office.

Murray, Charles. 1984. *Losing Ground: American Social Policy, 1950–1980.* New York: Basic Books.

Naples, Nancy A. 1994. "Contradictions of Agrarian Ideology: Restructuring Gender, Race-Ethnicity, and Class." *Rural Sociology* 59:110–35.

———. 1997. "Contested Needs: Shifting the Standpoint on Rural Economic Development." *Feminist Economics* 3(2):63–98.

———, ed. 1998a. *Community Activism and Feminist Politics: Organizing Across Race, Class, and Gender.* New York: Routledge.

———. 1998b. *Grassroots Warriors: Activist Mothers, Community Work, and the War on Poverty.* New York: Routledge.

———. 1998c. "Women's Community Activism and Feminist Activist Research." Pp. 1–27 in *Community Activism and Feminist Politics: Organizing Across Race, Class, and Gender,* ed. Nancy A. Naples. New York: Routledge.

———. 1998d. "The New Frontier of Qualitative Methodology," review of *The New Language of Qualitative Method* by Jaber F. Gubrium and James A. Holstein, *Contemporary Sociology* 27(4)(1998):345–47.

———, with Carolyn Sachs. 2000. "Standpoint Epistemology and the Uses of Self-Reflection in Feminist Ethnography: Lessons for Rural Sociology." *Rural Sociology* 65(2):194–214.

———. 2001. "Member of the Funeral: An Introspective Ethnography." Pp. 21–43 in *Queer Families, Queer Politics: Challenging Culture and the State,* eds. Mary Bernstein and Renate Reimann. New York: Columbia University Press.

———. 2002a. "The Dynamics of Critical Pedagogy, Experiential Learning and Feminist Praxis in Women's Studies." Pp. 9–21 in *Teaching Feminist Activism: Strategies From the Field,* eds. Nancy A. Naples and Karen Bojar. New York: Routledge.

———. 2002b. "Changing the Terms: Community Activism, Globalization, and the Dilemmas of Transnational Feminist Praxis." Pp. 3–14 in *Women's Activism and Globalization: Linking Local Struggles and Transnational Politics,* eds. Nancy A. Naples and Manisha Desai. New York: Routledge.

———, with Emily Clark. 1996. "Feminist Participatory Research and Empowerment: Going Public as Survivors of Childhood Sexual Abuse." Pp. 160–83 in *Feminism and Social Change: Bridging Theory and Practice,* ed. Heidi Gottfried. Champaign-Urbana: Illinois University Press.

———, with Carolyn Sachs. 2000. *Rural Sociology* 65(2):194–214.

———, and Manisha Desai, eds. 2002. *Women's Activism and Globalization: Linking Local Struggles with Transnational Politics.* New York: Routledge.

Narayan, Uma. 1997. *Dislocating Cultures: Identities, Traditions, and Third World Feminism.* New York: Routledge.

Nathan, Richard. 1987. Testimony before the U.S. Congress, Senate, Finance Committee, Subcommittee on Social Security and Family Policy. In *Welfare: Reform or Replacement? (Child support enforcement: II), Hearings before Subcommittee on Social Security and Family Policy,* Senate Finance Committee, 67–77. 100th Congress, 1st Session, February 20.

Nelson, Barbara J. 1990. "The Origins of the Two-Channel Welfare State: Workmen's Compensation and Mothers' Aid." Pp. 123–51 in *Women, the State, and Welfare,* ed. Linda Gordon. Madison: University of Wisconsin Press.

Nettles, S. Murray. 1991. "Higher Education as the Route to Self-Sufficiency for Low-Income Women and Women on Welfare." Pp. 155–67 in *Women, Work, and School,* ed. Leslie R. Wolfe. Boulder, Colo.: Westview.

Neubeck, Kenneth J., and Noel A. Cazenave. 2001. *Welfare Racism: Playing the Race Card against America's Poor.* New York: Routledge.

New York Civil Liberties Union [CLU]. 1969. "The Burden of Blame: A Report on the Ocean Hill-Brownsville School Controversy." Pp. 338–51 in *The Politics of Urban Education,* eds. Marilyn Gittell and Alan G. Hevesi. New York: Praeger.

New York Times. 1997. "Schools' Books on Gay Families Stir Seattle." *New York Times* 147:(Nov. 2):N20.

Newton, Judith, and Judith Stacey. 1996. "Ms. Representations: Reflections on Studying Academic Men." Pp. 287–305 in *Women Writing Culture,* eds. Ruth Behar and Deborah A. Gordon. Berkeley: University of California Press.

Newton, Judith. 1999. *Starting Over: Feminism and the Politics of Cultural Critique.* Ann Arbor: University of Michigan Press.

Nicholson, Linda J., ed. 1990. *Feminism/Postmodernism.* New York: Routledge.

Nielsen, Joyce McCarl., ed. 1990. *Feminist Research Methods: Exemplary Readings in the Social Sciences.* Boulder, Colo.: Westview.

Noble, Kenneth B. 1996. "Welfare Revamp, Halted in Capital, Proceeds Anyway: State Assumes the Lead." *New York Times* (March 10):1, 11.

Oakley, Ann. 1981. "Interviewing Women: A Contradiction in Terms." Pp. 30–61 in *Doing Feminist Research,* ed. Helen Roberts. Boston: Routledge and Kegan Paul.

O'Connor, Julia S., Ann Shola Orloff, and Sheila Shaver. 1999. *States, Markets, Families: Gender, Liberalism and Social Policy in Australia, Canada, Great Britain and the United States.* NY Cambridge University Press.

Offe, Claus. 1984. *Contradictions of the Welfare State,* ed. John Keane. Cambridge, Mass.: MIT Press.

Ofshe, Richard, and Ethan Waters. 1994. *Making Monsters: False Memories, Psychotherapy, and Sexual Hysteria.* New York: Charles Scribner's Sons.

Oliker, Stacey J. 1994. "Does Workfare Work? Evaluation Research and Workfare Policy." *Social Problems* 41(2):195–213.

———. 1995a. "The Proximate Contexts of Workfare and Work: A Framework for Studying Poor Women's Economic Choices." *Sociological Quarterly* 36(2): 251–72.

———. 1995b. "Work Commitment and Constraint Among Mothers on Workfare." *Journal of Contemporary Ethnography* 24(2):165–94.

Omi, Michael, and Howard Winant. 1986. *Racial Formation in the United States from the 1960s to the 1980s.* New York: Routledge.

Orlandella, Angelo Ralph. 1990. "Boelen May Know Holland, Boelen May Know Barzine, But Boelen 'Doesn't Know Diddle about the North End!' " *Journal of Contemporary Ethnography* 21(1):69–79.

Orloff, Ann S. 1993a. *The Politics of Pensions: A Comparative Analysis of Britain, Canada, and the United States, 1880–1940.* Madison: University of Wisconsin Press.

———. 1993b. "Gender and the Social Rights of Citizenship: The Comparative Analysis of Gender Relations and Welfare States." *American Sociological Review* 58(3):303–28.

Orner, Mimi. 1992. "Interrupting the Calls for Student Voice in 'Liberatory' Education: A Feminist Poststructuralist Perspective." Pp. 74–89 in *Feminisms and Critical Pedagogy,* eds. Carmen Luke and Jennifer Gore. New York: Routledge.

Ornstein, Allan C. 1974. *Metropolitan Schools: Administrative Decentralization vs. Community Control.* Methuchen, N.J.: Scarecrow Press.

Park, Lisa Sun-Hee. 1998. "Navigating the Anti-Immigrant Wave: The Korean Women's Hotline and the Politics of Community." Pp. 175–95 in *Community Activism and Feminist Politics: Organizing across Race, Class, and Gender,* ed. Nancy A. Naples. N.Y.: Routledge, 1997.

Pascall, Gillian. 1986. *Social Policy: A Feminist Analysis.* London: Tavistock Publications.

Patai, Daphne. 1994. "Sick and Tired of Nouveau Solipsism." Point of View essay in *The Chronicle of Higher Education* (Feb. 23).

———, and Noretta Koertge. 1994. *Professing Feminism: Cautionary Tales from the Strange World of Women's Studies.* New York: Basic Books.

Pateman, Carole. 1988. *The Sexual Contract.* Stanford, Calif.: Stanford University Press.

Pear, Robert. 1996. "Clinton Endorses the Most Radical of Welfare Trials." *New York Times* (May 19):1, 11.

Pearce, Diana. 1978. "The Feminization of Poverty: Women, Work and Welfare." *Urban & Social Change Review* (Winter–Spring):28–36.

———. 1990. "Welfare is Not *for* Women: Why the War on Poverty Cannot Conquer the Feminization of Poverty." Pp. 265–79 in *Women, the State, and Welfare,* ed. Linda Gordon. Madison: University of Wisconsin Press.

Peattie, Lisa, and Martin Rein. 1983. *Women's Claims: A Study in Political Economy.* London: Oxford University Press.

Pence, Ellen. 1996. "Safety for Battered Women in a Textually Mediated Legal System." Ph.D. dissertation. Graduate Department, Sociology in Education, University of Toronto.

———.2002. "Safety and Accountability Audit." Http://www.opdv.state.ny.us/coordination/safetyaudit.html.

Personal Narratives Group, ed. 1989. *Interpreting Women's Lives: Feminist Theory and Personal Narratives.* Philadelphia: Temple University Press.

Pezdek, Kathy, and William P. Banks, eds. 1996. *The Recovered Memory/False Memory Debate.* San Diego, Calif.: Academic Press.

Phalen, Shane. 1989. *Identity Politics: Lesbian Feminism and the Limits of Community.* Philadelphia: Temple University Press.

———. 1993. "(Be)Coming Out: Lesbian Identity and Politics." *Signs: Journal of Women in Culture and Society* 18(4):765–90.

Phoenix, Ann. 1994. "Practising a Feminist Research: The Intersection of Gender and 'Race' in the Research Process." Pp. 49–71 in *Researching Women's Lives from a Feminist Perspective*, eds. Mary Maynard and June Purvis. London: Taylor and Francis.

Piven, Frances Fox, and Richard Cloward. [1971] 1993. *Regulating the Poor: The Functions of Public Welfare.* New York: Vintage.

Polakow, Valerie. 1993. *Lives on the Edge.* Chicago: University of Chicago Press.

Pollner, Melvin, and Robert M. Emerson. 1983. "The Dynamics of Inclusion and Distance in Fieldwork Relations." Pp. 235–52 in *Contemporary Field Research*, ed. Robert M. Emerson. Prospect Heights, Ill.: Waveland Press.

Popkin, Susan J. 1990. "Welfare: Views From the Bottom." *Social Problems* 37(1):64–79.

Ports, Sukie. 1970. "Racism, Rejection, and Retardation." Pp. 50–92 in *Schools against Children: The Case for Community Control*, ed. Annette T. Rubinstein. New York: Monthly Review Press.

Post, David. 1992. "Through Joshua Gap: Curricular Control and the Constructed Community." *Teachers College Record* 93(4):673–96.

Profitt, Norma Jean. 2000. *Women Survivors, Psychological Trauma, and the Politics of Resistance.* Haworth Press.

Prus, Robert. 1996. *Symbolic Interaction and Ethnographic Research: Intersubjectivity and the Study of Human Lived Experience.* Albany: State University of New York Press.

Public Law 100-485, 2358. 1988. Family Support Act. Pp. 278–79 in *Digest of Public General Bills and Resolutions, Congressional Research Service.* Washington, D.C.: Library of Congress.

Pulliam, John D. 1982. *History of Education in America.* Columbus, Ohio: Charles E. Merrill.

Quadagno, Jill. 1994. *The Color of Welfare: How Racism Undermined the War on Poverty.* New York: Oxford University Press.

Quirk, Sherry A., and Anne P. DePrince. 1996. "Childhood Trauma: Politics and Legislative Concerns for Therapists." Pp. 19–30 in *A Feminist Clinician's Guide to the Memory Debate*, eds. Susan Contratto and M. Janice Gutfreund. New York: Haworth Press.

Rajan, Rajeswari Sunder. 1993. *Real and Imagined Women: Gender, Culture and Postcolonialism.* New York: Routledge.

Ramazanoglu, Caroline. 1993. "Introduction." Pp. 1–15 in *Up against Foucault. Explorations of Some Tensions between Foucault and Feminism*, ed. Caroline Ramazanoglu. New York: Routledge.

Randall, Margaret. 1987. *This Is about Incest.* Ithaca, N.Y.: Firebrand.

Ransom, Janet. 1993. "Feminism, Difference and Discourse: The Limits of Discursive Analysis for Feminism." Pp. 123–46 in *Up against Foucault: Explorations of Some Tensions between Foucault and Feminism*, ed. Caroline Ramazanoglu. New York: Routledge.

Rapping, Elayne. 1996. *The Culture of Recovery: Making Sense of the Self-Help Movement in Women's Lives.* Boston: Beacon Press.

Ratner, Ellen F. ed.. 1990. *The Other Side of the Family: A Book for Recovery from Abuse, Incest and Neglect.* Dearfield Beach, Fla.: Health Communications.

Ravitch, Diane. 1974. *The Great School Wars: New York City, 1805–1973. A History of the Public Schools as Battlefields of Social Change.* New York: Basic Books.

Reagon, Bernice Johnson. 1983. "Coalition Politics: Turning the Century." Pp. 356–86 in *Home Girls: A Black Feminist Anthology.* New York: Kitchen Table Press.

Reavey, Paula, and Brendon Gough. 2000. "Dis/Locating Blame: Survivor's Constructions of Self and Sexual Abuse." *Sexualities* 3(3):325–46.

Reay, Diane. 1996. "Insider Perspectives or Stealing the Words out of Women's Mouths: Interpretation in the Research Process." *Feminist Review* 53:57–73.

Reinarman, Craig. 1995. "The Twelve-Step Movement and Advanced Capitalist Culture: The Politics of Self-Control in Postmodernity." Pp. 90–109 in *Culture Politics and Social*

Movements, eds. Marcy Dranovsky, Barbara Epstein, and Richard Flacks. Philadelphia: Temple University Press.

Reinharz, Shulamit. 1992. *Feminist Methods in Social Research*. New York: Oxford University Press.

Reviere, Susan L. 1996. *Memory of Childhood Trauma*. New York: Guildford Press.

Rew, Lynn. 1989. "Childhood Sexual Exploitation: Long-Term Effects Among a Group of Nursing Students." *Issues in Mental Health Nursing* 10:181–91.

Rice, John Steadman. 1992. "Discursive Formation, Life Stories, and the Emergence of Co-Dependency: 'Power/Knowledge' and the Search for Identity." *Sociological Quarterly* 33(3):337–64.

Rich, Adrienne. 1980. "Compulsory Heterosexuality and Lesbian Existence." *Signs: Journal of Women in Culture and Society* 5:631–60.

Richardson, Laurel. 1990. "Trash on the Corner: Ethics and Technography." *Journal of Contemporary Ethnography* 21(1):103–19.

———. 1997. *Fields of Play: Constructing an Academic Life*. New Brunswick, N.J.: Rutgers University Press.

Riessman, C. Kohler. 1987. "When Gender is Not Enough: Women Interviewing Women." *Gender & Society* 1(2):172–207.

Riley, Joan. 1985. *The Unbelonging*. London: Women's Press.

Ristock, Janice L., and Joan Pennell. 1996. *Community Research as Empowerment: Feminist Links, Postmodern Interruptions*. New York: Oxford University Press.

Roberts, Dorothy E. 1993. "Racism and Patriarchy in the Meaning of Motherhood?" *American University Journal of Gender and the Law* 1(1):1–38.

———. 1995. "Race, Gender, and the Value of Mothers' Work." *Social Politics* 2(2):195–207.

———. 1997. *Killing the Black Body: Race, Reproduction, and the Meaning of Liberty*. New York: Vintage Books.

Roberts, Helen, ed. 1981. *Doing Feminist Research*. London: Routledge and Kegan Paul.

Ronai, Carol Rambo. 1992. "The Reflexive Self through Narrative: A Night in the Life of an Erotic Dancer/Researcher." Pp. 102–24 in *Investigating Subjectivity: Research on Lived Experience*, eds. Carolyn Ellis and Michael G. Glaherty. Thousand Oaks, Calif.: Sage.

———. 1995. "Multiple Reflections of Child Sex Abuse: An Argument for a Layered Account." *Journal of Contemporary Ethnography* 23(4):395–426.

Rose, Hillary. 1986. "Women's Work: Women's Knowledge." Pp. 161–83 in *What Is Feminism?* eds. Juliet Mitchell and Ann Oakley. Oxford: Basil Blackwell.

Rosenau, Pauline M. 1992. *Post-Modernism and the Social Sciences*. Princeton, N.J.: Princeton University Press.

Ruddick, Sara. 1989. *Maternal Thinking: Toward a Politics of Peace*. New York: Ballantine Books.

Rush, Florence. 1980. *The Best Kept Secret: Sexual Abuse of Children*. New York: Prentice Hall.

Russell, Diana E.H. 1986. *The Secret Trauma: Incest in the Lives of Girls and Women*. New York: Basic Books.

Sachs, Carolyn. 1983. *Invisible Farmers: Women in Agricultural Production*. Totowa, N.J.: Rowman and Allanheld.

———. 1996. *Gendered Fields: Rural Women, Agriculture and Environment*. Boulder, Colo.: Westview.

Sacks, Karen Brodkin. 1988. "Gender and Grassroots Leadership." Pp. 77–94 in *Women and the Policies of Empowerment*, eds. Ann Bookman and Sandra Morgen. Philadelphia: Temple University Press.

Sadker, David, and Myra Sadker. 1991. "Sexism in American Education: The Hidden Curriculum." Pp. 57–76 in *Women, Work, and School*, ed. Leslie R. Wolfe. Boulder, Colo.: Westview.

Said, Edward W. 1978. *Orientalism*. New York: Vintage.

Salamon, Sonya. 1992. *Prairie Patrimony: Family, Farming, and Community in the Midwest*. Chapel Hill: University of North Carolina Press.

Sandoval, Chéla. 1991. "U.S. Third World Feminism: The Theory and Method of Oppositional Consciousness in the Postmodern World." *Genders* 10:1–24.

———. 1993. "Oppositional Consciousness in the Postmodern World: U.S. Third World Feminism, Semiotics, and the Methodology of the Oppressed." Unpublished Ph.D. dissertation. University of California, Santa Cruz.

———. 2000. *Methodology of the Oppressed*. Minneapolis: University of Minnesota Press.

Sapphire. 1996. *Push: A Novel*. New York: Alfred A. Knopf.

Sartre, Jean-Paul. [1960] 1963. *Search for a Method*. Trans. Hazel E. Barnes. New York: Vintage.

Sarvasy, Wendy. 1988. "Reagan and Low-Income Mothers: A Feminist Recasting of the Debate." Pp. 253–76 in *Remaking the Welfare State: Retrenchment and Social Policy in America and Europe*, ed. M.K. Brown. Philadelphia: Temple University Press.

Schram, Sanford F. 1995. *Words of Welfare: The Poverty of Social Science and the Social Science of Poverty*. Minneapolis: University of Minnesota Press.

———, and Joe Soss. 2002. "Success Stories: Welfare Reform, Policy Discourse, and the Politics of Research." Pp. 57–78 in *Lost Ground: Welfare Reform, Poverty and Beyond*, eds. Randy Albelda and Ann Withorn. Cambridge, Mass.: South End Press.

Schuman, Joan, and Mara Glavez. 1996. "A Meta/Multi-Discursive Reading of 'False Memory' Syndrome." *Feminism and Psychology* 6(1):7–29.

Scott, Ellen, and Bindi Shah. 1993. "Future Projects/Future Theorizing in Feminist Field Research Methods: Commentary on Panel Discussion." *Frontiers* 13:90–103.

Scott, Joan W. 1992. "Experience." Pp. 22–40 in *Feminists Theorize the Political*, eds. Judith Butler and Joan Scott. New York: Routledge.

Scott, Kisho Y. 1991. *The Habit of Surviving*. New York: Ballantine Books.

Scott, Wilbur. 1990. *The Politics of Readjustment: Vietnam Veterans Since the Way*. New York: Aldine De Gruyter.

Seitz, Virginia. R. 1998. "Class, Gender, and Resistance in the Appalachian Coalfields." Pp. 237–55 in *Community Activism and Feminist Politics: Organizing across Race, Class, and Gender*, ed. Nancy A. Naples. New York: Routledge.

Shapiro, Shanti. 1992. "Trauma, Ego Defenses, and Behavioral Reenactment." Pp. 35–57 in *Sexual Trauma and Psychopathology: Clinical Intervention with Adult Survivors*, eds. Shanti Shapiro and George M. Dominak. New York: Lexington Books.

———, and George M. Dominak. 1992. *Sexual Trauma and Psychopathology: Clinical Intervention with Adult Survivors*. New York: Lexington Books.

Shear, Jeff. 1995. "The Ax Files." *National Journal* (April 15): 924–27.

Shohat, Ella, ed. 1998. *Talking Visions: Multicultural Feminism in a Transnational Age*. Cambridge, Mass.: MIT Press.

Siim, Birte. 1988. "Towards a Feminist Rethinking of the Welfare State." Pp. 160–85 in *The Political Interests of Gender*, eds. Kathleen Jones and Anna Jonasdottir. Newbury, Calif.: Sage.

Simmel, Georg. 1921. "The Sociological Significance of the 'Stranger.' " Pp. 322–27 in *Introduction to the Science of Sociology*, eds. Robert E. Park and Ernest W Burgess. Chicago: University of Chicago Press.

Skocpol, Theda. 1992. *Protecting Soldiers and Mothers: The Political Origins of Social Policy in the United States*. Cambridge, Mass.: Harvard University Press.

Smart, Carol. 1982. "Regulating Families or Legitimating Patriarchy." *International Journal of the Sociology of Law* 10(2):129–47.

———. 1995. *Law, Crime and Sexuality: Essays in Feminism*. Thousand Oaks, Calif.: Sage.

———. 1999. "A History of Ambivalence and Conflict in the Discursive Construction of the 'Child Victim' of Sexual Abuse." *Social & Legal Studies* 8(3):391–409.

Smith, Carolyn. D., and William Kornblum, eds. 1989. *In the Field*. New York: Praeger.

Smith, Dorothy E. 1987. *The Everyday World as Problematic: A Feminist Sociology*. Toronto: University of Toronto Press.

———. 1989. "Feminist Reflections on Political Economy." *Studies in Political Economy* 30:37–59.

———. 1990a. *Conceptual Practices of Power*. Boston: Northeastern University Press.

———. 1990b. *Texts, Facts, and Femininity: Exploring the Relations of Ruling*. New York: Routledge.

———. 1992. "Sociology from Women's Experience: A Reaffirmation." *Sociological Theory* 10(1):88–98.

———. 1993. "High Noon in Textland: A Critique of Clough." *Sociological Quarterly* 34(1):183–92.

———. 1997. "Comment on Hekman's 'Truth and Method: Feminist Standpoint Theory Revisited." *Signs: Journal of Women and Culture* 22(2):392–98.

———. 1999. *Writing the Social: Critique, Theory, and Investigations*. Toronto: University of Toronto Press.

———, and Alison I. Griffith. 1990. "Coordinating the Uncoordinated: Mothering, Schooling, and the Family Wage." Pp. 25–43 in *Perspectives on Social Problems, Vol. 2*, eds. Gale Miller and James A. Holstein. Greenwich, Conn.: JAI Press.

Snow, David, and Robert Benford. 1992. "Master Frames and Cycles of Protest." Pp. 133–54 in *Frontiers in Social Movement Theory*, eds. Aldon D. Morris and Carol McClurg Mueller. New Haven: Yale University Press.

Sokoloff, Natalie J. 1980. *Between Money and Love: The Dialectics of Women's Home and Market Work*. New York: Praeger.

Spalter-Roth, Roberta, Heidi I. Hartmann, and Linda Andrews. 1992. *Combining Work and Welfare: An Anti-Poverty Strategy*. Washington, D.C.: Institute for Women's Policy Research.

Spelman, Elizabeth V. 1988. *Inessential Woman: Problems of Exclusion in Feminist Thought*. Boston: Beacon Press.

Spiegel, Hans B.C., ed. 1969. *Citizen Participation in Urban Development Volume II—Cases and Programs*. Washington, D.C.: NTL Institute for Applied Behavioral Science.

Spivak, Gayatri Chakravorty. 1988. *In Other Worlds: Essays in Cultural Politics*. New York: Routledge.

———. 1999. *A Critique of Postcolonial Reason: Toward a History of the Vanishing Present*. Cambridge, Mass.: Harvard University Press.

Stacey, Judith. 1991. "Can There Be a Feminist Ethnography?" Pp. 111–19 in *Women's Words*, eds. Sherna B. Gluck and Daphne Patai. New York: Routledge.

Stack, Carol B. 1974. *All Our Kin: Strategies for Survival in a Black Community*. New York: Harper and Row.

———. 1996. "Writing Ethnography: Feminist Critical Practice." Pp. 96–106 in *Feminist Dilemmas in Fieldwork*, ed. D.L. Wolf. Boulder, Colo.: Westview.

Stanko, Elizabeth A. 1985. *Intimate Intrusions: Women's Experience of Male Violence*. London: Routledge and Kegan Paul.

Stanley, Liz, and Sue Wise. 1983. *Breaking Out: Feminist Consciousness and Feminist Research*. London: Routledge and Kegan Paul.

———, and Sue Wise. 1990. "Method, Methodology and Epistemology in Feminist Research." Pp. 20–60 in *Feminist Praxis*, ed. Liz Stanley. New York: Routledge.

State of Iowa, Department of Human Services. 1991. PROMISE JOBS Provider Manual. Iowa: Department of Human Services (March 26).

State of Wisconsin Legislative Audit Bureau. 1990. *An Evaluation of Learnfare Program Administration*. Madison: State of Wisconsin Legislative Audit Bureau, Department of Health and Social Services.

Stein, Annie. 1970. "Containment and Control: A Look at the Record." Pp. 21–49 in *Schools against Children: The Case for Community Control*, ed. Annette T. Rubinstein. New York: Monthly Review Press.

Steinberg, Marc W. 1999. "The Talk and Back Talk of Collection Action: A Dialogic Analysis of Repertoires of Discourse among Nineteenth-Century English Cotton Spinners." *American Journal of Sociology* 105:736–80.

Stern, Susan. 1994. "Social Science from Below: Grassroots Knowledge for Science and Emancipation." Ph.D. dissertation. City University of New York.

———. 1998. "Conversation, Research, and Struggles over Schooling in an African American Community." Pp. 107–27 in *Community Activism and Feminist Politics: Organizing across Race, Class, and Gender*, ed. Nancy A. Naples. New York: Routledge.

Stone, Adolph. 1969. "A Criticism of the N.Y. Civil Liberties Union Report on the Ocean Hill-Brownsville School Controversy." Pp. 352–62 in *The Politics of Urban Education*, eds. Marilyn Gittell and Alan G. Hevesi. New York: Praeger.

Strauss, Anselm, and Juliet M. Corbin. 1998. *Basics of Qualitative Research: Techniques and Procedures for Developing Grounded Theory*. Thousand Oaks, Calif.: Sage.

Survivor Resource Chronicle: Information For and About Survivors of Child Sexual Abuse. 1990. 5(3).

Tallen, Betty S. 1990. "Twelve-Step Programs: A Lesbian Feminist Critique." *National Women's Studies Association Journal* 2(3): 390–407.

Tappan, Mark B. 2001. "Interpretive Psychology: Stories, Circles, and Understanding Lived Experience." Pp. 45–56 in *From Subjects to Subjectivities: A Handbook of Interpretive and Participatory Methods*, eds. Deborah L. Tolman and Mary Brydon-Miller. New York: New York University Press.

Tarrow, Sidney. 1992. "Mentalities, Political Cultures and Collectin Action Frames: Constructing Meaning through Action." Pp. 174–202 in *Frontiers in Social Movement Theory*, eds. Aldon Morris and Carol McClurg Mueller. New Haven: Yale University Press.

Tavris, Carol. 1993. "Beware the Incest-Survivor Machine." *New York Times Book Review* 1, January 3, 16–17.

Taylor, Verta, and Nancy E. Whittier. 1992. "Collective Identity in Social Movement Communities: Lesbian Feminist Mobilization." Pp. 104–29 in *Frontiers of Social Movement Theory*, eds. Aldon D. Morris and Carol McClurg Mueller. New Haven: Yale University Press.

———. 1995. "Analytical Approaches to Social Movement Culture: The Culture of the Women's Movement." Pp. 163–87 in *Social Movements and Culture*, eds. Hank Johnston and Bert Klandermans. Minneapolis: University of Minnesota Press.

Thomas, Owen. 1987. "Freedom of Speech: Schools are the Center of a Conflict over Parents Rights to Restrict What Their Children Hear." *Christian Science Monitor* v.79(Nov. 24):16.

Thompson, Becky W. 1994. *A Hunger So Wide and So Deep: A Multiracial View of Women's Eating Problems.* Minneapolis: University of Minnesota Press.

Thompson, Edward Palmer. 1978. *The Poverty of Theory and Other Essays.* New York and London: Monthly Review Press.

Thorne, Barrie. 1995. "Symposium: On West and Fenstermaker's 'Doing Difference.' " *Gender & Society* 9:497–99.

Tolman, Deborah L, and Mary Brydon-Miller, eds. 2001. *From Subjects to Subjectivities: A Handbook of Interpretive and Participatory Methods.* New York: New York University Press.

Tonnies, Ferdinand. 1963. *Community and Society (Gemeinschaft and Gesellschaft).* New York: Harper.

Traub, James. 2002. "A Lesson in Unintended Consequences." *New York Times Magazine* (October 6):70–75.

Treichler, Paula. 1989. "From Discourse to Dictionary: How Sexist Meanings are Authorized." Pp. 51–79 in *Language, Gender and Professional Writing*, eds. Frank and Paula Treichler. New York: Modern Language Association.

Trombley, William. 1992. "Textbook Wars Flaring Up Anew." *Los Angeles Times* v.111(May 11):A3, A27.

Tyack, David B. 1974. *The One Best System: A History of American Urban Education.* Cambridge, Mass.: Harvard University Press.

U.S. Congress. House. 1986. Work, Education, and Training Opportunities for Welfare Recipients, Hearings before the Subcommittee on Public Assistance and Unemployment Compensation of the Committee on Ways and Means, House of Representatives, 99th Cong., 2d sess. March 13, 20; April 22; May 22; and June 17.

———. 1987a. Family Welfare Reform Act, Hearings before the Subcommittee on Public Assistance and Unemployment Compensation of the Committee on Ways and Means, House of Representatives, March 30; April 1.

———. 1987b. Medicaid Issues in Family Welfare and Nursing Home Reform, Hearings before the Subcommittee on Health and the Environment, House Energy and Commerce Committee, 100th Cong., 1st sess., April 24; May 12.

U.S. Congress. Senate. 1987. Welfare: Reform or Replacement? (Short-Term v. Long-Term Dependency). Hearings before the Subcommittee on Social Security and Family Policy of the Committee on Finance of the U.S. Senate, 100th Cong., 1st sess., March 2.

———. 1987a. Welfare: Reform or Replacement? (Child Support Enforcement), Hearings before the Subcommittee on Social Security and Family Policy, Senate Finance Committee, January 23; February 2.

———. 1987b. Welfare: Reform or Replacement? (Short-Term v. Long-Term Dependency), Hearings before the Subcommittee on Social Security and Family Policy of the Committee on Finance of the U.S. Senate, 100th Cong., 1st sess., March 2.

———. 1987c. Welfare: Reform or Replacement? (Work and Welfare), Hearings before the Subcommittee on Social Security and Family Policy, Senate Finance Committee, 100th Cong., 1st sess., February 23.

———. 1987d. Welfare Reform (Part 2), Hearings before the Senate Finance Committee, 100th Cong., 1st sess., October 14, 28.

———. 1988. Welfare Reform (Part 3), Hearings before the Committee on Finance, U.S. Senate, 100th Cong., 2d sess., February 4.

Van Maanen, John. 1988. *Tales of the Field: On Writing Ethnography.* Chicago: University of Chicago Press.

van Manen, Max. 1977. "Linking Ways of Knowing with Ways of Being Practical." *Curriculum Inquiry* 6(3):205–28.

Velez, William. 1985. "Finishing College: The Effects of College Type." *Sociology of Education* 58:191–200.

Vickers, Jeanne. 1991. *Women and the World Economic Crisis.* Atlantic Highlands, N.J.: Zed Books. Visweswaran, Kamala. 1994. *Fictions of Feminist Ethnography.* Minneapolis: University of Minnesota Press.

Vobejda, Barbara. 1987. "Judge Bans 'Humanist' Textbooks; Ruling is Victory for Fundamentalists." *Washington Post* v.110(March 5):A1, A19.

Vogel, Lise. 1983. "Questions on the Woman Question." *Monthly Review* 31:39–59.

———. 1993. *Mothers on the Job: Maternity Policy in the U.S. Workplace.* New Brunswick N.J.: Rutgers University Press.

Wagner, David. 1997. *The New Temperance: The American Obsession with Sin and Vice.* Boulder, Colo.: Westview Press.

Wakefield, Hollida, and Ralph Underwager. 1994. *Return of the Furies: An Investigation into Recovered Memory Therapy.* Chicago and La Salle, Ill.: Open Court.

Walby, Sylvia. 1990. *Theorizing Patriarchy.* Oxford: Basil Blackwell.

Walker, Alice. 1982. *The Color Purple.* New York: Washington Square Press, Pocket Books.

Walker, Gillian. 1990. "The Conceptual Politics of Struggle: Wife Battering, the Women's Movement, and the State." *Studies in Political Economy* 33:63–112.

———. 1994. "Violence and the Relations of Ruling: Lessons From the Battered Women's Movement." Pp. 65–79 in *Knowledge, Experience, and Ruling Relations,* eds. Marie Campbell and Ann Manicom. Toronto: University of Toronto Press.

Walker, Moira. 1998. "Feminist Psychotherapy and Sexual Abuse." Pp. 57–77 in *Feminism and Psychotherapy: Reflections on Contemporary Theories and Practices,* eds. I. Bruna Seu and M. Colleen Heenan. Thousand Oaks, Calif.: Sage.

Warren, Jennifer. 1991. "Schools Face Censors' Siege, Group Says." *Los Angeles Times* 110(Aug. 29):A3, A30.

Wasserfall, Rachel R. 1997. "Reflexivity, Feminism, and Difference." Pp. 150–68 in *Reflexivity and Voice,* ed. R. Hertz. Newbury Park, Calif.: Sage.

Wasserman, Cathy. "FMS: The Backlash against Survivors." *Sojourner: The Women's Forum* (Nov. 1992):18–19.

Watras, Joseph. 1997. *Politics, Race, and Schools: Racial Integration, 1954–1994.* New York: Garland Publishing.

Weedon, Chris. 1987. *Feminist Practice and Poststructuralist Theory.* New York: Basic Blackwell.

Weeks, Kathi. 1998. *Constituting Feminist Subjects.* Ithaca, N.Y.: Cornell University Press.

Weis, Lois. 1985. "Without Dependence on Welfare for Life: Black Women in Community College." *Urban Review* 17:233–55.

West, Candace, and Don H. Zimmerman. 1987. "Doing Gender." *Gender & Society* 1:125–51.

West, Guida. 1981. *The National Welfare Rights Movement: The Social Protest of Poor Women.* New York: Praeger.

Weston, Kath. 1991. *Families We Choose: Lesbians, Gays, Kinship.* New York: Columbia University Press.

White, E. Frances. 1990. "Africa on My Mind: Gender, Counter Discourses and African-American Nationalism." *Journal of Women's History* 2:73–97.

White, Louise G. 1994. "Policy Analysis as Discourse." *Journal of Policy Analysis and Management* 13(3):506–25.

Whyte, William F. 1955. *Street Corner Society.* Chicago: University of Chicago Press.

———. 1990. "In Defense of *Street Corner Society.*" *Journal of Contemporary Ethnography* 21:52–68.

———, ed. 1991. *Participatory Action Research.* New York: Sage.

Wilkinson, Kenneth. 1991. *The Community in Rural America.* New York: Greenwood.

Williams, Anne. 1990. "Reading Feminism in Fieldnotes. Pp. 253–61 in *Feminist Praxis,* ed. Liz Stanley. New York: Routledge.

Williams, Brackette. 1996. "Skinfolk, Not Kinfolk: Comparative Reflections on the Identity of Participant-Observation in Two Field Situations." Pp. 72–95 in *Feminist Dilemmas in Fieldwork,* ed. Diane. L. Wolf. Boulder, Colo.: Westview.

Williams, Fiona. 1989. *Social Policy: A Critical Introduction.* New York: Basil Blackwell.

Williams, Mary Beth. 1990. "Post-Traumatic Stress Disorder and Child Sexual Abuse: The Enduring Effects." Unpublished Ph.D. dissertation. The Fielding Institute.

Williams, Raymond. 1976. *Keywords.* New York: Oxford University Press.

Wilson, Elizabeth. 1977. *Women and the Welfare State*. London: Tavistock.

Wilson, William Julius. 1974. "The New Black Sociology: Reflections on the 'Insiders' and 'Outsiders' Controversy." Pp. 322–38 in *Black Sociologists: Historical and Contemporary Perspectives*, ed. James E. Blackwell and Morris Janowitz. Chicago: University of Chicago Press.

———. 1987. *The Truly Disadvantaged: The Inner City, the Underclass, and Public Policy*. Chicago: University of Chicago Press.

Wilson, Melba. 1994. *Crossing the Boundary: Black Women Survive Incest*. Seattle: Seal Press.

Winant, Howard. 1994. *Racial Conditions*. Minneapolis: University of Minnesota Press.

Wisechild, Louise M. ed. 1991. *She Who Was Lost Is Remembered: Healing from Incest through Creativity*. Seattle: Seal Press.

Wiseman, Michael. 1991. "Research and Policy: An Afterword for the Symposium on the Family Support Act of 1988." *Journal of Policy Analysis and Management* 10(4):657–66.

Wolf, Diane L., ed. 1996a. *Feminist Dilemmas in Fieldwork*. Boulder, Colo.: Westview.

———. 1996b. "Situating Feminist Dilemmas in Fieldwork." Pp. 1–55 in *Feminist Dilemmas in Fieldwork*, ed. Diane L. Wolf. Boulder, Colo.: Westview.

Wolf, Marjery. 1992. *A Thrice Told Tale: Feminism, Postmodernism, and Ethnographic Responsibility*. Stanford, Calif.: Stanford University Press.

———. 1996. "Afterword: Musing from an Old Gray Wolf." Pp. 215–22 in *Feminist Dilemmas in Fieldwork*, ed. Diane L. Wolf. Boulder, Colo.: Westview.

Wolin, S.S. 1981. "Higher Education and the Politics of Knowledge." *Democracy* 1:38–52.

Worrall, Anne. 1990. *Offending Women: Female Lawbreakers and the Criminal Justice System*. London: Routledge.

Wright, Mareena McKinley. 1995. " 'I Never Did Any Fieldwork, but I Milked an Awful Lot of Cows!' Using Rural Women's Experience to Reconceptualize Models of Work." *Gender & Society* 9:216–35.

Yapko, Michael D. 1994. *Suggestions of Abuse: True and False Memories of Childhood Sexual Trauma*. New York: Simon and Schuster.

Yates, Douglas. 1973. *Neighborhood Democracy: The Politics and Impacts of Decentralization*. Lexington, Mass.: Lexington Books.

Young, Iris Marion. 1980. "Socialist Feminism and the Limits of Dual Systems Theory." *Socialist Review* 50/51:169–88.

Zavella, Patricia. 1996. "Feminist Insider Dilemmas: Constructing Ethnic Identity with Chicana Informants." Pp. 138–59 in *Feminist Dilemmas in Fieldwork*, ed. Diane L. Wolf. Boulder, Colo.: Westview.

Zerbe, Carolyn. 1996. "The Feminist Therapy Institute Code of Ethics: Implications for Working with Survivors of Child Sexual Abuse." Pp. 79–91 in *A Feminist Clinician's Guide to the Memory Debate*, eds. Susan Contratto and M. Janice Gutfreund. New York: Haworth Press.

Zimet, Melvin. 1973. *Decentralization and School Effectiveness: A Case Study of the 1969 Decentralization Law in New York City*. New York: Teachers College Press.

Zinberg, Norma E. 1994. *Drug, Set, and Setting: The Basis for Controlled Intoxicant Use*. New Haven: Yale University Press.

Index